For my daughter,
Ashley Sylvia,
with love

Italy: From Revolution to Republic

ITALY: FROM REVOLUTION TO REPUBLIC

1700 to the Present

Spencer M. Di Scala

Westview Press
Boulder • San Francisco • Oxford

Copyright © 1995 by Westview Press, Inc.

Published in 1995 in the United States of America by Westview Press, Inc., 5500 Central Avenue, Boulder, Colorado 80301-2877, and in the United Kingdom by Westview Press, 36 Lonsdale Road, Summertown, Oxford OX2 7EW

Library of Congress Cataloging-in-Publication Data

Di Scala, Spencer.
    Italy : from revolution to republic, 1700 to the present / Spencer
M. Di Scala.
        p.   cm. — (History and warfare)
    Includes bibliographical references and index.
    ISBN 0-8133-1343-0 (pbk.). — ISBN 0-8133-1342-2 (case)
    1. Italy—History—18th century.   2. Italy—History—19th century.
3. Italy—History—20th century.   I. Title.   II. Series.
DG545.D5   1995
945—dc20
                                                                    94-48441
                                                                    CIP

Printed and Bound in the United States of America

    ∞   The paper used in this publication meets the requirements
        of the American National Standard for Permanence of Paper
        for Printed Library Materials Z39.48-1984.

Contents

PART FIVE
WAR AND FASCISM

PART SIX
THE REPUBLIC

Preface

Although Italy has a distinguished past, the country's modern history seems to generate a significant amount of controversy. Frequently, one-sided historical views vie for attention from students and the general public with commonplace assumptions based on insufficient knowledge and stereotypes. Interpretations also seem to differ wildly depending on events occurring in the country and filtered through poor press coverage, academic disputes, or Italian writers with their own ax to grind. Examples of controversial subjects include fascism, the strength of the former Italian Communist party (PCI), terrorism, and crime—all of which projected images in the foreign press of Italians as Fascists, Communists, terrorists, or *mafiosi*. In this interplay of clichés, Americans seem to have a special problem: the tendency to interpret Italy through the eyes of the descendants of poor emigrants who fled in the late nineteenth and early twentieth centuries. This inclination has produced an especially distorted understanding of Italy in a country that believes it has special ties with the peninsula.

Counterpointing this "popular" image of Italy are the academic ones that frequently reflect the Italian political milieu. During Mussolini's rule, Fascist interpretations of Italian history had influence; following World War II, liberal outlooks prevailed; and after the 1960s, leftist views predominated in the universities. Thus the Risorgimento, once interpreted positively as a dramatic fight to liberate the peninsula, encountered criticism because it allegedly failed to involve the masses. The Christian Democrats, praised by the U.S. government for successfully keeping Italy out of the Soviet bloc, were condemned by professors for excluding the "different" Italian Communists from power.

Although it has a point of view, this book attempts to provide different interpretations of Italian history where the usual ones appear inadequate or overly influenced by particular political positions. The technique employed supplies a diverse emphasis from the prevailing one where such a viewpoint seems warranted. This method includes putting events into historical context and comparing them with similar developments during the same period, rather than judging them according to the criteria of later generations. For example, the masses did have a significant role in Italian unification and, under Socialist guidance, in late nineteenth- and early twentieth-century Italian society and politics—within the context of the times. The reader will also discover that the historical debates over historical questions or periods have been brought directly into the text, in addition to the discussion in the bibliographical essay. Another consequence of this method is the emphasis on whatever detail is required to achieve clarity and understanding. This is the case in the treatment of Italian participation in both world wars, where misconceptions abound among the general public and historians who are not specialists on Italy.

One of the lessons of history is its continuity despite obvious breaks, and I have emphasized that here. Unlike other works, which either attempt to cover Italian history from antiquity or start with the unification of Italy in 1861, this book begins in the eighteenth century after a brief introduction covering the late sixteenth and seventeenth centuries. The reason for this structure is the radical alteration in Italy's position following the Renaissance. For Italy, the modern age that leads up to our time gradually began with the Enlightenment. The reader will also find the continuity theme reiterated through the heavy emphasis on culture, society, and economics. Sometimes periods that represented a break politically with previous times demonstrated continuity in other ways, for example, economics. This is the case with the Fascist period, whose continuity with the republic, on all levels other than the political, is striking.

Finally, the world situation in 1994 continues to be very fluid because of the Cold War's end. Always sensitive to international developments, Italy is in flux because of the so-called "bloodless revolution." Coming on the heels of calls for a "second republic" and a corruption scandal of enormous proportions, this development has decimated the governing class and the influence of the political parties that guided the country for fifty years. The causes and questions raised by this event are discussed in Chapter 21, but it will be a while until scholars will be able to reach anything but tentative—though extremely interesting—conclusions on its definitive effects.

Spencer M. Di Scala

Acknowledgments

This book benefited from critical readings by several top scholars in the field of Italian history whom I wish to acknowledge here. Alexander Grab, Antonio Landolfi, James Burgwyn, Alan Reinerman, Richard Drake, and Frank Coppa read the parts of the manuscript in which they are most expert. Alexander De Grand had the ungrateful job of reading the entire work chapter by chapter as it was being written and of proposing alterations during the heat of composition. The book is stronger because of his prompting. Corresponding to Alex De Grand's role at the beginning, Philip Cannistraro read the completed manuscript. His series of insightful suggestions, which I incorporated, allowed me to produce a much better final version than would otherwise have been the case.

Besides benefiting from the expertise of those reading the manuscript, I profited from discussions with colleagues such as Luciano Pellicani and Giorgio Spini on various topics relating to Italian history. My talks with Roberto Falaschi, Consul General of Italy for New England, on even the most exotic aspects of Italian affairs proved extremely stimulating. I also wish to thank Alfredo Molinari, science attaché at the Boston consulate, for sharing with me his very illuminating views on the development of Italian science, an area to which I have devoted some attention in this book. I also wish to thank Peter Kracht, senior editor at Westview Press, for the stimulating conversation on a snowy spring day during which this book was conceived and for his continued encouragement and support.

Like history itself, the writing of a book links the past, present, and future. My late parents, Antonio and Nancy Di Scala, stimulated in me a love of the subject. I thank my wife, Laura Clerici Di Scala, for creating an environment conducive to writing and for her wise suggestions on the text itself during the various stages of composition. To my daughter, Ashley, to whom this book is dedicated, I wish a continued blossoming of the kind that has amazed her parents during her young life. I hope that this book will make a contribution to the intellectual growth of all students of history, and when Ashley grows up, to hers as well.

S. M. D.

The Setting

A cursory glance at a map of Italy reveals important geographical features that profoundly influenced the boot-shaped peninsula's history. The most striking aspect is the mountainous and hilly terrain. To the north, the Alps—cited by the poet Dante as being the natural border of Italy—crown the peninsula and form Italy's boundaries with France, Switzerland, Austria, and Slovenia. Pockmarked by more than a thousand glaciers and with peaks over 13,000 feet in height, the Alps give a picture of rugged beauty. The most famous peaks include Monte Bianco (15,771 feet), Monte Rosa (15,203 feet), and the Matterhorn (14,692 feet). The Alps affect the country's climate by serving as a barrier to winds coming from the north and west and have been an important factor in the area's military history. In modern times, the starkly beautiful terrain accounts for the importance of the area's skiing and tourist industries. Besides the Alps, a long mountain range runs down the entire length of the peninsula into Sicily, the island at the toe of the Italian boot. With their highest peak at 9,560 feet, the Apennines are lower than the Alps but are 745 miles long and extend practically to the sea. A recent geological formation, the Italian Peninsula is subject to earthquakes, and a great deal of volcanic activity still exists. The country includes Europe's three active volcanoes (Vesuvius, Etna, and Stromboli), and various forms of volcanic action are visible in areas such as the Campi Flegrei and Pozzuoli, outside Naples, and islands such as Ischia in the Bay of Naples. Depending on location, these volcanic phenomena produce thermal springs—a source of revenue because of their supposed therapeutic effects—gas emissions, and unpleasantly abrupt alterations in ground levels.

Mountains and hilly areas represent 77 percent of the peninsula's territory, while plains make up 23 percent. Arable land is thus strictly limited, which has contributed to a high population density in the cities and towns and to vast emigration. The peninsula has also had an abundance of unhealthful marshlands, especially in the Veneto, Tuscany, and Lazio. Drained relatively recently, they were hotbeds of malaria and other diseases and hampered the peninsula's economic development. Fertile plains are practically restricted to the Po River Valley in the North, while small fertile areas exist around Naples, Catania, and other areas. The climate, which is cool and wet in the North and hot and dry in the South, also favors the Po Valley, which grows large quantities of rice, wheat, maize, and sugar beets. The fertile but tiny southern plains produce tomatoes and citrus fruits, both of which are important export crops.

Different climates and terrain help explain diverse dietary habits, products, and economic developments. The North historically produced more meat and dairy products. Northerners thus did their cooking in butter. Rice, introduced about five hundred years ago and favored by the wet conditions, became a staple instead of the pasta characteristic of the South. Soil and weather conditions in the Center and the South favor the growth of olive trees, which resulted not only in a cuisine making extensive use of olive oil but also in this product's becoming one of Italy's principal agricultural exports. Along with the production of olive oil, Italy's climate and soil favors the making of wine—the other important agricultural export. Wine-producing grapes grow over the entire peninsula, and the beverage goes well with both pasta and rice—which is "born in water and dies in wine." Italy is the world's largest wine exporter, a fact that has frequently created trade tension with France and Spain. As befits a country with wide climatic diversity, Italian wines range greatly. In the northern area of Piedmont, robust wines such as Barolo, Barbera, and Gattinara match the best French red wines in quality and are suitable for aging. The South produces wine of lower quality but of high alcoholic content; these wines, because they can be cut in various ways to create a less expensive beverage, historically have found a foreign and domestic market among the lower classes. Good local wines, best consumed on the spot, contribute to a thriving industry.

Climatic and geographical characteristics, however, have also produced differences that are more crucial to modern economies. Italy is one of the poorest European countries in natural resources, having no coal, iron ore, or petroleum to speak of, and recent discoveries of natural gas deposits are incapable of fulfilling the demands of a modern industrial economy. Given this situation, the North has had important advantages. It is located closer to northern Europe, and its plains facilitated the building of roads and easier communications with the rest of Europe; because of the more difficult terrain in the South, for example, a highway linking the entire South with northern Italy and Europe was not completed until the 1960s. The North has numerous rivers and large lakes that can be utilized for hydroelectric power—and industry—while southern rivers are dry during the summer and cannot be so used. While these advantages favored the development of an industrial base in the North in the late nineteenth century, the lack of an important energy source and poor communications help account for the South's failure to industrialize and thus to modernize its economy.

Besides economic disequilibrium, the difficult terrain facilitated the peninsula's division into many independent political units and hampered political, social, and linguistic unification. In ancient times, Roman military force unified the peninsula. This unity survived the fall of the empire in the West (A.D. 476) but ended with the Lombard invasions of the sixth century. With the revival of trade in Europe, which began during the tenth century, Italians took advantage of their strategic location in the central Mediterranean Sea and their proximity to the Middle East to dominate European trade with the more advanced Arab world. The four maritime republics (Venice, Genoa, Pisa, and Amalfi) restored the Mediterranean to Western control and made it safe once again for European traders. Thanks to their strategic location and trading skills, Venetian and Genoese merchants gained vast economic concessions among the Arabs and traveled as far as China. Merchant-dominated Italian cities such as Florence, Venice, and Milan boomed, reaching unheard-of populations of 80,000 to 100,000. The cities also achieved economic hegemony in Europe—especially in banking—overthrew medieval religious domination, and acquired secular political aspects which resemble modern times. The cities also produced goods such as woolen cloth and arms and tamed the land. Around Milan, the largest irrigation project since the fall of the Roman Empire was undertaken around 1100 and was worked on by Leonardo da Vinci in the fifteenth century. According to British historian Stuart Woolf, "By the twelfth and thirteenth centuries, the cities of northern and central Italy, as much of the countryside, had already acquired that characteristic physiognomy of towers and civic buildings, of markets and economic bustle, which amazed all foreign visitors and distinguished Italy from the rest of Europe." Italy had become "the land of the hundred cities" and had embarked upon that remarkable cultural domination of Europe that culminated in the Renaissance.

Within this context, Italian political units assumed different forms. In some areas such as Lombardy, the large cities expanded to take over the myriad smaller cities and towns and became organized as regional states. Other cities such as Rome and Naples dominated several regions, whereas others still shared political control of a single region (Parma and Modena). Tucked in the peninsula's northwestern corner (Piedmont), the Savoy dynasty busily gathered feudal possessions that it eventually organized as a highly centralized state in the seventeenth century.

By 1494, when the foreign invasions that spelled the end of Italian independence began, the peninsula, shaped by geography and history, had crystallized into these different states that lasted until unification occurred between 1861 and 1870.

Introduction: From "School of Europe" to Conquered Land

During the eighteenth century, the most famous *philosophe* of all, Voltaire, summed up Renaissance Italy: "The Italians had everything, except music, which was still in its infancy, and experimental philosophy, which was unknown everywhere until Galileo finally introduced it into the world." Yet in the eyes of many observers, and especially, it seems, of modern historians, within a hundred years of Emperor Charles V's sack of Rome in 1527, Italy appeared a "land of the dead." Is this view of post-Renaissance Italy accurate, and, if so, how is this rapid decline explained by historians?

The Invasions

During the Middle Ages, Italy was divided into a great number of independent political entities that eventually coalesced into five major states—Naples, Florence, Rome, Venice, and Milan—and several minor ones. Although the Swiss historian of the Renaissance, Jacob Burckhardt, argued that these states were the first in Europe with modern attributes, none of them developed enough strength to conquer and unify the entire peninsula.

Peculiar to Italy and marking its entire history was the Papal State, which the popes considered essential to ensure their independence from secular rulers anxious to dominate the Church. For centuries popes battled the German-based Holy Roman Empire, which claimed Italy and the authority to intervene in Church affairs.

The fight between papacy and empire enabled the Italian states to remain independent. Over the centuries, the empire steadily declined; but during the "Babylonian Captivity" and the "Great Schism" between 1308 and 1417, when the French nominated the popes and competing pontiffs claimed the allegiance of the faithful, the papacy's power did as well. The threat of political domination of Italy by either the Holy Roman Empire or the pope thus receded.

By 1454 the Italian states had consciously established a balance of power. This equilibrium meant that none of the major states could dominate the entire peninsula, because the others would ally against it. In effect, the territorial division of Italy had been officially recognized, guaranteed a multistate system on the peninsula, and made Italian unification impossible.

This development contrasted with events in France, Spain, and England that made strong national monarchies possible. In 1494 the Milanese ruler Ludovico il Moro, his power threatened by other Italian monarchs, invited French King Charles VIII into Italy to aid him. This move introduced a strong contender for European preponderance into the Italian equation. When France's rival, Spain, also entered Italy, the peninsula became a major battleground.

Although Ludovico's policy proved ill fated, great-power intervention was probably just a matter of time. Italy had been a battleground since ancient days, and only the decline of the two great medieval powers—the Church and the Holy Roman Empire—had produced political independence. During the Renaissance "the Italians had everything," rich cities and cultural, financial, and commercial superiority, but, separately, none of the small states could compete militarily with their newly united neighbors. Too weak to prevail militarily over either France or Spain, and too divided to act in concert and heed Machiavelli's "exhortation to take Italy and free her from the hands of the barbarians," the Italian states combined now with one, now with the other great power, in a vain attempt to salvage their independence through the application of balance-of-power principles. The savage fighting brought destruction, economic decline, and misery to the whole peninsula. The Spanish won the contest, and in 1559 the Treaty of Cateau-Cambrésis consigned Italy to Spain.

Italy During the Spanish Domination

Two major interpretative trends dominate historical views of post-Renaissance Italy. Not suprisingly, observers during the nineteenth-century Italian national revival viewed the period as a break with the preceding one and blamed Italy's "decadence" on war, foreign domination, and religious reaction. Subsequently adopted and honed by Marxist historians, this explanation became the standard interpretation. Proponents agree that, resting upon direct control of Milan and Naples, Spanish domination until 1713 favored a number of important economic and social developments that, though less rapid, produced more serious alterations than did the political changes.

Most important, in the late sixteenth and seventeenth centuries, the tendency of merchants to make large investments in land increased drastically. The prosperity of Medieval and Renaissance Italy had been based on commerce, which military operations rendered very risky. Though less spectacular, the profits from land were safer. In Milan, Florence, Venice, and other once-flourishing commercial centers, the urban upper classes gradually became transformed into a landed aristocracy that adopted the Spanish nobility's attitude of commerce as an undignified activity. Furthermore, always needing money, the Spanish authorities sold fiefs, noble titles, and the right to perform public services, such as collecting taxes and dispensing justice, to families once devoted to trade. According to these historians, this policy "refeudalized" Italy.

This process helps explain the near absence of an enterprising Italian bourgeoisie interested in change, as developed in France. It also encouraged the overcrowding of cities because peasants moved into urban areas to take advantage of, by such activities as begging, the aristocratic wealth concentrated there. As a result, this movement created not productive enterprises, but extremely poor living conditions and an imbalance between city and countryside. The cities consumed the food produced on the land without providing anything in return, such as capital.

International trends intensified the decline. Increased trade with the Americas and new routes around Africa shifted trade away from Italian cities such as Venice and toward French, Spanish, and English Atlantic ports. Furthermore, since Spain was constantly involved in wars against the infidel Turks, Italian insertion into the Spanish orbit increased Italy's exposure to naval attacks and piracy, devastating shipborne commerce and depopulating coastal areas, while increased taxation to pay for the fighting further impoverished the Italian Peninsula. Operas such as Antonio Vivaldi's *La Fida Ninfa* (first produced in January 1732) illustrate a lingering concern with the effects of piracy. Finally, Spain's military championship of the Counter Reformation, combined with the papacy's struggle to reestablish Catholic supremacy in Europe, accelerated Italy's decline by stifling the country's cultural life.

Reformation and Counter Reformation

The attempt of Martin Luther and other European reformers to purify the Catholic Church found many sympathizers among Italian theologians and intellectuals. Italian historian Delio Cantimori has described the rich and suggestive ideas of these thinkers, which were so widespread even in Rome that the future pope Paul IV complained: "At that time it seemed that one could not be considered a proper noble or courtier if one did not have some heretical or erroneous opinions."

Given the papacy's influence, the power of Spain, the weakness of the bourgeoisie, and the economically depressed peasantry, these Reformation ideas could not be transformed into a mass movement. Initially concentrating on the necessity to end corruption as a way to combat heresy, the Church rapidly turned to repression and doctrinal conservatism.

"If our own father had been a heretic," stated Pope Paul IV, "we would personally have carried the wood needed to burn him at the stake." In line with such a policy, this pope increased the Inquisition's powers, purged the Church hierarchy, imprisoned anyone vaguely suspected of harboring heretical ideas, and encouraged completion of the Index of Forbidden Books. Book shipments into Italy were scrutinized for offensive material, and book burnings became regular events. In 1573 the Inquisition summoned painter Paolo Veronese, criticized him for including "buffoons, drunken Germans, dwarfs, and other such absurdities" in a painting of the Last Supper, and ordered him to correct the picture at his own expense. In 1600 philosopher Giordano Bruno perished at the stake for his ideas. In 1616 Galileo submitted to the Inquisition's order to stop teaching that the earth went around the sun.

As a result of these persecutions, many intellectuals fled Italy, a diaspora that greatly impoverished the country and enriched the rest of Europe. At first this emigration affected religious reformers such as Bernardino Ochino, precursor of unitarianism, and Fausto and Lelio Sozzini, who greatly influenced the Reformation in Eastern Europe. In the seventeenth century, this "brain drain" became a flood that included artists, musicians, diplomats, statesmen, and specialized artisans.

During the same period, at the behest of King and Holy Roman Emperor Charles V of Spain, the Church convened the Council of Trent (1545–1563). This council reaffirmed all the Church's doctrines, conforming with the ideas of Charles's son Philip II and making him the Church's champion.

At the same time, the Church distorted Italian cultural life. Through its propaganda activities, domination of education, and political influence, the Church identified the glories of Italy with those of Catholicism and attributed to the Italians the historical function of safeguarding Catholic tradition and the Church's "liberty." This identification of Italian greatness with the Church inspired a "Guelph" spirit in Italian culture that remained powerful into at least the nineteenth century, when an Italian confederation with the pope as its head became one option for a united Italy. (During the Middle Ages, the Guelphs supported the papacy against the empire, hence the term's identification with the Church.)

The Debate

This synopsis may be considered the "standard" view of post-Renaissance Italy, but it has been challenged by historians such as American Eric Cochrane.

According to these revisionists, careful research reveals "refeudalization" as a myth. Furthermore, they believe, Charles V established a new order in alliance with the Italian states, not against them. Instead of misery, this Spanish "consolidation" supposedly produced a measure of peace and a new economic, commercial, industrial, and agricultural prosperity.

Furthermore, instead of viewing the Counter Reformation as a Spanish-inspired suffocation of Renaissance humanism, these observers praise it as a religious revival with deep Italian roots. Rather than interpreting the Counter Reformation as a subversion of Italian culture by the Church, revisionists emphasize a new and more modern definition of the nation during this period and point to an emerging nationalism. Just as they see no break in the economic sector, the revisionists discern not decadence but continuity of the secular culture of the high Renaissance. Indeed, their analysis of the age's artistic, literary, and scientific creativity is the keystone of their argument.

Both the "standard" and "revisionist" views have merit. It would seem an error to define as decadent the mannerist style of art and the Baroque Age that, between 1550 and 1750, produced Claudio Monteverdi, who in his lifetime brought opera from its primitive to its developed form, world-class artists such as the painters Annibale Carracci and Caravaggio, the poet Torquato Tasso, the sculptor Gian Lorenzo Bernini, and the religious thinker Paolo Sarpi. On the other hand, the revisionists do not deny that a relative decline in all fields occurred but tend to push it back, blame it on war and disease, and explain it in European rather than in Italian terms. And yet, the destruction, the suppression of ideas, the intellectual exodus, the subordination of Italian to Spanish interests under Philip II, and the repression of Paolo Sarpi's advanced ideas on the relationship between Church and State all occurred. Whether these events can best be explained by direct Spanish and papal intervention or by indirect pressure or trends that had Italian origins, as the revisionists believe, seems a less important issue.

Although the essence of the post-Renaissance era will continue to be debated, several facts seem clear. While continuity should be emphasized over a break, gradualism over a drastic shift, the Italian decline of the late sixteenth and seventeenth centuries seems both real and serious in all sectors. Italy not only lost its position as prime innovator and leader of the Western world but also regressed economically and politically. But the peninsula remained intimately linked to Western Europe, played a key role in the cultural developments of the eighteenth century, and was profoundly influenced by European events.

PART ONE

Enlightenment and French Revolutionary Italy

1

The Italian Enlightenment

A EUROPE-WIDE MOVEMENT, the eighteenth-century Enlightenment used ideas as "intellectual weapons" to alter the existing religious, political, and social situation. The intellectuals of this age, the *philosophes* (*illuministi* in Italian), aimed to transform their traditional, rigid, and inequitable society into a world with greater justice. They utilized "reason," critical judgment that corroded the "myths" underpinning the existing political and social structure. By employing reason, they could also analyze society, learn the principles governing behavior, and achieve a more perfect and rational world by applying these principles through education and influence upon powerful "Enlightened monarchs."

In short, the philosophes applied physicist Isaac Newton's scientific methodology to the study of society, reversing the prevailing attitude of reverence for the past and aiming for perfection in the future rather than lamenting the loss of the past's golden age. Using the rules of evidence, they questioned everything, destroyed the historical basis of the old regime, and set the stage for the "Age of the Democratic Revolution" in Europe and America.

In practice, the philosophes advocated eliminating the Church's political power, judging government by a utilitarian yardstick, rationalizing the economy by eliminating feudal vestiges and by establishing an equitable tax system, opening careers to talent instead of birth, drafting constitutions to limit the power of governments, securing civil rights, and reforming the justice system.

Reciprocal Influences

France's position as center of the Enlightenment sometimes causes observers to overlook the crucial contributions of Italian, German, English, Russian, and other thinkers, and Marxist analyses of the movement as the expression of a rising bourgeoisie have downplayed the Enlightenment's revolutionary character outside France. In Italy during the 1920s and 1930s, Fascist domination encouraged interpretation of the Italian Enlightenment as a purely native movement foreshadowing the Risorgimento—the movement for Italian unification. After World War II, Italian historian Franco Venturi refuted this nationalistic view, demonstrating both the Italian Enlightenment's richness and its complete integration within the "Atlantic" movement.

Although intellectual developments in France stimulated discussion in Italy, Italians also influenced European Enlightenment thinkers. The works of Alberto Radicati di Passerano, an exile from the intolerant Kingdom of Sardinia (Piedmont), dealt with several issues dear to Enlightenment intellectuals. After a bold analysis of religious leaders, for example, he wryly concluded that "it would be better . . . to be an atheist than to worship a Being chargeable with such enormous crimes and iniquities." Like French philosophe Denis Diderot, Passerano argued that ethical concepts originated not with a supreme being but in social habit and custom, chipping away at the concept that governments enforced ethical behavior established by God, a prime source of their authority.

If Passerano's ideas dealt with the more subtle aspects of the "myths" holding existing society together, writer Girolamo Tartarotti undermined grosser ones. In the 1740s, he struck a blow against prejudice and superstition by demolishing the belief in witches, which, he argued, contradicted both morality and the scientific precepts of the new age. His work stimulated a vast debate over magic and touched off a general attack in France, Austria, and Germany on the existence of witches, vampires, and ghosts.

The work of a Milanese thinker, Pietro Verri, might be cited as a further example of this reciprocal influence. Of all his important works, the *Meditations on Political Economy* (1771) caused the most commotion in Europe because it criticized the Physiocrats, influential economists who advocated taxes on all land as the only source of new wealth. Verri argued that Physiocratic ideas could not be implemented without keeping out foreign produce, contradicting the beneficial free trade that the Physiocrats believed their program would produce. Translated into French, German, and Russian, Verri's book stirred discussion among the most famous philosophes and provided Europe with a taste of the fundamental issues being engaged by Italian intellectuals.

But it was another Milanese thinker who had the most international influence. Cesare Beccaria's book *Of Crimes and Punishments* (1764) was translated into a host of languages (the French edition bore a famous commentary by Voltaire). In examining justice during his time, Beccaria made compelling arguments for institution of speedy trials, for informing the accused of their crimes, for limiting the power of judges, for proportioning the punishment to the crime, for equalizing punishments for the same crime, and for treating offenders equally regardless of social class; he also denounced the use of torture and the death penalty. In elaborating these principles, Beccaria placed jurisprudence on a modern footing in Europe and America.

The Long Peace

Besides intellectual aspects, political currents intertwined in eighteenth-century Italy. Historians seem to agree that the 1730s mark the depth of the Italian post-Renaissance crisis and that the decade witnessed a slow revival of the political, economic, and intellectual fortunes of the country.

They divide the century into two periods. From 1700 to 1748, the precipitous decline of Spain and the desire to pluck Spanish spoils in Italy provoked major conflicts. During the War of Spanish Succession (1700–1713), the French attempted to take over the entire Spanish Empire, including Italy, while Austria hoped to substitute its hegemony for Spain's on the peninsula. In the end, Austrian domination did indeed replace Spanish, making the Italian diplomatic situation more fluid.

The Austrians controlled only Lombardy (Milan) directly, even though they had indirect power in Tuscany (Florence). Spain retained influence in Naples, Sicily, and Parma through Bourbon rulers, but these states regained their independence. To obtain a consensus in their newly acquired possessions, the rulers implemented important reforms based on the prevailing Enlightenment culture. These attempts had the powerful support of Italian intellectuals, many of whom played an active role in the government, thus gaining valuable governmental experience.

With the decline of Spain and the emergence of a new European balance, the Italian diplomatic equation underwent major changes. The major beneficiary: Piedmont. Tucked in the northwest corner of Italy and pursuing the expansionist aims of its ruling Savoy dynasty, this state ably exploited the differences between France and Austria, new rivals for supremacy in Italy. Because of England's emergence as a Mediterranean power and its policy of preserving Piedmontese independence to counterbalance France and Austria, and because of its value to both France and Austria as a buffer state, Piedmont gained diplomatic maneuverability. By exploiting its privileged position, it acquired the large island of Sardinia, increased its mainland possessions, and won recognition as a kingdom. Thus, the eighteenth century witnessed the growth in prestige and size of the state that, a hundred fifty years later, would accomplish Italian unification.

European developments also produced a long peace in Italy. Following the War of Austrian Succession (1740–1748), the rivals for control of Italy—France and Austria—became allies. Consequently, European conflicts did not involve the peninsula until 1792, when revolutionary France and conservative Austria fought each other. For fifty years, the Italian states could concentrate on internal affairs. Different conditions in various sections guaranteed mixed results, but the reform attempts were always interesting in their own right and helped determine the future course of the various Italian regions.

MAP 1   Eighteenth Century Italy

The North

Enlightened reforms and their effects on social and economic development placed Lombardy, despite its subjection to Austria, in the forefront of the Italian states.

The Austrian Hapsburg queen, Maria Theresa (1740–1780), initiated a reform policy on practical grounds, not Enlightenment principles. Emerging from a war designed to dismember her disparate empire, Maria Theresa understood that only by streamlining the financial and administrative structure of her dominions could she increase production and the population's capacity to pay more taxes. In practice this policy meant a campaign against the remnants of Lombard feudalism, which hampered production—a goal that secured the cooperation of the Lombard philosophes.

The most crucial reform proved to be the vast land survey initiated by Maria Theresa's father but completed by the empress in 1759. This survey allowed the state to impose a fairer tax on land belonging to all classes, including the nobility. Besides addressing the equity issue, the survey ensured fiscal stability by implementing definitive taxes, thus stimulating agricultural production. A typical but rarely implemented Enlightenment demand, this reform pleased Pietro Verri and the Lombard illuministi, ensuring their collaboration in the reforms that followed.

During the seventeenth century, the Spanish had sold to landlords the right to collect certain taxes and tolls. Between 1760 and 1786 the Austrians returned direct control of these taxes and tolls to the state. As a result, the noble economic position suffered. Since the reform presented the nobility with the choice of either a reduction in income or a return to business activity, a part of the Lombard aristocracy engaged in improving its lands for profit. In short, this reform had results beyond the government's intentions, dealing a death blow to the residues of Lombard feudalism and creating the basis for its legal abolition in 1797. Furthermore, redemption of indirect taxes and tolls permitted Lombardy in 1776 to declare freedom of internal trade in grains and, ten years later, to permit their free export. Lombardy thus implemented a series of important reforms long advocated by European philosophes but that countries such as France had been unable to achieve.

In other areas of reform activity such as administration, the Church, and education, the Austrians achieved mixed success, but, on balance, the reform policy yielded permanent results. In the fertile Lombard lowlands, the great noble estates began breaking up, the land going to persons—noble and not—who founded vibrant agricultural firms. Intent on increasing production and profits, the agricultural bourgeoisie introduced new production methods and products such as cheese. This activity reversed the previous parasitic role of the city and created an equilibrium between the two, as may be seen in the cultivation of the silkworm in the country while the towns invested capital and produced finished silk products. The population spurt in the smaller Lombard cities signalled a new dynamism unknown in Lombard society since the Renaissance.

The emerging middle class produced by Austrian policy created a climate for greater participation in politics to further its economic interests, although this was expressed only with the arrival of the French in 1796. At this critical point, however, the Austrians reversed their policy of cooperation with the Italians. The circumstances of Maria Theresa's accession to the throne had forced her to collaborate with her subjects, but her son pursued a policy of centralization throughout his empire. After his mother's death in 1780, Joseph II strengthened his control over Lombard officials, ending collaboration with intellectuals and the middle class by 1790. Historian Alexander Grab emphasizes the limits of Austrian reform policy and believes that "Joseph II lacked a commitment to a deep economic reform program"; according to Grab, for further significant economic change to occur, "other political upheavals and a stronger bourgeoisie were necessary." Thus the Austrian fracture with Lombard illuministi and the middle class transformed collaboration into permanent conflict and ensured a receptive audience for French revolutionary ideas.

No reform activity of the kind noted in Lombardy marked adjoining Piedmont. This state lacked the stimulus of a new ruling house anxious to establish itself and did not follow a reform policy. Indeed, the Savoy dynasty judged reform dangerous to its control and persecuted Enlightenment culture. The travails of an important Piedmontese writer, Vittorio Alfieri, symbolize the poor relationship of this state with its intellectuals.

Other differences from the Italian pattern also show up. Piedmontese origins lay not in a large commercial city that had swallowed surrounding territory but in a collection of medieval fiefs over which the Savoy house had succeeded in imposing a centralized command after 1559. In accomplishing this aim, the government tamed the unruly aristocracy, converting it into a "service nobility" of the Prussian type, closely bound to the monarchy. Loss of its fiscal privileges did not transform the Piedmontese nobility into a business class, as had partially occurred in Lombardy, but into a military, bureaucratic, and diplomatic caste; it thus retained both its social status and landed character.

Though these changes increased government power, Piedmontese agriculture remained backward. Industrial activity did not develop because the government failed to encourage commerce through the eradication of feudal conditions and because of the lack of great cities. Piedmontese rulers did make weak attempts to encourage the growth of industry and commerce, but they rejected the Enlightenment reforms that would have favored such an expansion.

Piedmont achieved military and diplomatic successes in the eighteenth century, but it would not emerge as a serious candidate to lead the movement for Italian unification in the next century until it had moderated the less progressive aspects of its society, economy, and politics.

The fate of Venice and Genoa, once important mercantile republics, may be considered together. Venice emerged exhausted from the numerous attempts to destroy it during the late Renaissance and from a century-long conflict with the Turks. The discovery of America had pushed Venice into a long economic decline, and by the eighteenth century the republic had dwindled to diplomatic insignificance, even though its governmental structure remained an object of study and admiration for the philosophes.

But this structure stifled the state's chances at recovery. The Venetian nobility abandoned commerce for landed activity and concentrated wealth into a few hands while retaining the severe restrictions for entry into the ruling class that had existed in its glory days. These factors prevented the emergence of a commercial middle class and provided no incentive for the aristocracy itself to engage in commerce once more. Enlightenment ideas did penetrate and some industry did develop but not to a significant degree.

Similar to Venice in its restrictive governmental structure, Genoa also presents interesting dissimilarities. Given Genoa's small size and poor hinterland, the nobles continued to lend money to the great powers, but this moneylending never developed into modern investment activity nor did it stimulate industrial growth. Only in the ports of Leghorn and Genoa did mercantile activity expand, giving rise to a vocal bourgeois class that was impatient with noble privileges and, later, that supported Italian unification.

The Center

The government of Grand Duchy of Tuscany, the area surrounding Florence, conducted the most serious experiment in Enlightenment reform. In 1737 Francis of Lorraine, husband of Maria Theresa, became grand duke, bringing Tuscany under indirect Austrian control and initiating the reform process that their son, Peter Leopold (1765–1790), greatly accelerated.

Peter Leopold inherited an agricultural region that primarily produced grain, wine, olive oil, and fruit. There existed only a weak bourgeois class. The land belonged mostly to the nobility, the ruling family, the Church, or to special orders of knights founded to fight the Turks. The peasants worked the land on which they lived as sharecroppers to produce for themselves and the landowners, not for a market. The absence of a market, combined with the large tracts of unhealthful marshland, created a depressed peasant class perpetually indebted to the landlords and subject to frequent famines.

As in Lombardy, the new Austrian dynasty collaborated with the illuministi to implement a series of reforms. Expanding on a 1767 provision, Peter Leopold allowed unlimited exportation and importation of agricultural products in 1775. Eight years later, he eliminated internal tariffs and tolls, thus fulfilling also in Tuscany the philosophes' dream of free commerce. In addition, between 1747 and 1789, freedom to buy and sell land also arrived through strict limits on mortmain (perpetual ownership of land by the Church and other institutions forbidden to sell it). Between 1770 and 1781 the government, in the hope of eliminating serious obstacles to production, also abolished obsolete privileged corporations that had once dominated the Florentine economy.

During the same period, Peter Leopold limited the power of the central administration by giving greater autonomy to local government and implemented fiscal reforms. He replaced the many confusing taxes with a single land tax to be paid by all landholders and reduced the sharecroppers' burden by limiting the percentage of this tax that could be passed on to them. In addition, tax privileges enjoyed by ecclesiastical orders and privileged corporations also ceased.

However, a land survey that would have ensured the effectiveness of the reforms could not be completed, and the government's attempt to create a small landholding class failed. The grand duke broke up vast governmental holdings into small plots, arranging for their sale to peasants under easy terms. Unfortunately, these buyers proved too poor to meet the conditions of sale and consequently sold the land to rich city dwellers or to noble landholders. In a related area, the government achieved only mixed success in reclaiming marshland such as the Maremma, which was so unhealthful that, a popular song proclaimed, birds lost their tails if they flew over it.

The government partially succeeded in limiting the Church's influence by curbing mortmain, abolishing fiscal privileges, ending the Inquisition, and suppressing the Jesuits. But when Peter Leopold tried to implement Jansenism, policies to "purify" the Church favored by the philosophes, he failed. When he attempted to reform religious orders by abolishing perpetual vows, to simplify religious ceremonies, to cut the number of feast days, to reduce the pope's authority, and to forbid the veneration of relics, he encountered both hierarchical and popular resistance; riots broke out and the grand duke backed off.

Despite its intensity and the collaboration of the illuministi, Peter Leopold's reform effort had slight effect, illustrating the difficulty of producing real change against a recalcitrant social structure. In Tuscany, as in the other Italian states, the government reached the point when it had to decide whether to force greater reform at the risk of revolution or give up the effort.

In 1790, Peter Leopold succeeded his brother Joseph as the Austrian emperor, removing the chief stimulus for reform. The French Revolution had already begun, and Peter's successors abandoned reform. This increased conservatism of the Tuscan rulers made Tuscan intellectuals more receptive to revolutionary ideas. Like Lombardy, Tuscany faced a crisis situation at the end of the eighteenth century.

The Papal State faced greater problems than Tuscany and lacked its reform fervor. The pope's temporal domain, sliced in two by the Apennine Mountains, consisted of several disparate regions. Large noble and ecclesiastical landholdings and unhealthful marshlands characterized the most backward areas to the south, such as Lazio, where the sharecroppers lived a particularly depressed life. In these regions, little commerce went on in the cities, which served as administrative centers. Rome itself was important not as an economic center but as the capital of Christendom; indeed, its ability to siphon gold from the Catholic world dampened its rulers' will to undertake reforms. Northern regions, such as the Romagna, had a more resilient economy because of better communications with the North; silk and hemp stimulated industrial production, the University of Bologna maintained intellectual contact with Europe, and fairs and ports spurred trade. Even there, however, depressed agricultural conditions forced sharecroppers into the cities to beg, and a stunted, economically weak bourgeoisie remained subservient to the aristocracy.

Consisting of a mix of ancient feudal families, "nephews" descended from past popes and cardinals, and dignitaries of the papal court, this ruling class ran the papal government and the Church for its own benefit. Strengthened by imposition of a fairly centralized papal authority in the sixteenth century, this group resisted Enlightenment culture so successfully that the reform initiated with severe criticism of papal policy from abroad. Slowly the papal government implemented some measures such as the abolition of taxes and tolls in 1793, but these proved both late and inadequate to avert the crisis of the state in the late eighteenth century.

The little Duchies of Parma and Modena round out this survey of the Center. Both areas were centers of Enlightenment reform and culture, Modena being particularly noted for the activities of Ludovico Antonio Muratori, the historian of Italian cultural unity.

The South

In the South, the Kingdoms of Naples and of Sicily boasted Enlightenment writers who were of high quality but were defeated by a feudalistic social structure and the unwillingness of the rulers to adopt the drastic reform measures necessary to redress the poor economic and social conditions. Although these two kingdoms had the same ruler, they were administratively distinct and will be discussed separately.

Surveying his new possessions from his capital in Naples, the king, Charles of Bourbon (1734–1759), would have observed the most disparate kingdom on the peninsula. It consisted of six different regions that lacked a commercial and industrial base, possessed few roads, and organized agricultural production only for local markets. With a population of almost 410,000, the city of Naples, the largest city in Italy and one of the biggest in Europe, dominated the entire state. Naples, however, owed its size to its position as the seat of government, its appeal as a residential center for a nobility that refused to manage its lands, and its attraction for enormous numbers of peasants abandoning the land to find work as servants or to beg. Very little commerce or industry existed in the city, which lived off the countryside and best illustrated the economic disequilibrium that afflicted the kingdom.

In addition, Charles's Spanish forebears had bequeathed him a mixed heredity where the nobility was concerned. They had drastically reduced the nobility's governmental role at the center, but in the countryside the nobles had increased their power, retaining crucial functions such as tax collection and the dispensing of justice. In addition, out of two thousand towns, Charles had jurisdiction over less than fifty.

Rural economic and social conditions varied but were among the worst in Italy. Except in areas suitable for growing fruits, vegetables, grapes, and olives, extensive agriculture characterized by the primitive production of cereals alternated with long periods of leaving the land fallow. Tenant farmers worked large baronial holdings under miserable living conditions, with many forced to become day laborers or to leave the land.

Important trends, which might have signalled possible changes, did not alter this dismal picture. Throughout Europe, the eighteenth century witnessed enormous inflation. The Neapolitan barons, living in Naples and straining to keep up with the social requirements of a brilliant court, incurred large debts; to increase their income, they raised the fees and dues that peasants had to pay and, when that was not enough, sold off parts of their land or "rented" them to overseers. This new group—small propertyholders, merchants, moneylenders, administrative employees—opposed the feudal interests of the nobility and created a new tension in the countryside. The struggle, however, neither created an agrarian bourgeoisie nor substantially weakened the nobility, because the new class failed to develop new products or methods of production.

This disappointing result occurred despite the collaboration of notable illuministi with Charles's chief minister, Bernardo Tanucci, and his successors. Enlightenment intellectuals such as Antonio Genovesi and Gaetano Filangieri sought to eliminate the worst aspects of feudalism, but Neapolitan monarchs reacted weakly to the resistance of the privileged classes, and Tanucci did not agree with the more extreme measures the philosophes suggested. In 1741, for example, Charles ordered a land survey, but, unlike the land and production reform policies in Lombardy, poor implementation of reform policies in the

South ensured that the barons did not pay their fair share and that the poor would continue carrying the major burden of taxation, exacerbated by an expensive military policy. The kingdom remained economically backward; it exported unfinished products such as raw silk, olive oil, and grain and imported finished products while running a very high deficit.

Probably the Neapolitan Enlightenment succeeded best in its Church policy. With a disproportionately large number of priests, vast landholdings, important fiscal and legal privileges, and the government's inability to block the flow of vast sums to the pope, the Church presented a more serious problem in Naples than it did in other Italian states.

Energetic action to restrict Church influence began early. In 1741, a new concordat (an agreement regulating Church-State relations) limited the Church's fiscal privileges and the authority of Church courts. Soon thereafter the Inquisition was abolished, and Tanucci suppressed many monasteries, abolished mortmain for new acquisitions, expelled the Jesuits, confiscated their property, and abolished ecclesiastical tithes (taxes). The Church's power was still significant at the end of the century, but it had greatly diminished.

Ferdinand IV succeeded Charles but left policy to his wife, Austrian princess Maria Carolina, and to her English advisor, John Acton. Reform policies continued until 1792, when, fearful that Enlightenment ideas would produce a revolution as they had in France, the two reversed course.

Despite the high intellectual quality of the Neapolitan Enlightenment and its strong international ties, it produced fewer results than the Enlightenment movement did in either Lombardy or Tuscany. Illuminista collaboration ended in Naples, as it had in the other Italian states, on a note of failure and resentment that would plunge the kingdom into a greater crisis.

In the other Bourbon-controlled kingdom, Sicily, the social situation resembled that of Naples, but because low consumption allowed high grain exportation, the nobility retained a stronger economic position than its Neapolitan counterpart. Moreover, the Sicilian nobles had won important political privileges from the previous Spanish rulers. A small bourgeois class existed in some cities, but its lack of capital condemned it to perpetual weakness, making it dependent on English capital, for example, for development of the wine industry in Marsala. Finally, an active baron-dominated Parliament rounded out the noble advantage.

Until 1781, Neapolitan administrators cooperated with the barons. This changed with the arrival of Domenico Caracciolo, an energetic philosophe who had lived in Paris. His ambitious program would have weakened Sicilian feudalism by limiting the barons' power to confiscate goods and dispense justice, eliminating their political and financial control of the towns, establishing a mechanism to redeem feudal rights, and attacking the barons' financial privileges.

The barons fought back by portraying the Neapolitans as new conquerors attempting to abolish the ancient rights of the Sicilian "nation." Following a pattern all too typical of the eighteenth century, the barons won the support of the very people who would have benefited from the projected reforms. In addition, members of the nobility gradually transformed their fiefs into free land, converting themselves into large landowners while preserving their economic and social privileges.

Daily Life

As might be expected, living conditions at this time varied greatly, depending on social class and region. In the towns, luxurious Renaissance villas, monuments, theaters, fountains, and monumental stairs built for gala occasions (e.g., the Spanish Steps in Rome) contrasted with very poor housing. Low population density characterized urban centers, despite a demographic recovery allowing Rome to reach 163,000 and Florence 72,000. In smaller towns, convicts used cart-drawn water barrels to clean streets, which were unpaved and unnamed and on which stood unnumbered houses. Mild weather encouraged people to live outdoors, selling things, cooking food, washing clothes in the fountains, and relieving themselves in the courtyards. Because of the heat, people rose early and all activity ceased at noon; everyone slept then, resuming their tasks only after the sun had gone down, having dinner very late, and retiring late.

Tradespeople and shops concentrated in specific areas, which eventually took the names of their trades. Wooden signs bearing a symbol of the trade identified the shops. For example, a brass plate identified a Roman barber; and since men with high-pitched voices took the place of women in musical performances, he proudly advertised: "Here we castrate the singers in the Papal chapels."

Travellers remarked upon how well tended the land in the countryside seemed, despite the extreme poverty of the peasants. German poet Goethe wrote: "It would seem impossible to see better-kept fields." In the North, fertile lands, irrigation networks, and landowner interest eased the sharecroppers' lot, but in the South an adverse climate, absentee landlords, isolation, and the lack of public works crushed the sharecroppers. Peasants frequently lived in huts with only a hole in the roof to let out the smoke. In Sicily, most men possessed only a short, brown, sleeveless waistcoat, with a heavy brown or black wool cloak for the winter; women wore dresses of black linen or serge, a handkerchief on their heads, and, on Sundays, a white mantle if they owned one.

As might be expected, peasants and the poor in general did not receive an education, since the Italian states did not establish a public school system. Occasionally a priest who noticed a boy of uncommon intelligence might teach him or arrange for his education in a seminary (not necessarily to become part of the clergy), but the lack of an educational system accounts for the very high illiteracy rate that later afflicted modern Italy. In the middle of the nineteenth century, illiteracy in the South was at 80 percent, but a hundred years earlier it was probably higher and more diffused.

Southern peasants frequently rebelled against their situation. A popular song dating from the fourteenth century demanded: "You promised me six 'handkerchiefs' [pieces of land], and I'm here to claim them . . . for that which you carry on your back [own] is not yours." In the seventeenth century, serious revolts shook the region, but the lack of a strong middle class hampered the evolution of these revolts into revolution. Until the famine of 1763–1764, agricultural conditions probably remained static or even improved. That development, however, worsened the conditions of the sharecroppers and tenants. Lacking reserves, technical skill, and the ability to resist a nobility imposing harsher conditions of land tenure, and forced to borrow money that they could never repay, many of these peasants became day laborers or found other means of subsistence. These developments help explain the great increase in begging that observers report in the eighteenth century.

In the cities, the government's control of food prices and tendency to restrain the worst abuses of the nobility mitigated the poverty there. Begging was rife, but the poor had a better hope of receiving charity and of finding employment in the guilds or as servants in the large number of palaces owned by the aristocracy or the Church hierarchy.

Not all nobles fared better than the common folk. Foreign tourists reported that poor aristocrats resided in large palaces that they could not afford to heat, but, luckily, the wealthy ones were usually generous to foreigners. This was a boon to travellers like Goethe, warned to avoid the "Golden Lion" in Catania: "It is worse than if you had fallen into the clutches of the Cyclops, the Sirens, and the Scyllas all at the same time."

Governments subjected wealthy nobles to dress codes appropriate to their station in life. In Venice, nobles had to wear a toga based upon the dress of the ancient Roman Senate. When capes became fashionable in the seventeenth century, a law punished noblemen caught wearing them in public with five years' imprisonment and a heavy fine. Noblewomen who wore any color other than black suffered a similar fate, since only prostitutes wore bright colors and rouge. These attempts at control failed especially during the eighteenth century, when magazines introduced French and English fashions.

Noblemen hired tutors, usually clergy, to educate their sons, but these were frequently useless. Serious sons of the nobility and the middle class went to Jesuit academies, which were fairly widespread throughout the peninsula. The Jesuits imparted strict discipline and religious instruction to their charges, in addition to a solid grounding in Latin and the classics. After the suppression of the Jesuit order in 1773, the Jansenist-influenced Congregation of Pious Schools became more important. These fathers introduced subjects more appropriate to eighteenth-century interest in economic and agricultural affairs. Italian also was a more important part of the curriculum, and many later supporters of Italian independence came out of these schools.

As might be expected, the increasing importance given to education did not extend to women. Daughters of well-off families generally went off to convents to await marriage, but they were educated primarily in the acquisition of social and domestic skills. Sometimes they learned some reading and writing, but generally parents, who believed it dangerous for women to know how to read because they might be misled by bad books, felt learning the rosary to be far more appropriate. Despite these limitations on their education, there are interesting reports of highly cultivated women in eighteenth-century Italy, and in the major Italian cities, salons run by women—usually noble—were, as in France, major centers of culture.

In eighteenth-century Europe, women were excluded from the recently founded scientific academies—following a long-established practice in the universities. "In Italy, however, a few women succeeded in carving out a niche for themselves. They were excluded neither from the universities and the scientific academies nor from the knowledge expounded by those universities." In fact, Laura Bassi Verati was granted a lectureship at the University of Bologna (in the Papal State) on October 29, 1732, eventually receiving one of the highest salaries at the institution—1200 lire a year.

As a rule, however, women led restricted lives. They did not go out, except to church, and chaperones always accompanied them. Their parents chose their husbands without taking their wishes into consideration, even though the bridegroom was sometimes expected to make some ritual show of love. In Venice, women could dissolve marriages for such reasons as "barbarous treatment by the husband," but during divorce proceedings had to retreat to a convent. Venice prohibited public affection between husbands and wives, contributing to the evolution of the *cicisbeo,* a noble "servant." Frequently encountered in Carlo Goldoni's plays and a staple of upper-class Venetian marriage contracts, the cicisbeo accompanied the noblewoman everywhere, was present during her most intimate functions, but was never her lover. A Venetian satirist described his duty: "to stay constantly by the side of the wife of a third party and by express contract and obligation to be bored by her for days at a time."

Religious attitudes differed greatly from those in modern times. During church services, people chatted, walked around, gathered in crowds, and conducted their business. Religious festivals also provided entertainment. People appeared genuinely attached to their religion—many attended mass daily, recited the rosary nightly, and observed Lent—but they saw no reason to alter their behavior. Brothels burned candles to the Virgin Mary and charged an extra fee to have masses said on special occasions. People gave in to their passions, went to confession, and began all over again.

This pattern shocked no one. Goethe observed a rich nobleman famous for his expensive vices begging for money to ransom slaves captured by the Barbary pirates. When the poet remarked upon the contradiction, he received the following response: "But we are all like that! We gladly pay for our own follies ourselves, but others are expected to provide the money for our virtues." When it came time to reap the rewards of a virtuous life, funerals of the rich were lavish and the deceased was remembered with the grandiose monuments with which Italian churches are decorated. In Sicily, the corpse was frequently dressed in its finest garments and brought seated into the decorated church as musicians played their instruments. In the states most affected by the Enlightenment, however, a reaction against these customs set in; states such as Lombardy and Tuscany regulated funerals even to the point of restricting the number of candles families could have (depending on their social status) and forbidding the use of coffins except for high clergy and nuns.

Culture and Crisis

Whereas contradiction characterized private life, the interaction of philosophy and politics and the manifest failure of reform marked the public life of eighteenth-century Italy. Enlightenment philosophy, however, precluded a return to old methods, spurring the illuministi instead to examine the causes of their failure and on to new action.

European and Italian philosophes had counted upon rulers imbued with their ideas—"Enlightened monarchs"—to reform their countries and in the process justified their leaders on the basis of utilitarianism. The philosophes eventually realized that the monarchs ruled for their own benefit, in essence, exploiting them. At this point, they replaced "Enlightened Monarchy" as a basis for rule with Jean-Jacques Rousseau's "general will," a difficult political concept, which, however, easily translated into "majority rule." In France, a country with an economically powerful and politically sophisticated bourgeoisie, this transition helped produce the Revolution. In Italy, the bourgeoisie's strength varied but nowhere attained the strength of its French counterpart. Thus the collapse of Enlightenment reform due to the withdrawal of government support could not immediately lead to revolution, but it did produce a crisis that made Italian intellectuals receptive to radical social, economic, and political solutions, including the idea of national cohesion.

In Naples, Tanucci rejected the ideas of Antonio Genovesi, a professor of political economy, to free the grain trade and to eliminate government interference in the economy as a means of modernizing the state, alleviating rural poverty, and preventing such terrible catastrophes as the famine of 1763–1764. Famine also hit Tuscany in the 1760s, but by the 1790s the reform movement had petered out or failed. Thus Italy approached the end of the eighteenth century in a severe economic and moral crisis characterized by widespread discontent.

If indeed "a substantial part of the Italian Enlightenment debate can properly be read as testimony to the scale of pauperism," it is comprehensible that with the failure of reform revolutionary ideas current in the rest of Europe should become attractive to Italian intellectuals. In the 1770s and 1780s, for example, Freemasonry appealed to growing numbers of Italian intellectuals, signalling their withdrawal from conventional politics. In the South especially, faith in radical, egalitarian, and communistic methods of solving Italy's problems increased. Influential Neapolitan philosophe Gaetano Filangieri might remain basically optimistic, but he forcefully identified Europe's paramount problem as the minority's monopoly on wealth, and "the remedy to be aimed at," to make certain that "everything be in the hands of the many."

The search for new solutions produced faith not only in egalitarianism and republicanism of the American type but also in a revival of national feeling, the idea that the lot of Italians would improve if the peninsula were united and if the people could work together. But what made the Italians one people? Discussion centered on several elements that emphasized pride and national character. Intellectuals debated the implications of the ideas of Neapolitan philosopher Giambattista Vico, a philsophical giant of the age, in order to understand the relationship between language and nationality. Vico's student Genovesi challenged his colleagues by lecturing at the University of Naples in Italian. Genovesi's reasoning was double-edged: As long as Latin, incomprehensible to most Italians, dominated education, there could be no mass education and no national solidarity; and no nation could develop an independent culture so long as its most important works were written in a foreign language. Accordingly, Genovesi and other scholars wrote in Italian and convincingly argued for the scholarly stature of Italian.

During the same period, "history also became a source of national pride," and Italians turned their emphasis from European to Italian history. Ancient Rome, whose language had dominated the cultural life of the peninsula but now hindered the view of Italians as one people, was deemphasized. In Modena,

Ludovico Antonio Muratori investigated the Middle Ages as the source of modern Italy. He published majestic, accurate collections of medieval documents designed to demonstrate the continuity of Italian history through the ages. One historian believes that because of this kind of activity, "a national feeling resulting from a recognition of a common cultural heritage, common historical traditions, common economic interests, and common language" made progress during the eighteenth century.

This view does not contradict the cosmopolitan essence of the Italian Enlightenment, but it suggests the multiple antecedents of the Risorgimento. Between 1700 and 1789, European influences found quick acceptance in Italy, despite the resistance of an older culture, and transformed the static situation of the previous century into a dynamic one. Historian Giorgio Candeloro believed that the political, social, economic, and cultural conditions that emerged during the period combined with the impetus of the French Revolution to create a necessary "preface" to the Risorgimento.

In short, the Italian and European cultural strains, and their complex interaction with Atlantic society and politics, must be understood to analyze the Italian Enlightenment on its own merits and to appreciate its implications.

2

Italy and the French Revolution

THE FRENCH REVOLUTION's impact on Italy has aroused fierce debate. Did the Risorgimento originate during the Enlightenment, the dawn of national awareness, or was it another nineteenth-century spin-off of the French Revolution? Historians have not reached a consensus on this question, but many believe that the social and political changes induced by the Revolution—and therefore its influence on the Risorgimento—would have been impossible without the Enlightenment.

Greeting Revolution

The last chapter described how Enlightenment measures stimulated only the limited development of a modern bourgeoisie. The growth of groups profiting from inflationistic economic trends and antifeudalistic governmental action through the acquisition of land, management of noble holdings, or rents, a "primitive" capitalism, increased tensions with the ruling classes and contributed to the impoverishment of many peasants. In addition, because of the Europe-wide price rise, real wages dropped and poverty increased dramatically. This social crisis coincided with the cultural and political crisis, the growth of radical ideas, and the new emphasis on cultural and linguistic unity.

Thus, the Italian situation had become critical by 1789, when the French Revolution exploded. Between then and 1795, the Revolution found both popular support and a warm welcome from disillusioned Italian intellectuals. Disorders erupted in several states, as in Naples, where demonstrators wished "to do as the French are doing," or Piedmont, where crowds shouted "Long Live France!" The intellectuals had already gone beyond cultural considerations, advocating Italian political revival. Piedmontese playwright Vittorio Alfieri, who dedicated one of his works to "the American liberator," George Washington, symbolized this feeling. Intellectuals published draft constitutions, favored French ideals, and transformed Masonic lodges into Jacobin organizations. The turmoil caused by the Revolution favored the intellectuals' activities by exacerbating the economic crisis: Prices rose, trade difficulties increased, and the fiscal burden worsened as arms spending increased. Furthermore, the governments responded to French developments by truncating reform policies, allying with the Church, and repressing the opposition. Intellectuals and governments set upon a collision course, but Italians imbued with French revolutionary principles could make slight headway without outside help.

Statecraft in a Revolutionary Era

The wars of the French Revolution that began in 1792 ended the long peace between France and Austria, who once more fought for supremacy in Italy. One important difference, however, marked this struggle. Frightened by revolution, Italian monarchs did not negotiate for advantages but connected with Austria. Despite French attempts to secure Piedmontese support, this state quickly allied itself with Austria. In short, Piedmont threw away its strategic advantage and allowed itself to be exploited diplomatically by Austria. Naples and Tuscany preferred to remain neutral, but the British coerced them into war. French policy appeared torn between traditional diplomatic initiatives and revolutionary aims. While French agents attempted to convert Italian dissatisfaction into revolution, their government acted to exploit revolutionary fervor for expansionist ends.

The primary reason for this development was the course of the French Revolution itself. The Revolution's "moderate" phase ended in late 1792, when France found itself at war with most of Europe. There followed a radical period when the Jacobins seized control, which lasted until July-August 1794, during the French revolutionary month of Thermidor, when they lost power. The French overhauled their form of government in 1795, setting up the Directory (a government that consisted of five directors chosen by two councils). These changes had important effects on Italy. The Directory pursued a conservative domestic path and exploited French revolutionary ideals to extend French influence abroad. These policies created the premise for a fight with the Italians because they remained committed to Jacobinism after its defeat in France and resented French expansionism. In addition, France and the conservative European powers, united in a series of coalitions, continued fighting during the years the Directory remained in power. These conflicts had important effects on Italy because the French first became dominant on the peninsula, then were defeated, and then returned for several years until their definitive defeat. A host of shifting territorial arrangements in Italy during the French revolutionary and Napoleonic periods reflected these events.

After war broke out in 1792, the French quickly occupied Savoy and Nice, but then the French army bogged down. In March 1796, however, Napoleon Bonaparte, from the formerly Genoese island of Corsica, became French commander on the Italian front. On April 12 he unloosed a campaign that broke through enemy lines, defeated the Piedmontese, and chased the Austrians out of Italy. He came within seventy-five miles of Vienna before the Treaty of Campoformio was signed in 1797. With the Austrian defeat, Napoleon, who enjoyed considerable autonomy from the weak Directory, controlled the entire peninsula.

Italian Jacobinism

The French conquerors made a host of complex, constantly shifting territorial alterations in Italy. They established several republics governed by a Directory (as was the case in France between 1795 and 1799) and that embraced areas previously part of different states. This provided many Italians with the important experience of living, working, and governing together.

In the North, Napoleon established the short-lived Cispadane Republic (consisting of the papal legations of Bologna and Ferrara and of the Duchy of Modena), and the Transpadane Republic (which included the Duchies of Milan and Mantua), later merged into the Cisalpine Republic. By October 1797 the Cisalpine Republic was further enlarged and included three and one-half million inhabitants who had formerly been subjects of several different states. The French reorganized Genoa into the Ligurian Republic and, in February 1798, incorporated the pope's domains into the Roman Republic after the pope's exile. This last development provoked a Neapolitan attack, with Austrian and British support, resulting in a Bourbon defeat, the royal family's escape to Sicily, and establishment of a Neapolitan Republic in January 1799.

Despite replacement of the radical Jacobins in Paris with a moderate Directory in Paris, Jacobin influence pervaded the peninsula during this period. Indeed, informed scholars from Italian Giorgio Vaccarini to English historian Stuart Woolf agree that the staunchly republican Italian Jacobins, or "patriots," posed the question of Italian revival in political and social terms, calling for unity, independence, and a republic. Giorgio Candeloro argued that a pan-Italian "Jacobin-patriotic" movement formed between 1789 and 1795 and, by posing the Italian problem in political terms, constituted a "revolutionary" development.

The story of the French revolutionary impact in Italy, therefore, could not be linear, since the French discouraged an Italian revolution for domestic and diplomatic reasons. Thus, although heavily influenced by France, significant intellectual independence, a degree of political autonomy, and a complex relationship with the "Revolutionary Fatherland"—not simple "satellite" status—characterized the republics of this era.

Even before the French conquest, for example, Piedmontese Jacobins conspired with Filippo Buonarroti. Buonarroti, a law graduate of the University of Pisa, former official of the French Jacobin government, and participant in Gracchus Babeuf's communistic "conspiracy of the equals" in 1796, would become the major European conspiratorial figure in the early nineteenth century. Buonarroti and his Italian friends planned a Piedmontese uprising that would gain popular support by attacking feudalism and instituting a republic as the first step in the liberation of all Italy.

This plan failed because of the conspirators' arrests in Paris and Napoleon's rapid advance. The conspiracy had positive results in terms of political experience for the Italians, but negative repercussions on France's Italian policy because it branded Italians as radical followers of Babeuf. Ironically, French officials concluded that they should not "republicanize" Italy because the Italian youth, "excited and carried away by ideas borrowed from our revolution, . . . want to stir things up, without knowing how, without calculating their resources, without any clear and balanced ideas about what sort of thing they want to set up." In the debate about Italy's future, in which the Jacobins demanded an independent and unified Italian republic, the Directory favored conservative currents and viewed the peninsula as an area to be exploited economically to pay for France's wars. In fact, after initial pro-French euphoria, this attitude caused many Italians to turn against the French and support the counterrevolutionary movements of 1799.

Napoleon's political ambition also proved critical. His military successes gave him a great deal of independence from Paris, and he used it to gain support. This meant allowing the Italians some freedom to debate the crucial issues but not allowing these ideas to be translated into action. At the same time, Napoleon controlled the conquered areas, intervened in the republics' domestic affairs, and drew their boundaries to ensure continued Italian military dependence on France. Napoleon's decision to award the Venetian Republic to Austria despite the protests of Italian patriots was the most clamorous example of this policy.

Within the context of French revolutionary Italy, therefore, Italian Jacobin ideas had little chance of being realized; nevertheless, they had an important effect on the future.

What were some of the points discussed?

Although differences existed on the process, composition, and political form a united Italy would assume, the Jacobins never wavered in their total commitment to a unified, independent Italian republic. They also believed that French revolutionary ideals would free Italy and regenerate Italian society, but they identified these ideals in the most radical phase of the French Revolution, which had ended in France. Italian Jacobins had absolute faith in education as a means of eliminating Church influence and inspiring egalitarian democracy; and they viewed the creation of a small, independent, peasant property-holding class as essential to the future of their country. But how to create such a class and how to eliminate poverty? Here debate raged, as it had in France. Jacobin Melchiorre Gioia advocated cutting up Church estates for distribution to the poor; others wanted equal distribution of land, imposition of a maximum income, or the abolition of property. All supported state intervention on behalf of the poor through public assistance.

Within this context, Italian Jacobins stirringly debated the meaning of *democracy,* a term that frequently appeared in the titles of their newspapers. For them, democracy and republicanism were inseparable. More interesting, they favored representative government over the precepts of Rousseau, the thinker who most influenced French Jacobins, agreeing with moderate political philosopher Charles Louis Montesquieu. Though Jacobinism has come to be identified with totalitarianism, some observers find the origins of the "making of Italian democracy"—a term originally applied to a much later period—in this "Jacobin triennium."

But Italian Jacobinism ran into difficulty as early as 1797. Jacobins advocating the liberation and regeneration of Italy and humanity called for French evacuation of their country so a revolution could proceed in a unified republic without foreign interference. Napoleon responded by repressing patriotic exponents and organizations. By 1798 leading Jacobins flocked out of Lombardy, the radical center, admitting defeat by moving on to Rome and Naples.

The Early Republics

Practical developments in the various republics set up by the French reflected the badly divided Italian situation. The French government and, eventually, Napoleon lumped together as enemies both "reactionaries" who favored the old order and "anarchistic" Jacobins arguing for radical change and Italian unity. Furthermore, the confusing rival claims of Italian cities and regions tried their patience, as did Italian attempts at independent policies designed to further patriotic aims. By now the French were primarily interested in exacting payments from the Italians to help finance their wars, in coercing the republics to raise their own armies for French ends, and in taxing to pay for French forces stationed on Italian soil.

The French imposed moderate governments that would follow these policies. When the Cispadane Republic in the North proved unruly, Napoleon abolished it, reordered its territory, and established the Cisalpine Republic. The constitution of this and the other republics reflected the French governmental setup, with an executive consisting of five directors and a legislature composed of two houses elected by a restricted suffrage. Rigid administrative centralization was also imported from revolutionary France, and Napoleon personally named the highest officials. But he still faced fierce opposition from democrats influenced by French Jacobin ideals who demanded social justice measures such as price controls and progressive taxation.

In Milan, heart of the Cisalpine Republic, the financial crisis caused by French exactions and Napoleon's hostility defeated advanced democratic demands, but a series of reforms paralleling those of the early French Revolution—abolition of feudalism, tithes, and primogeniture; the confiscation of Church lands; the institution of civil matrimony; and the declaration of equality of men and women—were undertaken. As had been the case in France, these measures generally favored both the middle class and peasants.

The more moderate southern Jacobins obtained fewer results. In Rome, the Jacobins could operate primarily through their political clubs and newspapers, and in Naples the French quickly eliminated the more democratic leaders. Indeed, in Naples the failure to grant significant reforms beyond the abolition of primogeniture spelled disaster for the Parthenopean Republic.

Counterrevolution

Because France's overly powerful position disrupted the balance of power, the European war resumed in 1799. The allies of the "Second Coalition" aimed to reduce French dominance in Italy. At the same time, French exactions, the plundering of wealth and artworks, the identification of Italian Jacobins as pro-French traitors, and revolutionary anticlericalism inflamed the common people. These elements produced an explosion, at the same time popular and reactionary, against the French invaders and their Italian supporters.

This development had its most important manifestation in Naples. Proclaimed on January 22, 1799, the Parthenopean Republic moved rapidly to give Naples an administration of the French type, but it acted on a law abolishing feudalism only on April 25, when the peasants had already risen against it. This procrastination proved to be the republic's undoing.

In January, Cardinal Fabrizio Ruffo had already organized the *Armata cristiana e reale*, also called the Army of the Holy Faith (Sanfedista), to retake Naples. He landed in Calabria and, by playing upon the peasants' blind faith, loyalty to the king, and hatred of taxes, he provoked a mass uprising against the republic. The peasants extraordinary marching song proclaimed themes that motivated them:

> To the sound of the beating drum
> Long live the little people;
> To the sound of tambourines
> the poor have risen.
> To the sound of bells
> long live the populace;
> To the sound of violins
> death to the Jacobins.

As for French revolutionary principles:

> The French arrived
> they taxed us;
> Liberté . . . egalité
> you rob me
> I rob thee!

In April 1799, Austrian victories in Lombardy placed French forces in jeopardy, and they withdrew from Naples, leaving the Neapolitan Jacobins to fend for themselves. Ruffo marched north, taking the capital after a heroic resistance. "Defenceless men, women, and children were butchered in hundreds by the lazzaroni [lower classes]," wrote historian R. M. Johnston. After a heroic resistance, the patriots signed a capitulation that guaranteed their lives. In July, however, King Ferdinand IV, pushed by English Admiral Horatio Nelson and Queen Maria Carolina, unilaterally declared the agreement null and void. In a move condemned in all Europe, the restored government slaughtered the flower of Neapolitan intelligentsia with a ruthlessness remembered to the present day.

The Neapolitan counterrevolution, the most famous incident of its kind, raises interesting questions and had important implications. The most important question is, Why did the revolutionary government fail to achieve popular support? The answer seemingly lies in the failure to abolish the vestiges of feudalism quickly and the underestimation of the depth of popular feeling; but the skill with which Ruffo played upon peasant religious devotion and hatred of foreigners and high taxes was also important. According to the classic account of the counterrevolution by Vincenzo Cuoco, the intellectuals themselves concluded that the people were misled and that there existed "two peoples, divided by two different climates and two centuries of history." Also, "nowhere else has a monarch ever sentenced to prison, death, and exile prelates, gentlemen, generals, admirals, writers, scientists, poets, philosophers, jurists, and nobles—the intellectual and spiritual flower of the country." Revenge and a desire to decapitate future revolutions explain the Ferdinand's action, but Nelson aimed to destroy French influence and guarantee future British dominance over Naples and its strategic ports—in addition to impressing his mistress.

Finally, the implications. During the Parthenopean Republic's brief life, culture flourished. In the *Monitore napolitano*, the major vehicle of intellectual discussion, Jacobins such as Eleonora De Fonseca Pimental, one of the reaction's most illustrious victims, analyzed Neapolitan conditions and debated crucial reforms. The republicans also considered the fate of all Italy. In June 1799, in coordination with Italians from different parts of the peninsula, an appeal for the proclamation of a "single, indivisible, and independent Italian Republic" came to an unfriendly French Directory. Later declarations blamed French failure to endorse this goal as a reason for their defeat in Italy.

Philosopher and historian Benedetto Croce stressed the importance of failed noble experiments consecrated by tragic defeats as a prime motivating force in history. He argued that, for this reason, the massacre of the Neapolitan patriots had enduringly positive consequences for the entire peninsula. In the South it "created a revolutionary tradition and education by example," and it forced the Neapolitan monarchy to rely upon the plebian element, "transforming the Enlightened monarchy of Charles of Bourbon into the paupers' monarchy" that ended in 1860. It taught modern Italian liberals not to rely on the word of foreign governments. And, most important, it "planted the first seeds of Italian unity" by making Italians understand the need for a revolutionary movement based on the cooperation of the most "cultured" classes from all parts of Italy.

French-dominated northern Italy fell under a combined Austro-Russian assault in 1799, and elements similar to the Neapolitan counterrevolution could be discerned elsewhere—especially in Tuscany and Lombardy. Although some reforms of the early French Revolution were implemented, the Directory's Italian policy had failed. The French government's rapaciousness had alienated the people, and French hostility to the idea of Italian unification had diminished loyalty to France.

Napoleon in Italy

The Directory's domestic policies and its foreign failures produced the coup d'etat of 18 Brumaire (November 9, 1799), which brought Napoleon Bonaparte to power in France. His Italian origins and his professed special interest in Italy hinted at support for its future unification. The French ruler had no intention of favoring independence, but his rhetoric reinforced the nationalist ideals of the French Revolution. In addition, by consolidating Italy into a few states, he brought together former inhabitants of different political constituencies and provided them the opportunity to work together. Along with French reforms, this development created a more efficient political class, unattached to the old regimes, that would have an important role in the early Risorgimento. The increased economic opportunities created by wider markets and the experience of fighting in the same army under the same flag explains the qualitative leap forward of the idea of Italian unity during the Napoleonic period.

Prudent historians, however, will consider the negative aspects as well. Despite the existence of native states that struggled to formulate independent policies, the peninsula remained a conquered land that had a subordinate place in Napoleon's schemes of empire. The need to subsidize French military costs and the "Continental System," which favored French industry, limited economic opportunities. And though armies may convey a feeling of national glory, the draft, the expenses, the casualties, and the recognition that Italian soldiers were fighting for foreign aims caused resentment.

After taking power, Napoleon addressed foreign affairs, defeating Austria in the Battle of Marengo in northern Italy on June 14, 1800. Further victories produced the Treaty of Lunéville with Austria (February 9, 1801), which recognized French dominance on the peninsula. Thereafter, until his fall, Napoleon retained control of Italy, except for the islands of Sicily and Sardinia, where the exiled kings of Naples and Piedmont remained under British protection.

Napoleon's territorial reorganization of the peninsula occurred in two phases, from 1800 to 1802 and from 1805 to 1809. Practical considerations concerning the empire as a whole, not any continuity in Napoleon's thought or action toward Italians, dictated the changes. At first Napoleon reestablished the old republics, then reorganized them into the Italian Republic with himself as president. As usual, the French-dominated states reflected French governmental organization and became kingdoms after Napoleon declared himself emperor in 1804. By 1809 Napoleonic Italy had taken on final form, with the Kingdom of Italy in the North, the Kingdom of Naples in the South, and large areas (including Piedmont and the city of Rome) ruled directly as parts of Imperial France.

The Italian Republic and the Kingdom of Italy

Following an abortive attempt at reviving the Cisalpine Republic, Napoleon created the Italian Republic in the North (1802). Once again, the republic's

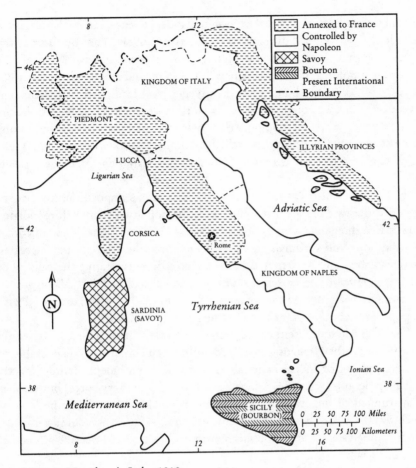

MAP 2   Napoleonic Italy, 1812

constitution paralleled the French constitution imposed by Napoleon and that reserved all power to him. Napoleon made himself president of the new republic but chose as his vice president Francesco Melzi d'Eril, a prominent Milanese patrician of moderate liberal views who was deeply hostile to Jacobinism and a strong supporter of property rights and Italian independence. Napoleon delegated a fair amount of autonomy to Melzi, but disputes still occurred because of the vice president's support of Italian independence.

Melzi imposed French-inspired governmental institutions and laws and relied on the wealthy landowning class to make them function. Representative bodies modeled on Napoleonic France were instituted at the center, and a French-style administrative structure was established at the local level. Melzi considered an efficient state structure essential for eventual independence, but he did not favor the radicals and found it difficult to secure active involvement by the wealthy classes even though his economic policies favored them. He had some success in creating a political personnel, a new tax system, and an effective police, but his suspicion of critics limited his effectiveness and facilitated Napoleon's intervention. Thus, although the Italians worked on comprehensive legislation, delays caused the French to impose their own law codes; this legislation, among the most advanced in Europe, signalled a definitive break with the old regime, but certain aspects, such as reintroduction of the death penalty, caused resentment.

Church policy also provoked disputes. Napoleon's imposition, in 1803, of the concordat that France had signed with the pope two years before violated Melzi's Enlightenment conception of Church-State relations. The concordat gave the pope and cardinals more authority over the Church and increased prestige in the state. An irritated Melzi issued a decree restating the validity of earlier laws that, in the Jansenist tradition, had curbed the Church's power. In this manner, he attenuated the concordat's effect until Napoleon quarreled with the pope and set off another power struggle with the Church.

Melzi also had a different conception of the role that an Italian army would have. He and other Italians considered an independent army indispensable to the development of Italian national consciousness and independence—exactly what Napoleon feared. The French ruler favored a military force, but only as an instrument of imperial policy. Despite many difficulties—not the least of which was the lack of homogeneity and desertions—Melzi introduced a military conscription system and a republican army took shape and became a focus of patriotic fervor.

Within its circumscribed sphere, Melzi's diplomacy challenged Napoleon. Perhaps as a step toward eventual unification, Melzi hoped to expand the republic's frontiers, especially in Venetia, and undertook talks to achieve that end. Napoleon disapproved of this activity and stopped it. In fact, Napoleon limited Melzi's options, refusing to allow the Italian Republic to exchange diplomatic representatives with other states and obliging it to go through French diplomats; in addition, French involvement of the republic in wars without consultation further revealed the republic's dependent status.

In 1804 Napoleon proclaimed himself emperor. Even more than before, he enforced uniformity upon his client states, removing their leaders if they resisted his orders. In Italy he transformed the Italian Republic into the Kingdom of Italy and named as viceroy his stepson Eugène Beauharnais, who was much more subservient than the independent Melzi. French institutions and policies were introduced with greater determination than previously, but Napoleon's subordination of the kingdom's interests to his own and the increasing pace of his wars created enormous cracks in the structure.

The landowners had profited from Melzi's policies, which had brought stability, allowed them to buy public lands cheaply, and liberated them from the incubus of Jacobinism. Furthermore, the price rise of agricultural goods had more than compensated them for tax increases and the loss of feudal privileges. The commercial and industrial bourgeoisie had benefited from the establishment of a large state free of customs barriers, the unification of weights and measures, existence of a single currency, the expenditures of the Italian and French armies, and the building of new roads. The textile and silk industries boomed, and Italian products found markets in England, France, Germany, Austria, and Switzerland.

Napoleon's desire to subordinate the Kingdom of Italy economically to France and his attempt to ruin the British economy through the prohibition of trade with his enemy (the Continental System) eventually suffocated these promising economic developments. French economic policies favored French landowners and bourgeoisie by blocking the exportation of Italian products to France, favoring the importation of French products, and disrupting old patterns of trade with parts of Italy annexed to France. The Continental System exacerbated the effects of this discrimination by closing Italy to trade with Britain and by subjecting it to a British blockade. As in other parts of the empire, the Continental System provoked economic disaster and turned property owners and merchants against Napoleon.

In addition to economic factors, French military policy also provoked opposition. The positive effects of an Italian army have already been noted, but the constant utilization of that force in all parts of Europe for the benefit of the French Empire, and the great number of casualties, made conscripts—most of whom were peasants—less eager to serve. In the later years of the kingdom, draft dodging and desertions increased, providing greater impetus to the banditry that afflicted the state.

Adding to this phenomenon was the unhappiness of the lower classes, whose lives had not been substantially improved during the Napoleonic domination. Indeed, the conservative policies, of both the Italian Republic and the Kingdom of Italy, that had strengthened the landowners had as the other side of the coin the lack of improvement for the poor. Although there was a widespread revolt in 1809, the lower classes seem to have been characterized by an increasingly "passive awaiting of events which sooner or later would have decided the fortunes of Europe and of Italy."

This attitude had its counterpart even in the middle class and among noble moderates who had benefited by government jobs. Napoleon's desire to surround himself with technicians who would execute orders without elaborating independent programs prevented formation of a reform party such as had existed in the eighteenth century, despite the existence of a large state that might have been the nucleus of a united Italy. As time went on, French policies deprived proponents of independence of all hope. Despite Napoleon's attempt to fire their enthusiasm through official organizations, they dropped out of politics.

These elements made the Napoleonic Kingdom of Italy a structure with little content, destined to disappear with its creator.

The Kingdom of Naples

In southern Italy, the Bourbon monarchy restored by the lazzaroni in 1799 punished the nobility because some of its elements had supported the Parthenopean Republic but failed to deliver on promised fiscal reforms or to break up feudal property. Mirroring the monarchy's failure to garner mass support was its ambiguous foreign policy, which alienated the large powers. Naples's precarious situation allowed Napoleon to declare Ferdinand IV deposed, and a French army occupied the capital in February 1806. The king and his court fled once again to Sicily, from where he encouraged a repeat of the 1799 uprising. This effort presented a serious problem to the French because the attempt became embroiled with brigandage. Strong government forces put down the revolt, but brigandage remained an endemic problem.

Napoleon's brother Joseph became the first French King of Naples until he left to be King of Spain in May 1808. A French cavalry general and Napoleon's brother-in-law, Joachim Murat, replaced Joseph in July of the same year.

As had been the case in northern Italy, both men introduced reforms of the French type. Indeed, these measures, many of which had been discussed during the Enlightenment but had not been implemented, affected southern Italy more than the Napoleonic regimes influenced the North. Because of the South's less-advanced starting point, however, these reforms could not bring the region's social structure to the North's level in the years of French rule from 1806 to 1814. Indeed, although the Napoleonic reformers—French and Neapolitan—struggled to improve economic and social conditions, they opposed radical action to modernize southern society.

As usual, the new rulers applied Napoleonic legislation to Naples. They instituted law codes and rationalized and simplified the fiscal system, which gained a modern footing. They abolished feudalism, and many Church lands were confiscated and sold to the benefit of the bourgeoisie and other wealthy landowners. Although these developments improved the lot of the provincial bourgeoisie, they did not result in the modernization of southern agriculture. The southern peasant remained poor, and land hunger continued to be the region's major problem.

Despite these issues, the Napoleonic regimes in Naples seem to have aroused a greater energetic response than their northern counterparts. To consolidate themselves, the rulers sought compromises with leading Neapolitan exponents, bringing them into their governments in important positions. Under Napoleon's brother Joseph, the French element predominated and the king closely followed Napoleon's policies. Murat, however, gave predominance to the Neapolitans, achieved semiautonomy from Napoleon, and worked toward independence. He balanced the budget, helped industry, spurred education, and, most important, developed a well-trained army out of which issued many future patriots. He also established communication with patriots hoping to unify Italy.

As a result, unlike in northern Italy, government functionaries formed in Napoleonic Naples did not "drop out" of politics. On the contrary, they became ever more active in the hope of gaining a greater participation in government, even entering the numerous secret societies formed during the period. Murat opposed creation of an effective parliament, but his desire for greater Neapolitan autonomy and, later, his support of Italy's independence proved an important meeting ground. For all its weaknesses, during this period the Kingdom of Naples kept alive the hope for Italian unity and independence.

3

The First War For Italian Unity

By THE TIME Napoleon invaded Russia in 1812, he faced passive or outright opposition throughout his empire. A guerrilla war raged in Spain while in Italy widespread dislike of the Napoleonic order affected all regions and classes. The Continental System suffocated the middle class, which Napoleon's economic and legislative reforms had initially stimulated; his desire to create loyal, apolitical functionaries and his aversion to persons with potential political programs alienated the rich bourgeoisie and nobility, the bedrock of his social stability policies; his fight with the Church culminated in the pope's arrest and alienated the clergy. The peasantry, damaged by a pro-landowner and high tax policy, was now further exasperated by conscription and the heavy casualties of the Napoleonic Wars.

Nevertheless, French reforms and Italian reaction to them helped significantly in extending the principles of unity and independence for the peninsula. Italy remained rural, the peasants uneducated, and most Italians lacked a national consciousness, but if the desire for unity had previously taken root among radicals and influential intellectuals, it now spread to at least part of the middle class and would soon take on a life of its own. By creating new states, no matter how dependent, the French raised Italian national consciousness. Although it would not be true to say that the desire for unification was widespread among Italians, by 1812 they understood both the economic benefits that a larger trading area would bring and that France exploited a conquered Italy for its own purposes. For intellectuals at least, the jump from there to a demand for unification would not be a large one.

Growth of the Secret Societies

Since the Napoleonic police system prevented open opposition, Italians formed secret societies. Originating in eighteenth century Freemasonry, these societies had diverse political orientations, organizations, and rituals but became conspiratorial after 1794. This development first occurred in France among groups anxious to restore either Jacobinism or the monarchy. In Italy, reactionary societies also existed, but the nationalistic-patriotic societies have particular importance because many active fighters for Italian unification would emerge from them. Especially active in the South during the Napoleonic period, they were the first widespread, influential groups advocating independence and a constitution.

Members of the Society of the Rays, dissolved in 1802, initiated these clandestine liberal groups in which, despite usually vague programs, republican, Buonarrotian, and French revolutionary ideas predominated. The largest such society was the Carboneria, or society of the charcoal burners (*carbonari*), most active in the South because of the prodigious activity of a French official who served both Joseph Bonaparte and Murat. Indeed, Murat and his government had contacts with the Carboneria during its early years; a break occurred only in 1813 to 1815, when—influenced by British agents whipping up feeling against the French—the carbonari demanded a liberal constitution, which Murat refused to grant, ostensibly because it would weaken his power.

The Failure of the "Pure Italians"

By December 1812, the consequences of Napoleon's Russian defeat had become clear. Of the Kingdom of Italy's 27,000-man army, for example, 1,000 survived. This disaster increased underlying anti-Napoleon feeling and contributed to a growing sentiment for independence. But many negative factors conspired against the realization of this hope.

In 1812 the British had forced the Bourbons to issue a constitution in Sicily, a move that bolstered the false claim that the reactionaries favored a constitution and independence. Furthermore, though the secret societies desired a constitution, they lacked a well-defined program and a coordinated organization. They operated in an atmosphere of war weariness and mistrust that, given their clandestine nature, they could not hope to overcome. In these circumstances, the patriots faced for the first time a problem that would recur throughout the Risorgimento: how to utilize a constituted state—and its bureaucracy, army, and diplomacy—for their goal of uniting Italy.

In the North the patriotic movement was especially fragmented. The "pure Italians," led by Count Federico Confalonieri, had a particularly unrealistic program. With Napoleon tottering, they hoped to eliminate French influence, gain British support to prevent an Austrian restoration, and obtain the Kingdom of Italy's independence by accepting any king agreeable to the allies. When Napoleon abdicated, Eugène Beauharnais's supporters convoked the Senate, hoping to petition the allies to recognize him as sovereign of an independent kingdom, but the senators refused. Despite this setback, Eugène prepared to declare himself king, provoking a mass revolt led by Confalonieri and his friends. Austria used this pretext to intervene. As the Austrians moved into Lombardy, a depressed Eugène handed the area over to them.

Since British officials had favored Lombard independence, Confalonieri appealed to Lord Castlereagh, in charge of foreign affairs, to support an independent and constitutional North Italian regime. Tied to an Austrian alliance, Castlereagh refused. His statement that the Lombards had nothing to fear from a "paternal Austrian government" provoked a defiant statement from Confalonieri announcing that Italians would never accept Austrian domination. On June 12, 1814, Austria officially annexed Lombardy, signalling the swift failure of the "pure Italians."

Murat and the War for Unity

Like Prince Eugène, Joachim Murat fought in Russia at Napoleon's side, but, unlike Eugène, Murat criticized Napoleon and, despite some hesitation at turning against the emperor, was determined to save his Neapolitan throne. At the end of his ill-fated Russian expedition in December 1812, Napoleon left Murat in charge of his defeated army and went to raise a new force in France; anxious to take charge of his own kingdom during a delicate diplomatic moment, however, Murat suddenly relinquished this command to Eugène and returned to Naples.

Murat had been distancing himself from Napoleon for some time. Influenced by his Neapolitan councilors, King Joachim had resisted implementation of the emperor's orders when they adversely affected the Neapolitan people. Furthermore, Pietro Colletta, a contemporary observer, testified that these advisers had previously convinced Murat that he should adopt a policy favoring Italian independence and perhaps unity. Seeking to remain in Italy as an independent sovereign after Napoleon's defeat, Murat initiated negotiations with the Austrians and the British.

As talks dragged on, a faltering Napoleon remained powerful enough to pressure Murat to aid Eugène in northern Italy. In August 1813 Murat did so, but without his army and leaving his wife Caroline (Napoleon's sister) to continue negotiations with the allies. Following Napoleon's defeat at the Battle of Leipzig in November 1813, Murat returned to Naples and in December and January occupied Tuscany and large parts of the Papal State. Irritated by Murat's diplomatic and military actions but preoccupied by Napoleon's continued resistance, the allies finally reached agreement with Murat. Austria recognized him as King of Naples and promised territorial gains at the pope's expense; in turn, Murat renounced his claim to Sicily and promised to join the war against Napoleon by attacking Eugène. The British also concluded an armistice with the Neapolitan king.

Murat declared war on Eugène but remained psychologically incapable of engaging his former friends on the battlefield; since he was not a major factor in the final defeat of the Napoleonic regime in Italy, he had little say in the peninsula's disposition. While he procrastinated the Austrians and British defeated Eugène and brought the old Italian rulers back in their train. To avoid alienating the allies, Murat returned to the pope the occupied areas of the Papal State and, at this crucial point, found himself facing a serious revolt in his own realm.

Murat's foreign policy may be criticized for its ambiguousness or praised as realistic, but historians agree that he made a fundamental error in domestic policy: his apparent refusal to compromise on the demand by the carbonari for a constitution. Clearly, such a move would have caused problems with the Austrians, but Murat incorrectly calculated his action's potential within Italy. Indeed, despite his contacts with the Carboneria, he not only proved incapable of gaining its support but also alienated the burgeoning movement based upon the secret societies, leaving the field free to British and Bourbon agents who emphasized freedom from the French and a constitution. The result was widespread revolt, which Murat ruthlessly suppressed. Continuous revolts by the carbonari in October 1813, in March and April 1814, and in March 1815 enveloped several southern regions and gravely weakened Murat's negotiating and military positions vis-à-vis the British and Austrians. Murat promised a constitution too late; timely promulgation of an instrument the Neapolitans already possessed in draft form would have advanced the Italian cause immeasurably.

With the opening of the Congress of Vienna, at which the great powers discussed the shape of post-Napoleonic Europe, Murat's position deteriorated. The British distrusted him, and the Russians and the restored French Bourbons pressed for restoration of the Neapolitan Bourbons. The Austrians had recognized Murat but only for strategic reasons no longer operative after Napoleon's defeat. In fact, the Austrian foreign minister and architect of Restoration Europe, Clemens von Metternich, also favored the return of the more pliable Ferdinand IV, but Metternich, because he sponsored the sanctity of contracts as the basis of a new European order, would not take unprovoked action against Murat. Murat, however, provided Metternich the pretext for intervention after March 1815.

During that month, Napoleon escaped from exile in Elba and made a bid— the Hundred Days from March 20 to June 29, 1815—to become sovereign of

France once more. Murat believed that Napoleon's return would tie down the great powers in northern Europe for a long time and that he could gain territorial concessions in return for Neapolitan neutrality. In fact, Murat communicated with Napoleon's followers before the emperor escaped, but his calculations turned out to be wrong on both counts.

Murat declared war on the Austrians and moved into the Papal State. In Rimini, he issued a famous proclamation promising a constitution and exhorting the Italians to join him in a war for independence and unity. This appeal fell flat because of war weariness, lack of coordination with the patriotic movement, and his poor track record on the constitutional question. A series of military defeats quickly followed. On May 12, 1815, too late, Murat finally issued a constitution. Less than a week later, he left for exile in Corsica. Metternich then restored the Bourbons.

In October 1815 Joachim Murat landed once more on Neapolitan soil, seeking to reconquer his "beautiful Kingdom." He was immediately captured and shot; as a soldier, he asked permission to command the firing squad and died a hero's death: "Courage, good soldiers, shoot!" Fearing a popular reaction, the Neapolitan authorities held up news of the execution.

In the church where he was buried, townspeople heard the sounds of chains, observed the building suddenly illuminate itself, and heard King Joachim try to leave his tomb. Fear filled the village until a holy woman told the people that an angel had informed her that Saint George, whose church Murat had rebuilt, knew that the king would soon die and had called him to martyrdom to save his soul. "Knowing that they had been the instrument of salvation, the people calmed themselves."

Murat and the "Italian Question"

The historiographic debate on Murat has followed the course of his ghost—at first agitated and then disappearing from view. This first war for Italian unity, however premature, deserves special mention as the first concrete step in a long process.

An attempt to secure as much independence as possible from Napoleon and a policy directed at bolstering the pride of his Italian subjects marked Murat's reign in Naples. These factors explain why Murat's actions went beyond the usual French administrative reforms of the period. King Joachim not only attempted to construct a modern state and to stimulate agriculture and industry, he zealously implemented important educational measures ranging from the elementary to the university level. He also hoped to revive the kingdom's cultural pride by encouraging artistic endeavors, archaeological research, the study of ancient languages, and the rebuilding and beautification of cities. These measures demonstrated a genuine desire to restore the kingdom's ancient glory, which could subsequently serve as a springboard for political revival. In fact, the British reported that his actions made him very popular in all Italy.

Indeed, as a result of his policies, word flew in Murat's own domains and in Italy that he wished to unify Italy. By 1812 he had begun preparations for a war to be fought "under the French flag, but, who knows, perhaps under the Neapolitan flag." This attitude alienated the allies and Napoleon. The person who has studied Murat the most, Angela Valente, has argued that the British were ready to leave him undisturbed in Naples had he not insisted on uniting Italy. She has also discovered letters to Napoleon, written in 1813, in which the theme constantly emerges that the emperor could save himself by heading a popular movement for Italian independence and unity: "It is the road to salvation and will ensure enduring glory to the great Napoleon." Murat's belief that the Italians would rise en masse should Napoleon proclaim a war for Italian unification peppers Neapolitan documents of the period and appears to be the origin of Murat's own war for Italian unity.

Why did Murat's appeal fail to raise the Italians? Among the reasons already mentioned, historians emphasize the failure of an early promulgation of a constitution. Valente suggests that Murat was much more concerned with this issue than previously believed. She has discovered a draft of a Neapolitan constitution that Murat ordered drawn up in May 1814, along with evidence of the king's continuing interest. According to her, only Murat's fear of a violent Austrian reaction at a time of delicate political negotiation prevented him from issuing the document and thus winning the support of the southern patriotic movement.

Would this support have made a difference? Historians think not. They emphasize the rural nature of Italian society at this time and the vague and sometimes contrasting hopes of the patriotic movement at this early stage. Crystallized in the secret societies, the desire of patriots for independence had become identified with their anti-French feelings, despite Murat. Their Jacobin origins were muted by conservative elements, and the mixture emerged as a vague constitutional feeling. Ironically, this state of affairs allowed the allies to exploit the patriotic movement for the purpose of restoring the old regimes and keeping Italy divided.

In 1815 the international and the Italian situations did not appear mature for Italian independence and unity, but the first war for both had been fought. This is a particularly important point. Despite the very real divisions among Italians of different regions, dating from the fall of Rome to the present, Neapolitan policy favoring unity and the kingdom's willingness to engage in a war on behalf of the peninsula's independence, especially at this early date, is surely remarkable. The fact that this policy was initiated by a Frenchman and would have greatly strengthened his personal power is less remarkable, even though it helps explain the historiographical silence. After all, Italian unification would finally be accomplished by a dynasty of French origins more honed in the subtle ways of power than the dashing and impetuous French revolutionary cavalry general.

PART TWO

Restoration Italy

4

A "Geographical Expression"

Hᴵꜱᴛᴏʀʏ ᴘʀᴏᴠɪᴅᴇꜱ few examples of the single-minded determination with which the victorious allies of the anti-French coalition applied their policy after Napoleon's defeat. Statesmen such as Metternich tried to restore the political order as it had existed before the French Revolution insofar as it was possible, but in the long run conservatives could not suppress the national and constitutional aspirations unleashed in Europe by the French. In their attempts to contain the effects of the economic, social, and legislative changes of the revolutionary era, the restored rulers met with little success. On the other hand, Austria proved remarkably successful in keeping control of the areas in which it had established its political domination—in Italy until 1860 and in Germany until 1866.

In both Italy and Europe during the Restoration, the tension between an evolving society and a repressive political order drove events. With the industrial revolution's progress and the spread of liberalism, how quickly a particular society changed and to what extent governments endeavored to block the political ramifications of that evolution became crucial variables determining the history of different areas.

General Principles

Even before the Final Act of the Congress of Vienna (June 9, 1815), Austria, England, Russia, and Prussia established a twenty-year alliance against possible renewed French aggression in the postrevolutionary era (Treaty of Chaumont, March 9, 1814). The powers supplemented this pact with the Holy Alliance (September 1815). Originally based on the vague mysticism of Russian Tsar Alexander I, this agreement became a prime instrument of antirevolutionary intervention under Metternich's influence. With Castlereagh's cooperation, the great powers instituted the "Concert of Europe," which called a series of congresses in the 1820s and sanctioned the powers' intervention against revolts

43

shaking the smaller states. This mechanism allowed the Austrians to crush Italian patriotic revolutions and to preserve their domination of the peninsula. The Restoration's antirevolutionary and balance-of-power fixed points found their major challenge on the Italian Peninsula. The conflict caused numerous revolutions throughout the nineteenth century and, in the unification process of 1859 to 1861, the European balance's first substantial modification after the Congress of Vienna.

As in the rest of Europe, the social, political, and administrative situation was also in turmoil in the restored Italian states. Despite loyalty problems, the restored rulers retained both the essence of French revolutionary reforms and the natives who had made up the Napoleonic bureaucracy because they could not dispense with the efficiency of either. But to ensure their power, the restored absolutistic regimes handed over to their noble allies control of the army and the administration. An alliance with the large landowners and the Church further bolstered the nobility's strong position. Noble domination, however, conflicted with the economic and political growth of the industrial and commercial bourgeoisie. Immediately after the Napoleonic Wars, however, overproduction and a price collapse momentarily weakened the bourgeoisie and favored the reactionary elements in European society. But the years after 1818 saw an extraordinary acceleration in economic growth, stimulated by railway building; this economic development set the stage for a renewed political challenge to the reactionary ruling groups by the bourgeoisie, which had liberal and national aspirations.

Austrian Domination and Its Limits

Balance-of-power politics signified strengthening the victorious allies and the small countries ringing France. In Italy, this meant handing over Genoa to Piedmont and Venice to Austria. These changes violated "legitimacy," one of the Congress of Vienna's vaunted watchwords, since both republics had a centuries-long history. The Congress's other precept, "compensation," strengthened Austria's control of the peninsula.

Venice went to Austria because the empire had given up the Austrian Netherlands, a strategic liability, to the kingdom of Holland. The Venetian hinterland, now geographically linked to Austria, made the empire more powerful. In addition, the monarchs of three small Italian states were tied to the Austrian dynasty, while the papacy viewed Austria as its prime protector. The King of Naples had been restored by Austrian intervention against Murat, and a friendship treaty mandating an Austrian commander for the Neapolitan army and prohibiting a constitution bound the monarch to Austria. Finally, control of strategic cities in Lombardy-Venetia known as the "quadrilateral" rounded out Austrian military domination of Italy.

Although Austria had practical control over Italian affairs, two elements limited domination. With the restoration of a European balance after Napoleon's defeat, Piedmont regained both its independence and the great power guarantee of its territorial integrity that it had enjoyed in the eighteenth century—whereby neither France nor Austria could reduce it to subservience. In the early nineteenth century, the Savoy dynasty followed a conservative, pro-Austrian policy; but its Italian aspirations remained active, and internal changes would later catapult Piedmont to the forefront of the unification movement.

In addition, the patriots could now focus on one state as the enemy of Italian independence and unity. While the debate over the future shape of an Italian state waxed furious and lacerated the national movement, the patriots came together to fight against the Austrian Empire.

Restoration Italy: Shape and Substance

With the exception of the disappearance of Venice and Genoa, the map of Restoration Italy superficially appeared similar to that of the eighteenth century. In the South, Austria had initially recognized Murat as Neapolitan king and the Bourbons had to await Murat's defeat to be restored. The Papal State resumed its previous shape thanks to the diplomacy of Cardinal Ercole Consalvi.

In the North, the Napoleonic Kingdom of Italy's breakup caused major disruptions. Its territory went to four different states, reestablishing not only political but also economic frontiers. Where during the Napoleonic period it had been possible to exchange goods freely, customs barriers reappeared—dealing a bitter blow to commerce. For a time these restored barriers even hampered internal trade between Lombardy and Venetia, both Austrian possessions, and between different regions of the Piedmontese state.

Despite economic handicaps, the Lombard economy boomed, thanks to continued development of new products and the engagement of the aristocracy in business enterprises. Lombardy also profited from the long peace after 1815. but the Austrians allowed the Lombards no autonomy and absorbed two-thirds of their economic surplus to offset the Austrian Empire's chronic deficits. This situation helps explain the intense hatred that the Lombards had for their rulers and the disorders that shook the area periodically.

In Piedmont, the government's cultural and political repression helps explain why the Kingdom of Sardinia shared only minimally in the economic boom occurring to its east. While in the rest of Italy Enlightenment measures influenced by French revolutionary principles replaced Napoleonic legislation, the

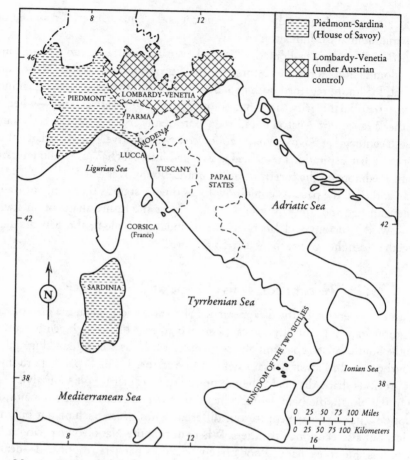

MAP 3   Restoration Italy

Savoys restored preexisting measures uncontaminated by modern ideas. They allowed the Jesuits to return (the order had been dissolved in the eighteenth century) and discriminated against religious minorities. King Victor Emmanuel I refused to wear clothes styled after the beginning of the French Revolution. Piedmontese Joseph De Maistre became the theoretician of the European reaction, and patriotic intellectuals such as Silvio Pellico were forced into exile. One result of the Piedmontese repression, however, was the growth of secret societies opposing the government.

The Papal State witnessed a struggle between moderates and reactionaries but eventually reverted to its old ways. Pius VII's government included a real statesman willing to judge French revolutionary legislation on its merits—Cardinal

Consalvi. He refused to restore the personal privileges of the barons and, for the most part, recognized the sale of Church lands that had occurred during the French occupation, even though former owners were often partially indemnified for their losses. Considering papal–Austrian relations during this period, Alan Reinerman has made an interesting case for Consalvi's cooperation with Metternich against the reactionary party—the Zelanti; in effect, Consalvi's moderate policy coincided with Metternich's views because Metternich was convinced that obscurantist policies would produce a "church-state conflict that was sure to weaken the conservative front and open the way for liberal gains." In the long run, however, neither collaboration with the Austrian leader nor European recognition of his statesmanlike qualities saved Consalvi after Pius VII's death. In 1823 Pope Leo XII was elected with Zelante backing against Metternich's opposition, and Consalvi's reforms were undone. Reinerman has described some of the measures that followed as "not merely reactionary but truly medieval."

In contrast to Piedmont and the Papal State, the Tuscan Restoration took the form of Ferdinand III's moderate conservatism—laws and the rule of men influenced by the Tuscan Enlightenment. Napoleonic legislation was repealed, but advanced Tuscan laws replaced it. On the whole, tolerance marked the Restoration in Florence, and only Vienna's intervention blocked the grand duke from issuing a constitution.

Surprisingly, Naples also returned to its Enlightenment tradition instead of practicing repression. No massacre of the 1799 type occurred or was even contemplated, and Prince Canosa, the police minister, lost his position because of resentment against his persecution of carbonari, Muratists, and Freemasons. The king's principal adviser, finance minister Luigi de' Medici, encouraged cooperation between Bourbon loyalists and Muratists. A concordat with the Church was not as harsh as early negotiations indicated. French legislation and reforms remained practically intact, and feudalism was not reestablished. Indeed, with the administrative absorption of Sicily by Naples, creating the Kingdom of the Two Sicilies (Ferdinand IV now became Ferdinand I), the Bourbon government extended French reforms to the island.

Combined European and Italian elements thus characterized the Restoration. Depending on the area, renewed territorial division, intensified Austrian domination, and the return of embittered or resigned dynasties created either an oppressive or a languid atmosphere. The nobility, reinforced by large landowners and the newly rich of the Napoleonic era, kept the struggling commercial and industrial bourgeoisie in a subordinate position while, thanks to the Europe-wide alliance of throne and altar against a fresh revolutionary outbreak, the Church increased its economic power and its influence over education and culture. But though Italy lagged behind France and Belgium, the development of productive forces in agriculture, industry, and commerce—aided by the survival of French Revolution–inspired reforms and institutions—could not be halted. This economic activity would make a powerful contribution to the alteration of the Restoration's political and social structure.

Restoration Culture

A constant struggle of intellectual tendencies, none of which achieved dominance, and the slow but steady breakdown of old currents of thought marked the culture of the Italian Restoration.

As in the rest of Europe, romanticism emerged in Italy during this period. The most important review advocating romantic ideas was the Milanese *Il Conciliatore,* and Ugo Foscolo, a poet best known for his masterpieces *Dei Sepolcri* and *Le ultime lettere di Jacopo Ortis,* made artistic activity an important component of national identity. In Florence, the *Antologia,* edited by Gian Pietro Vieusseux, was more oriented toward the social sciences and accepted contributions from all schools, although romanticism eventually set the tone for the magazine. Politically, the moderate liberals who ran the review hoped to link up with reform elements in the Tuscan government and to do battle with the official culture of Restoration Italy. For this reason, the emphasis on historical studies never produced a reactionary or conservative outlook in the country's romantic movement, as it did in both France and Germany. Indeed, attracted by French historian Victor Cousin's concept of conciliating order and liberty, and emphasizing gradual but progressive reform against Jacobin radicalism, Italian thinkers stressed a moderate monarchical liberalism that would become the Risorgimento's winning card.

The most important thinker of this moderate liberal current, Gian Domenico Romagnosi, evolved a program for a national monarchy in which the royal prerogative would be counterbalanced by the nation. Cesare Balbo, a young man destined to have an important role in the Risorgimento, also implied that constitutional liberty derives from the restoration of ancient liberties and institutions, not from the votes of constituent assemblies. Important currents of political thought that had long-term effects appeared during the Italian Restoration, as they did during the Restoration monarchy in France.

A similar development occurred in the religious thought of the Restoration. Catholicism's hostility to the legacies of the Enlightenment and the French Revolution contributed to the repressive atmosphere, but some religious thinkers dreamed of reconciling liberty and authority. The most authoritative figure here was Antonio Rosmini, a priest who struggled with the "Christian" concern of protecting the human person against the "despotism" of modern society, which he considered more efficient than that of the old regime. Primarily concerned with social equilibrium and social justice, Rosmini would produce a draft of a papal constitution in 1848. (In addition to Catholic thinkers, historian Giorgio Spini has stressed the influence of Italian Protestants, whose concept of life as a duty and history as a mission spurred Italians to view national problems in "religious" terms.) In short, the Restoration was the seedbed of liberal Catholicism, a movement that made a major contribution to the Risorgimento.

A straight line connects this liberal Catholicism with the most successful writer of the period, Alessandro Manzoni, a consummate practitioner of the historical novel so popular during this period. Beginning as an anticlerical and not "offically" a romantic, Manzoni was attracted to Catholicism as a moral imperative.

Manzoni's masterpiece, *The Betrothed*, tells the tale of Renzo and Lucia, two lovers caught up in the political and social vicissitudes of Spanish-dominated seventeenth-century Milan. Here "we have a fusion of themes—the political or patriotic conscience mingles with the Catholic conscience." Contemporaries easily associated the Spaniards with the repressive Austrians, but the novel operates on two other levels important for Italian history. Manzoni recounts the history of an age through the eyes of the victims of grand politics and explains what individuals armed with little but faith in God must do to survive. The novel has been seen as the history of the Italian people, oppressed but retaining its dignity and vitality.

The other reason for the novel's importance is Manzoni's conscious and successful development of an Italian language that could serve as "a means of communication for all sorts of concepts for all the Italians." Historian Giuliano Procacci has emphasized that when writers of the period wished to paint a true picture of popular characters, they had to have recourse to their local dialect, but Manzoni created a vibrant Italian language that could be understood by all—not just intellectuals—without being dialectical or provincial. And according to literary critic Christopher Cairns, Manzoni consolidated "linguistic theories about the Italian language in art, the modern analogue, in this sense, of the *Divine Comedy*." Manzoni's work capped the process, which was begun in eighteenth-century Naples and was discussed in Chapter 1, of trying to elevate the Italian language to a scholarly level. Besides its historical significance, *The Betrothed* survives as a literary masterpiece that has become an integral part of every cultured Italian's heritage.

In addition to Manzoni, a world-class poet worked in Restoration Italy. Giacomo Leopardi, the hunchback son of a virulent reactionary, fit the European mold of a melancholy and suicidal romantic. It is hardly surprising that Leopardi, who lived under terrible personal circumstances, differed from many other romantics in considering nature a hostile force that must be dominated by humanity. Leopardi recalled Italy's past glory, lamented the country's fate, and denounced both the Austrians and the French. His overtly patriotic poems are not his best work, but these themes are reflected in all his poetry, which "provide a consummation, in a sense, of the ideas of that generation of writers which launched the Italians on the idealist path toward the *Risorgimento.*"

Other Italian novelists, poets, and playwrights of the period could not match the towering literary stature of either Manzoni or Leopardi, but they infused with national feeling the models they adopted from the Italian Renaissance, German romanticism, and English literature. Influencing the content of these writings were the memoirs of Italians who had fought with Napoleon. Unwilling to rest on their laurels, these memorialists emphasized the distinction and honor with which Italians had fought in the most arduous Napoleonic campaigns; they aimed to redress Italy's modest military tradition in recent times and suggested that Italians could redeem themselves on the battlefield. Throughout the Restoration and the Risorgimento, this military theme dominated a steady stream of literary works dealing with the foreign invasions to which the peninsula had been subjected over the centuries. The most famous included Giovanni Battista Niccolini's *Giovanni da Procida* (1817) and *Arnaldo da Brescia* (1837), Tommaso Grossi's *I Lombardi alla prima crociata* (1826), transformed into a popular opera by Giuseppe Verdi in 1843, Massimo d'Azeglio's *Ettore Fieramosca* (1833) and *Niccolò de' Lapi* (1841), Giovanni Berchet's *Fantasie* (1829), and Domenico Guerrazzi's *L'assedio di Firenze* (1836).

Besides literature, opera also became a patriotic weapon that had to be disguised to elude the period's heavy censorship. Gioacchino Rossini's *William Tell* (1829), a story of heroic resistance against oppression, clearly alluded to the Italian case. A haunting aria in Vincenzo Bellini's *I Puritani* (1835) describes the hardship of the exile, a common figure as a result of the many Italian revolutions of the age; in this opera, a stirring duet concludes: "It is beautiful to confront death while shouting: Liberty!" The musical heir of these composers, Verdi, included choruses in all his operas during the Risorgimento—such as "Va' Pensiero" in *Nabucco*—that were easily susceptible to patriotic interpretation.

Although the Restoration was not a particularly brilliant period for the plastic arts, it did produce a world-class sculptor in Antonio Canova. His most significant work related to a patriotic theme, *Tomb to Vittorio Alfieri* (1810), dates from shortly before Napoleon's fall. It shows a crowned "Italia" that some consider the first iconographical treatment of "Italy," pointedly made during the French occupation. Writer and Risorgimento hero Massimo d'Azeglio, in addition to the work previously mentioned, painted romantic landscapes, some of which have been interpreted as antiforeign.

So Art became enlisted in the struggle for independence.

5

Failed Revolutions: The 1820s and 1830s

After 1815, the Italian situation appeared unstable. Although governments in some states pursued moderate policies, all ignored vital changes in political mentality and social and economic conditions that had occurred during the French revolutionary and Napoleonic periods; indeed, continued fear of losing their power made the rulers partners of a reactionary Austria. Revolutionary principles continued in the form of nationalism and liberalism, which dominated nineteenth-century Europe. Both concepts, supported by many different peoples politically bound together by the mystical attraction and practical power of a strong monarch, posed a mortal threat for the Austrian Empire, because nationalism implied independence for all nationalities and liberalism advocated constitutional limitations on the sovereign's power.

Italy represented a major threat to Austria because the desire for independence and unity that the French Revolution had stimulated among "Jacobin-Patriotic" intellectuals from different parts of the Italian Peninsula had spread beyond radical circles. As did their European counterparts, Italian liberals and radicals of the 1820s and 1830s looked to France for help. In those years they set off a series of revolutions. The disorders failed, but they produced some important lessons. First, the ideological underpinning of unity had to become less vague, and it had to give a picture of the future Italy to create favorable Italian and European pressure essential to Italian liberty. The debate on this issue produced three major "models," which are discussed in the next chapter. Second, the failures of the 1820s and 1830s—along with the events of 1848–1849—demonstrated to Italian patriots that the European revolutionary movement would not or could not come to their aid. Half a century of disappointment would drive most Italian revolutionaries, in order to unify their country, to seize the realistic options that opened to them in the 1850s. The revolutions of the early Restoration were important stages in this evolution.

The Neapolitan Revolution

In 1820 a military revolution against King Ferdinand of Spain occurred. This revolution proclaimed the Spanish Constitution of 1812. A liberal shibboleth, this document presented one overwhelming problem to the rulers of the period, even if they had been inclined to accept constitutions: It greatly weakened the monarch's power. Thus, even when a ruler declared his acceptance under revolutionary pressure, all understood that he could never sanction a document transforming him into a virtual figurehead. Ferdinand VII was typical in biding his time until French troops could rescue him in 1823.

The Spanish Revolution had profound effects in Italy, especially in the Kingdom of the Two Sicilies. In July 1820 Luigi Minichini, a *carbonaro* priest, touched off a revolution based on the Spanish model. This movement, which began in the provinces, secured the support of Guglielmo Pepe, a general in the Neapolitan army who had previously served Murat. Bourbon efforts to stop the revolt failed because the carbonari had infected the army. Furthermore, the king had retained many officials who had held office under Murat because the kingdom needed their experience. Called "Muratists" because they favored a policy of moderate reform such as had been pursued by King Joachim, they were no carbonari. But Muratist leaders ultimately proved unreliable because they disliked the government's subservience to Austria, its hostility toward granting a constitution, and its reduction of the public works budget.

Unlike the Muratists, the carbonari were confused and very divided, but they exhibited strongly Jacobin tendencies. Many members of the secret society yearned for a constitution, and the most progressive leaders strongly favored independence and unity for all Italy. Moreover, there were regular contacts between the Neapolitan carbonari and members of the same and other sects in the Papal State and northern Italy, and their vague constitutional stirrings had solidified into a specific demand for the Spanish Constitution of 1812. Beyond this desire it would be an error to attribute much social, political, or organizational cohesion to the Carboneria, but its spectacular growth after the withdrawal of Austrian troops in 1817 and the constant, if ineffectual, planning for insurrectional activity demonstrated dissatisfaction with the restored regime. In the South, carbonari lodges have been seen as the successors of eighteenth-century Freemasonry, previously discussed; like Freemasonry, the Carboneria society was strong primarily in the provinces and attracted small businessmen, small property owners, minor officials, and members of the local militias. Membership in the lodges has been variously estimated at from 300,000 to 1 million. Although these estimations are certainly exaggerated, (after all, the nature of secret societies is to be secretive), they do indicate that the carbonari achieved a significant measure of popular support.

Muratist complicity made the Carboneria formidable beyond its inherent strength because involvement of the Muratists gave an impression of coherence and consistency that the society lacked. But the strongly democratic carbonari tendencies made the Muratists uncomfortable, and they also disapproved of the Spanish Constitution as too radical. Consequently, they kept tabs on carbonari, refused to join the society, and hoped to exploit the carbonari for their own purposes.

This scheme failed because the carbonari seized the initiative, forcing the more prestigious Muratist leaders to follow. The rebels marched on the capital and, on July 13, 1820, Neapolitan King Ferdinand I swore allegiance to the Spanish Constitution with the same enthusiasm as his Spanish namesake. A Muratist-dominated government took power amid popular rejoicing. The Neapolitan Revolution seemed to have succeeded and to have achieved genuine popularity.

The speed of the changes pointed to widespread support for a constitutional regime, but within a brief nine-month period the revolution had been ignominiously defeated. Victory revealed the intrinsic weaknesses of the constitution, the carbonari, and the Muratists. The carbonari followed up their initial success with democratic measures, including tax reductions and partial decentralization, but Muratists fearing rapid change dominated the bureaucracy and army; in the newly elected parliament, democratic carbonari-backed deputies maintained an uneasy equilibrium with the Muratist-landowner majority by resorting to popular pressure.

Despite these internal problems, diplomacy determined the revolution's future. Because constitutions weakened the royal power holding together the Austrian Empire, Metternich opposed them—and he particularly objected to Neapolitan developments for the example they would set in North Italy. Indeed, a secret treaty with the Bourbons gave Austria the right to intervene in case Naples granted a constitution. But the 1820 events had caught the Austrian statesman by surprise and short of troops on the peninsula. Moreover, he faced competition from France and Russia, both interested in reducing Austrian dominance in Italy; on the other hand, Metternich's rivals were also adamantly opposed to the Spanish Constitution.

In attempting to take advantage of the diplomatic situation and forestall Austrian intervention, Muratist leaders assured the great powers that they had no intention of "exporting" the revolution. Understanding the danger posed by the Spanish Constitution of 1812, the Muratists also tried to modify that document, but the carbonari would not allow that sacred instrument to be tampered with. The inability to alter the Spanish Constitution ensured Ferdinand's continued hostility, despite his public acceptance of the revolution, and enhanced Metternich's capacity to exploit the issue. Furthermore, as proof that they did not wish to spread disorder abroad, the Muratists refused to transform the revolution into a campaign for national unity; this decision proved to be a major blunder. Metternich intended to crush the revolution once he had cleared away the diplomatic obstacles. Given the circumstances, the revolutionaries had few chances of succeeding, although linking the Neapolitan Revolution to national unity might have mobilized the peninsula into action at a time when Austria was momentarily weak. Such a course might have furthered the cause of unity and would have strengthened the southern image in the future unified Italy. Patriots in Piedmont and Lombardy were sympathetic to unification and also stood ready to act. The Neapolitan Revolution confirmed that without the guiding principle of national unity, Italian revolutions of this period could only be dead ends.

Sicilian events bolster this conclusion. Unhappiness with the loss of autonomy (1816), economic crisis, reforms, hatred of Neapolitans, and the demand for the Sicilian Constitution of 1812—as opposed to the Spanish Constitution—stimulated a revolt against the Neapolitan Revolution, fierce fighting among different Sicilian factions, and Neapolitan military intervention. Conversely, the conviction of many Sicilians that only by becoming part of a wider *Italian* movement could Sicily attain autonomy from the Neapolitans represented a step forward for the patriots.

Sicilian developments supplied Metternich with a further argument for intervention. After smoothing out the diplomatic kinks (Congresses of Troppau, October 1820, and Laibach, January 1821) and with King Ferdinand's exit from his lands, Metternich moved his troops into Naples and easily suffocated the revolution in March 1821.

The Piedmontese Revolt

In northern Italy, Neapolitan events encouraged a conspiracy with strong national overtones in late 1820. Rumors of an imminent invasion of Naples encouraged a concerted plan for an uprising against Austrian domination of the peninsula in the Kingdom of Sardinia and Austrian-controlled Lombardy-Venetia. Despite the different problems of North and South and the internal divisions of the revolutionaries, the agitation of 1820–1821 illustrates the strict interdependence of Italy's most diverse regions and the capacity of Italians to initiate their own revolutionary activity.

The Restoration's harshness in the North had stimulated opposition among the middle classes and the aristocracy, and the carbonari remained active in the region. In Piedmont, Victor Emmanuel I realized the failure of his reactionary policy and briefly flirted with reform before ending the attempt out of fear of the Neapolitan and Spanish revolutions. Widespread dissatisfaction spread among liberal aristocrats—including the influential Massimo d'Azeglio and Cesare Balbo—resulting in the conversion of a great number to an alliance with middle-class carbonari who advocated adoption of the Spanish Constitution. As in Naples, this demand and the inability of liberal aristocrats to moderate the stance of their allies would prove fatal.

In Piedmont the conspirators hoped to enlist the House of Savoy in their activities by appealing to its dynastic ambitions. As the Austrian army prepared to move against Naples from Lombardy-Venetia, conspirators hoped to coordinate simultaneous revolts in Piedmont and Lombardy-Venetia, declare a constitution, drive Austria out of Italy, and establish a strong north Italian kingdom under the Savoy monarchy. The aggrandizement of Piedmont, they reckoned, would ensure Victor Emmanuel's collaboration and induce him to swallow a constitution. As insurance, the conspirators also negotiated with Charles Albert, heir to the throne after Victor Emmanuel's reactionary brother Charles Felix.

This plan found ardent supporters in Lombardy-Venetia who chafed under Austrian repression and who believed they needed a regular army such as the Piedmontese could provide to drive out their oppressors. Emperor Francis ruled his Italian kingdom with an iron fist: German reigned as the official language; Austrians and Slavs ran the civil service and officered Italian military units, raised by conscription; severe restrictions discriminated against Italian products if they competed with Austrian ones and other regulations practically prohibited Italians from traveling; modern history was a forbidden subject at the university; only the official newspaper could appear as a daily; censors examined cultural reviews before they were printed or brought into the country; and the government banned outright many authors.

These conditions bred conspiracies among the aristocracy, the middle class, professionals, and businessmen. The Austrians responded with legislation forbidding secret societies, the institution of the death penalty for taking part in revolutions, and hard labor for life for failing to prevent revolution or for failing to denounce persons engaging in revolutionary activities. These measures permitted the police to arrest persons suspected as members of secret societies and to extort information. By 1820, just as Piedmontese and Lombard liberals planned their revolt, mass arrests and trials had become the norm, making it difficult for the conspiracy to succeed. In October the Austrian police arrested two important leaders, Count Federico Confalonieri and Silvio Pellico. Both men had founded *Il Conciliatore*, a literary review that mixed romanticism with patriotic ideals in a necessarily subtle manner, which, however, did not prevent their becoming police targets. Such methods wiped out the Lombard part of the conspiracy but not the greater opposition. Sentenced to fifteen years of hard labor, Pellico published *My Prisons*, a classic account of his incarceration at the Spielberg prison; Confalonieri had his death sentence commuted to life at hard labor. Pellico's book and Confalonieri's dramatic story as told by his wife inspired the Risorgimento generation to struggle against Austrian domination.

Despite the arrest of their Lombard coconspirators, the Piedmontese rebels pushed ahead with their plans. On March 9–10, 1821, Alessandria, the kingdom's chief fortress and a city known for its democratic tendencies, rebelled; the rebels proclaimed the Spanish Constitution and support for Italian unity and independence. At this point, Victor Emmanuel suddenly abdicated, causing the conspirators' plan to go awry. Charles Albert became regent because the new king, Charles Felix, was out of the country. As already mentioned, the conspirators had been in contact with Charles Albert and claimed they had his support (whether this was true has been debated ever since), but the regent subsequently proved to be an unreliable ally. As rebellion spread throughout the kingdom, Charles Albert succumbed to pressure and officially proclaimed the Spanish Constitution; but his tortuous reasoning and halting justification revealed his fear of Charles Felix—who turned against him anyway—and his willingness to submit to the new king's orders. When Charles Felix ordered him to retire to a loyal fortress, Charles Albert meekly complied instead of leading the revolution as the rebels had hoped. Charles Felix promptly requested the Austrian intervention that crushed the Piedmontese movement in April 1821.

Historians rightly emphasize the contradictions that doomed the Piedmontese revolt; but the episode marked the entrance into the fray of a moderate party that wished to achieve Italian unity and independence in conjunction with the Savoy dynasty. Although radical democrats dominated the unification movement for the next twenty years, the failed revolutions of 1820–1821 converted many moderate liberals to the cause. The native rulers had proven powerless before an overwhelming desire for change, but Austria had demonstrated both its hostility toward constitutions and its ability to maintain its domination by military means. Italian moderates who wished to apply the principles of French and British liberalism to Italy now recognized the need for independence from Austria as a prerequisite for Italian constitutional development. This realization proved decisive in the long struggle for unification.

Continuous Revolution

Events following the agitation of 1820–1821 confirmed the existence of two "parties" favoring Italian unification—democratic-republican and moderate-liberal-monarchical. The immediate Austrian crackdown and the intense Italian reaction of the 1820s and 1830s produced not only radical democratic but also moderate exiles such as Santorre di Santarosa, who was implicated in the Piedmontese events. Influenced by French liberals such as Victor Cousin, the moderates preferred a constitution similar to the French Charter of 1814 rather than the Spanish Constitution of 1812, especially after the Spanish Revolution's defeat in 1823. The decade of the 1820s, which witnessed a diaspora of Italian intellectuals throughout Europe, created a new "liberal" political emigration paralleling the radical-republican-democratic one that had existed since French revolutionary days; as in the republican case, these moderates interacted with Europeans of a like persuasion and, through their contacts and writings, made the Italian cause "respectable" and gained support for it.

Furthermore, Italian exiles of different political colors won sympathy for their own cause by fighting and dying for liberty in other countries, such as Spain and Greece. The recognition of Greek independence in 1830, which was particularly popular and significant, proved that Austria could be isolated diplomatically and its policies defeated by international pressure—a lesson skillfully exploited by Italian patriots.

Besides the exiles' contacts with foreigners, in the 1820s and 1830s the exiles and conspirators within Italy also increased their communication enormously. For example, the old revolutionary Filippo Buonarroti was still alive and appeared to the police to be pulling the strings of numerous European radical conspiracies. In 1828, Buonarroti published his recollections of Babeuf's failed communist conspiracy of 1796, which was the model for the secret society's modern form. But despite his European prominence and his historical importance in introducing "the ideology of state communism and dictatorship" into European socialism, Buonarroti's influence in Italy was probably limited to the *Apofasimeni* ("desperate ones"). The significance of this group is primarily associated with Carlo Bianco di Saint Jorioz, its organizer, and his influence on Giuseppe Mazzini, one of the nineteenth century's most prominent revolutionaries.

In 1830 another wave of revolutions surged over Europe. The French overthrew the Bourbons and replaced them with the more liberal Louis Philippe, and the Belgians successfully declared their independence from Holland. For a brief time, it seemed to European democrats that France might resume its role as revolutionary guide. Spurred by the possibility of French aid, the "July Revolution" encouraged Italian patriots to act.

Geographically limited to the Duchies of Modena and Parma and the Papal State, the 1831 Italian revolutions are important because they stated the desire of all patriotic factions for unity and independence more explicitly than had the previous revolutions. The late 1820s had seen confused plots involving liberals and princes, such as Francis IV of Modena and Napoleon's descendants, who some patriots believed could be hitched to the patriotic cause. By 1830, however, the Modenese liberal Ciro Menotti had organized revolutionary committees in several cities with the purpose of achieving "the independence, the unity, and the liberty of all Italy" through a "representative monarchy" and a king to be chosen by a national assembly. To strengthen his hand, Menotti made contact with Italian exiles in Paris, but dominated by Buonarroti, these exiles demanded "the Italian Republic, one and indivisible, from the Alps to the Sea."

When revolutions erupted in central Italy in February 1831, the tricolor of Italian unity (green, white, and red) appeared everywhere, while many papal and ducal troops deserted to the patriotic cause. The idea of unity, at least, seemed to have been consolidated, but not the form that an eventual Italian state would assume. In Paris, the exiles once again called for a republic and warned Italians against the wiles of kings who would try to divide the people by offering them constitutions. But the monarchical "party" lacked a candidate to be king of a united country.

The revolutions of 1831 failed, as had those of 1820–1821. Rome itself did not revolt, and the revolutionaries hesitated to attack it for fear of precipitating Austrian action—a vain hope. France had been hinting that it would not intervene to help the revolutionaries and when Louis Philippe's government explicitly declared that French blood would be spent only for France, the myth of the revolutionary fatherland willing to do battle for Italian independence collapsed. In the meantime, Metternich's successful diplomatic maneuvering allowed Austrian military intervention to crush yet another Italian revolution. More would follow.

PART THREE

The Risorgimento

6

Three Models for Unification

Fʀᴏᴍ ᴛʜᴇ 1830s until unification, Italian intellectuals ardently discussed not whether the peninsula would be unified but how unification might take place and what would be its future. In interweaving these questions, they produced responses that further stimulated the desire for independence and unity.

The Enduring Myth

By the early 1830s progress toward unification had reached a peak and then stagnated. The idea of unity had achieved widespread acceptance among Italian opinion makers, but the means of achieving this goal remained elusive. The Carboneria and other secret societies had failed: They had demonstrated their capacity to overthrow existing governments but not to challenge Austrian hegemony; their opposition to current conditions appealed to large numbers of people, but their lack of a rigorous ideology failed to galvanize them, and their elaborate rituals masked ineffectiveness.

The man who would reinvigorate the struggle for Italian liberty, Giuseppe Mazzini, became a carbonaro in 1827, the same year he obtained a law degree. A sickly child who later became the epitome of the romantic revolutionary, given to playing the guitar and smoking cigars, Mazzini had aimed at a career in medicine, like his father, but gave up that hope after feeling faint while observing an operation. He seemed destined to become a revolutionary, supported by a devoted mother and basking early in the revolutionary recollections of his father. The elder Mazzini pushed his son to choose literature as a vocation but encountered the stubborn resistance of his wife. Giuseppe's mother regarded her son as a messiah, fueling the mythical quality that came to surround him. She recounted that at age eleven, her son ran up to a beggar, threw his arms around him, and asked her to give him something. The beggar exclaimed, prophetically, "Love him dearly, signora. He is one who will love the people." All this happened in front of a church, as befits the man whose slogan would become "God and the People."

Another story of mythical proportions is commonly invoked to explain Mazzini's entrance into the fray for Italian liberty. On a Sunday in April 1821, defeated revolutionaries, planning to sail for Spain to continue the struggle for liberty, crowded around a dock in Genoa. They asked for money from Maria Mazzini and her teenaged son—an incident that remained etched in the boy's memory forever. This revolutionary—dressed in black, mourning for his country, driven into exile, condemned to death, who continually conspired for Italy's freedom, who struck fear in the hearts of the continent's police, and who inspired the most heroic events of 1848 and of Risorgimento hero Giuseppe Garibaldi—could not avoid having his life take on the mythical attributes that underpin great movements.

As a carbonaro Mazzini encountered only disappointment, outdated rituals, ridiculous missions, and intractable old leaders. The secret society's failure during the disorders of 1830 was for Mazzini the last straw. Betrayed by a senior member of the society, the police arrested Mazzini in November. In jail he encountered once again the emphasis on ritual, rather than action, when a fellow prisoner tapped him rhythmically on the head, conferring a higher Masonic dignity upon him instead of providing contacts to aid in resisting their captors. Finally convinced of the old society's irrelevance, Mazzini abandoned it and established a new organization as the instrument of Italian unification, Giovine Italia (Young Italy).

At a time when the national movement's failures caused many patriots to doubt the practical possibility of unifying the peninsula, Mazzini proclaimed that Italy must be free and independent, with Rome as its capital.

The Theory

Influenced by the revolutionary atmosphere of the 1830s, Mazzini insisted on greater autonomy and dignity for the Italian movement by carving a niche for it in the European revolutionary-philosophical context.

The idea of progress animated Mazzini's philosophical system as it had enlivened that of the eighteenth-century philosophes, but, unlike them, Mazzini tied progress as a historical law to God's will and nationality. In a kind of "left" romanticism, Mazzini argued that individuals and nations had a special "mission" within God's universal plan for humanity's improvement. Each nationality, therefore, must have control of its own affairs in order to fulfill God's will. There could be no doubt about the existence of an Italian nation, which twice before had led the world, even though it now found itself prostrate because of foreign domination and the weakness of its citizens; acquiring knowledge of their mission and devoting all their energies to it became a moral imperative, a faith, a duty, for Italians as for other peoples.

Although faith in God's idea of progress stalled during the Restoration under reactionary hammer blows and the exhaustion of the French revolutionary generation, Mazzini argued, the romantic era rebelled against authority and preached moral renewal. Even if that movement itself had become lost in the meanderings of medieval mysticism, its appeal to youth had produced a ferment that could not be blocked. The nineteenth century, with youth as its watchword, would overwhelm conservatives who erroneously concluded that Louis Philippe's triumph in France had ended social revolution. Far from killing "the great social revolution," Mazzini believed that the French Revolution of 1830 had merely announced it.

Thus it became the duty of the young to overthrow systematic repression in Europe, which blocked the moral education of the people and the progress willed by God. In describing the atrocious conditions that prevailed not only in Italy but in most of Europe—censorship, the threat of capital punishment for reading proscribed books and foreign newspapers, the closing of universities—Mazzini asked, "Who will give progress to this people?" His answer: "Insurrection is the only course . . . possible; a general, determined rising of the multitude: the holy war of the oppressed." The slogan: "God and the People."

Unlike other forms of nationalism, Mazzini's religious-romantic-nationalism placed all nationalities on an equal footing, since God had anointed each with a special mission. His nationalism was devoid of the intolerance toward other nationalities' independence, which, for example, marred German nationalism and the ideas of some Italian moderates. Considering the ill repute into which nationalism later fell, it would be unjust not to recall the progressivism of Mazzini's brand, which defended the dignity of all nationalities and their obligation to eliminate the shackles binding them and others. Mazzini insisted that "European revolution today will be made in the name of national independence." These national revolutions would produce a new map of Europe, which Mazzini sketched, coinciding with the existing geographical distribution of thirteen or fourteen identifiable national groups; the details he wisely left to "the future and the people's vote." Once terminated, the European struggle for freedom would create equal political entities based on popular sovereignty and prepared to fulfill their special missions within God's plan for humanity's progress. Empires such as the Austrian and the Turkish, based on the tyrannical and selfish administration of diverse nationalities destined to develop in different directions, would disappear.

Italy's mission was intimately bound up with its history and its struggle for liberty. It must lead the way to the new order because its fight for national unity necessarily involved the quest for the unity of humanity. In seeking this unity, the Italian nation had to overcome two powerful obstacles—Austria and the papacy. In destroying the first, Italy would advance the cause of oppressed nationalities, encourage the formation of independent states, create the premise of a future European federation, and promote God's cause. Italians could only free themselves by freeing others.

If Austria's collapse would bring liberty, obliterating the papacy would create a new unity. In the past, the Eternal City had united humankind twice, under the Caesars (Action) and the popes (Spirit); the "Third Rome," that of the people, the successor of both, would "unite, in a faith that will make Thought and Action one, Europe, America and every part of the terrestrial globe." Thus Mazzini's religious fervor should not be confused with organized religion; neither popes nor priests interpret God's law, but the people, and their religion is progressive nationalism.

Historian Gaetano Salvemini wrote that, despite weaknesses that may be discerned in the Italian patriot's philosophy, by fusing medieval utopian ideas, Rousseau's *Social Contract*, and the doctrines of nineteenth-century French thinker Saint-Simon, Mazzini emphasized "many democratic ideas that belong to our own time." But Mazzini's modernity emerges more fully when the question of how he would unite Italy is posed. Neither a military strategist nor a tactician, Mazzini did not create the method by which he advocated the physical destruction of Austrian power, but he made an extraordinary selection from among the available methods and enriched it with his own ideology.

Mazzini's philosophy, in fact, found its military complement in that of Carlo Bianco di Saint Jorioz. Bianco had been part of the Piedmontese agitation of 1821, after which he participated in the Spanish Revolution. After a period of imprisonment there, he traveled to other parts of Europe and settled in Paris. In 1830 he published a book, *Della guerra nazionale d'insurrezione per bande applicata all'Italia (The National Insurrectionary War by Means of Guerrilla Bands, Applied to Italy)*. This work, the first theoretical treatise on guerrilla warfare, drew from the lessons of the Spanish uprising against Napoleon and of the Greek war for independence. According to Bianco, a popular uprising using the methods of guerrilla warfare was the only way to free Italy. Despite Bianco's closeness to Buonarroti at this time, Mazzini, with whom Bianco later collaborated, made Bianco's military concepts an integral part of his own system and publicized them; it can be argued that Bianco's ideas animated the military aspects of the 1848 revolutions and the 1860 expedition of The Thousand, which culminated in unification.

Thus the program of Young Italy (1831), after emphasizing national insurrection and intimately tying it to the education of the people, makes the following extremely significant methodological statement: "Insurrection—by means of guerrilla bands—is the true method of warfare for all nations desirous of emancipating themselves from a foreign yoke. This method of warfare supplies the want—inevitable at the commencement of the insurrection—of a regular army; it calls the greatest number of elements into the field, and yet may be sustained by the smallest number. It forms the military education of the people, and consecrates every foot of the native soil by the memory of some warlike deed."

It seems ironic that English-language writers neglect this full-blown antecedent of what have become known as "wars of national liberation" and that have been so successful in China, Cuba, and Vietnam. Italian historians, although aware of this aspect of Mazzini's thought, generally fail to emphasize it as well. The inner contradictions of a desperate populace rising up against foreign occupiers, yet failing to turn against native grandees, perhaps helps to explain this attitude. But Mazzini's overwhelming desire to liberate Italy and prevent the national struggle from degenerating into a divisive social conflict prompted him to stress the military aspects of liberation and even to adopt practical measures against its transformation into a class war.

To this fundamental reason must be added Mazzini's differences with Buonarroti, the period's chief champion of social revolution. For Buonarroti, the French Jacobin experience of the 1790s had demonstrated how revolutions generate class warfare, and the French Revolution of 1830 had confirmed it; the poor must therefore organize themselves militarily to prepare for the coming social war. The leadership of revolutions consequently devolved to an elite, a concept that introduced a dictatorial principle into class action. This idea also worked for Buonarroti on the international level, with France as the general and less-advanced countries like Italy as the soldiers. Though he recognized that an insurrection must be prepared in secret by a few leaders, to avoid dictatorship and terror, Mazzini emphasized the people's role. Do not, he wrote, "condemn the yearning masses to inertia; do not delude yourselves into thinking that you operate for them; do not entrust to only one class the great work of national regeneration." Even more important for the Italian context, Mazzini acknowledged that there could be revolutionary collaboration between France and Italy but insisted that the Italians must take the lead in the struggle to free themselves; this was at the core of the nation's larger mission. Clearly this last point was more adapted to the Italian situation than Buonarroti's, energized the peninsula's patriotic movement, and eclipsed Buonarroti's influence. In fact, Mazzini's thesis originated the slogan of the 1848 revolutions: "L'Italia farà da sè" ("Italy will do it by itself").

Mazzini's challenge to Buonarroti has made it seem to some modern commentators, especially of the left, that the Italian thinker neglected the social question. Indeed, for the reasons already discussed, Mazzini did not address the issue as directly as Buonarroti. Mazzini emphasized national revolutions—essentially political movements that would avoid class warfare but create the conditions for social change and the material progress of the masses. These developments could occur exclusively in a republic. Only republican institutions, he believed, could enact the social legislation that would embody the law of God and humanity that people be "free, equal, and brothers," because they guaranteed free expression of the "general will"; monarchies "necessarily" injected privilege and an intermediate element, aristocracy, into the national equation, thus undermining equality and liberty. Mazzini considered monarchies obsolete, and unification as a kingdom would necessitate a new Italian revolution.

If Italy should not be unified as a kingdom, neither should it be a federation, which would weaken the nation, make it a prey to its neighbors, and "strike at the root of the great mission Italy is destined to accomplish towards humanity." Mazzini emphasized that unity did not signify administrative centralization or destruction of local autonomy but that "political organization" should be "one and central."

Like his demand that Italians should take the lead in their own liberation, Mazzini's dogmatic insistence that without unity there could be no nationality brought about a qualitative change in the Italian national movement. Unlike other patriots, who believed that unification was preferable to a divided peninsula, Mazzini advocated unity as an indivisible entity because he believed it to be the sole possible solution to the Italian problem. According to Mazzini, the entire history of the peninsula tended toward unity. Although, on analysis, his evidence for this concept can be disputed, it is true that developments since the eighteenth century had been working against the peninsula's division into separate states and that progressive forces advocating change worked for national unity. Mazzini lent fire to this tendency by injecting it with the passion born of religious, philosophical, historical, and national conviction and, consequently, the inevitability of success.

In this manner, Mazzini evolved his powerful model of the new Italy: a democratic, socially compassionate, indivisible republic, based on popular sovereignty and distinguished by a duty to lead other nations in achieving the liberty that would permit them to fulfill their God-given missions. This model caught the imagination of the patriotic movement and of future generations.

Practice

After Mazzini's arrest in November 1830, Piedmontese authorities gave him the choice of exile or living in a small town. Mazzini left his country for Marseilles. There he founded Young Italy, a practical expression of his revolutionary ideas.

Young Italy surpassed the Carboneria thanks not only to its goals, which were outlined earlier, but also to its modern organization. At the top, a "Central Group" consisting of Mazzini and his closest associates named three-person "provincial groups" for every Italian province. These groups appointed organizers who recruited two categories of members, "Federals" and "Federal-Propagators," in each of the province's cities. The latter members, chosen from persons who possessed "heart [courage] and mind," had the task of initiating the former, selected from persons of "heart" but who did not have the "mind" to choose appropriate people. Each member must take a nom de guerre with which to be recognized within the Young Italy society and swear an oath reaffirming the organization's ideology. Except for secret signals permitting members to recognize each other, this oath was Young Italy's only ritual. At first membership was restricted to persons under forty years of age, but Mazzini later modified this condition by allowing admission to persons who "had sucked the aspirations of the century," that is, he made youth dependent upon spirit. Mazzini hoped in this manner to distinguish his organization from the Carboneria, which was paralyzed by a timid membership and by a complex, meaningless ritual.

Immediate, resolute action also distinguished Young Italy from the Carboneria. To prepare the field for revolution, Mazzini signed an agreement (September 1832) with Buonarroti. But the old conspirator had reorganized his Italian societies with the aim of gaining control of Mazzini's movement, and the rivalry between the two leaders marred Young Italy's revolutionary debut. In addition, their conflicting ideas on social revolution and Buonarroti's conviction that an Italian revolution should not be attempted without the lead being taken by France produced a complete break between Mazzini and Buonarroti in 1834.

Between 1830 and 1832, Mazzini's organization quickly found adherents in several Italian regions, especially Liguria (Genoa), Piedmont, Lombardy, and Venetia and, to a lesser extent, Tuscany, the Kingdom of the Two Sicilies, and the Papal State. Mazzini chose Piedmont for his first revolutionary action. The insurrection there was to be based on the army and coordinated with an uprising in Genoa and revolutionary incursions from Switzerland and France. These ambitious plans went awry almost immediately. The Piedmontese government discovered the conspiracy in the army almost by accident in April 1833 and resorted to torture and execution to maintain control. Despite this serious setback, Mazzini doggedly pushed ahead, but quick military action thwarted the Genoa uprising; in Switzerland, the general entrusted by Mazzini to lead the revolutionary invasion gambled away the money raised to arm a thousand volunteers. Other patriots gathered, but the Swiss authorities disarmed them. A revolutionary column invading from France encountered defeat at the hands of Piedmontese *carabinieri*.

The fizzle of Mazzini's first revolutionary challenge caused the crisis of his organization, a death sentence in absentia, and flight to England, but not failure. An English historian put it best many years ago: "The immediate result of Mazzini's teaching was to fan to a blaze the embers of Italian nationality." Patriots later important in the national movement had responded to his call to action. These included Giuseppe Garibaldi, who made his own revolutionary debut in the projected Genoese uprising, and Vincenzo Gioberti—the priest who would make the Risorgimento respectable—who was sent into exile for his Mazzinian sympathies. For this reason, even though Mazzini's "titanic" model for a future Italy could not be implemented, "None the less he made Italy."

The Italian Primacy

Mazzini argued that Italy should be united to fulfill a God-given mission. But both the mission and its methods were radical. Furthermore, Mazzini's intimately religious temperament detested the traditional religious forms that had dominated the peninsula for years. These views made Mazzini the mortal enemy of Italian moderates who believed in unification for economic and other reasons but abhorred Mazzini's revolutionary ideology. In short, "the great mass of educated Italians, who had too much common sense or too little courage for Mazzini's gospel, were looking for a milder creed which would reconcile patriotism and prudence."

From the beginning, this "moderate party" split into two factions. One faction was predominantly Catholic and centered in Lombardy, thanks to the cultural influence of Manzoni and Rosmini, but a Turinese priest emerged as its most powerful spokesman.

Vincenzo Gioberti's youthful flirtation with Mazzini's ideas ended with the taming of the Mazzinian mission for Italy. Italians indeed had a special "mission"—the spiritual leadership of the Catholic world—Gioberti argued in his extremely influential *On the Moral and Civil Primacy of the Italians* (the *Primato*) (1843). Gioberti tied Italy's greatness to the Church—a familiar tenet—but brilliantly linked the Church to unification, thus removing the radical edge that Mazzini and Buonarroti had given Italy's "mission" while retaining the crucial concept that Italy must necessarily be the "redeeming" nation. Before Gioberti, the demand for unification had been the province of revolutionaries; by single-handedly inventing "neo-Guelphism," Gioberti gave the independence movement respectable ideological credentials. Gioberti achieved this by tying the papacy's regeneration to Italy's resurrection. He attributed the papacy's decline to the split between religion and civil society caused by the French Revolution; the resurgence of Italy and the papacy together would heal this division by reconciling the Church with liberty and progress. As in Mazzini's case, Gioberti provided the Risorgimento with a universal aspect, but one that deemphasized revolution and caught the imagination of moderate liberals by mandating cooperation between the Church and the national movement. He thus provided a vehicle of political expression for well-off groups such as large landowners, progressive nobles, and liberal clergy anxious to revive the peninsula's fortunes but unwilling to throw over their religion, social status, and traditional values. Gioberti's lasting importance lies in his mobilization of these influential groups for unification, not in his model for an independent Italy.

Gioberti reconciled Italy's political independence with its spiritual mission by envisioning a loose confederation of existing states under the pope's presidency. His unification model consisted of an economic union with consultative institutions open to moderate reform. Thus Gioberti hoped both to eliminate the serious divisions among Italians as to Italy's future makeup and to win the support of Italian rulers for unity. But this proposed neo-Guelph confederation stood out for its impracticality. The current pope, Gregory XVI, inspired no confidence in anyone, including Gioberti. In fact, the priest himself acknowledged that only a new pope could implement his program. It is a tribute to the stunning boldness of Gioberti's project that his ideas influenced the election of a pope who seemed capable of realizing his plan. Although the unexpected election of a "liberal" pope briefly breathed life into Gioberti's vision, it would quickly become exposed for the impossible dream it was, and even Gioberti would abandon the conceptual model of a unified Italy as expressed in the *Primato*.

But liberals had been fired by Gioberti's vision of moderate leadership for the national movement. Instead of the pope, they focused on the Piedmontese monarch as the only ruler with the energy and perhaps the will to free Italy while preserving traditional values.

"Hamlet," or the Quandary of Moderates

In his bid to win the support of the princes for his unification model, Gioberti appealed to King Charles Albert of Piedmont-Sardinia to help free the Italians. While welcoming Gioberti's role in gaining respectability for the independence movement, Piedmontese moderates had no faith in the papacy's ability to reform itself or to lead the independence movement. The strength of the Piedmontese moderate movement resided in its connection with the government.

Many liberals were statesmen and bureaucrats proud of their traditions. They resented Austrian domination of the peninsula and papal interference in their government and agreed that unity could greatly enhance Piedmont's power. They did not favor unification on Mazzinian terms but instead called on Turin to fight for a federated Italy complete with a customs union.

As with the previous two models, influential literary works stimulated the idea of unification under Savoy leadership. Terenzio Mamiani's *Nostro parere intorno alle cose italiane* (*Our Opinion on Italian Things*) (1841) argued that Italians could unify themselves by fighting for their freedom under an Italian monarch. Given the disparity of forces in the field, the struggle would have to await a moment of Austrian weakness. In the meantime, Italians must prepare themselves by initiating the patriotic education of the masses, winning over the wealthy and the clergy to the movement, and implementing a program of educational, religious, and social reforms. Mamiani advocated agreement between liberals and Catholics but disagreed with Gioberti's emphasis on a paramount position for the Church.

Whereas Mamiani's tract illustrates the moderates' prevailing skepticism of Gioberti's concrete solution to the Italian problem, Cesare Balbo's *Le speranze d'Italia* (*The Hopes of Italy*) (1844) had an important influence on the liberal milieu. As with Mamiani, Balbo's dialogue with Gioberti confirms moderate disagreement with the ideas of the Turinese priest. A Catholic who was sympathetic to Gioberti's views, Balbo pronounced them impossible to apply practically. Balbo gave four possible unification scenarios, all dependent on the elimination of an Austrian role in Italian affairs: concerted action by Italian monarchs; a popular insurrection; foreign intervention; or satisfaction of Austrian appetites outside of Italy. For Balbo, the first three were impossible or dangerous. He therefore held out the hope that with the decline of the Turkish Empire the Western powers would hand over Ottoman territory to Austria to bolster it against Russia, which they all feared, and as an inducement to the Austrians to withdraw from Italy. Capping this diplomatic deal, Piedmont would absorb Lombardy and Venetia to form a strong north Italian kingdom and create an Italian confederation free from Austrian domination.

Although Balbo's solution to the Italian problem may appear to have an unrealistic flavor today, it had an important impact when he proposed the idea because it expressed the feelings of the Piedmontese ruling circles with whom Balbo had close connections. The Savoys had long aimed at absorbing Lombardy and Venetia, a goal Piedmontese diplomats never abandoned. Furthermore, both Piedmontese moderate liberals and conservatives favored Austrian expansion at Turkish expense, a plan that had French encouragement. Not only would this solution resolve the Italian problem and expand Piedmontese power, but it also would reinforce Catholic Austria against eastern Orthodox Russia. Unlike Mazzini, neither Balbo nor the Piedmontese government sympathized with the national aspirations of eastern Europeans under Austrian domination. For Balbo and the Piedmontese rulers, who with Gioberti identified civilization with the advance of Catholicism, the plan approached perfection.

Thus, while it might have seemed puerile to hope that Austria could be made to give up Italian territory, Balbo viewed the decline of the Ottoman Empire as an important occasion to connect two important problems threatening the peace of Europe. Although his plan did not work out, Balbo emphasized the importance of Piedmontese and European diplomacy in attaining a solution to the peninsula's problems and linked Piedmontese expansionism and Italian independence in a nonrevolutionary manner.

But the major obstacle to Piedmontese guidance of the national movement was none other than King Charles Albert himself, the person to whom Balbo's entire book was a veiled appeal. Charles Albert's indecisiveness illustrated in the 1821 conspiracy characterized the monarch throughout his life. His uncle, the conservative Charles Felix, never forgave his role in that revolution and favored denying him the throne until persuaded otherwise by Metternich. This uncertainty made the Piedmontese court a center of intrigue and left its mark on the heir of the throne after he became king.

Because of his past, Charles Albert ascended the throne to serious doubts at home and abroad as to his future performance. Mazzini greeted him with a strange appeal to support the national cause, which he followed up in 1833 by an attempted revolution. Reactionary policies characterized the new reign's first years. Charles Albert supported the attempts of French conservative monarchists attempting to overthrow King Louis Philippe and signed a military convention with Austria. He discouraged moderates looking to him for leadership of the national movement, and the violence with which he repressed the revolutionaries of 1833 ranks as one of the Risorgimento's worst chapters. The psychologically unstable, physically delicate ruler led a strange life, adopting peculiar diets, falling prey to quacks, and fueling intense political and religious intrigue. He himself is supposed to have remarked that he stood "between the dagger of the Carbonari and the poisoned chocolate of the Jesuits."

Despite the inauspicious start to his reign, Charles Albert resisted becoming the tool of reactionaries. A strong factor that helps explain this resistance was his family background and youthful experience: His father fought with Napoleon and his mother entertained French troops while he was educated in Geneva with a stipend from Napoleon. Reinforcing these factors, probably his strong Piedmontese patriotism and his stubborn commitment to good government accounts for his resistance to the reactionaries. He strengthened his kingdom through a series of administrative and legislative reforms that partially satisfied the bourgeois demand to modernize the economy while retaining the Crown's prerogatives. Some of his economic reforms and a desire to reduce Piedmontese dependence on Austria brought the two countries to the brink of war. He unleashed an attack on Church power, considered a prime reason for Piedmontese backwardness. He gradually weeded out conservative ministers from his government, replacing them with moderate liberals, and suggested he might grant a constitution. He encouraged nationalists by stating that he would strike a blow for Italy when the opportunity came and by remarking: "If Piedmont lost Austria she would gain Italy, and then Italy would be able to act for herself."

Despite these developments, Charles Albert never overcame the fundamental ambivalence of his character. As his "liberalism" increased his standing among his subjects, he seemed fearful of his growing popularity. When war with Austria seemed imminent, he hastily retreated and sought arbitration. He accompanied his actions against the Church with a promise to the Jesuits that they would be safe. In sum, it remained unclear whether Charles Albert would respond to the appeal of moderate liberals to become the champion of Italian independence. To patriots, he was truly "the Hamlet of Italy."

Even with this uncertainty, an important change occurred in the Italy of the 1830s and 1840s: Italian moderate opinion now favored independence. This stance signaled a crucial break—one that enormously advanced the cause of independence—in the conservative-reactionary front that had allowed Austria and its Italian allies to reassert their dominance in 1815, 1821, and 1831. In this sense, a "cultural revolution" had indeed occurred.

This development was represented not only by writers such as those examined in this chapter but also by a wider cultural phenomenon. Between 1839 and 1847 scientists and technicians from all parts of the peninsula met together in congresses. These meetings advanced the cause of unity by discussing common Italian problems, by contributing to the elaboration of a moderate national program, and by helping build the country's future ruling class. The popularity of scientific meetings and associations was so strong that even Metternich had to permit them and Charles Albert sympathized with the movement.

By the 1840s the dominant political culture in Italy demanded independence. Except for Mazzini's, the other models called for a confederation; but Mazzini's radical democratic ideas alarmed the moderates, who rejected the weak pope as leader of the national movement and turned to Piedmont. Charles Albert vacillated but gave timid promises to help.

The people, the pope, and Piedmont represented the three best hopes for independence and unification. In retrospect, it seems clear which one had the best chance for success, but historical events usually unfold in unexpected ways.

7

Revolutions of 1848: The Great Shakeout

P RISCILLA ROBERTSON, author of a classic work on the 1848 revolutions in Europe, writes about the Italians: "In habit and attitude . . . they were the most democratic people in Europe, except possibly for the Swiss." Behavior in two areas bolster Robertson's argument: relationship among the classes and the position of women.

With regard to the first, she notes the courtesy and respect with which the aristocracy treated the lower classes, contrasting this behavior with that in other parts of Europe. Robertson believes that ownership of property by the common people and the great economic strides that had been made in the North accounted for this relationship. The remarkable influence of women in Italian life complemented this "easy friendliness and self-respect" of the workers. Robertson emphasizes the political commitment and the prominence of women in Italian society, which exceeded that of women in France, Germany, and England.

Among the major European revolutionaries, Mazzini alone denounced any qualifications tending to limit women's equality with men. Women not only participated in the Risorgimento, they were its "fiercer patriots." They included Giuditta Sidoli, Mazzini's lover and his "intellectual passion," and Anita Garibaldi, who fought alongside her husband and died in the field. The fictional heroine of Camillo Boito's *Senso*—subject of a film by Luchino Visconti—was caught up in the passions of sex and Risorgimento wars and was able to exact a terrible price for her betrayal by an Austrian soldier. The London *Times* correspondent observed that "it was hard for Englishmen to allow for the freedom of manners which Italian women enjoyed, coupled with perfect respectability."

These aspects of Italian society illustrate the democratic climate of the 1848 revolutions that attempted to put Mazzini's preaching into action.

Economics

Besides the development of the cultural and ideological milieu that favored unification, the peninsula's participation in Europe's rapid economic and commercial growth after 1820, discussed in Chapter 4, intensified the demand for national independence. In Italy, however, this economic development proceeded
unevenly and at a slower pace than in other parts of Europe. The patriots attributed this lag to the political and territorial order that Austria imposed on
the peninsula.

Lombardy led in economic growth. Building on eighteenth-century reforms,
production had become capitalist, and the aristocracy engaged in business to a
greater extent than in other parts of the peninsula. Prosperity varied according
to the physical characteristics of the region's zones, but the value of silk exports,
for example, more than quadrupled between 1814 and 1841; the cotton, metallurgical, and mechanical industries all got their starts during this period, and
the expansion of banking testifies to the growth of capital accumulation.

Even though Lombard economic progress outstripped the rest of Italy, it
trailed more-advanced parts of Europe. Lombard capitalism was still primarily
based on land ownership, and the chief export and source of wealth, silk, which
depended on the vagaries of foreign demand, was increasingly threatened by
growing Asian competition. Of all the peninsula's regions, Lombardy came
closest to developing, but had not achieved, a modern economy based on production as a response to increasing internal demand. Lombardy's status as an
Austrian colony blocked this qualitative leap. For although Lombards benefited
from some positive aspects of Austrian rule such as good roads, decent administration and a measure of local autonomy, they suffered serious economic and
tariff discrimination, which favored Austrian-owned enterprises and hampered
Italian-owned businesses. Furthermore, the peninsula's division into many small
states protected by tariff barriers deprived the fledgling Lombard industries of
natural markets and stunted future development. Finally, Lombards watched
helplessly as the Austrians drew one-third of their empire's revenue from Lombardy (which accounted for only one-sixth of the population) and unofficially
shut them out of the best government jobs.

These elements explain why widespread anti-Austrian feeling agitated the
richest part of Italy. Patriots attributed Lombardy's economic growth primarily
to Italian enterprise against overwhelming odds and emphasized the heavy negative aspects of Austrian rule. Moreover, they believed that future Lombard
industrial development depended on the region's economic integration with the
rest of Italy and free trade for the entire peninsula. But as long as foreign rule
continued, Austrian protectionist concerns took precedence over Italian economic development. Indeed, the more Lombard economic activity accelerated.

the greater the dispute with Austria became. Economic growth in Lombardy before 1848, therefore, stimulated revolutionary developments and decisively contributed to the struggle for Italian independence.

After Lombardy, Piedmont boasted the second-fastest-growing economy in Italy. This was an important change from earlier years and greatly enhanced the Risorgimento's cause. Economic progress in Piedmont stemmed from administrative and legislative reforms, the encouragement of free trade, and other economic reforms advocated by patriots and European economists. Charles Albert reversed his predecessor's protectionist policies by eliminating export duties on raw silk, lowering the tariff on grain and other products, and by signing twenty-six commercial treaties with foreign states. These measures, which were put into effect between 1840 and 1847, favored the growth of modern credit institutions, spurred greater economic activity among the bourgeoisie, intensified the rate at which capitalist firms transformed economic relationships on the land, and encouraged the progress of new industries. Economic development also stimulated research, exchange of information, congresses of scientists, and creation of groups such as the Agricultural Association in 1842. Most active in these activities were moderate liberals such as Count Camillo Benso di Cavour, future leader of the national movement.

As with his politics, innumerable contradictions accompanied Charles Albert's economic policies. The king hoped to stimulate the economy without relinquishing his absolutistic power, a goal that made it more difficult to eradicate old methods and ideas. With all their limits, however, the Piedmontese reforms of this period prepared the ground for the economic policy of Cavour during the next decade and contributed greatly to the momentum favoring unification.

Economic growth failed, however, to reconcile patriots to Italy's dependent political status, and stagnation in the South confirmed their desire for unity and independence. Rome was a prime example of this feeling. Between 1823 and 1846, Popes Leo XII and Gregory XVI blocked the minimum reforms that the changes in nineteenth-century Italian, European, and even Roman society required. Metternich and the European powers, anxious to put the papacy on a more solid basis, pressured the government for reforms without avail. The extremist Zelanti continued to determine policy, propped up by the Austrians and irregular paramilitary terrorist formations who "came to bear an increasing resemblance to the *squadristi* of Fascist Italy, performing the same function of intimidating political opponents by arbitrary extralegal violence, and causing at times similar concern to their supposed masters."

Italians and Europeans attributed the worst poverty, economic degradation, and financial stagnation in Italy to the nature of papal government, which was controlled by a narrow political class of prelates who perceived reform as a dire threat to their power. Despite Gioberti's theories, the Papal State appeared as an anachronism whose survival depended on continual Austrian military intervention against frequent attempts to overthrow an oppressive government. In a perverse way, the extent of governmental mismanagement, and the revolutionary agitation that the government's reactionary policies provoked, significantly influenced the Risorgimento; mismanagement transformed the problem of the Papal State into a common Italian one and focused European attention on Italy's plight.

Further south, in the Kingdom of the Two Sicilies, Enlightenment and Napoleonic reforms had failed to transform a landed and money-lending bourgeoisie into a modern productive class engaged in business and industry. King Ferdinand II pursued protectionist and reform policies aimed at mollifying the bourgeoisie, not stimulating economic changes that might threaten his absolutistic rule. For the patriots, the problem was that the southern bourgeoisie's landed character paralyzed the liberal national movement. Southern patriots sought to change the government, but the bourgeoisie relied on it for economic favors and for protection from the brigandage resulting from widespread poverty. Although a strong desire for unification characterized southern intellectuals, the kingdom's social and political structure limited their options to insurrection. No moderate movement, which might hope to collaborate with the king, developed as it had in the North. Thus the Bourbon dynasty and a backward economy precluded the South from assuming a leadership role in the Risorgimento and cost the region dearly after unification.

Rumblings

As in the rest of Europe, numerous rumblings preceded the "year of revolutions" on the peninsula. In Italy, unlike in other areas, the overwhelming demand for national independence, not economic factors, drove events. Moreover, the disorders in different parts of the country did not remain isolated, as they had in the past, but influenced each other. Eventually the events of 1848–1849 spurred the intervention of Italians from the entire peninsula and all political persuasions.

After the initial defeat of his insurrectionary activities, in 1834 Mazzini withdrew to London, where he suffered a period of doubt. He reemerged, his faith unscathed and his ideology unchanged. Painfully rebuilding his conspiratorial organization, Mazzini amplified the social dimension of his activities by devoting more attention to the workers, but his radicalism still made him anathema to many progressives who otherwise might have supported him.

At the same time, exiles influenced by Mazzini but not controlled by him linked up with local opponents of the pope and the Bourbons and initiated several important but ill-fated insurrections. Forced to emigrate after the numerous Italian revolutions, these exiles had become freedom fighters in liberal causes in Europe and America and hoped to exploit their military experience in the struggle to free their homeland. They focused on the Papal State and the Kingdom of the Two Sicilies because these states had been shaken since 1834 by endemic rebellions. Harsh measures and frequent executions failed to quell the ongoing disturbances, which issued from local, uncoordinated conspiracies. Hoping to supply that coordination, exiles from Spain and Malta converged on the Romagna and the Bourbon domains in 1843. Mazzini had advised against the action because he judged its preparation insufficient, and the capture and execution of the conspirators proved him correct. The brutality of the repression that followed the disorders in the Papal State inspired the Bandiera brothers, sons of an admiral and sailors in the Austrian navy, to spark a revolution in the South. Betrayed by spies, they refused an Austrian offer of clemency and "invaded" the Kingdom of the Two Sicilies with only nineteen men. They were captured by Bourbon troops and executed.

The revolutionary attempts of this period demonstrated a misunderstanding of Mazzini's tactics; he advocated insurrection to stimulate guerrilla warfare but did not believe that isolated patriot bands could stimulate insurrection. Nevertheless, the desperate activism of Italian patriots characterized the Italian situation in the years leading up to 1848, and the patriots' sacrifice won Italian and foreign sympathy for the national cause.

The rebellions in the South also increased moderate influence on governments not directly affected by the uprisings lest the agitation spread to their states. Precisely, this process occurred in 1845–1846. The continual failure of revolutionary agitation in the Papal State caused liberals to investigate whether more peaceful means of change existed. Massimo D'Azeglio, an intimate friend of Cesare Balbo with impeccable social connections, was dispatched to the Romagna to determine whether he could advance the moderate liberal cause there. D'Azeglio's mission was a discrete success despite widespread skepticism about Charles Albert. Soon after D'Azeglio's departure, however, a new revolt erupted. The participants made several mild requests, which were refused. This emphasized the unreasonableness of a papal government that forced its subjects to take up arms to achieve minimal change.

Upon his return to Turin, D'Azeglio reported to Charles Albert on his visit. The monarch's astounding response: "Tell them to be quiet and not move, since, for now, nothing can be done; but also let them be certain that, when the occasion presents itself, *my life, the lives of my children, my arms, my treasure, my army, everything will be spent for the Italian cause.*" Given Charles Albert's past history, even D'Azeglio sounded a cautionary note, but this time the king would make good on his promise.

D'Azeglio kept the momentum going. Encouraged by the king, he published his ideas on the Italian situation as it related to the Papal State. The resulting *Degli ultimi casi di Romagna* (1846) (*On the Last Incidents of the Romagna*) was one of the Risorgimento's most influential works. D'Azeglio explained his reasoning in his memoirs: "Revolution, no. We already have had enough. War, no, because we have neither the means nor the strength. . . . Therefore, put the question in a camp where every individual always has some force, . . . the camp of opinion and publicity."

D'Azeglio attacked the papal government, stating that it had lost all popular support, that it remained in power thanks only to the Austrians, and that it must reform or perish. He duly paid homage to those patriots who had sacrificed their lives in the many uprisings but argued that they had no right to speak on behalf of the people. He urged them to renounce conspiracies and violence and to fight for independence by developing a vast public opinion movement at home and abroad—a "conspiracy in the sunlight"—supplemented by military discipline to be employed when the opportunity presented itself. In short, no more secret conspiracies but a vast "open conspiracy."

D'Azeglio's lively, influential, and widely read pamphlet completed the liberal moderate program, even though, characteristically, Charles Albert refused permission to publish it in Turin. The appeal to public opinion invested the moderates with a "democratic" aura with which to combat radical influence, while the Piedmontese would soon supply the Risorgimento with an efficient army and a well-organized diplomatic corps. Moreover, D'Azeglio's work had the enthusiastic endorsement of the other moderate leaders. Even Mazzini commented: "The great national idea is expressed with decision, without reticence, and with admirable courage." And Mazzini had the most to lose.

The Surprise Pope

Although these considerations would become clear over the next few years, in 1846 the diverse models for unification still competed and, amazingly, the least likely suddenly became the most probable.

On June 1, 1846, the "retrograde, stubborn, lazy, reactionary to the highest degree" Pope Gregory XVI died. Ironically, the ideas expressed in Gioberti's *Primato* and by the liberal moderates had penetrated the highest ranks of the clergy. Furthermore, popular pressure in the form of petitions and the crisis of the Papal State itself convinced a number of cardinals that Gregory's policies must end. These men engineered the election of the cardinal from Imola as a compromise at a conclave that had originally pitted a highly favored conservative against an opponent considered overly liberal.

The new fifty-four-year-old pope, Pius IX or Pio Nono (Giovanni Maria Mastai-Ferretti), came from the Romagna and favored change. He was reasonable rather than liberal, counted friends of the moderate political persuasion, and had read Gioberti, Balbo, and D'Azeglio. It is not surprising, therefore, that moderate and neo-Guelph ideas influenced him. His election stunned Metternich and the Austrians.

In his first official act, Pius IX appointed a commission to study the question of an amnesty for political prisoners, demanded by popular opinion. Although conservative prelates served on this body, it included the novel presence of influential liberals and it granted the amnesty on July 16. Variously judged as generous and limited, the amnesty was very important because of the context in which it was issued: The most reactionary state in Europe seemed to have made a complete turnaround.

The resulting explosion of popular joy and Gioberti's famous prophecy created the myth of Pio Nono. The people of the Eternal City saluted him with a torchlight parade, continuously begged for his blessing, and detached his horses from his carriage so they could pull it themselves. Similar tumultuous scenes repeated themselves in other cities, in churches, and in theaters, while Bologna's central piazza echoed with the strains of a hymn Rossini composed and directed in the pope's honor. The peninsula witnessed an extraordinary chorus of enthusiasm for the pope and Italy. Where Mazzini had failed to raise the people, Pio Nono had succeeded; what the moderates had judged as extremely difficult, and perhaps dangerous, Pius IX had done effortlessly. An observer has noted that these events of 1846 "initiated the national revolution of 1848."

But a fundamental reality remained: Pius IX was not a liberal, and although historians have argued that he sympathized with Italian independence and unity, he was unwilling to lead the movement. To this factor must be added indecision. He supported reforms but not to the extent demanded by the patriots who gained control of the Roman crowd and nudged it from neo-Guelphism to radical democracy. In his biography of the pope, historian Frank Coppa quotes Pius as saying, "We will cede as long as our conscience permits us, but arriving at the limit which we have already preestablished, we will not, with the help of God, go beyond it by one step, even if they tore [sic] us to pieces."

Gradually the joyful exhibitions turned into demonstrations for measures about which Pius IX was lukewarm or did not wish to implement. Pressed by the people throughout 1847, and either "inebriated by the applause" or lacking the strength to oppose it, Pius yielded to the crowd's pretensions, which only emboldened it. When he found the conviction to stop the process, the neo-Guelph bubble burst.

The People's Revolution

The strong involvement of the masses in the Risorgimento characterized not only Rome but other parts of Italy during this period. In the repressed South, where no Pio Nono appeared to save the desperate situation, patriots and exiles planned coordinated uprisings in Naples, Palermo, and other areas, in addition to Tuscany and the Papal State.

Within this conspiratorial context and the dramatic Roman backdrop, the first revolution of 1848 exploded in Palermo on January 8. Despite their appearance of being isolated and yearning for independence from Naples, Sicilian patriots had solid contacts with the national movement. Simultaneously a revolt began on the continent; the king granted some concessions and fired his hated police chief, actions that heartened rather than satisfied the rebels. Popular demonstrations for a constitution ensued. Ferdinand II angled for Austrian intervention and, when he failed to get it, published on January 29 a constitution based on the French Constitution of 1830. Even though this act inspired some southern moderates to hope for an alliance with Ferdinand II to free Italy, fear and a desire to split Neapolitans and Sicilians (who supported a different constitution) motivated the king.

Ferdinand's action brought pressure on other Italian rulers to follow suit. When news of the Neapolitan Constitution reached Piedmont, massive demonstrations occurred in the kingdom's two chief cities, Turin and Genoa. These events finally forced Charles Albert to choose; he had been following a policy of encouraging the liberals on the independence issue, granting administrative reforms but retaining political power in his own hands. The demand for a constitution meant he could no longer pursue that policy. In fact, the king opposed a constitution because it weakened his position and because he had promised his predecessor that he would never grant one. Conservatives encouraged him to hold fast, but his advisors argued that it would be wise to grant a constitution speedily rather than be forced to do so under the popular pressure that would inevitably build up. A moderate commentator exposed the contradictions of those opposing a constitution: "Those of you who do not wish to diminish the King's authority by allowing the Nation's participation through political representation, those of you who oppose written guarantees or sanctions against the abuse of power, those of you who say that public opinion is a sufficient check, have you thought about which guarantee you count on? That of revolution, neither more nor less." Under the force of these arguments, Charles

Albert's resistance waned; finally he received a dispensation from the oath he made to Charles Felix that he would not agree to a constitution. On February 8, the government published the *Statuto*, also based on the French Constitution of 1830; this instrument, discussed in Chapter 8, became the constitution of united Italy.

The people greeted the *Statuto*'s promulgation with great enthusiasm. Widespread demonstrations of support occurred and quickly turned anti-Austrian and anti-Jesuit. The new constitutional order also mandated replacement of the current government with one more acceptable to the liberals, and in March a cabinet headed by Balbo took office.

Demonstrations had caused the government to plan reforms in Tuscany as well. News from Naples and Turin, however, forced the grand duke to go beyond reforms and to publish a constitution on February 17.

These events had repercussions in Rome. As previously mentioned, patriots there had been pushing Pius to speed up the pace of reform and to increase support of the national movement. The papal government initiated talks with Charles Albert on creation of a customs union but refused Piedmont's offer of an alliance directed against Austria. The renewed agitation in Italy found Roman patriots and demonstrators increasingly disenchanted with the slow pace of reform and Pius IX becoming more upset with his subjects' demands, but once again the two misunderstood each other. On February 10 Pius issued a statement attributing past reforms to his own benevolence, not to the rights of the people; he called for calm, invited the Romans to desist from making requests not conforming to his duties (a constitution?), and sought to defuse a demand for military reorganization directed against the Austrians by claiming that no danger of war existed. Pius nullified his stern message, however, by ending with an eloquent call upon God to bless *Italy*. The pope intended to end the continuous demonstrations demanding support for the national movement, but given the Italian context and the gathering revolutionary storm that would soon break out over Europe, everyone interpreted the pope's message as conferring his benediction on the patriotic movement. That evening, enthusiastic demonstrators cheered the pope, who, once more, tried unsuccessfully to clarify his position. He wound up the evening by blessing all Italy once again.

The concession of constitutions in Naples, Turin, and Florence, a mounting petition drive in the Papal State, and increasing European disorder convinced members of the papal government that it had become necessary to grant a constitution, despite Pio Nono's initial opposition. At the same time, a debate occurred on which qualities would best combine democratic principles with the Papal State's religious nature, but the pope ignored this discussion. On March 14 he published a constitution establishing two legislative houses but giving the pope and the College of Cardinals supreme power over legislation; the constitution also banned the secular legislature from passing laws in areas of mixed secular-ecclesiastical concern—extremely difficult to define—and conferred political rights only on practicing Catholics. Under the circumstances, these weaknesses went unnoticed and popular ecstasy greeted the constitution's promulgation and raised Pius's popularity to new heights.

By the time Pius issued his constitution, revolution had radically altered the European landscape. In late February King Louis Philippe had been overthrown and the Second Republic established in France. In mid-March the revolution spread to Vienna, an event that proved crucial for Italy and other Austrian-dominated areas.

The events of early 1848 resulted in constitutions being given in all major Italian states except Lombardy-Venetia. Convinced that any concessions to constitutionalism or nationalism would end in the breakup of their polyglot empire, the Austrians harshly repressed the slightest sign of national feeling in their Italian possessions. They arrested well-known leaders in both Lombardy and Venetia, but the struggle's novel aspect is that, at least in urban areas, it spread into the popular consciousness. Austrian officials and their subjects engaged in an imaginative "cold war" calculated to inflict maximum irritation on each other. The most famous of these events was the antismoking campaign. In an effort to deprive the government of revenues from its tobacco monopoly, the Milanese gave up smoking and pressured anyone not participating in the boycott to follow their example. Austrian authorities distributed free cigars to their soldiers, who sauntered down the streets blowing smoke in the faces of citizens; fights ensued, with Austrian troops killing and maiming unarmed civilians.

With the outbreak of the Viennese revolution and the ignominious flight of Metternich from his capital, the Italian possessions exploded. The Austrians had poured reinforcements into Italy, but they were unprepared for the fierce street fighting that broke out in Milan on March 18—the "Five Days." This uprising seems to have begun spontaneously but was rapidly transformed into a guerrilla war directed by a "War Council." This council had as its guiding light Carlo Cattaneo, a federalist republican who had believed in gradual progress toward independence but who concluded that the national feeling demonstrated by the uprising made his ideas obsolete. On March 22 the Austrian commander, Joseph Radetzky, was forced to pull his army out of Milan, proving Mazzini's theory that civilians could defeat professional armies. Encouraged by similar developments throughout Austria's Italian dominions—especially the expulsion of the Austrians from Venice—and the news that volunteers from Naples, the Papal State, and Tuscany were rushing to aid the Lombards, Cattaneo and the War Council proposed raising a democratic volunteer army to drive the Austrians out of the peninsula as a prerequisite to a definitive political solution. Unfortunately, the conversion of Cattaneo, the "reluctant revolutionary," to something uncomfortably resembling Mazzini's "people's war" raised an alarming specter, which compromised the national independence movement.

The Divided War for Liberation

Although the desire to liberate themselves from Austrian domination and their support for a "free Italy" unified the rebels, politics divided them. Differences existed among republicans such as Cattaneo and Mazzini, who was more radical but willing to subordinate everything to achieve unity. Bad blood, however, split Lombard republicans and aristocrats, who favored Charles Albert and advocated fusion of Lombardy with Piedmont. Led by Count Gabrio Casati, the aristocratic party feared not only the Austrians but the radical-democratic implications of a popular war. Lombard moderates formed a provisional government and appealed to Charles Albert to intervene. The Piedmontese king consented but arrived after the Milanese had driven out the Austrians.

This tardiness made the republicans even more suspicious of Charles Albert. The king's indecisiveness has already been noted, but Cattaneo had a simpler explanation of his motives. He believed that Charles Albert had intervened for dynastic reasons, "to save the most retrograde part of Italy" and to transform the conflict from a "people's war" into a "safe" conventional one. The Piedmontese army, therefore, had come to replace the Austrians, not to save the Lombards.

In sum, with the Austrian army still intact, the Italians began squabbling about issues such as fusing Lombardy-Venetia with Piedmont and about where the capital would be located. Cattaneo conducted a campaign to block fusion by calling for the election of assemblies to decide that and other questions. He condemned as treason Mazzini's attempt to reach a compromise with the king and later denied any validity to a May referendum overwhelmingly favoring fusion, which clearly indicated popular support for the Piedmontese solution. Cattaneo's memoirs graphically illustrate republican suspicion of Charles Albert's motives, and the fulminations found there symbolize the republican-monarchist split in the national movement. This republican hatred of the "royal war" culminated in the fragmentation of Mazzini-oriented groups, the revival of local rivalries, and the proclamation of small independent republics. The Piedmontese, in turn, resorted to self-destructive stratagems to block these tendencies. For example, since Venice had proclaimed itself a republic under the leadership of Daniele Manin, the Piedmontese refused to move against Austrian reinforcements in an attempt to frighten Venetia into declaring union with Piedmont.

These divisions sabotaged the "war for national liberation" before Austrian influence on the peninsula could be eliminated, transforming the conflict into a conventional one between armies. This change and the recovery by the conservatives in Vienna shifted the military advantage to Austrian commander Radetzky, who retreated into impregnable fortresses and regrouped.

Other aspects of the Italian situation also favored Austria. Spurred by popular enthusiasm, Rome, Florence, and Naples had sent troops to aid the national cause. As hegemony of the national movement passed to Piedmont, however, the frightened rulers of these states withdrew their forces. In Rome, Pius finally found the courage to oppose the reform movement, while the Kingdom of the Two Sicilies fell prey to disorders and secession. Suspicious of possible French aid, with Radetzky rejecting British mediation, and having refused an Austrian offer to content themselves with Lombardy, the Piedmontese faced the Austrian army alone. Furthermore, Charles Albert continued his contradictory policies, allowing conservatives suspicious of the national movement space to maneuver and injecting indiscipline into the army. After several small victories, the Piedmontese lost the Battle of Custoza in July. A slow retreat and the loss of Milan followed on August 6, 1848, and an armistice was signed three days later.

Anger and accusations of betrayal directed at Charles Albert followed the loss of Lombardy. In Turin, a Gioberti government took command but was soon replaced with a more democratic cabinet. Anxious to vindicate himself as soon as possible, Charles Albert wished to resume the war, and the government agreed. Because of his previous defeats, the king relinquished command of his dispirited and politically divided army to Polish General Wojciech Chrzanowski. On March 23, 1849, the Piedmontese once again met defeat at the Battle of Novara. Failing to find the death he sought on the battlefield, Charles Albert abdicated in favor of his son, who took the name of Victor Emmanuel II, and left for Portugal. "There are moments which redeem an entire life," said a contemporary observer; Charles Albert finally found redemption at Novara.

The Roman Revolution

Even as the national revolution began unraveling, dramatic events occurred in Rome. Pius was shocked by the commander of his troops, who told his soldiers that they were waging a new crusade. Reports of a possible schism with the Austrian and South German Catholics also alarmed the pope. As a result, on April 29, 1848, Pius issued the famous allocution making his position clear. He declared that, as leader of all the Catholics, he would not wage war on the Catholic Austrians.

Pius had finally distinguished between his sympathies as an Italian and his duty as pope, but the reaction was immediate, sharp, and unanimous. "He has betrayed us," tearfully declared Angelo Brunetti, known as Ciceruacchio, chief tribune of the people. Instability followed the allocution, and Pius's appointment of moderate Pellegrino Rossi to head a government failed to stem it. Rossi's energetic reform policies and resistance to demands that he support the national cause alienated both conservatives and democrats. On November 15 a fanatic stabbed him to death. Demonstrations ensued, and the crowd imposed a cabinet committed to Italian independence. On November 24 Pio Nono fled to Gaeta, in the Kingdom of the Two Sicilies.

The Catholic powers vowed to save the pope. Naples and Spain, even republican France, offered Pius military assistance while the Romans exulted to Verdi's patriotic *La Battaglia di Legnano*, deposed the pope, and declared a republic. Verdi's opera tells how the Italian city-states routed German Emperor Frederick Barbarossa in 1176; with the defeat of the national movement in the North, the Eternal City became the center of the Risorgimento. Freedom fighters poured into Rome, including Giuseppe Garibaldi, who had spent years in South America.

The Roman Republic put itself in the hands of Giuseppe Mazzini, who revealed himself an excellent organizer capable of winning the people's support. Despite difficult conditions, hardly any disorders marred the republic's existence. The Romans discussed and adopted the most democratic constitution of the period and adopted a series of significant social reforms. The republic abolished the Inquisition, special courts, clerical control of schools and universities, and censorship. On February 21, 1849, the republican Assembly mandated the takeover of Church property by the state and passed measures to ensure that the land would actually reach the peasants. The republic also introduced the concept of a paid clergy.

These measures encountered criticism, but they dramatically illustrate the competence and courage of Rome's democratic administration. Mazzini's party showed great promise in resolving the Papal State's ancient ills and, given more time, might have transformed its economy in a manner that the popes had perennially demonstrated themselves incapable of doing.

The People Defeated

But time had run out for the national movement's democratic wing. By 1849 reactionaries had regained control in Austria and Germany. Italian liberals had negotiated for French help, but republican France was too radical for the Pied-montese and too conservative for the democrats. In May and June 1848, French radicals who might have supported Italian liberty suffered defeat. The election of Napoleon I's nephew, Louis Napoleon, as president of the Second Republic encouraged some Italian democrats, but he was primarily interested in strength-ening his own position. In Tuscany, where the people had expelled Leopold II, the Austrians intervened ferociously. The restored grand duke reinstituted ab-solutistic rule and on May 6, 1852, revoked the constitution he had granted in 1848. In the Kingdom of the Two Sicilies, Ferdinand II suspended the Nea-politan Parliament forever on March 13, 1849. The king then proceeded to re-conquer Sicily, which had previously declared its independence. By the end of May all resistance to the Bourbons ceased.

These events and the Austrian siege of Venice left the Roman Republic as the only beacon of hope for Italians. Garibaldi organized Rome's defense in the ex-pectation of an Austrian attack. Naples and Spain sent troops to restore the pope, but they proved too weak to accomplish the mission. Indeed, Garibaldi planned to invade Neapolitan territory to revive the Neapolitan Revolution. Mazzini suc-cessfully opposed the move, anxious to avoid exacerbating the diplomatic situa-tion. He believed that rivalry with the Austrians and republican sympathies might encourage the French to aid the Romans. Instead the French president hoped to strengthen himself internally by exploiting the Italian situation. Louis Napoleon gambled on garnering both domestic Catholic and liberal support by restoring the pope but pressuring him to retain the constitution he had previously granted. A heroic defense defeated Louis Napoleon's army at first, but its commander violated an armistice and sneaked in reinforcements. Thus the French destroyed the Roman Republic and restored Pio Nono.

The patriots scattered from Rome and the other defeated revolutionary states. Garibaldi escaped from the French in a desperate attempt to reach Venice, but many of his men were captured and executed, and his wife died in his arms. On August 26, following a tenacious defense that won the respect of its Austrian besiegers, Venice finally capitulated. The people's revolution had been crushed.

With the exception of France, all of the rulers who were overthrown in the gigantic European revolutionary movement of 1848 were restored. This fact has led observers to ask whether or not the revolutions of 1848 constituted a "turn-ing point."

In Italy they had a clarifying effect by eliminating two models for unification from contention. Neo-Guelphism turned out to be an illusion. The 1848 events demonstrated that no matter how sympathetic individual popes might be on Italian national issues, they would subordinate their feelings to their role as international leaders of the Catholic world and would call in foreign powers to intervene on their behalf. Moreover, the papacy reverted to its ancient role as a major obstacle to the peninsula's unity because the restored Pius IX no longer toyed with liberal ideas.

Mazzini's model also emerged fatally wounded from the events of 1848. Although Mazzini did not plan the uprisings, his ideas inspired and marked them. He had theorized the revolution of the people as the answer to military occupation. From a military viewpoint, 1848 proved him correct, but "there was an immense gap between the people as dreamed of by Mazzini and as awakened by revolution." The victorious people failed to implement his ideal of a free, united, and indivisible Italy, reviving instead class and local divisions. Furthermore, whereas Mazzini had demonstrated prudence and a keen awareness of the Italian and European diplomatic context, republican leaders such as Cattaneo had demonstrated an inflexibility and suspiciousness that alienated the national movement's moderate wing. In addition, the developments of 1848–1849 revealed the limitations of Mazzini's methods. They might succeed in overthrowing princes but could not defeat the great powers. Indeed, 1848 proved that Italy could not "do it by itself"; the national movement needed Europe's help against Austria, and only an established power had a chance of securing that aid. Mazzini, the sworn enemy of the European establishment, could never institute a dialogue with the powers. Although Mazzinian ideals continued to fascinate part of the national movement and exercised a pull far into the future, support for Mazzini greatly diminished over the next few years. Even his sympathizers became convinced that Mazzini lacked the practical qualities necessary to free the peninsula from foreign domination.

The destruction of neo-Guelphism and the decline of Mazzinianism left the moderate model for independence under Piedmontese leadership as the most plausible solution to the Italian problem. Charles Albert's abdication removed a major obstacle to Piedmont's leadership, and the Statuto, the only surviving Italian constitution, quickened the kingdom's evolution into a liberal state. Absolutism had returned to Rome, Naples, and Tuscany, eliminating them as centers of the Risorgimento; buttressed by Austrian or French armies, those governments could no longer pretend to have real popular support, buttressed as they were by Austrian or French armies. With the Austrians exacting as well a terrible price from the inhabitants of Lombardy-Venetia—where they also unsuccessfully attempted to stimulate a class war—Piedmont attracted the sympathies of Italians comparing their situation to that of the only independent state on the peninsula.

The revolutions of 1848 had brought independence within sight, despite local differences and political divisions. In 1849 this dream had suffered defeat but remained alive. Indeed, the revolutions had simplified the terms of the Italian problem and had set into motion a process that culminated in unity and independence.

8

Cavour and the Piedmontese Solution

IN 1848 THE ITALIANS had led Europe in revolution, and in 1849 their heroic resistance against overwhelming French and Austrian force won the admiration of Europeans. In the 1850s, amid all the gloom, Italian nationalists could take heart because the Risorgimento had been forcefully posed as a European problem and because Piedmont had been converted to the cause of independence.

The "Second Restoration"

As expected, the restored regimes clamped down hard on their populations. In Lombardy-Venetia, military authorities under Radetzky ruled until 1857. This regime conducted a particularly harsh repression, with summary executions of persons discovered with arms in their possession and frequent beatings of suspected patriots. On August 12, 1849, the Austrians conceded an amnesty for all but the most compromised patriots, but the police retained wide powers to crush any suspected opposition. Sustained by the memory of the Five Days, the people opposed a sullen resistance. No dialogue between the imperial government and its Lombard and Venetian subjects of any class existed, and physical force alone kept the Austrians in power.

Besides intolerable political conditions, the Lombard economy stagnated. This slowdown occurred despite a more liberal tariff policy, dictated by an Austrian desire to bring its possessions into the Prussian-dominated Zollverein. Diseases debilitating the silk and winemaking industries caused great hardship, but Austrian administration had primary responsibility for the downturn. The Austrians greatly increased taxes to make their Italian subjects pay the costs of the 1848 revolutions, the financial crisis that ensued, and an increased share of the empire's enormous deficit. Moreover, the Austrians failed to encourage railway building, the engine of economic development in Europe at this time, and also subordinated Lombardy's economic well-being to their strategic goals. In the decade following 1848, Lombards and other Italians looked wistfully at the economic progress of Piedmont and concluded that independence was the necessary prerequisite for such progress.

Conditions in Rome and Naples also deteriorated. With the support of Europe's Catholics, Pius IX successfully resisted French pressure to retain the constitution he had granted in 1848. Pius broke with the national movement forever, setting his face against liberalism and democracy. Reaction gripped the state as the government repealed legislation adopted by the Roman Republic and conducted a propaganda campaign against the memory of 1848. Corruption reigned in the economic sphere as well, and reform abruptly ended. In the religious area, the Curia attacked liberal Catholicism and waged war against any hint of Church reform. The formerly unwelcome Jesuits spearheaded the anti-liberal campaign on the theoretical plane through their new review *La Civiltà Cattolica*. Discontent among all classes grew and conspiracy flourished, but French troops in Rome and Austrian soldiers holding down the outlying areas made a fresh revolution unlikely. After the brief parenthesis of Pio Nono's "liberal" biennium, the Papal State had reverted to its old self.

The same happened in the Kingdom of the Two Sicilies, where the reaction matched that of 1799 in ferocity, if not in bloodshed. The kingdom also languished economically because the king would not consider any reform that might stimulate another revolution. Worsening economic conditions, however, fueled numerous conspiracies, which continued to threaten the throne.

Though on a superficial level the "second restoration" resembled the one following 1815, European and Italian conditions were different. On the diplomatic side, the unity that had characterized the Vienna settlement cracked. The 1848 revolutions had encouraged a Prussian move to become preeminent in Germany. With the help of Russia, Austria blocked that attempt in 1850 (the "humiliation of Olmütz"), but soon thereafter the Prussians prevented Austria from joining the Zollverein, an economic organization that would keep alive the idea of German unification under Prussian leadership. The struggle for domination in Germany had begun. Furthermore, Russia hoped that its destruction of the Hungarian Revolution on behalf of Austria and Austria's embroilment in Germany would result in attaining a free hand in Turkey. The revival of Bonapartism in France, where Louis Napoleon seized dictatorial power in 1851, complicated these mistaken calculations. Austria had hoped to win French support against England, which was taking increasingly liberal positions—another miscalculation. In 1853 this diplomatic maneuvering resulted in the Crimean War, with France and England fighting to contain an expanding Russia and Austria remaining an embarrassing neutral. The conflict finally shattered the European equilibrium and furthered the Italian cause.

As usual, economics contributed to the changing European diplomatic picture. Although most of Italy's economy stagnated, in the rest of western Europe the period up to 1873 witnessed a general price rise, rapid economic development, increased pressure for free trade, and the shift of political power from the aristocracy to the bourgeoisie. These economic changes help explain why England—an advanced industrialized state anxious to expand its markets—favored alterations that would pacify the continent and favor trade. Economic interests, therefore, encouraged a diplomatic resolution of issues such as the "Italian problem," which had generated so much disorder. The decline of revolutionary influence and the growing attraction of the moderate camp in the national movement favored this scenario.

Mazzini and His Enemies

Despite his defeat in 1849, Giuseppe Mazzini remained optimistic about the ultimate success of the revolutionary method. Returning to London, he resumed his old habits: living modestly, smoking cigars, going to dinner at the homes of prominent Englishmen, and planning fresh revolutions. He claimed certain victory in the future because 1848 had proven that the oppressed masses would lead the Italian Revolution. Mazzini interpreted the defeats as temporary setbacks due primarily to divisions among revolutionary factions. As a consequence, he concluded that 1848 had confirmed his revolutionary ideology.

Mazzini failed to understand that his refusal to modify his ideology alienated many European revolutionary leaders. Hoping to bring radicals under one umbrella organization, he established the "Central Committee for European Democracy" in England and the "National Association" in Italy. Radicals attacked Mazzini because they believed that the revolutions had demonstrated the importance of the social question, which the Genoese patriot refused to subordinate to the struggle for liberty.

In Italy these opponents included Giuseppe Ferrari, an associate of Cattaneo's during the 1848 revolution. Because of Mazzini's single-minded obsession of unity at any cost, Ferrari argued, the revolutionary leader had compromised himself with Pius IX, the Church, and Piedmont during the uprisings. A republican federalist, Ferrari favored political revolutions in the different Italian states, even if these did not immediately produce unification—a violation of Mazzini's tenet of indivisibility. Influenced by the new socialist ideas circulating among European intellectuals, Ferrari proclaimed that liberty and independence were "only lies where the rich crush the poor"—a secondary issue for Mazzini. Even more than Ferrari, socialist thinker Carlo Pisacane attributed the failure of the 1848 revolutions to class warfare and to Mazzini's emphasis on unity rather than liberty. Even if they did not have an immediate impact, the ideas of this young Neapolitan, who died in 1857 in the struggle for independence, provide crucial testimony to the rising importance of social issues in the Risorgimento. The heated discussions among Italian radicals ended any possibility of unified action by radical patriots.

Ironically, Mazzini also lost his more moderate following. The revolutionary apostle of Italian unity animated conspiracies all over Italy, culminating in an attempted revolution in Milan in February 1853. The move failed because of a serious split between the Milanese bourgeoisie and the popular classes. This defeat polarized the national movement and swelled criticism of Mazzini from friends who were losing faith in him. They proposed the union of all patriotic forces regardless of political persuasion, which meant postponement until after unity of a decision on whether Italy should be a republic or a monarchy. In effect, they favored collaboration with Piedmont. The intransigent Mazzini responded by forming the Action party, a fighting group committed to immediate action, unity, and a republic. The hemorrhaging in Mazzini's camp had already begun when Piedmontese developments accelerated it.

Cavour and the Transformation of Piedmont

In 1849 the liberal transformation of Piedmont appeared most unlikely. Thrust on the throne by the forced abdication of Charles Albert, Victor Emmanuel II had not been groomed to succeed his father, perhaps because of persistent rumors about his true paternity and because his mother and his wife were Hapsburgs. Notwithstanding his nickname "the Gentleman King," his long-running affair with an earthy drum major's daughter, popularly known as "la bella Rosina," scandalized his subjects, and his manners shocked Queen Victoria.

According to legend, Victor Emmanuel earned his appelative by refusing to revoke the Statuto under pressure by Radetzky, but English historian Denis Mack Smith casts doubt on this story. He believes that the new monarch promised to revoke the constitution, asking for and receiving a pledge of Austrian support. The urgency of peace at any price after the disastrous Battle of Novara and Victor Emmanuel's success in securing a good deal from Radetzky, however, fuels suspicion that the young king shrewdly manipulated the Austrians. Facing military collapse, a revolution in Genoa, and the insistence by Piedmontese democrats that the war be continued, the new monarch could hardly withdraw the Statuto.

Despite Victor Emmanuel's intentions, the constitutional development of the conservative charter in a more liberal direction marks the 1849 to 1859 decade. The Statuto's brief text reserved to the king absolute power to name and dismiss the ministers. It bolstered the Crown's position by failing to establish the office of prime minister, by creating a Chamber of Deputies elected by restricted suffrage and lacking the the power to confirm or dismiss governments, and by instituting a Senate appointed by the king that could veto legislation passed by the Chamber. Yet unlike the French Constitution of 1830, on which it was patterned, the new constitutional order immediately permitted liberal political expression and the emergence of liberal statesmen.

The elections of July 15, 1849, produced a majority politically to the left of the king and of his government headed by Massimo D'Azeglio. As a result, the Chamber of Deputies quarreled with the government over ratification of the peace treaty with Austria. Unable to reach agreement, the king dissolved the Chamber in late November and issued a critical statement asking for support. In this famous "Moncalieri Proclamation," authored by D'Azeglio, Victor Emmanuel complained about the Chamber's "hostile" acts toward him; he had maintained his promises by dissolving the Chamber and calling for new elections, but, he stated, if the voters failed to elect a favorable majority, they, and not he, would be responsible for any future disorders and other consequences.

Although this proclamation and subsequent government electoral interference established a precedent encouraging future intervention in elections, it produced positive results. Elections held on December 9 gave the government a two-thirds majority, but a high percentage of voter participation was the key factor in this outcome. This factor revitalized Parliament by encouraging the middle classes to become involved in politics and ending conservative suggestions to demote the Chamber to a consultative assembly. The electoral debate also reenergized the patriotic movement. Furthermore, the constitution proved crucial in bolstering Piedmont's prestige and in attracting patriotic supporters from all over Italy; D'Azeglio understood these factors very well and resisted requests to suspend the Statuto.

The constitutional system also propelled onto the political scene a remarkable individual who would set the future course of Piedmontese liberalism and Italian independence: Camillo Benso, Count of Cavour. Cavour was born on August 10, 1810, the second son of Marquis Michele Benso, police chief of Turin from 1835 to 1847, and Adele de Sellon, a Protestant from Geneva who later converted to Catholicism. His father's flexibility as a conservative who adapted well to more liberal times seems to have influenced the young Cavour's intense intellectual life. Cavour also interacted with Swiss and French intellectuals related to his mother. Cavour was attracted to moderate liberalism as a young man.

Since his elder brother inherited the title, Cavour pursued a military career, but the army ill-suited his character. After being punished for defending the July Revolution in France, Cavour resigned his commission in November 1831. He travelled widely in Britain, France, and Switzerland, familiarizing himself with the more-advanced western European political tradition and economic system and applying his knowledge to Piedmontese commerce and agriculture. Anxious to establish his economic independence, he participated in a number of business enterprises, including banking, railway construction, stock market investments, candle manufacturing, and commerce in wheat and rice—in addition to gambling. His most spectacular endeavor took place at his estate in Leri, where he established a showpiece of modern agricultural and business methods. In 1842 he helped found the influential Agrarian Association; by 1848 he had achieved fame as a businessman with a reputation as a serious student of Piedmontese economic affairs. He decided to enter politics, in which he always had an interest.

Cavour was a supreme pragmatist; thus, it is hardly surprising that, politically, he believed in a middle road. He supported change but opposed sudden or violent alterations and therefore frowned upon revolution. Cavour favored eliminating feudalism's economic and social vestiges in Piedmont; but beyond that he judged eighteenth century–style absolutism obsolete and hoped to construct a political structure based on cooperation between the bourgeoisie, the progressive nobility, and a monarchy sensitive to the nation's wishes. Convinced that property was the foundation of a modern economy, he rejected radical democracy, socialism, and communism. His inborn pragmatism caused him to dismiss the romantic interpretations of nationality propagated by Mazzini and Gioberti: He viewed the Risorgimento as a vast movement destined to raise Italy to the level of the most-advanced European countries.

For these reasons, Cavour believed in moderate politics as the most sensible. He aimed to modernize Piedmont's economic system, address pressing social issues, and make the kingdom into a major player in the European diplomatic constellation. Cavour forcefully and successfully brought the Italian problem to the attention of the powers in terms they could comprehend. In achieving this goal, he brought to the moderate model for independence a necessary element that it had always lacked—a brilliant statesman operating within a viable constitutional system. Cavour's qualities proved irresistible to the national movement because they appeared just as Gioberti's neo-Guelphism and Mazzini's radical democracy faltered.

Because his middle stance alienated both right and left of the Piedmontese political spectrum, Cavour faced a difficult struggle within his country's new constitutional order, but he had a major influence in the operation of the system from the start. Unsympathetic with the liberal direction in which the constitution seemed to be developing, Piedmontese conservatives and some moderates considered forming a bloc that would have threatened that evolution. What might have cemented this coalition was the strong feeling among leftists, moderates, and some conservatives that Piedmont's ecclesiastical legislation—which gave the Church too much power—had to be modified to fit the new constitutional situation. Clashes between the reactionary Catholic hierarchy and the government made resolution of this issue urgent.

Cavour acted on this issue in late 1849 when he succeeded in getting Count Giuseppe Siccardi named as Minister of Justice and Ecclesiastical Affairs. In February 1850, supported by Cavour, Siccardi presented bills that reduced the Church's influence. These "Siccardi laws" liberalized Piedmont's ecclesiastical legislation by eliminating a number of antiquated Church privileges and, by splitting conservatives and moderates, made an anti-Statuto alliance impossible. More important, Cavour distinguished himself in the debate by boldly pressing the government for further reforms. His action established the basis for an agreement between the moderates, now indisputably headed by Cavour, and the left in the Chamber of Deputies.

In October 1850 Cavour entered D'Azeglio's cabinet and served in two cabinet posts until 1852. During that time he guided Piedmont's economic and financial affairs but also had influence in other areas. A convinced free-trader, Cavour put into place important commercial treaties with Britain, France, Belgium, Austria, and other countries. Passed against conservative opposition, these agreements eliminated protectionism, increased trade, helped modernize the economy, and placed Piedmontese economic policy on a par with other European countries. Cavour carried forward an ambitious program of railway building, key to the country's further modernization and to increasing business activity. His attempted banking reform was rejected, but he succeeded in reorganizing the state's financial administration. Cavour also sought to bring Piedmont's growing budget deficit under control. He increased taxes on business and in other areas, but his opposition to progressive income taxes, the heavy borrowing for railway building, and the cost of future wars for independence made him less successful in this area.

In implementing his economic program, Cavour ran into recalcitrance from his cabinet colleagues and opposition from conservatives in the Chamber. Ironically, the bulk of his measures passed because of support from moderate leftists led by Urbano Rattazzi, and this de facto cooperation provided the basis for a future political alliance. The head of the government, D'Azeglio, had allowed Cavour relative freedom but opposed the state's further liberalization, which Cavour considered essential. This situation suggested a new majority composed of Cavour's moderate right and Rattazzi's moderate left, a change spurred as well by foreign developments. On December 1–2, 1851, President Louis Napoleon Bonaparte assumed dictatorial power in France, causing Austria to seek a rapprochement with its old enemy. This agreement, which proved illusory, would have squeezed Piedmont between two reactionary powers and favored

Piedmontese conservatives opposing the progressive evolution of the constitutional order. This scenario seemed to be playing out when French and Austrian pressure forced the government to present a bill imposing press restrictions. As a cabinet member Cavour could not openly oppose the bill, but he differentiated his position from the government's and made a pact with Rattazzi in which the two statesmen promised to support the constitution, independence, and further liberalization.

This *connubio*, or "marriage," ensured the liberal development of Piedmont by creating a new majority powerful enough to block conservative backsliding and to support progressive legislation. It also favored the national movement in a general way, but by allying with a party intimately identified with the Risorgimento and the 1848 revolutions, Cavour announced Piedmont's paramount role in the independence struggle. The *connubio* also incarnated a new alliance between the bourgeoisie, which favored independence, and the nobility's most active segment. The new lineup undermined conservative and extreme left influence and was a pole of attraction for the center.

The delicate political operation furthered both the Risorgimento and the liberal transformation of a state that had been among the peninsula's most reactionary. As in the case of all great political compromises, this one had costs. In the maneuvering that produced a Cavour cabinet in November 1852, for example, the Piedmontese statesman agreed not to utilize all the power at his disposal to pass a bill instituting civil marriage. Opposed by Victor Emmanuel, the measure met defeat in the Senate by one vote and had to wait until 1865 to be enacted. These necessary concessions to Piedmont's political and social realities were so small in comparison to Cavour's achievement in rooting constitutionalism in Piedmont that English historian Denis Mack Smith's criticism of Cavour's alleged "transformism" and of his high-handedness misses the mark. (A term usually applied to postunification politics and discussed in Chapter 10, transformism indicates the abandonment of one's principles for political gain.)

Indeed, Piedmont's liberal political, economic, and Church policies during Cavour's stewardship propelled the northern state into the national movement's undisputed leader. Cavour made agricultural loans easier to obtain, modernized the credit industry, ended residual feudal dues, and reformed the law on joint-stock companies; all greatly aided business. With regard to the Church, Cavour launched the attractive slogan "a free Church in a free state." What this policy would eventually have come to mean is a matter of dispute, but in 1855 a law struck at the Church's power once again. All religious corporations not devoted to teaching, preaching, or care of the sick were dissolved. But the state was also concerned enough to raise the stipends of the lower clergy and provide pensions for disabled clergy, so it levied a tax on benefices. Victor Emmanuel opposed this legislation and intervened against Cavour in concert with the Church and Pius IX. Their success might have reversed Piedmont's liberal development, but in a complex series of brilliant parliamentary maneuvers, Cavour ensured continued liberal leadership of the country by outfoxing both king and pope.

Thus in the ten years after the 1849 defeat of the national movement, Cavour's policies put Piedmont at the head of all Italy for economic development and political progressivism. The free trade regime spurred agricultural development and the silk industry and put textile and cast iron manufacturing on a modern footing, while banking reforms created the basis for a future centralized banking system. In addition, the nineteenth-century index of and major stimulus to economic activity, railway building, showed a tremendous jump. In 1848 Piedmont had 8 kilometers of railway, compared to 357 in the other Italian states. By 1859 Piedmont counted 850 kilometers in operation and an additional 250 under construction, including work on the major Frejus tunnel through the Alps, compared with a total of 986 for the rest of the peninsula. The railways were built either by the state or with state subsidies.

The prodigious economic activity brought with it an improvement in the conditions of life for the bourgeoise, and the right of association, recognized by the Statuto, allowed the growing number of workers to create their own organizations. Since this economic and political development occurred during a decade of stagnation for the rest of Italy, Piedmont became an example to emulate and a magnet for other Italians and demonstrated a hint of the benefits that independence and unity could bring.

A "Sterner Plan"

Cavour's successes contrasted with continued failures in the Mazzinian camp and would leave independence under Piedmont's guide as the only option in the patriotic camp. It is estimated that as many as 50,000 exiles from the Risorgimento's disruptions made their homes in Piedmont. One of them, Marquis Giorgio Pallavicino-Trivulzio, a Lombard democrat and survivor of Austrian prisons, proved particularly important as the moving force in the transmigration of republicans to the monarchical camp. Pallavicino insisted that patriots should forget about their republicanism because Italian independence was the most important issue for them, and only monarchist Piedmont offered any real hope of freeing Italy. He successfully convinced many exiles from the 1848 revolutions to drop Mazzini and come over to Piedmont.

Paris exile Daniele Manin, hero of the Venetian Republic and well connected within the European liberal milieu, was Pallavicino's most influential convert. Manin's position began maturing in the early 1850s, and in 1855, he stated that the republicans stood ready to sacrifice their demand for a republic if the House of Savoy led the fight for Italian independence. Along with a growing number of republicans, Manin admitted that the form of government Italy would have was secondary to the creation of an Italian state. While making this sacrifice, however, Manin forcefully posed another question. In the debate on independence, the question of unification had been neglected or obscured. An independent Italy could not remain a geographical expression, Manin argued, therefore: "Italy cannot be *unified* unless it is *independent,* and cannot remain *independent* if it is not *unified.*" Manin thus renounced his demand for a republic but in return insisted that monarchists accept the old republican demand for a united Italy.

In effect, Manin asked Piedmont to set aside its dynastic interests to become the core of an Italian state. Piedmontese foreign policy indeed appeared headed in that direction at a time when European diplomats seemed ready to favor an enlarged Piedmont but only as a way of blocking unification. Despite his own sympathy for unification, Cavour the realist believed that it could not be achieved. He supposedly told Giuseppe La Farina, an influential leader of the democrats-turned-monarchists: "If the Italians demonstrate themselves mature for unity, I hope that the opportunity will not be long in coming; but I warn you that of all my political friends, none believe in the possibility and that its approach would compromise me and the cause we believe in." Nonetheless, Cavour met secretly with members of the group favoring unity, including Garibaldi, to coordinate activities.

As previously mentioned, Mazzini had established the Action party to implement his ideas on unification. Disturbed by the loss of prominent leaders, he attempted a rapprochement with Pallavicino by offering cooperation on unification and agreeing to delay consideration of Italy's future form of government. This attempt failed because Mazzini continued his conspiratorial activities. Between 1853 and 1856, several Mazzini-inspired disorders occurred, but all failed.

Mazzini's focus remained northern Italy, where he had a base among the workers and where he was convinced that the revolution had the best chance of spreading throughout Italy and Europe. But other patriots believed that the Kingdom of the Two Sicilies was the weak link in the reactionary chain, pointing to the long string of revolutions that had begun there and that had touched off disturbances in the North. They convinced Mazzini to pay more attention to the South, and in 1856 Mazzini and Carlo Pisacane agreed to promote an insurrection in the region—the "southern initiative." Because Sicily offered the best hope of guerrilla warfare, the conspirators chose it as the preferred location to land an armed band, but the Bourbons registered successes there before the action could be undertaken. Sapri, south of Naples, seemed the next best hope, and in 1857 Pisacane and his friends tried to set off a revolution there. Pisacane failed to raise the population, was defeated, and committed suicide.

Despite widespread sympathy for Pisacane's fate, his *Political Testament*, published after his death, revealed the depth of his radicalism and alienated both the democrats attempting to link up with Piedmont and European opinion. More important, the disastrous end of the Sapri expedition totally discredited Mazzini's methods.

The immediate political repercussions included a deep crisis in the Action party and the foundation of the "National Society" in August 1857. This organization represented the definitive defection of democrats once influenced by Mazzini to Cavour. Written by La Farina and approved by Cavour, the Society's manifesto subordinated all questions to Italian independence and unification. The Society stated that it supported the Savoy dynasty and any Piedmontese government as long as they supported Italian freedom and unity. Besides this moral support, the Society delivered over to Cavour a network of former Mazzinians that covered all Italy. The Society proved invaluable in the creation of public opinion favorable to unity, in the calling of volunteers, and in the referenda and the other actions that produced a united Italy in 1861.

At the time, Pallavicino observed that Mazzini was down but would probably rise again. But historian Raymond Grew's sterner verdict is more accurate: "Its [the National Society's] formation was the most dramatic sign that republicans were turning to Cavour, that nationalists would accept unification under Piedmontese monarchy, that the era of Mazzini was really over."

Diplomatic Initiatives

The Italian situation clarified just as crucial diplomatic alterations occurred in Europe. The conjunction of the two provided Cavour the opportunity to demonstrate himself a master statesman capable of exploiting changes in the European system on behalf of his aims on the peninsula—despite the enormous disproportion in power between Piedmont and the large states with which he dealt.

The reactionary diplomatic order established after 1815 had been made possible by a substantial confluence of interests among the big powers. Austria and Russia had cooperated to preserve their dominance in eastern Europe and Italy, as seen by the Russian reconquest of Hungary on behalf of Austria, which allowed the Austrians to concentrate their forces on the peninsula in 1849. In later years, conservative ideology might possibly have served as the basis for an Austro-Russian alliance had it not been for competition between the two powers over the Turkish Empire's spoils. After 1849, the conservative system had been reestablished but was shaky. In essence, Europe tended to divide into two camps. The bourgeoisie had enormously strengthened itself in France, even after Louis Napoleon declared himself Emperor Napoleon III in 1852. This reality brought France's foreign policy closer to liberal Britain's, even though the British feared the expansionistic tendencies that the Second Empire inherited from Napoleon I.

The continued decline of Turkey and the weakness demonstrated by Austria during the 1848 revolutions emboldened Russia. Tsar Nicholas I believed that gratitude for his intervention against the Hungarian revolution, besides the time required to recover from the 1848 revolutions, would induce Austria to allow him a free hand in Turkey, and the French regime's weakness caused by recent domestic political changes would prevent Napoleon III from interfering with his Turkish ambitions. In the Tsar's calculations, only Britain remained an obstacle that necessitated an agreement. But Nicholas had miscalculated. Rapid economic development had reinvigorated France, while the British feared that Russian successes in Turkey would lead to Russian hegemony in Europe; and Austria's gratitude did not counterbalance its opposition to Russian gains in Turkey or its fear that cooperation with Russia would provoke France and Britain to encourage a Piedmontese move against Austria's Italian possessions. When Nicholas moved against Turkey, the British and French declared war (March 27, 1854) to contain Russian expansionism.

The French and British needed allies to wage a war that stretched their lines of communication to the limit. They hoped for Austrian assistance. Knowing that if they were engaged in a war in the East the Italians would revolt, the Austrians requested a French guarantee of their Italian possessions. The French seemed willing, but Austria chose to create a "neutral" bloc with Prussia and the German states. Austria then exploited this bloc to pick up Turkish territory. In the meantime, French and British forces bogged down in their siege of the Russian stronghold of Sevastopol, on the Crimean Peninsula. The Austrians tried to broker a peace, but such a conclusion suited neither side. Given their desperate situation, the allies still attempted to draw Austria in despite their irritation at its actions. It was during these negotiations that the Austrians extracted from the French their agreement to conserve the Italian status quo while the war continued in the East.

Piedmont and the Italian cause thus risked being crushed in the high-stakes great-power maneuvers. As the Eastern crisis simmered, Piedmontese liberals, including Cavour, interpreted it as an ideological struggle between liberalism and conservatism that would result in a reordering of Europe on national lines. A broad consensus favoring Piedmontese participation on the side of Britain and France against reactionary Russia and Austria existed in Piedmont. This illusion vanished as British and French diplomats anxious to appease Austria enjoined Piedmont to remain quiet on the national issue. Despite his rebuff, Cavour feared that Piedmont would become isolated and would be forced to accept French troops marching across its territory to link up with Austrian soldiers should the empire join the war against Russia; these considerations forced him to keep open the possibility of Piedmontese intervention while the wooing of Austria continued during the summer and autumn of 1854. On the allied side, Britain hoped to use the Piedmontese to counterbalance the superior military contribution of their French allies, who they never fully trusted, but it also believed that Piedmontese intervention would encourage the Austrians to join the war, since the Piedmontese could not move against the Italian possessions of its new "ally" while engaged in war on the same side.

As the Piedmontese became boxed in, in early 1855, they decided to make the best of a bad situation. The foreign minister, Giuseppe Dabormida, accepted an invitation to join the war but demanded that after the war Britain and France allow Piedmont to participate as an equal in the peace negotiations, pressure the Austrian government to return property confiscated from Lombard and Venetian exiles, and pledge to discuss the Italian situation. Reluctant both to alienate Austria and to give a secondary power a major voice in European affairs, the allies flatly refused. In addition, the French and British ambassadors in Turin gave Piedmont two days to adhere to the alliance or drop the matter. The French representative asked Victor Emmanuel to intervene against Dabormida. Faithful to the warlike qualities of his dynasty, the king supported Piedmontese intervention at any cost. Furthermore, Victor Emmanuel opposed the previously mentioned government legislation to dissolve a number of religious convents. Using the war issue as an excuse, the king prepared to dismiss Cavour and replace him with a conservative minister. Getting wind of the plan and convinced that nothing further could be done to alter the diplomatic realities, Cavour cleverly got himself named foreign minister and brought Piedmont into the conflict.

Cavour managed this complicated situation so well that the historical literature frequently pictures him as having planned Piedmont's intervention in the Crimean War. Internally, he used the war to prevent a conservative involution of Piedmontese politics, maintain a liberal constitutional system, and strengthen his links with the national movement. Externally, the allies preferred Austrian intervention, but Piedmont's status as a belligerent increased its prestige and lent weight to its opinions, especially since Austria remained neutral. After the conflict, Cavour cleverly exploited his position in a manner that allowed him to have an influence beyond that of the head of a second-rate power, but he could not have "planned" these developments. As A. William Salomone wrote:

"Perennially on the job, restlessly ready to begin again after every bad turn, he was keen-eyed enough to learn the secret of extracting the potential of success from almost every failure." Cavour's brilliance, like Otto von Bismarck's, the artificer of German unity, lay in his ability to adapt to adverse conditions and to make rapid decisions, even though he had a less powerful state to work with. Unlike Bismarck, however, he used these qualities to preserve liberalism, not destroy it, and to integrate the dynasty into the Italian national fabric, not dominate it.

The Crimean War's finale and the peace conference, held in Paris on February 25, 1856, illustrate how events do not go according to plan and Cavour's uncanny ability to draw advantage from the complex diplomatic reality of mid-nineteenth-century Europe. As the conflict dragged on, Cavour continued to hope that it would develop into an ideological war of liberalism versus conservatism. Napoleon III briefly considered steering the conflict in this direction but backed off because he feared the revolutionary implications of this policy, especially in Italy; ripe conditions there would indeed threaten the Austrian Empire, but a revolution in Italy might spread to France (the revolutions of 1848 had begun in Sicily in January). Furthermore, fearing that the longer the conflict endured, the more it threatened imperial interests, Austria sent Russia an ultimatum and the peace conference was scheduled.

Although Piedmont's participation was initially uncertain, it did participate in the Congress of Paris as an equal, but Cavour found the great powers unwilling to act against Austria on Italy's behalf. Cavour put forward several schemes to strengthen Piedmont's territorial and dynastic position, all of which went nowhere. France and Britain sympathized with Cavour, but they were still unwilling to offend Austria. On April 8, over Austria's objection, a discussion did occur on the Italian problem. Austria's continued occupation of some papal territory and the repressive policies of the Two Sicilies were interpreted as encouraging revolution; both contemporaries and historians judged this debate very important, but Cavour came away dissatisfied. During his trip to Paris, however, Napoleon III asked Cavour to draft a memorandum on the Italian situation. The direct contact established with the emperor and the Austro-Russian split, which cracked the diplomatic prerequisite for the European order established after 1815, were the chief results of the Congress of Paris and the Crimean War. At home, Parliament enthusiastically approved Cavour's diplomatic activity, thus enhancing his political position. Significantly, Cavour announced that Piedmont's liberal system had put the state on a collision course with Austria.

On January 14, 1858, an event occurred that focused European attention on the Italian problem: Felice Orsini led an attempt to assassinate Napoleon. Despite the difficulty of linking this event to subsequent developments, it appears to have had an effect. Orsini was a Mazzinian (although blamed for his supposed involvement, Mazzini had nothing to do with the conspiracy) who related the Italian cause to Europe's "renovation," who viewed Napoleon as the head of the reactionary party, and who therefore resolved to kill him. Orsini's desperate act aroused sympathy for the Italian cause, including, strangely enough, that of Napoleon himself. Indeed, dissuaded by his advisors from pardoning Orsini, Napoleon allowed him to turn the trial a into showpiece for the Italian cause; in return, he asked Orsini to renounce assassination and appeal for Napoleon's aid in a letter published in Piedmont. The Orsini affair reinforced Napoleon's fear that the Italian situation encouraged revolutionary activities that threatened his throne. Although the emperor had undoubtedly been thinking about doing so before, the attempt on his life encouraged him to unite with Piedmont as a means of defusing the revolutionary movement in Italy, and perhaps Europe, and to do so quickly.

Cavour's contacts with Napoleonic circles culminated in a famous meeting between Napoleon and Cavour at Plombières, which Cavour detailed for Victor Emmanuel in a memorandum on July 24, 1858. At this meeting, Napoleon declared himself ready to help Piedmont expel Austria from Italy. A condition of such action was that Austria declare war and that the struggle not become a "revolutionary" conflict. Cavour then suggested several ways of provoking an Austrian attack while allowing Piedmont to appear the aggrieved party and permitting Napoleon to intervene. The two men settled on the acceptance by Victor Emmanuel of an appeal by the people of Massa-Carrara, crushed by their Austrian-backed ruler. This pretext would cause a crisis with Piedmont, Piedmontese military preparations, and an Austrian ultimatum.

The two men then discussed the peninsula's postwar appearance. Piedmont would take Lombardy-Venetia and part of the Papal State to form a strong northern Italian kingdom; the pope would retain Rome and its surrounding territory; Tuscany and the remaining papal territory would be united into the Kingdom of Central Italy; the Kingdom of the Two Sicilies would remain intact to appease Russia (it had supported Russia during the Crimean War), although Napoleon ventilated the idea of placing Joachim Murat's son on the throne if the Neapolitans should revolt. Finally, to compensate the pope, he would be made head of an Italian confederation. France would be compensated with the Piedmontese regions of Savoy and perhaps Nice. To complete the new French order on the peninsula, Napoleon requested the hand of Victor Emmanuel's daughter Clotilde for his cousin Jerome, nicknamed Plon-Plon. Reflecting the concerns of the age, the major part of the memorandum concerned Cavour's attempt to convince the king to accept the marriage of his religious fifteen-year-old daughter to the thirty-six-year-old playboy, later mentioned as the possible monarch of the projected Kingdom of Central Italy.

The Plombières agreement illustrates very well the complicated nature of Italian, French, and European diplomacy of the period. The agreement would not have created a united Italy, which would have damaged French interests; indeed, it conflicted with the policies of professional French diplomats, causing Napoleon to conduct the talks on a personal level, in secret, and against the wishes of his pro-Austrian foreign minister, Count Alexandre Walewski.

What did Napoleon hope to achieve?

As always in interpreting Napoleon's actions, observers must take personal factors into account. As a young man, Napoleon had participated in the central Italian revolutions of 1831, and his elder brother had died then. The emperor also viewed himself as carrying on the imperial tradition of his uncle, Napoleon I, who had been most active in Italy. The previously mentioned desire to end revolutionary turmoil on the peninsula was also a major factor. Most important, however, Napoleon aimed at making French influence supreme in Italy, the glory of which would immensely strengthen his throne. The best way to achieve this goal would be to expel Austria from Italy and create a strong northern Italian kingdom tied to France that would dominate the peninsula. The connection with progressive-oriented French rule instead of reactionary Austria would make the Italian states more stable and less susceptible to revolution. The French link would be reinforced by the dynastic connection through Jerome and, perhaps, Lucien Murat.

Although Cavour recognized the benefits that would accrue to Napoleon, he exhorted Victor Emmanuel to endorse the Plombières agreement. If the plan worked, Cavour wrote: "Your Majesty, sovereign in law over the richest and most powerful part of Italy, would be sovereign in fact over the whole peninsula." But Cavour's reasoning went far beyond the dynastic argument he had to employ for the king's benefit. Even though the agreement did not envision a unified Italy, Austria's expulsion would rearrange the age-old order on the peninsula and make a native state supreme. Given the level of anti-Austrian feeling in Italy, it also seemed unlikely to Cavour that the war would not stimulate revolutions—and his links with the National Society and moderates all over Italy ensured Cavour's ability to deal favorably with the eventuality without allowing the revolutions to get out of hand. In addition, the French initiative presented the only opportunity to alter the Italian situation imposed by the great powers in 1815 and, therefore, important enough to risk French hegemony. Cavour also calculated that French control would be temporary; the suspicious great powers feared an attempt to rebuild Napoleon I's empire and would intervene to block French domination of the peninsula. Furthermore,

Piedmont's increased power and prestige after the war would enhance its ability to participate in the continent's balance-of-power politics and thus attenuate French influence. The final element in Piedmont's favor was its vigorous liberal political system, which powerfully attracted the peninsula's bourgeoisie in a manner Napoleon's absolutism, despite its progressive elements, could not do.

This key point allowed Cavour to adjust his policies and maintain support for them during the unpredictable, unforeseen, and complex developments of 1859 and 1860 that finally created united Italy. In sum, Napoleon unwittingly constructed a favorable context for unification, but this achievement required Cavour's "métier of the real politco, of the genuine statesman, of a maker of states."

The 1859 War and Its Aftermath

The war issuing from the Plombières meeting was fought against an amazingly confused and changing backdrop; the war's favorable outcome for the Italians illustrates not only Cavour's diplomatic skills but also the maturity and force that the national movement had achieved by that time.

After Plombières the anxious Austrian ambassador to Paris asked: "What sort of deal have these two conspirators made?" Nobody knew, but the secrecy galvanized European diplomacy to seek ways to stop a war it strongly suspected would erupt. As news of the particulars slowly leaked out, Walewski and the French government pressured Napoleon not to go ahead, and talks formalizing an alliance treaty with Piedmont stalled. At the same time, Princess Clotilde decided to accept the marriage to Jerome, and Napoleon seemed determined to press forward. In a meeting with the diplomatic corps on New Year's day, 1859, Napoleon startled the Austrian ambassador by telling him that he regretted that relations between their two countries "are not as good as I would have hoped." On January 10, Victor Emmanuel made the famous "cry of anguish" discourse to Parliament stating that he could not remain insensitive to the pain of his fellow Italians. This speech, coordinated with Napoleon, set the stage for the conflict, aroused great enthusiasm on the peninsula, and stimulated the movement of volunteers from all over the peninsula to aid Piedmont in the coming war for independence.

On January 26, France and Piedmont signed an "offensive-defensive" alliance whose terms were somewhat less favorable to Piedmont than the Plombières discussion had led Cavour to believe. Piedmont was now obliged to pay the costs of the operation and cede Savoy and Nice while accepting a less precise definition of Piedmont's future boundaries. On the other hand, the treaty nailed down the size of the French military contribution. Most interesting, the instrument contained clauses restricting the possibility of a revolutionary war. In February the Piedmontese Parliament authorized the government to contract a large loan to pay for the conflict, while in France a pamphlet directly inspired by Napoleon gave his solution for the "Italian problem." The publication pointed to Austria as the major obstacle to the ideal resolution of the issue corresponding to the wishes of the Italians themselves—establishment of a federation of states. But though the plan for war seemed on track, Napoleon made the first of his several clamorous reversals.

Except for Napoleon, the entire French establishment, including the empress, opposed the Piedmontese alliance. Bankers making loans to Austria and the Italian states feared for their present and future investments. Catholics fretted about the possible loss of papal territory. Diplomats considered it folly to weaken Austria because it would signify the rise of Prussia and possible German unification under that state. Even should that eventuality not occur, the conflict threatened a wider war in which lingering memories of Napoleon Bonaparte would trigger a great-power alliance against France.

These fears proved unfounded, because the Crimean War had split Austria and Russia and had made a repeat of the old anti-Napoleonic alliance unlikely. In addition, although some groups in Russia and England supported Austria, both Russian and British public opinion sympathized with the Italian national movement, and the issues were not strong enough for either country to intervene. Britain, however, attempted to mediate the dispute. Added to Napoleon's internal problems, this international pressure caused him to get cold feet. As the crisis proceeded, Piedmont went on a war footing, but British mediation produced an agreement for a congress, which Austria would not attend unless Piedmont disarmed. Despite Cavour's vehement protest, France and Britain decided that Piedmont should do so.

This development was a disaster for Cavour. He could not hope to defy the great powers. Furthermore, the proximity of the war for independence had inflamed Italy, and the sudden collapse of nationalistic expectations would certainly have been directed against Cavour. Informed of Napoleon's decision at 1:30 A.M., Cavour jumped up on his bed and exclaimed: "There is nothing left for me to do but to get a pistol and blow my head off!" The Austrians, however, forcefully intervened to save the count. Unwilling to discuss the Italian situation as equals with Piedmont at a congress, misinterpreting the problems of the peninsula as a Turinese plot, fearing to appear weak and jeopardize their position in Germany, alarmed at the economic consequences of remaining on a war footing during protracted negotiations, and convinced they could knock out Piedmont before the French army arrived, the Austrians on April 21 ended all negotiations and delivered Piedmont an ultimatum demanding immediate disarmament. "It was one of those jackpots you win only once in a century," commented Massimo D'Azeglio. Cavour refused the ultimatum and the war began. Napoleon and Cavour had plotted at Plombières to portray Austria as the aggressor, but Emperor Francis Joseph did a much better job.

Besides French assistance, the crucial factor in the "Second War for Independence," as compared to 1848–1849, was the unity exhibited by the Italians. In Piedmont, patriotic feelings and dynastic loyalty replaced political division. Unlike their role in 1848, the republicans played a minor role, at least in northern and central Italy. Indeed, although Mazzini kept democratic options open as to the future political form of Italy, he put demands for a republic on the back burner and explicitly accepted war against Austria under Piedmont's guidance on the grounds that Austria was the enemy of all Italian development. Volunteers rushed to join the military effort, with Garibaldi given a command of his own. The National Society in effect acted as an auxiliary organization for Cavour and intensified its actions throughout Italy, ensuring that the political divisions of 1848 did not reappear. Its efforts were particularly effective in central Italy.

The military effort during this conflict was not particularly notable, except that the railway was used for the first time in great strategic maneuvers. Convinced he possessed military genius equal to that of his uncle, Napoleon took personal command of the campaign. Luckily the Austrian commanders matched his incompetence. The opposing armies fought two significant battles, Magenta and Solferino, in which the Piedmontese also acquitted themselves well. Solferino proved especially important and bloody and contributed to Napoleon's second sudden reversal. Without informing Cavour, on July 11 Napoleon met with the Austrian emperor at Villafranca and ended the war. The agreement provided that Lombardy would be ceded to France, which would hand it over to Piedmont. Venice would remain under Austrian suzerainty and would join a confederation to be established under the pope's presidency. The rest of Italy would return to the situation that had existed before the war.

The usual complex interplay of international relations and Italian developments explain Villafranca. After the shock of the Austrian ultimatum had worn off, the powers redoubled their actions in favor of peace. In addition, Prussia had mobilized and France could not ignore this potential threat, even though the Prussians aimed not at France but at weakening Austria in Germany. From the military viewpoint, the French had won two victories, but the war was far from over. But the main reasons for Napoleon's actions are to be found in Italian developments. His hope of containing revolutions quickly proved illusory. Insurrections occurred in Tuscany, Parma, Modena, and in the eastern part of the Papal State known as the legations. With the divisions of 1848 gone, these areas immediately manifested their desire to be annexed to Piedmont, which Cavour initially delayed because of French disapproval. Napoleon understood that the Italian situation was out of control and that if the war continued, he could not prevent the annexation of central Italy to Piedmont. Instead of French hegemony over the peninsula, he faced the prospect of a strengthened state on his border and so called the war off.

Cavour resigned in protest at this new manifestation of Napoleonic "treachery," but instead of reestablishing the old order, Villafranca proved the last, failed attempt of the powers to arrange the peninsula according to their plans and without the consent of its inhabitants. Villafranca could be enforced only through the use of arms. For reasons of prestige and given its previous role, France could neither use force nor allow Austria to do so. Napoleon made this clear from the beginning both to the Austrians and to the Italians, even though French diplomacy exerted considerable pressure for the return of the rulers who had been overthrown in central Italy. Also crucial in this equation, Britain and Russia judged Austria's position in Italy lost and favored an Italy independent of foreign influences.

Given the lack of a military option, central Italian leaders such as Bettino Ricasoli in Tuscany acted with considerable political skill in a confusing and complex environment. The divisions that had lacerated the national movement in 1848 barely resurfaced. Furthermore, in close cooperation with the National Society, the patriots skillfully demonstrated the support that unity had among the people. The affected areas elected assemblies that voted overwhelmingly for annexation to Piedmont in August and September 1859. The major question was now diplomatic. In December, Napoleon again reversed himself and signified possible acceptance of a new territorial order in Italy. Convinced of the impossibility of enforcing Villafranca, he now aimed at cession of Nice and Savoy in return for his agreement to the annexation of central Italy. In January Cavour returned to power in Piedmont and conducted the negotiations.

After agreement had been reached, the question was put to the people. Since there was little real opposition, the patriots temporarily in charge of the Center worried about the turnout and did their best to encourage potential voters. The size of the vote exceeded their expectations, and in March 1860 the former states of central Italy chose annexation by large majorities. Plebiscites were also held in Nice and Savoy, which voted for annexation to France. Questions have been raised about the fairness of the central Italian plebiscites, but compared with those in the ceded areas, conducted under effective French military occupation, and by the standards of the day, those gauges of popular opinion seemed convincing.

On March 25, 1860, elections for the Chamber of Deputies took place in the old Piedmontese domains and in the new territories. As expected, they produced an overwhelming victory for Cavour. In a stunning turnaround, the war of 1859 had produced an enlarged liberal northern Italian kingdom, but the surprises had by no means ended.

Garibaldi and the Thousand

Cavour demonstrated consummate diplomatic skill in managing the events of 1859 and 1860, but they had achieved an enlarged northern Italian kingdom, not unification. Since the Piedmontese statesman operated in a rational world that did not allow for idealism, unification still appeared doubtful. It was the romantic spirits within the national movement who pressed forward in this quest.

With the absorption of northern Italy by Piedmont, attention focused on the South. Mazzini launched the idea of regaining the initiative for the national movement's republican wing through action in the South. Francesco Crispi, a close follower of Mazzini, travelled to Sicily in July and August 1859 to contact antigovernment conspirators there. After the death of Ferdinand II in 1859, his unimaginative son Francis II created more discontent by continuing his father's policies, but effective police repression on the mainland made revolution difficult. Sicily offered greater promise for revolutionaries because it was less controlled and because the Bourbon rulers were more hated. On the island, Crispi organized an insurrection for October, but the attempt failed.

Inspired by the Mazzinian precept of guerrilla revolution, Crispi ignored the defeat. He turned to Giuseppe Garibaldi, the premier guerrilla fighter, and asked him to lead a Sicilian revolution. Garibaldi answered that he did not believe a revolution possible but said he would be willing to undertake the task only if the basis for the revolt would be Italian unity under Victor Emmanuel. Garibaldi's attitude reflected that of Sicilian patriots. This position was widespread even among the democrats, and Mazzini himself had acknowledged the impossibility of attaining a republic.

In early April 1860, a revolution erupted in Palermo. Crushed in the Sicilian capital, the insurrection spread to other parts of the island and assumed the aspect of a guerrilla war. Despite its ubiquitous character, the insurgency seemed headed for defeat without outside help. Crispi and other leaders urged Garibaldi to intervene. Difficult communications and conflicting reports that the revolution had ended caused Garibaldi to vacillate, but on May 11, 1860, he set sail with a thousand volunteers amid myriad difficulties, including being forced to leave with outmoded weapons and without ammunition (which he picked up later). Cavour feared diplomatic repercussions if Piedmont aided the expedition, and a serious disagreement with Victor Emmanuel II ensued. The king favored the expedition and tried to act independently of his minister.

Landing on the island at Marsala, Garibaldi found Sicily defended by a well-disciplined and well-armed force of 25,000. This army, however, was engaged in fighting the revolution, which helps explain Garibaldi's eventual success. In addition to his linkup with the bands fighting the Bourbons, the military experience and quality of his volunteers and Garibaldi's own tactical and strategic brilliance also account for his victories, as does the inefficiency of the supreme Bourbon command. Nevertheless, the small force faced its most difficult period during the first three weeks. The crucial battle occurred at Calatafimi, where a fierce *garibaldino* bayonet attack offset enemy superiority in arms. Soon thereafter, a brilliant feint sent some of the best Bourbon troops on a wild goose chase while Garibaldi moved into Palermo on May 27. The city promptly rose, and Garibaldi held onto the capital despite a fierce artillery bombardment. Protracted negotiations led to abandonment of the city by the Neapolitans, and Garibaldi proceeded to reduce the rest of the island.

Cavour reacted cautiously. He dared not oppose the wave of favorable popular opinion the expedition had generated and allowed the various committees collecting funds to resupply the general. Modern rifles, volunteers, and medical supplies were sent to Sicily on ships that the American consul-general in Genoa had reflagged as American. This operation saved Cavour from diplomatic embarrassment, but the harsh European reaction Cavour expected because of Garibaldi's adventure never arrived. The powers had become used to the idea of Italian unity and European public opinion continued to be very favorable. Nonetheless, serious political, social, and diplomatic problems brewed.

Faced with his dynasty's destruction, Francis II initiated a diplomatic offensive, attempting a compromise with Turin and consulting Napoleon. The French suggested a number of concessions, and on June 25 Francis promised a constitution and installed a new cabinet. These measures fell flat, however, as an insurrection began in Naples. Francis's timid and ineffectual action had reinforced the "annexationist" party among moderates on the continent, and social issues ensured its dominance. In Sicily the alliance between Garibaldi and the insurrectionary bands was breaking down as the common objective of expelling the Bourbons came within reach. The peasants saw an opportunity to achieve their ancient goal of land redistribution, but the nobles and bourgeois had jumped on Garibaldi's bandwagon because, with the crumbling of the old order, they wished to be in a position to stop social change: "If we want things to stay as they are, things will have to change," says a character in the novel *The Leopard*. "D'you understand?" In Sicily, *garibaldini* leaders participated in the crackdown, while on the continent, where peasants had similar demands, liberals concluded that a quick unitary solution under Piedmont offered the best hope for a stable and efficient government.

Initially Cavour considered compromising with Francis but changed his mind as the desire for annexation grew in the South; but Cavour found it difficult to act because the Neapolitans considered Garibaldi a hero and were anxiously awaiting him. To short-circuit imminent diplomatic efforts favoring the Bourbons, Cavour pushed for quick annexation of Sicily, but Garibaldi hoped to exploit the island as a base for operations on the continent. Once again, Cavour feared the diplomatic consequences of this operation, although it appears that Victor Emmanuel secretly encouraged Garibaldi. The French especially opposed Garibaldi's threat to eliminate the Kingdom of the Two Sicilies and sought British cooperation to block a Garibaldi attempt to cross the Strait of Messina. British refusal removed that obstacle, but the duel between Cavour and Garibaldi continued on other fronts.

Cavour saw that Garibaldi's spectacular success had suddenly and dramatically shifted the initiative to the Action party. Seizure of continental Neapolitan territory would greatly enhance Garibaldi's prestige and transform Victor Emmanuel into an appendage of the popular general. In addition, Garibaldi was determined to continue on after he had taken Naples and to attack Rome, and Mazzini also encouraged him to move against Venice, still under Austrian control. These actions would risk bringing in the French and the Austrians against the national movement and destroy what the Risorgimento had accomplished.

To block Garibaldi, Cavour evolved a plan to stimulate a "revolution" under moderate auspices that would overthrow the King of Naples before Garibaldi reached the capital. This action would allow the Piedmontese to recoup their prestige, seize control of the national movement, and preserve its monarchical character. The plan failed because the Neapolitans preferred to wait for Garibaldi. In mid-August, the redshirts crossed onto the continent and fought their way up the Italian boot. After the failure of his projected revolution, Cavour fell back on a different scheme to achieve his ends. He would advance through papal territory to the northern border of the Kingdom of Naples while promising Napoleon that Rome would remain inviolable.

This move would result in annexation of papal Umbria and Marches, contributing to the restoration of Piedmontese prestige and moderate control of the national movement. Furthermore, the Piedmontese army would be in a position to intervene in the South, if necessary, preventing Garibaldi from moving on Rome. Cavour's plan to checkmate the democrats depended on Napoleon's consent, which would ensure French neutrality and block Austrian intervention to save the pope. Napoleon understood that Cavour's action would probably produce a unified Italy, but if Garibaldi attacked Rome, the French monarch would have been faced with the choice of losing face by abandoning the Eternal City or fighting alongside a French Catholic who commanded the papal volunteers but who happened to oppose Napoleon's regime. Besides, if a unified Italy was in the cards, the emperor preferred it be controlled by moderates over whom he had some influence. When Cavour's envoys explained the plan to him, therefore, he answered: "Do it, but do it quickly."

In September 1860 Cavour stimulated revolts that served as the royal Piedmontese army's pretext for crossing the papal frontier. On September 18 the Piedmontese defeated the papal army at Castelfidardo, completely accomplishing Cavour's goals. The moderates had seized the initiative, and Cavour announced that Piedmont strongly supported a unitary solution to the Italian question, thereby stealing the democrats' thunder. The Roman mission made Garibaldi furious because it blocked his projected attack on Rome. The general, however, was considerably weakened militarily by the Battle of the Volturno in October, when he barely contained a large Bourbon army, and by a serious pro-Bourbon insurgence behind his lines. The military situation meant that Garibaldi was dependent on Piedmontese arms to defeat the Neapolitans. When Victor Emmanuel crossed into the Kingdom of Naples, Garibaldi greeted him at Teano as "King of Italy." Speculation that Garibaldi wavered as to whether to hand over the South seems to be contradicted by a conversation with Mazzini in late September indicating that Garibaldi had decided not to make problems on this score and to put off any eventual expedition to Rome or Venice. Garibaldi's sole request of the king was to ask him to fire Cavour, but despite ongoing friction between Victor Emmanuel and the Count, the Gentleman King refused. Garibaldi was furious with Cavour because of the Roman issue and because Cavour had ceded Garibaldi's birthplace, Nice, to France, but the general could do nothing because Cavour had Parliament's confidence. Later Garibaldi's disenchantment with united Italy's political constitution and the way in which his followers were treated turned him into a severe critic of the new state.

Cavour found himself in a stronger position than he had ever been. The major question with regard to the South was whether it would be "annexed" to Piedmont like central Italy had been or whether a constituent assembly would be convoked and present conditions for union. Since Garibaldi had retained legal and military control of the area, the second option seemed a possibility. Mazzini urged Garibaldi to insist upon an elected assembly that would draw up a "national pact" and shake moderate control of the national movement. Cavour, however, easily outmaneuvered the democrats on this question because such a course might have jeopardized the most important goal of the democrats themselves—unity. Moreover, Cavour skillfully exploited the desire of the southern bourgeoisie to bring a rapid end to an unsettled situation through annexation.

He presented a bill in the Piedmontese Parliament "accepting" annexation and pledging to work for unity with Rome and Venice. Meanwhile, the moderates maneuvered to hold plebiscites in Sicily and on the Neapolitan mainland. The democrats—concentrating on continuing military action against Bourbon remnants and on the desire for unification—lost this battle. On October 21, Naples and Sicily voted overwhelmingly for union. Marche and Umbria followed suit on November 4.

After the final destruction of Bourbon forces, the flight of Francis II, and the ironing out of minor diplomatic problems, Parliament officially proclaimed the Kingdom of Italy on March 17, 1861.

The Debate

Even though Venice and Rome did not become of part of the new kingdom until 1866 and 1870, Italian unification had been achieved. The culmination of a long and complex process, and of high drama involving the participation of colorful individuals, the Risorgimento could not fail to become a favored subject of historians. As might have been expected, the first reflections glorified the party that had been successful in uniting the peninsula. Although the "losers," Mazzini and the Action party, condemned the manner in which unification had occurred, early historiography exalted Cavour, Victor Emmanuel, and other important players on the moderate side. Historians concentrated on the "heroic" developments of 1859 and 1860 that had produced a unified state and not on the Risorgmento's roots or its slow development. Cavour's glorification transformed him from a statesman who could profit brilliantly from his errors into the perfect manipulator of European diplomacy who unified Italy according to a predetermined plan. This tendency extended to the other famous actors of the Risorgimento, so that instead of being considered as persons with opposing ideologies, they became collaborators. Popular mythology made Mazzini "the pen," Cavour "the mind," and Garibaldi "the sword" of unification.

Like all great historical events, the Risorgimento soon became a tool for different political groups. Until the 1890s, Italian prime ministers were "expected" to have participated in the Risorgimento, but a different tendency also manifested itself. After the drama of the Risorgimento ended, many Italians had difficulty settling down to the ordinary work of building and running a new state. Since Italy did not become as great a power as they had expected, these Italians felt that the promise of the Risorgimento had not been fulfilled, and they became highly critical of the way Italy had been unified. Over the next fifty years, this attitude produced numerous and vicious denunciations of the parliamentary system and the policies of the new state. In the 1920s the Fascists exploited this corrosive criticism in their successful drive for power, denying the liberal nature of Cavour's work and the real accomplishments of the state produced by the Risorgimento.

At that point, philosopher and historian Benedetto Croce rose to the Risorgimento's defense. Croce emphasized the progress made by the Kingdom of Italy after unification and argued that Italian unification was "the masterpiece" of European liberalism. In arguing against the Fascist interpretation of Italian history, Croce certainly gave an overly optimistic view, but opponents of fascism understood the historical context of his interpretation and, in general, Croce's version prevailed.

After World War II, however, Marxist historians criticized Croce. The Marxist "school" condemned the Risorgimento for uniting Italy with little popular participation. The impetus for this development was the publication of Antonio Gramsci's prison notebooks. Gramsci, a founder of the Italian Communist party, argued that to combat the moderates, the Action party had to create an alternate economic and social program of the radical Jacobin type that would appeal to the rural masses making up 80 percent of the peninsula's population. But, he wrote, the democrats retained a partially agrarian character that limited their freedom of action with regard to the landholding classes. In other words, the Actionists no less than the moderates feared a degeneration of the Risorgimento into "communism." Since Austria occupied Italy, it was easy enough for the democrats to emphasize the national struggle and neglect the social character of the revolution to create unity. Gramsci, however, believed that, despite the difficulties, an alliance with the peasants was possible. He interpreted the Risorgimento as "a revolution that failed."

This view seems motivated by the desire of leftist Italian intellectuals to shake free from Croce's enormous cultural influence, by the persistence of the "southern problem," and by an effort to discredit the existing political system. The "failed revolution" concept not only seems unhistorical but even from a Marxist viewpoint appears illogical. If the revolutionary aspects of the Risorgimento were so easily put aside, existing conditions did not favor victorious peasant agitation of a modern kind. Consequently, only dictatorial methods could have ensured a radical "Jacobin" solution; leaving aside the central issue of the long-term consequences of such methods, those favoring this kind of force at the time utterly lacked the means to implement "revolutionary" policies. Furthermore, activists must and do choose priorities when making political decisions, and the first priority in the 1800s could only have been to expel the Austrians, even at the cost of social reform. The Communists themselves made a similar choice during World War II when they put aside social revolution to join with a reactionary Italian government to drive out the Nazis. Applying the failed revolution principle to other events would reduce Italian and all history to an absurd series of missed opportunities. As for the southern problem, which indeed persisted, it seems unclear that a constituent assembly would have resolved the question, although it might indeed have jeopardized unification. The major criticism here is that the Piedmontese extended their laws and administrative system to the South. Aside from the plausible argument that the newly united country had to take that course to prevent Italy from falling apart after unification, the differences between the Piedmontese and Neapolitan administration do not appear as great as commonly supposed, since both originated in the centralizing tendencies of revolutionary France.

Indeed, Gramsci's emphasis on an agricultural revolution as a means of generating capital accumulation for industrialization, and the resulting criticism of the Risorgimento because this revolution did not occur, derives from the Marxist interpretation of the French Revolution. Liberal historian Rosario Romeo contested this model. In analyzing Italy's economic and political history, Romeo insisted on emphasizing the constraints faced by Italian statesmen during and after the Risorgimento. Employing statistics as a means of proving his point, Romeo argued that the 1860s and 1870s saw significant increases in capital, and that the capital thus accumulated went first into building basic services such as a railway network. Capital investment in industry followed and stimulated economic growth after this essential process. Romeo does not deny that these economic developments occurred at first through a political compromise between the bourgeoisie and semifeudal landowners at the expense of rural areas and the South, but he believes that these conditions were temporary and characterized industrialization everywhere. Although some of Romeo's statistics have been called into question, his thesis stands as an attractive alternative to Gramsci's.

It seems legitimate for historians to analyze errors, as does Marxist Giorgio Candeloro in pointing to the Risorgimento's failure to enlarge the electoral system or to elaborate a new administrative system suited to the integration of different parts of the peninsula; they can plumb with Raymond Grew the roots of how and why the persons who made the Risorgimento "narrowed" its political focus by reducing popular participation; they can sympathize with the defeated personages. But historians "cannot reduce the Italian national revolution merely into a function of the unrealized potentialities of the Risorgimento."

In tracing the origins of problems, historians must also take care not to burden one age with the mistakes of future eras. It is more reasonable to emphasize the successes of a movement, in addition to its failures, not in absolute terms but in relation to similar movements during the same period. For example, in comparing Italian and German unification, it is clear that no figure comparable to Mazzini gained such prominence in Germany, and no one wielded influence like he did, either at the time or in the future. In like manner, even though Cavour can be criticized for his constitutional shortcomings, Piedmont's past as Italy's most reactionary state and the distance it covered toward liberalism during his tenure must also be emphasized. Furthermore, Italian unity resulted from the interplay of actions taken by Piedmontese liberals and the democratic movement based on a revolutionary ideology—even though they conflicted— whereas a conservative dedicated to raw power and unwilling to make concessions to more liberal forces guided the Prussian military and diplomatic activities that unified Germany on the basis of Prussian and dynastic supremacy and an exasperated nationalism. In Prussia, as in Piedmont, a moderate liberal movement was underway before Bismarck came to power, but he definitively defeated it while Cavour stimulated liberalism in his country.

These different aspects of Italian and German unification would determine the different roads taken by the united countries, despite superficial resemblances. From a social viewpoint, in Italy the gulf between aristocracy and bourgeoisie had been considerably narrowed. Although the nobility maintained a powerful position in the army and the diplomatic corps of united Italy, it also engaged fully in commercial and banking activities, and the bourgeoisie, even though linked to the land, engaged in commerce and the professions; in Germany, the nobility remained a closed and compact class of landholders that preserved some feudal privileges and retained political control of Prussia and the unified state; the German bourgeoisie, although economically better off than its Italian counterpart because of greater resources and the faster formation of a national market, had less influence in the political arena. United Germany was more politically backward than united Italy, even though the Italian constitutional system had problems, which will be elaborated upon in the next chapter. Although they were similar states in the late eighteenth century, Piedmont emerged radically different from Prussia because of the cultural and political revolution brought about by the Risorgimento. Risorgimento statesmen achieved ministerial responsibility for united Italy, even if imperfect, while Bismarck eliminated that possibility for united Germany, severing it from western constitutional development. In a few years after unification Piedmont became integrated into Italy, whereas Prussia dominated Germany up to 1918. Northern domination of southern Italy can be partially explained by objective economic reasons, but, politically, cabinets had to be geographically balanced and by 1887 the country had a southern prime minister.

Finally, even in defeat, the democratic ideals of Mazzini and the example of Garibaldi continued to ferment in Italy and to maintain a European and worldwide influence down to present times. In this sense, these activists no longer appear as the "losers" of the Risorgimento.

PART FOUR
The "Age of Prose"

9

Cavour's Heirs: The "Right" Reigns

O<small>N</small> J<small>UNE</small> 6, 1861, Camillo Cavour died at age fifty. Upon hearing of his death, Napoleon said: "The driver has fallen from the box; now we must see if the horses will bolt or go back to the stable."

This statement expressed Europe's doubts that Italy would hold together. The "driver" had left at a crucial time. The peninsula had been united after centuries of political division, which had produced different customs, traditions, and dialects. Venice and Rome remained out of the kingdom, and making them part of Italy presented numerous diplomatic difficulties. Melding the disparate parts of the peninsula and building a single state out of long-divided areas would prove even more formidable. Risorgimento wars and the takeover of debts of the old states created enormous financial problems. Besides these issues, the question of whether the more socially backward parts of the peninsula could successfully transition to liberal institutions remained unresolved. Given the extent of the new kingdom's tasks, the new state's inability to become a great power hardly comes as a surprise.

Completing Unification

When Cavour died of "fever", the Kingdom of Italy had been declared, but unification remained incomplete. Cavour's heirs (the "Right") had to integrate the peninsula into one state—a qualitatively different and less heroic job than the exhilarating struggle for independence; as Victor Emmanuel II remarked, the age of poetry had given way to an age of prose.

European politics had determined the manner in which Italy had been unified and strongly influenced its future political development. The annexations excluded a federal structure, while the threat of political disputes leading to foreign intervention and collapse made calling a constituent assembly impossible. The different parts of the peninsula had been attached to a preexisting state that had its own dynasty, constitution, and administrative structure. It is hardly surprising that Cavour and his successors—anxious to forestall complications that could undo the unification so painfully achieved—extended Piedmont's political system, its economic policies, and its administration to the rest of Italy. By amalgamating political and economic liberalism with a rigid administrative structure, Cavour and the Right created a strong state that survived the shocks of postunification but that did not solve the southern or social questions.

With a social structure similar to Piedmont, the North adapted fairly well to the new legislation, but the South did not. Moderate leaders had assumed that the passage of power from the Bourbons and Garibaldi into their hands would resolve the South's problems, but the real issue was the disparity in the economic and social development between the two regions. For example, unlike Piedmont's policy, Bourbon tariff policy had been protectionist. After unification, the new rulers extended free trade policies to the South without regard to southern conditions or the economic emergency that existed in the area. Policies such as this one exacerbated the South's crisis and contributed to the brigandage there, which was part protest and part pro-Bourbon revolt. Adding to the insensitivity of the northerners, the new state dissolved Garibaldi's volunteer army under unfavorable conditions; this move created resentment and deprived the government of a valuable and committed military force that could have been employed against the "brigands." After unification, Italy had to commit 100,000 troops to end a stubborn guerrilla-type war in the South and to dominate a revolution in Sicily.

In addition to the southern issue, the Right had pledged to incorporate both Venice and Rome into Italy. Of the two, Venice seemed the greater problem because of Austria's military prowess. Before his death, Cavour concentrated on making Rome the new state's capital. The rationale for the Papal State's existence had always been to protect the pope's independence. With only a rump area still belonging to the pontiff, however, Cavour believed this argument no longer held. He hoped to convince the pope to give up Rome in return for a guarantee by Italy that he would retain freedom of action. Both Pius IX and his minister Cardinal Giacomo Antonelli disagreed, and negotiations failed.

The opportunity to take Venice came in 1866. The struggle between Austria and Prussia for control of Germany culminated in that year. Italy and Prussia signed an alliance providing for an Italian attack on Austria's Italian possessions in case of war between the two Germanic powers. The problems of the Italian military in amalgamating previously separate forces, the failure of central command, and the "sectional conflict, personal animosities and partisan conflict" resulted in two indecisive engagements, on land at Custoza and on the sea at Lissa. Prussia, however, defeated Austria in the conflict, known as the Seven Weeks' War, and Venice became part of Italy as a result.

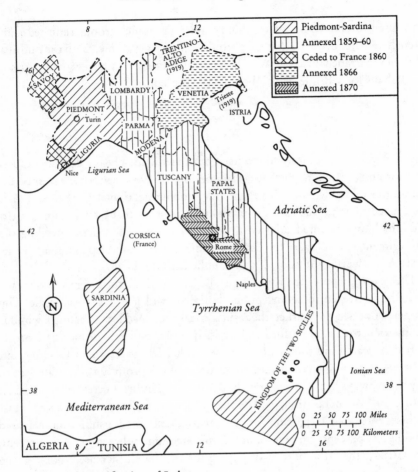

MAP 4   The Unification of Italy

Rome proved the harder nut to crack. Despite bad blood between Napoleon and the pope, French honor and the presence of French troops originally sent in 1849 forced France to protect the Holy City. Complicating the diplomatic situation, Garibaldi's pledge to take Rome, if implemented, would have provoked military intervention not only by France but by the entire Catholic world. The Right negotiated a French evacuation, which it could only achieve by guaranteeing Rome's borders while contemporaneously coveting the city for Italy's capital; it feared both the diplomatic consequences of an attack by Garibaldi and a popular backlash if forced to intervene against the hero. In 1864 an agreement secured the withdrawal of French troops and removal of the capital from Turin to Florence as a pledge of good faith. During this period, Garibaldi attempted to take Rome twice; the second time French troops returned and a French minister declared that Italy would "never" get Rome. With the outbreak of the 1870 Franco-Prussian War, however, the French withdrew their garrison; the Italians took Rome, which became the capital.

Finances

The new Kingdom of Italy found itself burdened with a heavy debt that caused an enormous deficit, in the 1861–1865 period, of 47 percent over receipts. Expenditures in connection with Piedmont's modernization after 1848 and loans contracted in 1859–1860 by the provisional regimes that later became part of the kingdom accounted for two-thirds of the new state's debt. Swelling this Risorgimento "bill" were the country's military and other spending after unification. Between 1861 and 1865 the public debt doubled.

The governments of the Right hoped to remedy this situation in several ways. First they resorted to selling public buildings and land on a vast scale. This property flooded the market; the result: Prices remained low, creating a windfall for the rich who could afford to buy it. In 1867 the lands of monastic orders were confiscated and sold, with the same results. The government also sold state railways, but private companies could not make a profit and the state had to buy the railways back. In addition, both direct and indirect taxes were increased. Before 1865 direct taxation, paid by the rich, increased by 54 percent, and transfer taxes increased 40 percent. In comparison, taxes on consumption increased a modest 11 percent, while revenues from state monopolies grew by 25 percent. Up to 1865, then, the burden of paying for the deficit increased more on the wealthy than the poor.

Thanks to a continuing inability to stem the deficit and an economic crisis in 1866, however, the burden shifted. The Right determined to eliminate the deficit by orthodox economic methods advocated by future finance minister Quintino Sella, and through stringent spending controls. In 1869 the Right increased several taxes and, most important, instituted the hated *macinato* (grist mill) tax. This indirect measure hit the poor hardest because it taxed the grinding of different grains, especially wheat, essential for making the bread and other food products that represented a large percentage of the lower class's budget. In comparing tax revenues in 1865 and in 1871, it has been calculated that while direct and transfer taxes increased 63 and 50 percent, respectively, taxes on consumption, paid primarily by the lower classes, increased 107 percent. Implementation of the grist mill tax provoked agitation throughout the country, especially the North, but it proved essential in solving the financial crisis. On the other hand, the tax was unfair, put Italy on the road to becoming the highest-taxed country in Europe, and greatly increased social tensions.

Besides increasing taxes, the Right resorted to an important financial measure to improve Italy's economic position: the inconvertibility of bank notes. At this time, European currencies could be exchanged for gold on demand, but the Italians eliminated this practice for the lira beginning in 1866. This *corso forzoso* proved remarkably successful; because of the difficulty of securing gold to pay for imports, the country was forced to reduce imports dramatically, while exports increased. Besides this salutary effect, the policy put the lira on a sound basis and got Italians used to paper money. These results could be seen after 1881, when convertibility was reintroduced but resulted in little demand for gold and no appreciable inflation.

From the fiscal viewpoint, the Right's policies proved so successful that their political opponents—who proclaimed themselves more sensitive to lower-class concerns—found it necessary to perpetuate those measures even though they placed the major economic burden on the poor.

The Church

In addition to the grave financial problems it faced, the Right confronted the Church's hostility. The Church greeted unification with anger because the new state had absorbed most of the papal possessions. Pius excommunicated the Piedmontese leaders responsible for annexing papal territory and punished the priest who, despite this expulsion, had given Cavour the last rites.

After the Kingdom of Italy's birth, the pope concentrated on saving Rome. He walked a tightrope between the Italian state and Garibaldi, both anxious either through diplomacy or force to secure Rome for Italy, and Napoleon III, pledged to protect the Holy City for political reasons but uncomfortable with the commitment. As the pope's political power waned, he reinforced himself in the spiritual realm. In 1864 the withdrawal of the French contingent provided the occasion for publication of the *Syllabus of Errors*, a controversial condemnation of modern civilization; and when the Italians took Rome in 1870, a Church council declared the pope infallible when officially defining Church doctrine (*ex cathedra*). These measures indicated the pope's desire to do battle with secular states and strengthened his influence among the Italian clergy.

The Church's hostility to the new state had major effects in two distinct but ultimately linked areas. In domestic affairs, the Church announced the *Non expedit* in February 1868. This decree ordered Italian Catholics not to participate in Italian political life and to boycott national elections. This meant that there would be no organized national Catholic party in Italy, although, in effect,

Catholics did engage in politics through the *Opera dei Congressi*, political committees tightly controlled by priests. On the one hand, the official Church boycott exacerbated an important weakness of the new kingdom by reducing the already low level of political participation on the national level, caused, above all, by the high illiteracy rate (there were some property qualifications, but it was the literacy requirement that excluded most men from attaining the right to vote); on the other hand, the boycott muffled the effects of Church hostility in Parliament at a particularly delicate time in the nation's life.

With the fall of Rome on September 20, 1870, the Italian clergy intensified its attacks on the government from its pulpits. The government retaliated by prohibiting Church services when they became openly political manifestations. In addition, government inspections occurred at seminaries to ensure that the education taking place conformed with the "fundamental necessities" of culture, and a law was passed allowing for conscription of priests. It will be recalled that the same period witnessed Bismarck's Kulturkampf ("struggle for civilization") in Germany, compared to which the Right's campaign was a policy of pinpricks. In fact, Italian leftists admired Bismarck's anti-Church policy and objected to the mildness of the Italian measures.

Diplomatic considerations, however, obliged the Right to pursue a cautious policy toward the Church. The Vatican pressed European Catholic powers to intervene against Italy and restore the Papal State, but Napoleon's overthrow in 1870 as a result of the Franco-Prussian war proved particularly dangerous. During its early days, the Third French Republic, which replaced the Second Empire, was very conservative and subject to clerical influence. This development caused bad blood between France and Italy—exacerbated by what the French perceived as "ungratefulness" in the failure of Italy to intervene on France's side in the recent war and by resentment against the Italians for having taken Rome when the French withdrew their troops to fight the Germans. Public opinion whipped up by French bishops brought the two countries close to an open break.

The Italian government sought to mollify France and the other European powers. Rejecting concessions that might have given Rome an international character because of possible diplomatic complications and papal intransigence, Prime Minister Giovanni Lanza's cabinet presented Parliament a "Law of Papal Guarantees" on January 23, 1871. This bill proposed resolving the Church problem through separation of Church and State and a guarantee of liberty and independence for pope and Church. Consequently, the state gave up various rights it had vis-à-vis the Church, made the pope a practical sovereign in Italy, instituted punishment for assassination attempts and insults against his person, arranged for the diplomatic immunity necessary to fulfill his mission, allowed full freedom to use papal buildings and Roman churches, and appropriated a yearly budget equal to what the pope had received in the budget of the former Papal State. The law provoked protests among Italian anticlericals because, they argued, it gave the pope a special position within the Italian constitutional order that no other individual or religious institution enjoyed; this opposition did not prevent successive governments of the Right and the Left from enforcing the law, finally passed on May 13, 1871.

Although the pope rejected this settlement on the ground that it was an internal Italian measure that could be unilaterally revoked at any moment, the law achieved its purposes. Despite the pope's continued whining and the clergy's propaganda, it defused European diplomatic hostility as it became clear that Pius had real freedom, even though he proclaimed himself a "prisoner" in the 11,000-room Vatican. A representative of a government friendly to the pope summarized the situation best when he said: "This old man, who every week flings insults in your face . . . , does you far more good in Europe's eyes than all the honesty and moderation which you have demonstrated in your policies toward the Papacy! Those speeches prove that the Pope remains the freest and most independent man on earth." The Right had shrewdly made the papacy seem unreasonable in European eyes, thus removing any pretext for foreign intervention on its behalf.

In the domestic arena, the Law of Papal Guarantees had flaws in that it did not completely separate Church and State, but it regulated Church-State relations in Italy for fifty years according to the best political compromise that could be achieved at the time. Even though Pius IX denounced the measure and succeeding pontiffs consciously kept the dispute alive, the Vatican tacitly accepted the law and claimed most of the rights that the state granted it under the legislation. On the other hand, the Left, that also denounced and denigrated the law, made no move to repeal the measure after it came to power and, on the contrary, vigorously enforced it. By enabling the new state successfully to get past a delicate issue that threatened its fragile existence so soon after unification, the Law of Papal Guarantees represents a monument to the wisdom of the Right.

Fall of the Right

During its tenure in power, the Right was dogged by the serious political opposition of the Left. The Left was composed of former Mazzinians who had abandoned the Genoese republican and had gone over to the Piedmontese camp in the 1850s to make unification possible. The old Risorgimento question of whether Italy should be united as a monarchy or a republic constituted the original distinction between these two political groupings and thus persisted in the newly formed kingdom. In 1865 a new break occurred between Mazzini and some of his most important followers—Francesco Crispi, Benedetto Cairoli, and Agostino Bertani. In a famous letter to Mazzini, Crispi wrote that the Italian Constitution could be reformed and that he preferred to enact Mazzini's principles into law rather than utilizing the insurrectionary method that, Crispi believed, divided leftists. In his words: "The monarchy unites us, but the republic would divide us." Thus, Crispi and his friends dropped the fight for a republic but not for an extension of liberty and social legislation by legal means. And on this basis the Left fought the Right in Parliament.

Before 1870, the major issue dividing Left and Right was the issue of Rome. Influenced by its anticlerical and revolutionary origins, the Left criticized the Right's "timid" Roman policy. The Left advocated storming the Holy City, making an idealistic appeal to the people and gloriously avenging French suppression of the Roman Republic in 1849, whereas the Right counted on diplomatic maneuvering. When Lanza took Rome as the result of the French withdrawal, the Left attacked him for entering the city in an embarrassed, unheroic, and almost apologetic manner. Subsequently, the Left blasted the Right on the Law of Papal Guarantees, arguing that the measure violated freedom of conscience and set up Catholicism as a "state religion." The Left rejected the Right's diplomatic objective on the ground that the pope would never be reconciled to loss of his temporal power.

Besides the Church, the two groups fought bitterly over other issues, especially tax policy and the detested macinato. The Left denounced the measure and promised to repeal it immediately once in power. The Right also neglected Italy's pressing social problems, the Left insisted, and failed to widen the country's electoral base. At the same time a debate erupted on the government's free trade policies, which had gravely damaged the South. Indeed, in the South the Left gathered strength because of increasing resentment against the Right's "Piedmontization" of the area, poor treatment of Garibaldi's volunteers after unification, the free trade regime that crippled the region, and frequent use of the police to quell social agitation. These policies increased opposition to the new state to such an extent that socialistic ideologies flourished, and in 1874 anarchists led by Russian revolutionary Mikhail Bakunin tried to overthrow the government.

Ironically, despite these disputes and its bitter denunciation of the Right, the Left had nothing substantially different to offer. In fact, the two groups resembled each other; their members came from the same social class; they were well-off, educated, eloquent patriots who had participated in the Risorgimento and who had overthrown old states, princes, and laws, including the pope's temporal power. Neither group was reactionary—a losing policy identified with the Austrians and the old states. In addition, the Right included important proponents of progressive policies identified with the Left—widening of the suffrage, extension of civil liberties, and government intervention on the side of the poor—while opponents to those ideas existed within the Left. Furthermore, when the Left came into power, it either delayed changing or did not touch legislation passed by the Right, setting the basis for a historic compromise.

The Left's constant hammering and the South's decisive support produced a major change in the 1874 elections. The Right won 275 seats, preserving a slight majority, but the parliamentary "arithmetic" opened the possibility of negotiations that would produce an eventual majority for the Left. Neither Right nor Left was a "party" in the modern sense; both were divided into many groups, centered around prominent individuals, that could suddenly shift their political allegiance. On March 18, 1876, a cabinet of the Right headed by Marco Minghetti lost a vote on the macinato question when a group of Tuscan deputies who disagreed with his railway policy deserted him. A government of the Left replaced Minghetti, and in November new elections were held. The new interior minister, Giovanni Nicotera, brought the government's power to bear in favor of the Left. As a result, the Right won only about 20 percent of the seats in the Chamber. It never rose again.

Despite the criticisms that could be leveled against the Right and the polemics of which it was made the object during its rule, the Right has significant accomplishments to its credit. It completed unification and ended the pope's temporal power, even if not in the "heroic" manner envisioned by the Left and historians. At the same time, the Right set the tone for Church-State relations for half a century through the Law of Papal Guarantees. It also steered a successful course in foreign policy on the papal issue, shattering the pope's hopes to restore his temporal power. Finally, the Right did achieve a balanced budget under difficult economic conditions. When the Left came to power, its actions demonstrated that it appreciated the value of those achievements, even if its words never did.

10

Two "Parliamentary Dictators"

Between 1876 and 1896 Leftist leaders Agostino Depretis and Francesco Crispi dominated Italian politics. Both had been Risorgimento heroes and followers of Garibaldi, but the similarity ends there. Depretis, calm, prudent, and calculating, frequently shared power with the well-meaning but politically inept Benedetto Cairoli. The fiery, temperamental, and controversial Crispi governed from 1887 to 1896. His own worst enemy, Crispi stormed back from a period of political "exile," caused by his allegedly bigamous marital status, to implement domestic and foreign policies that still stir debate. Unfortunately, this argument has impeded a serene discussion of this period's accomplishments.

Depretis and His Policies

Although the term "revolution" with which contemporaries greeted the Left's coming to power in 1876 is overblown, the event should not be undervalued. Recalling the Left's origins in Mazzini's messianic ideology and the revolutionary antecedents of its leaders, contemporaries speculated whether the king would accept turning over power to his former enemies. That he did so is a positive comment on the monarch's flexibility, the parliamentary state's solidity, and the Left's capacity to evolve politically.

As the end of the Right's term approached, a debate arose within the Left. Deploring the continued stagnation of the South's economy, Giovanni Nicotera ventilated a proposal by which his group would break off from the Left and ally with groups from the Right sympathetic to southern aspirations. Depretis responded by presenting a comprehensive program in a speech at Stradella on October 10, 1875 (reiterated the next year). He hoped to meet Nicotera's objection by promising, when the Left came to power, free, compulsory, and lay elementary education, an expanded suffrage, and the expenditure of public monies to address the problems of the country's areas that had suffered most under the "misgovernment" of the old states or that were unable to improve economic conditions by themselves. By making these proposals—which addressed the concerns of the "real country" as contrasted to the "legal" one to which the Right appealed—Depretis sought to demonstrate that the Left had a wider social base than the Right.

When the Left achieved power, however, it discovered that its program could not be implemented as originally drafted. As previously stated, Leftist leaders had thundered against the Law of Papal Guarantees and demanded its immediate repeal. Faced with diplomatic realities, they now rigorously enforced it. Depretis stated that although he would give no further concessions to the Church, neither would he withdraw past concessions. Furthermore, anticlerical legislation proposed by the Left did not depart from the guidelines set down by the Right. Even when the Left passed a law providing for free and compulsory school attendance in 1877, it made provisions for religious instruction if parents requested it.

Nor could the Left implement radical departures from the financial policies of the Right. Out of power, the Left had promised an immediate repeal of the hated macinato tax, but its governments found that financial considerations prohibited quick action. Leftist cabinets did eliminate the macinato, but only gradually by 1884. More important, although the Left reduced some other taxes as well, it made no major alterations in the tax system. In addition, the Left did not keep its promise to spur economic development in the South by spending significantly more public funds there, although it did promote a fundamental inquiry into the problems of the South by Stefano Iacini and Sidney Sonnino. From then on, Italian officials understood the importance of the southern problem and realized that rebuilding the South's economy would require decades.

Continuing the work of the Right, the Left vigorously promoted the building of railways, which were essential for the country's economic development, and their purchase by the state. But, unlike the Right, Depretis championed giving concessions to private businessmen to run them.

The Left's energy should be noted as well in two other areas: civil liberties and suffrage extension. Giuseppe Zanardelli, a minister in several governments of this period, forcefully argued in favor of the right of assembly and association. He opposed preventive action by the government, defended the right of people to be free from arrest until they actually violated a law, and courageously argued his case against critics who accused him of being soft on the law and order issue. In 1878 an assassination attempt on the king and other disturbances forced the Cairoli cabinet of which Zanardelli was a part to resign, but he successfully drafted a progressive penal code that went into effect in 1890.

In the related area of suffrage extension, which Depretis had promised in his Stradella program, several governmental crises, financial problems, and fear of opposition by the Right postponed action. In 1881, however, Zanardelli introduced a bill giving the right to vote to literate males over twenty-one who paid at least nineteen lire a year in taxes. The number of persons eligible to vote under the new law rose from 600,000 to 2 million (from 2.18% of the population to 6.97%). The reform increased the influence of the urban lower middle classes, many of whom knew how to read and write, and encouraged the formation of new working-class parties. The change recognized the growing importance of the urban industrial, intellectual, and commercial classes of the North as opposed to the landowning classes. The legislation went as far as it was possible to go without extending the suffrage to illiterates and to women.

Depretis and the Left expected a hard fight from the Right on all these issues, but with the exception of civil liberties, the struggle did not materialize. It has already been mentioned how members of the rival groups had similar social origins; the large majority in favor of the suffrage law revealed that two distinct parties advocating radically different programs no longer existed. Groups nominally belonging to the Right frequently discovered themselves voting for Leftist government proposals while members of the Left voted against them.

In 1882 Depretis took official notice of this development. He announced that the Right had evolved to the point that it had become indistinguishable from the Left. Since the Right had become "transformed," its leaders would be welcomed in his cabinets. Objecting that it had been the Left that had been transformed, the Rightists accepted Depretis's offer. From then on, when leaders of "Left" or "Right" formed cabinets, they included representatives of the "opposition" faction. In fact, the Chamber of Deputies now consisted of a very large liberal party, based upon the middle bourgeoisie, whose factions collaborated but conserved the titles Right and Left. Only the Extreme Left and, later, the Socialists separated themselves from this party by an ill-defined and flexible line. This grouping of minority political organizations became the only pole of opposition in Parliament. The term "transformism," however, acquired a connotation of betrayal of principle and corruption that it retains.

On the whole, Depretis's tenure had positive effects on the country. He had the fame of being a parliamentary "dictator," and Felice Cavallotti, colorful leader of the Extreme Left, accused him of corruption, suppressing liberty, collusion with industrialists, and secret deals with the Church; but though Depretis mastered the art of maneuvering deputies and taking full advantage of any means to achieve his goals, he was no dictator. Giuseppe Marcora, a radical deputy, saw him as "individually honest, a liberal, and an enemy of all excesses"; Marcora concluded that Depretis was "much better than his reputation." Indeed, Depretis's pragmatism and calming effect on the Chamber of Deputies helped win backing for his reform program. Depretis also piloted the new country through the traumatic time of Victor Emmanuel II's death in 1878, and, unlike his successor, he avoided major foreign adventures. This prudence made Depretis unacceptable to intellectuals anxious to assert Italy's greatness after unification, and his transformism brought him unpopularity among the people.

Crispi's Domestic Legislation

Among Depretis's possible successors, Francesco Crispi distinguished himself. A prominent Risorgimento fighter, radical, and friend of Garibaldi, Crispi scaled the heights of political power in the new state as minister of the interior, but his personal life caused scandal. In 1878 he married in a civil ceremony Lina Barbagallo, the woman with whom he had been living and who had given him a daughter whom he loved dearly. Unfortunately Crispi, always drawn to beautiful women, had in 1854 married a woman who had followed him into exile during his Risorgimento days. Agostino Depretis was a witness to the marriage and had also purchased the wedding ring for the bride. Crispi declared that the earlier ceremony was invalid because it had been conducted by a Jesuit without proper authorization, that he had entered the union out of a sense of duty, and that the subsequent strange behavior of his first wife had ended the union, but a virulent press campaign made him a political pariah.

Despite this incident, Crispi made a slow comeback. He emerged as leader of the "Pentarchy," a group of deputies demanding that Depretis pursue a more energetic African policy. In January 1887 a column of five hundred Italian soldiers was destroyed at Dogali, giving credence to Crispi's criticism. In July 1887 an already ill Depretis brought Crispi into his cabinet as minister of the interior, thus designating him as his successor. Upon Depretis's death, King Humbert I asked Crispi to form a government.

Mixed emotions greeted the controversial Crispi's rise to power. The Vatican feared him as a staunch anticlerical, and his uncompromising antagonism toward the Right alarmed the leaders of that group. Tired of Depretis's prudence and welcoming Crispi's passion and boldness, however, many Leftists greeted his accession. In fact, while Crispi took serious action neither against the Church nor the Right, his government listened to the country's progressive lobby. And although he took a hard turn to the right during his later years as prime minister, a series of progressive measures that had a lasting influence mark his early tenure.

Most important, his government overcame the previously mentioned opposition to Zanardelli's penal code that the statesman from Iseo, now Crispi's justice minister, implemented in 1890. The code abolished the death penalty, partially addressed the changing economic and social structure of the country and the political demands of the lower classes by reducing punishment of crimes against property, and tacitly admitted the legality of strikes by not declaring them illegal. This last provision, however, did not prevent governments from intervening in favor of the employers by utilizing other, economic, means. On the issue of preventive detention that had caused so much debate in 1878, the new code compromised. Police regulations implementing the Zanardelli code maintained restrictive measures requiring groups to notify the police twenty-four hours before meetings and allowed law enforcement officials to dissolve associations. In addition, *domicilio coatto* (internal exile) by which the police could force "dangerous" persons to remote areas of the country without a trial also remained; police officials favored this weapon against the growing anarchist and socialist movements, discussed in Chapter 11. Reflecting the tensions between Church and State during the period, the penal code also established sanctions against priests who attacked the state and its institutions and who violated its laws.

Despite obvious compromises, the Zanardelli penal code and the regulations governing police behavior represented a significant liberalization compared with previous legislation. The Zanardelli legislation lasted until the Fascists replaced it with more restrictive laws in 1926 and 1930.

Besides the penal area, other legislation during the Crispi period attempted to address lower-class interests and to modernize the country. His treasury minister, Giovanni Giolitti, believed that in modern democracies economic issues are paramount and must be resolved in favor of the people, whose participation is the hallmark of such regimes. As a result, in 1889 Giolitti piloted a law through the Chamber of Deputies modifying the procedures for the awarding of public works contracts, thus allowing cash-strapped workers' cooperatives to compete on a more even basis with well-heeled private companies. In 1888 another measure extended local autonomy. It enlarged the right to vote in local elections and permitted the city councils of provincial capitals and of towns over 10,000 to elect their mayors (by 1896 all towns could elect their mayors). Creation of a special commission presided over by an appointed officer of the central government, the prefect, limited actual control, but the legislation dramatically expanded participation in local government. Crispi also established a system of appeals against administrative incompetence and abuses, on the national and local level, which became the basis of continued Italian practice in this area. Attempts to implement this system since the 1870s had failed before Crispi succeeded in 1889 and 1890. In a series of laws passed in 1887 and 1888, Crispi further strengthened the prime minister's office and its control over the bureaucracy. The government received wider powers to replace and retire prefects and to institute or abolish ministries. A law also abolished the office of "secretary general," an administrative position in each ministry that had become highly politicized, and replaced it with that of undersecretary, a member of the government who acted as a "vice minister."

Finally, two laws rounded out this prodigious legislative activity: a public health law and one reorganizing charitable institutions. Adopted in 1888, the first law set the basis for future Italian legislation in the field, and the second reorganized and modernized charitable institutions, simplifying their complex structure and secularizing many of them. Crispi's legislative activity in the domestic sphere thus left a permanent mark on the country. His foreign policy and its internal implications, however, have remained controversial.

Foreign Policy

Even while Cavour's heirs remained in power before 1876, relations between the newly unified state and France soured. The Franco-Prussian War had caused the overthrow of Napoleon III's empire and its replacement by the Third Republic. Dominated by conservatives during its initial phase, the new regime believed Italy ungrateful for French help in the unification struggle and resented the Italian takeover of Rome after the withdrawal of French troops. This resentment, the country's declining diplomatic position, and a rapprochement with the Church made France fertile ground for the pope's maneuvers against Italy over the issue of his lost territory. As a result, the Right began casting around for allies. The changed European diplomatic, political, and cultural situation made the Italians turn to the strongest European power, Germany.

The Left's rise did not alter this major shift, despite the closer cultural links of Leftist statesmen with France and the victory of parliamentarianism there in 1877. Until 1881, however, distaste for Bismarck's Austrian allies and the priority the German statesman gave to that tie hindered an Italo-German pact. In that year Franco-Italian relations worsened dramatically because of colonial competition. Given the proximity of Tunisia to Sicily, many Italians had emigrated there, and the Italian government had pursued a policy of economic penetration as a prelude to bringing the North African territory under its control. This policy brought Italy into conflict with the French, who wished to attach the area to their Algerian protectorate next door. Despite Italian convictions that they would win the struggle for Tunisia, they lost it. Italian statesmen attributed the loss to their lack of powerful allies and determined to seek a German alliance. Bismarck made it clear that the road to Berlin ran through Vienna, so the Italians swallowed their pride and made up with Austria-Hungary (as the empire became known after 1867). Although relations between the two Risorgimento enemies remained poor beneath the surface and became progressively more poisoned, in 1882 Italy and Austria-Hungary joined Germany in the Triple Alliance.

Crispi's accession in 1887 exacerbated relations with the French. Although Italian democrats in his party admired France, Crispi loathed it—and he did not hesitate to go his own way. Moreover, Crispi had excellent relations with Bismarck, France's archenemy, and the press hailed the Italian leader as Bismarck's close adviser. The French suspected an Italo-German plot to attack them, despite German failure to support Crispi's Francophobe policy. As tensions between the two countries escalated, each followed a policy of pinpricks. Taking seriously information fed to him by a secret informer, Crispi set off a war scare by telling the British that the French were about to attack Italy and prompting the dispatch of British warships to Genoa. This situation caused military expenses and the budget deficit to increase rapidly. Although a shooting war never came off, in 1888 a ten-year "tariff war" caused by the protectionist policies of both France and Italy erupted. Both countries increased duties and imposed quotas on each other's goods, but the Italians were no match for the economically more powerful French.

Crispi's anti-French policies left no permanent mark on relations between the two nations, but his foreign adventurism and diplomatic miscalculations brought further misery to the country. Despite his friendship with Bismarck, Crispi misunderstood the fundamental function of the Triple Alliance as a conservative instrument for preservation of the European status quo, and he attempted to utilize the pact to win a colonial empire. This policy necessitated downplaying Italian interests in Europe, especially in the Balkans and in the Irredenta, the Italian-speaking territories that remained part of Austria. Consequently, Crispi pursued a friendly policy toward Austria that raised the ire of newly allied France and Russia and alienated domestic opinion. Because of his mistaken interpretation of the Triple Alliance, the expected payoff—German and Austrian support for Italian colonial ventures—never came. In 1890 the French strengthened their protectorate over Tunisia; Crispi protested and stated that Italy was not isolated as it had been in 1882—but he failed to secure substantial German-Austrian support against the move. When Crispi sought diplomatic aid for his expansion plans in East Africa (Ethiopia) by getting the Germans to pressure the French and British, he received this rebuke: "The Triple Alliance is a conservative pact, not a profit-making company." After Bismarck left the scene in 1890, the European diplomatic situation shifted in favor of France, which, in addition to concluding a Russian alliance, became closer to England. This emerging "camp" would not miss the opportunity to strike at the Triple Alliance through Italy.

Despite the lack of diplomatic support and the economic problems of his country, Crispi doggedly pushed ahead with his plans to take Ethiopia. Between

February 1891 and November 1893 the Crispi government was replaced by cabinets headed by Antonio Di Rudinì and Giovanni Giolitti. Cool to Crispi's African venture and wishing to patch up relations with France, their brief tenure did not permit any real changes in foreign policies. Furthermore, domestic problems including banking scandals and a revolt in Sicily increased the temptation, upon Crispi's return to office (the reasons for Giolitti's fall and Crispi's return are discussed later), to undertake a foreign adventure to distract the nation from these problems.

In East Africa, Crispi had already laid the groundwork for expansion of the existing Italian colonies and the conquest of Ethiopia. In typical European fashion, the Italians hoped to take advantage of complex internal disputes and on May 2, 1889, signed the Treaty of Uccialli with Menelik, a local contestant for power. The Italians believed that they now had a protectorate over the area but had only succeeded in uniting the local forces against them. Hostilities broke out over the differing interpretations of the Uccialli treaty. In 1895 the Italian commander Oreste Baratieri requested reinforcements, but Crispi refused because of opposition from the northern bourgeoisie ironically allied with antiwar radicals and Socialists. Although the European bourgeoisie generally favored colonialism, in Italy the industrial revolution had begun in the North, necessitating a period of peace and stability, and the industrialists opposed "squandering" resources in Africa. As a result, their representatives in the government, particularly treasury minister Sidney Sonnino, refused to sanction further aid for the military effort in Africa. Indeed, Crispi's support came not from the dynamic groups implanting a new industrial base in the North but from the southern bourgeoisie tied to the central administration and anxious for new opportunities in the colonies.

In addition, Crispi interfered in the military operations. Contradictory orders from Rome reached Africa, and the soldiers, many of whom had political aspirations, argued among themselves. On March 1, 1896, separated Italian columns confronted a vastly superior native force and met defeat at the Battle of Adowa. About 4,000 Italians and 2,600 native troops died, along with 9,000 Ethiopians. The resulting demonstrations and political backlash ended Crispi's long tenure in office.

Military factors alone do not explain the defeat. Crispi's plan to exploit the Triple Alliance as a cover for African expansion produced a misguided policy of Austrian appeasement that damaged Italian interests in the Balkans and irritated the Russians—who joined the French in supplying the Ethiopians and encouraging native resistance to the Italians. In addition to the diplomatic failure, Crispi misjudged the power of new domestic forces within Italy, which, ironically, gained impetus from economic measures passed by his administration; he also underestimated the capability of these groups to ally against his policies despite their differences. In Milan, the center of modern economic activity, industrialists and persecuted Socialists joined forces against him. Emerging from a social and economic crisis, the nation was in no mood to engage in colonial adventures. It understood that the government followed a colonial policy for reasons of prestige and imitation of the big powers and that there were no economic gains or attractive areas of settlement to be won.

The military events, however, created a desire for revenge that burned more brightly the further Adowa receded and would come to full fruition under the Fascist regime of Benito Mussolini. Indeed, Nationalists would later praise Crispi, and Fascists claimed him as a forerunner. Crispi and Mussolini attempted to impart dynamism to Italian foreign policy; but their inability to adapt Italian foreign policy to the country's level of domestic economic and social development, and their erroneous interpretation of the European diplomatic situation meant, in the end, that they had only their mistakes in common.

11

Social and Economic Dilemmas

IN JUDGING THE SOCIAL AND economic policies of Italy after unification, historians frequently fail to emphasize the difficulties of creating a unified state. The Risorgimento patriots had been too preoccupied in forging unity to devote much attention to the economic and social issues that would confront them afterward. Furthermore, the Italian peninsula presented unique problems. It exhibited a disparity probably found in no other European country. The old states had a long, entrenched history, having been cited by Renaissance historian Jacob Burckhardt as the first modern ones; this factor rooted separate administrations, economic policies, systems of law, mentalities, and dialects in different areas. Although standard Italian had been the first tongue to establish itself in early modern Europe, ordinary people spoke dialects frequently unintelligible to inhabitants of different regions.

After unification, Piedmont resolved these problems in a superficial but perhaps the only politically viable manner, given international conditions: by extending its administrative, economic, and legal structures to the rest of the peninsula. This policy caused long-term resentment and revolts, but crucial short-term questions had to be solved as well and immediately. Consider the basic issue of budgeting, which affects all areas of social and economic life: "No one knew, for example, how much tax evasion there was; only an oracle could have forecast what military expenditures would be to cope with brigandage or keep an army at fighting trim for fear of international complications; and even a supernatural power would have been hard pressed to know how much the founding fathers would pay out for public works, especially railroads."

During the first forty years after unification, an economic web of immense complexity threatened the new state. Italian statesmen understood the need for a modern infrastructure to create a national market and to link the country to Europe, and they substantially completed that task by 1880. This accomplishment brought notable trade increases, but it did not automatically resolve the major economic imbalances of the peninsula, which had existed for centuries.

The weakest parts of the country dragged down the economy, which, in turn, had dire social and political results. As in other nations, pressure groups and compromises determined government policies, which had both positive and negative effects. The government also had to cope with the international economic slump that hit Europe between 1873 and 1896; Italy's responses resembled those of other European powers, but as a vulnerable resource-poor developing country, it could not compete with its more-advanced neighbors.

North and South: The Great Divide

Lack of raw materials, especially coal and iron crucial to the "first" industrial revolution, has been cited as a primary reason for the slow pace of Italy's industrialization. Economic historian Shepard B. Clough, for example, wrote that the "shortages of raw materials were undoubtedly the most crucial [factors inhibiting industrialization], for if the natural resources had been great, they would have attracted the necessary capital and the necessary technicians." When examining the country's retarded economic development, therefore, the paucity of natural resources must always be kept in mind, even though the economic story of postunification Italy is much more complex and requires as a starting point a review of existing social and economic conditions during the late nineteenth century.

An underlying factor always assumed to have slowed economic growth but that, unlike raw materials, seems not to have been crucial is population growth. In 1881 Italy's population stood at almost 28.5 million. There had been a steady increase since the eighteenth century, and the first twenty years after unification did not present a drastic demographic change. High birth and death rates typical of preindustrial societies characterized the country. After 1880, because of improvements in public health measures and better food and living conditions, annual population increases averaged over 10 percent due to a decrease in the death rate and an increased birth rate—another typical development. But then emigration exploded, especially after 1895, the "takeoff" period for the Italian economy (see Table 11.1).* From 1900 to 1914 emigration averaged almost 616,000 per year—bringing the annual population increase on the peninsula down to .7 percent during the nation's industrial takeoff and becoming an essential ingredient in its social and economic equilibrium. By 1901 the population stood at 32 million, considerably less than it would have been without emigration.

---

* As will be noticed throughout this work, different sources provide slightly different statistics.

TABLE 11.1   Italian Emigration:
Annual Average before World War I

1861–1870	121,040*
1871–1880	35,764**
1881–1890	187,920*
1901–1913	601,500***

* No figures available for return immigration.
** Figure is net of return immigration.
*** No figures available for return immigration from European and
Mediterranean countries.

Generally, with industrialization the birth rate decreases as living conditions improve, and emigration declines. In Italy neither of these developments occurred. The lopsided nature of the country's industrialization, which took place only in the Northwest, explains this difference. Accompanying this factor, emigration changed character. Before the 1870s it had been seasonal, directed toward Europe, and involved the entire country; afterward, it became southern and permanent and had the Americas as its focus. In short, the country experienced not only incomplete industrial and economic development but also a seriously unbalanced one that accentuated the differences between North and South. The dualistic nature of Italian society and its economy can be explained by the complex interaction of history, the international agricultural crisis from 1880 to 1895, and governmental policies.

As noted in previous chapters, extreme regional differences marked Italian agriculture. The most advanced area, Lombardy, continued building on the Enlightenment reforms of the eighteenth century, which had encouraged transformation of its agriculture into a capitalistic system. Piedmont as well benefited from the economic reforms of the nineteenth century, which contributed to its leading role in the Risorgimento. To the south, around Bologna, draining of the Emilean marshes and the capitalistic transformation of the land had begun, poising the region for a rapid economic development.

In other Italian regions, such hopeful conditions did not prevail. In the North, Venetian agriculture remained backward, with sharecroppers and tenant farmers primarily producing raw silk for exportation and maize. Widespread pellagra, a disease caused by niacin deficiency, and poor living conditions spurred emigration. In the central regions of Tuscany, Umbria, Marches, and Lazio, the nobility and city bourgeoisie retained their power by maintaining sharecropping. Nonetheless, the peasants of these regions fared better than Venetians and southerners, by applying improved methods to the production of wine, olives, and fruit, for which there was an increased demand in Italy and abroad. The profits went primarily to the landlords, and the areas lagged behind Lombardy and Piedmont, but the products at least allowed peasants to enjoy a healthier diet than that of people in Venetia and the South.

The South suffered the worst social and economic conditions. The reforms of the eighteenth century had either failed or produced half-capitalistic enterprises based on exploitation of the peasants. Conditions varied according to the geographical features of the regions. In the mountains, calculated at 40 percent of the old Kingdom of the Two Sicilies, living and working were harshest. Economic changes had cut the profitability of sheepherding, a major activity for the population. In the 1870s the population began growing, increasing pressure on the already poor soil and water; coinciding with this development, emigration to America began. In proportion to their population, the mountainous regions of the South (Calabria, Basilicata, Molise, and the Abruzzi) lost the greatest number of people to emigration.

The flatter areas devoted primarily to extensive cultivation of cereals and sheepherding (about 30%) suffered severe droughts and lacked irrigation. Primitive cultivation methods prevailed on large latifundia and small plots. These *latifondi* consisted of big holdings accumulated by landlords over the years from former possessions of feudal lords, from the Church during the Napoleonic and postunitary period, and from usurped domain lands that had once belonged to the state. On the continent, the latifundia generally belonged to the bourgeoisie and in Sicily to the nobles. The owners usually did not live on the land but rented it out to people who had it worked by day laborers and salaried peasants. The extremely low salaries produced low yields per acre but very high profits for latifundia owners and renters, thus discouraging investment and technological innovations on the land. Misery and lack of investment, however, also produced a harvest of social agitation and peasant demands for a share in the former state lands that the owners had usurped. This unrest contributed to the brigandage phenomenon following unification, but after its defeat the peasant had no escape except emigration. Fearing a decline in the labor supply, large landowners first enlisted government aid to brake emigration, with no avail, then realized its importance as a "safety valve" and encouraged it.

In Sicily, the bad social and economic conditions strengthened the Mafia. As already mentioned, in the eighteenth and nineteenth centuries, nobles stimulated a misplaced patriotism to sabotage Enlightenment reforms and the Bourbon administration, also employing criminal elements to maintain their power. This alliance survived unification, and the new state found it easier to accept than to destroy the local power structure. After unification the Mafia flourished even more. In the words of Denis Mack Smith, "It was used by landowners who needed strong-arm men to collect rents and intimidate labour; and by the *ga-bellotti* [people who made a profit from renting land from the owners and had it worked by others] who, as well as coercing their workers, had to intimidate the owners in order to rent the *latifondi* on easy terms." In addition, liberal democratic institutions, combined with a voting base narrowed by illiteracy and poverty, increased the difficulties of combating the existing system. With a restricted electorate of only about 1 percent, landowners and their peers could easily manipulate elections through Mafia influence. The police force could not intervene unilaterally as it had during Bourbon rule, so the liberal system "offered a better field for bribery and intimidation than autocratic government had ever done." In 1861, for example, a new law gave considerable influence to village notables, constraining Italian prefects to work with local "Grand Electors" with Mafia connections to help the government win elections. If the prefect failed to deliver electoral victories, the government would transfer him, and if he tried to keep the elections honest, local bosses with Mafia connections would use their influence to remove him; if both failed, the Mafia would resort to assassination. If anything, the new state's weakness strengthened the Mafia in Sicily and enhanced the political influence of other southern Italian criminal "organizations" such as the Camorra and the 'Ndrangheta.

Despite the prevalence of the latifundia, numerous land-owning peasants persisted in the South. They possessed several small parcels of land, distant from each other and usually insufficient to support a family. They made long treks daily to work their own land and, at least part of the year, the land of others. Unlike northern peasants, they did not live on the land but in large towns from which they would set out each day.

Well-watered parts of the region to some extent counterbalanced this dismal picture of southern agriculture. More fortunate areas produced specialized products for export to foreign countries and to northern and central Italy. These sections included parts of Campania, Sicily, and the Puglie and have been estimated at about 25 percent of the South. Their products included wine, olives, and citrus fruits. The most notable early development occurred around the cities of Bari and Lecce, the first to be connected by rail to the rest of Italy and Europe. The Bari-Lecce area profited from the free trade system imposed by Piedmont after unification that devastated most of the South's agricultural system by exporting wine to France. In 1880 French vines had been hit by phylloxera, but the disease spared this area for about the next twenty years. Even these more fortunate areas, however, suffered from the vagaries of politics and economics. With the outbreak of the tariff war in 1888, the French retaliated against Italian agricultural products, and wine exports did not reach the level of the 1880s even after the "war" ended.

Although total Italian agricultural production increased between 1866 and 1875 because of better communications with the rest of Europe, this increase did not alter the fundamentally backward nature of the country's agriculture, despite bright spots. In addition to the disparities just outlined, investors preferred to sink their money into bonds the government issued to service the huge debt, rather than invest in technical innovations on the land. In the South, landowners preferred to accumulate more property by buying up expropriated Church and domain property rather than introduce technical changes, because existing social conditions allowed them to make substantial profits using outmoded methods of cultivation. The state's fiscal policies exacerbated matters by weighing heaviest on the poorest areas.

In his 1881 investigation of agricultural conditions, Stefano Jacini cited the low production of land, the antiquated methods, the heavy taxation policies, and the misery of the peasants and drew a gloomy conclusion: "Agricultural Italy presents itself to us as a chronic and cancerous patient." Jacini suggested government intervention and reducing the fiscal burden to help agriculture, but international developments and domestic response would make this solution impossible.

Agricultural Crisis and Emigration: The Southern Problem

The international agrarian crisis that hit Italy between 1881 and 1894 had its roots in long-term technological trends. Railways had appeared in the first part of the century, but it took years to build a thick network, especially in large countries such as the United States. Because of its vast plains and favorable climate, American agriculture produced great harvests of grain cheaper than could be done in Europe. By the 1870s, completion of the American railway system and improvements in steamship transportation allowed American grain and other cereals to reach Europe and be sold there for less than the Europeans could produce it. European prices of wheat, corn, and other agricultural products drastically declined, threatened farmers with ruin, and presented European governments with a dilemma. If they did nothing, the development would favor urban consumers by lowering the price of bread and other foodstuffs. That policy had two disadvantages: It provoked intense opposition among politically powerful large landowners in a position to threaten the government's viability and left countries vulnerable to being starved out in case of war. But raising the tariff would alienate industrialists who would have to pay their workers more to cover subsidies to landowners. As a result of these considerations, European countries erected protective barriers to protect both their farmers and industry and intensified their colonial expansion to find markets. The crisis had different but crucial results in all countries. In Germany, for example, the government compensated the industrialists for the higher wages they had to pay their workers by building a big navy, which resulted in lucrative contracts for industrialists.

In Italy there would be a similar outcome. The crisis first appeared in a drastic price decline for grains and corn, accompanied by a jump in grain imports and price stabilization at a lower level in the 1876 to 1880 period. The imports declined with passage of a new tariff in 1887. After 1900 imports increased again, this time due to the rising food needs of the population and Italy's inability to meet them. In addition to the grains, the price of other Italian agricultural goods—including wine, olive oil, and raw silk—dropped as well.

At the beginning of the crisis, no consensus existed in favor of protectionism, although the first demands for it were heard. The Risorgimento generation, still in power, strongly favored free trade. The complex inquiry into agricultural conditions undertaken by Jacini (1877–1884) eschewed protection, calling for direct government intervention and tax cuts to improve technology and favor more private investment on the land. Debate on the Jacini report witnessed Depretis defending free trade and some large landowners demanding protection and a lowering of the land tax. A North-South split developed among the landowners, with the northerners requesting a new land survey as the basis for unifying land values over the entire peninsula, and southerners objecting because the survey would mean paying taxes on the part of their possessions that they had usurped from the domain lands. The southern landowners had more clout, given the importance of the South to the Left's electoral base. Depretis, however, obtained the southerners' support by scheduling a land survey that would have taken fifteen or twenty years to complete.

A quick switch to protectionism therefore seemed unlikely until international complications arose. In 1887 the Italians suffered a colonial defeat at Dogali; as previously mentioned, the defeat forced Depretis to modify his government by taking in Crispi, the major proponent of colonialism. Depretis had to request more funds for an army better equipped to pursue a vigorous colonial policy, to be financed by increasing the tariff (definitively passed on June 21, 1887). This situation meant that the government could not afford to cut taxes and increase services for agriculture, as Jacini insisted. The desire of the Italians to play a great-power role in international affairs, plus the poverty of their country, meant that Italy devoted a greater percentage of its income to military expenditures than did the more-advanced countries; this policy siphoned scarce resources away from the domestic sector without putting the country in a league with the other European powers.

Furthermore, the tariff had important social and economic implications. It permitted the latifundia to survive the onslaught of cheap American grain, which meant that emigration would continue. Emigration in turn contributed to the rescue of large landowners by becoming a "safety valve" lessening the social tensions that might otherwise have exploded into revolt. In 1888 a law supported by the *Meridionalisti* (advocates for the South) allowed free emigration. The southern bourgeoisie profited by acting as recruiting agents for steamship lines transporting emigrants to the United States under appalling conditions.

Some emigrants returned with their American savings to buy land, joining their land-hungry compatriots continuing the struggle against the landlords, but the fight had been lost. The agrarian crisis and government policies ensured the survival of the inefficient latifundia, low production, and social inequities; they blocked the emergence of new types of land tenure, greater production, and better wages—which would have reduced emigration and created greater wealth for the entire country. Instead, poor agricultural conditions in the South helped limit the country's industrial growth to the Northwest and greatly intensified the severe economic imbalance between North and South. And the southern problem has dragged down the entire country ever since.

Industrial Development and Protectionism

Economic historians agree that important gains in agricultural production per unit precede or accompany rapid industrial expansion and continued growth. Increased agricultural productivity allows a country to export more products, earning more foreign exchange that can be invested, raises per capita income so investment capital becomes more available, and expands the domestic market for industrial products as machinery becomes crucial to increase productivity further.

As outlined in the last section, the backwardness of southern agriculture ensured that the required productivity increase in the agrarian sector would not occur. During the 1870s, the cost of establishing the new state, the expense of building an infrastructure, the consequently low savings rates, price declines of industrial products, and technical changes in heavy industry that gave the edge to older, more experienced, and better-capitalized foreign firms help explain the failure of Italian industry to develop more rapidly. But why did the country lag so far behind the rest of Europe from 1880 to 1896, after the government had built an infrastructure, when emigration reduced population pressure, and despite the existence of important nuclei of engineers, technicians, and skilled laborers? Here agricultural backwardness appears as a main culprit restricting the domestic market so it could not support a sustained takeoff in the areas crucial to the industrial revolution—iron and textiles. Confirming this explanation are the following events: The industrial takeoff in the North after 1896 coincided with a great increase in agricultural productivity in Lombardy, Piedmont, and Emilia, while the South did not experience this development and failed to follow suit in the industrial sector.

In 1880 industry represented a small part of the total economy, characterized by no sector that could serve as the starting point of a "big spurt." Agriculture dominated, followed by the service sector (such as commerce and finance), which had increased after unification and had tied the peninsula more closely to the rest of Europe. Cotton manufacturing, because of the favorable treatment accorded to it in the tariff of 1878, developed rapidly but, thanks to the large lead of the older industrialized countries, could not play the role of leader as it had there. Also accorded favorable treatment in 1878, wool had a notable, if slower, development. The silk industry remained important but was handicapped by plant illnesses, Asian competition, and concentration on production of semifinished items for export. Because the government and foreign capitalists placed orders for cheaper iron products and locomotives abroad, railway and shipbuilding did not stimulate these industries.

The lack of a policy to industrialize the country reflects an important debate. It took time for statesmen of the period to understand that Italy had to industralize rapidly if it were not to regress. Although most agreed that action in favor of some industries had to be taken, they believed in a balanced development of the country, with agriculture leading the way and industry playing a supporting role. After this idea was abandoned, a new debate began. The proponents of a modern iron and steel industry demanded a general protective tariff for iron products. Their antagonists, however, argued that the costs of implanting the iron sector would be prohibitive; they believed in free importation of iron products that would provide cheap material to the mechanical industry, where they argued Italy could compete with foreign countries. They also called for a protective tariff on machine products and government orders to stimulate the industry.

The 1887 tariff gave the victory to the partisans of a strong iron and steel industry. The machine industry received some added protection, but not enough, according to economic historian Alexander Gerschenkron, who made a good case for the greater ability of the mechanical sector to compete with its rivals had it received greater support. As it had done in Germany ten years earlier, the tariff signalled the alliance of industrialists and large landowners to secure protection for their products. In another parallel with Germany, the government stimulated the metal and mechanical sectors by placing orders for a big navy. Under the leadership of navy minister Benedetto Brin (1884–1891), the leading proponent of large warships, Parliament appropriated huge sums and advanced the money to large firms created to exploit the new opportunities.

The government also boosted spending for railways and this time was partially successful in its attempt to ensure that domestic industry filled the orders. These operations also stimulated the finance area to reorient its investments from government paper to the industrial sector. But the banking system was poorly organized and regulated, and in 1893–1894 it collapsed amid charges of widespread corruption. Its subsequent reorganization on modern lines, however, and the creation of something like a central bank set the stage for further industrial development.

Thus the state emerged as a major player in the country's industrialization, but at a high price. Industry became inordinately dependent on government contracts, and though it profited, it also suffered because of the vagaries of state orders and indirect subsidies. Taxpayers and consumers footed the bill for expensive Italian products, and all Italians paid more for foodstuffs. The government policies that produced the rapid, though lopsided, industrialization of 1896 to 1914 also increased the already high political and social tensions that marked the century's end. Protectionism played an important role in the industrialization of most countries, but it cost the Italians more.

Education

Linking social and economic problems with political tensions and intensifying the North-South imbalance were schooling and education. Modern industrial democracies depend heavily on literacy, and here Italian educational policies turned in a mixed performance.

The most dramatic manifestation of this proposition is the slowness with which the illiteracy rate went down after unification. In 1871 the illiteracy rate for the entire population was 72.9 percent. In 1881 the percentage had declined to 67.3. As might be expected, illiteracy was higher in the South than in the North, but the statistics reveal a more significant discrepancy: a tendency for illiteracy to drop faster in the cities. The 1901 census revealed that although illiteracy fell over a nineteen-year period by 27.6 percent in urban areas, it went down only by 20 percent in the countryside. The rural nature of the South and its lower starting point meant that a high illiteracy rate persisted longer in the region. For example, those areas that had the lowest illiteracy in 1861 (Lombardy and Piedmont) dropped below 50 percent in ten years and below 25 percent by 1901, whereas the South, including the islands and part of the Center, still had an illiteracy rate above 50 percent in 1901.

The most important factor in bringing down illiteracy is elementary education. Since the old governments had done little to encourage public education, a law named after Count Gabrio Casati and passed in Piedmont in 1859 was extended to all Italy after unification. This law struck at clerical influence and reorganized education on the European model; that is, it was concerned primarily with the education of elites in the secondary schools. It paid only rudimentary attention to elementary education, obliging the towns to provide free education for two years (four years for towns over 4,000, or that had a secondary school) and provided minimum wages for teachers. It obliged fathers to send their children "of both sexes" to school under punishment of law. Besides the insufficient time provided to teach literacy to children who knew only the local dialect, many towns (prevalently in the South) could not afford to meet their obligations to finance the schools, and the law provided no sanctions to fathers who did not send their children to school. In addition, the need to work the land to help their families meant that many children could not afford to go to school—even though their records showed attendance.

The Left recognized the inadequate nature of the law and a debate ensued after 1870. Arguing that the state should take more responsibility for the eradication of illiteracy and, consequently, schooling, and wishing to increase the number of persons eligible to vote, the Left pushed for free, compulsory education similar to other European nations. In 1877 Parliament passed the Coppino law, which provided for three years' compulsory education for children of both sexes from ages six to nine and provided sanctions for parents who did not comply. The new law made insufficient provision for financing the schools, so that, in fact, many children received only two years' schooling. Over a period of years, however, governments of the Left greatly increased appropriations for education in a number of areas, including school construction and teachers' salaries. Nonetheless, the quality of elementary education and attendance remained low, and the formulas for distribution of the funds helped the richer North and worked against the South.

The country fared better in the quality of public secondary and higher education. The number of students increased greatly but still remained well below the proportions of other European countries. Public education overshadowed private and was highly centralized, even though universities achieved some autonomy in determining their academic programs, geared to producing professionals. In the secondary schools the state paid most attention to educating the elite through a rigorous classical education. Technical education remained inferior, to the point that future prime minister Luigi Luzzatti overhauled it in 1869. This reform, untouched until 1923, improved matters but did not erase the subordination of the technical schools, which remained a persistent weak spot in Italy's industrialization effort.

The Catholic Social Movement

Education had been a battleground between the Church and the secular power. The fight broke out in Italy later than in many European countries, since the

Church retained control of education in the old states. In the major exception, Piedmont, the Casati law had anticlerical aspects but did not eliminate religious teaching by priests in the public schools. When the debate over compulsory education began after 1870, intransigent Catholics opposed it because their schools could not compete with free public schools and because they opposed children being forced to attend schools that taught liberal values. Although the Coppino law established obligatory schooling, it did not specifically abolish religious instruction. This lack caused major polemics between Catholics and their opponents because some local jurisdictions retained religious instruction while others abolished it, depending on the political situation in the area. The national government consistently refused to take a clear stand on the issue. Furthermore, the fight fueled the introduction of "positivist" philosophies and empirical programs into Italian schools as a means of combating Catholic "spiritualism."

The educational battle illustrated the anticlerical aftermath of the Risorgimento, caused by the taking of the Papal State, the Church's unwillingness to accept that development, its order requiring Catholics to abstain from national politics, and the Pope's attempt to secure the intervention of foreign powers. The state struck back in 1866 and 1867 by extending to all Italy the earlier Piedmontese legislation expropriating Church property not used for religious purposes, by instituting a special tax on most of the rest, and by punishing Church interference in political activities. On the other hand, economics more than religious persecution spurred the government's hand on Church property, and the authorities meted out mild punishments. Furthermore, affiliation with the Catholic Church shut no one out of a career in state service.

These factors favored a future reconciliation. Despite the political intransigence of Church authorities, the period up to 1900 began a healing process between State and Church as many Catholics accepted the reality of unification and tried to reconcile their faith with their patriotism. With the death of Pius IX in 1878 and the election of Leo XIII, an attempt at cooperation with the national government replaced hostility. Although a policy of cooperation was implemented most clearly in Germany and France, Italy moved in the same direction even though the particular problems caused by the country's being the site of the papacy's center caused the policy to be implemented unofficially and with caution.

Forbidden from overt participation in national politics, the Catholic movement dedicated itself to social concerns. Not only did the Church's centuries-long tradition encourage this development but so did the rising threat from a new atheistic and radical force—socialism. Moreover, the Catholic movement's strength in this area created the premise of an alliance with the liberals, who also feared socialism. The new century would witness a muting of the old disputes with the state and a partnership between Catholics and liberals based on antisocialism.

The more-advanced North, where Socialist organizations proliferated, remained the Catholic focus. Respect for property, the denial that an inherent struggle existed between owners and employees, a lack of aggressiveness, an emphasis on Christian cooperation instead of struggle based on economic interests, and a failure to challenge the existing system marked the Catholic social movement. Although extremely active in charitable activities and championing the dignity of labor and its right to decent wages, the Catholics hesitated in organizing unions or favoring strikes, activities that would have alienated their rich noble and bourgeois supporters. Catholics romanticized the past, emphasizing cooperation and corporate medieval institutions; they debated the feasibility of mixed unions of employees and employers. They devoted their considerable energies to creating a vast network of economic and social organizations to help peasants and workers: mutual aid societies, cooperatives, and rural savings banks (culminating in the Bank of Rome, the Vatican's financial arm). Coordinating these economic activities, and local political initiatives was the Opera dei Congressi, a lay organization controlled by the Church and whose efficiency no political party could match. The Opera ensured that its religious view permeated Catholic social activity and that no radical ideas would germinate from it.

In 1891 Leo XIII's encyclical *Rerum Novarum* gave theoretical unity to these social activities. It modernized the Church's mission, declaring that labor was not just another commodity whose value depended on supply and demand, opposing the exploitation of workers, emphasizing justice in economic relationships, and arguing for protection of child and female labor. The encyclical also reaffirmed the Church's traditional role as defender of the poor, stated its preference for a corporate organization of society, argued against the extension of the state's powers over society, and condemned liberalism and socialism. In this manner the Church equipped itself to meet the Socialist menace and avoided the radical implications of its social policy until after World War I.

At the same time, *Rerum Novarum* set the basis for an Italian Christian democracy. A professor at the University of Pisa, Giuseppe Toniolo, theoretician of Church primacy in social and economic activity, organized a congress of Catholic intellectuals in October 1892 and founded a review devoted to the social sciences. Consciously committed to providing a "scientific" basis to Catholic activities as Marx and Engels had done for the Socialists, Toniolo advocated social legislation and measures favoring workers and the poor, but on a foundation of class cooperation, not class struggle.

Don Romolo Murri, the priest who was the real founder of Italian Christian democracy, hoped to defeat socialism by linking the already strong Catholic social activism to politics. In 1898 Murri founded *Cultura Sociale*, a title that recalled the Socialist *Critica Sociale*. Since a Socialist triumph would create not communism, Murri believed, but a radical democracy, the Catholics would be the real winners in the struggle between the Socialists and the state because the Catholic social movement would be in a position to mobilize much larger masses than their rivals. For both Toniolo and Murri, true democracy translated into a great victory for Christian democracy, but whereas Toniolo understood that the Church would not condone a political campaign designed to destroy the existing liberal state and believed it would collapse of its own weight, Murri had absorbed Socialist rhetoric about the destruction of liberal institutions. Murri condemned the liberal state as an expression of the evil bourgeoisie and therefore antithetical to Catholic principles. As he wrote to Filippo Meda, a Catholic leader willing to dialogue with the state, he believed in "the necessity of a reorganization [of society] from below, inspired by the Church, and there-fore in opposition to the mission of the modern state."

Murri did not push revolution as a means of destroying the state, but he did advocate complete political intransigence on the part of Catholics, beyond that authorized by the Vatican, as a means of destroying the state in the name of Christ. Thus, ironically, Christian democrats rejected the state and favored a harder opposition than the more vocal clerical intransigents who, though they opposed Italian governments because of anticlerical legislation or expropria-tions, favored an eventual accommodation. Indeed, peace discussions between Church and State actually began and were advanced by that noted anticlerical, Francesco Crispi.

When the talks fell apart, the government misidentified the clericals as the state's most tenacious opponents. In 1898 riots took place all over Italy, leading to mass arrests. The government arrested clerical intransigent leaders such as Don Davide Albertario along with Socialists and Anarchists. Shocked at being lumped with the leftist opponents of the state, the Church recognized reality and slowly changed its policy to one of cooperation with the government against their common Socialist enemies. The Catholic social movement went along, but Christian democratic opposition to real reconciliation represented a major weakness for the liberal state.

Anarchists and Socialists: Rise of the "Social Question"

Not surprisingly, Italy's economic dislocations during the late nineteenth cen-tury prompted opposition by those most affected. This movement availed itself of the ideas prevailing in other, more-advanced European countries—a condemnation of bourgeois power and the organization of society directed toward the exploitation of the working class. Radicals preached destruction of bourgeois-controlled governments and the passage of power to the workers.

Two broad currents existed as to how these goals should be accomplished, anarchism and socialism. The first to dominate the revolutionary movement in Italy, Anarchists advocated immediate social revolution, sparked by themselves, without much thought to analyzing the conditions favoring it or what the new society might look like. Mikhail Bakunin, a Russian Anarchist, disseminated socialist ideas in Italy on behalf of the London-based Workers' International in the 1860s. He destroyed the influence of Mazzinianism among Italian workers and gained the allegiance of many Italian intellectuals against Marx during the 1860s and 1870s. Persons of high quality who joined the movement included Carlo Cafiero, whose wealth financed the Anarchist movement; Errico Malatesta, its longtime leader; lawyer Francesco Saverio Merlino, later a Marxist revisionist; Andrea Costa, who would create a forerunner of the Italian Socialist party; and Russian revolutionary Anna Kuliscioff, Costa's lover, a future founder of the Socialist party, and the "Signora" of Italian socialism.

Bakunin and his friends advocated the immediate overthrow of the state by violence. In 1874 and 1877 Anarchist bands attempted to spark a nationwide revolution, but the police had little trouble suppressing their activities because of the lack of popular support. After 1877 the failure of Anarchist methods became clear, and prominent leaders deserted the movement. In 1878 Anna Kuliscioff pointed out that miserable social conditions are prerequisites of revolts but that revolutions must issue from the people and could not be made without them. In August 1879 a famous letter from Andrea Costa pronounced anarchism a failure because it had neglected the economic conditions and needs of the people, "and when we raised the flag of revolt, the people did not understand us and we were left alone."

Costa advised his comrades to enter Parliament and in 1883 became the first Socialist to serve there. But he remained an Anarchist at heart, advocating destruction of existing political institutions by infiltrating and undermining them, rather than transforming them into tools that the proletariat could use. He proposed the union of all socialist factions in Italy and broadening the movement's base by establishing a political party. In 1881 he pursued this ideal by founding the Partito Socialista Rivoluzionario di Romagna, intended as the nucleus of a nationwide political organization, but the party failed to achieve this aim.

In 1882 workers in Milan founded the Partito Operaio Italiano (Italian Workers' party, POI), the Italian Socialist party's direct forerunner. This organization hoped to take advantage of the recently widened suffrage and signalled the shift in working-class influence from the artisan Romagna to what would become the Italian industrial heartland. Although socialist intellectuals around the Milanese newspaper *La Plebe* had a hand in founding the organization, the party distrusted "bourgeois" socialists and restricted membership exclusively to workers, a policy that proved disastrous. In 1886 the government seized upon a dispute with Felice Cavallotti, popular leader of the Radical Democrats who feared POI competition, and dissolved the party. Although *operaista* leaders reorganized, their organization never recovered. It had reached a membership of 40,000.

The task of creating a Socialist party now fell to Filippo Turati and Anna Kuliscioff. A former Radical Democrat and poet who had been part of an important artistic movement in Milan, Turati had converted to Marxism. Turati and Kuliscioff had fallen in love in Naples after her affair with Costa had cooled down; returning to Milan, they lived together until her death in 1925 (although Turati would go home at night to sleep with his mother until she died in 1912). Together they founded the Milanese Socialist League, a "cell" enunciating the principles that inspired the future Italian Socialist party, and in 1891, *Critica Sociale*, the review that spread Marxist ideology in Italy.

Turati and Kuliscioff believed in a nonviolent, gradual road to socialism in which socialist ideas would penetrate all the institutions of the old society. Violence was irrelevant and illusionary because the proletariat itself had absorbed bourgeois principles and because it had been held in subjection and ignorance for so long. If the workers were so "backward, " as many socialist leaders claimed, how could the working class lead the way to the higher organization of society represented by socialism? From the beginning, Turati denounced the "dictatorship of the proletariat," which he claimed introduced an oligarchic principle into socialism that he predicted would produce a dictatorship of intellectuals against the proletariat. Only by educating the workers and enacting social legislation to mitigate the terrible conditions under which they labored, setting the basis for a spiritual growth, could that fate be avoided. Social and economic reforms could be achieved making use of Parliament; this goal required the establishment of a Socialist party to coordinate political action not only to pass social legislation but also to defeat reactionary governments hostile to the proletariat's progress and to help extend the democracy necessary for socialism. Self-redemption and autonomous political action would slowly teach workers their own best interests and how to organize to achieve them. The "revolution," therefore, would be the culmination of a great evolutionary movement.

These ideas initially won out, but the left wing, or "revolutionaries," opposed them in the Italian as in the other European socialist parties. The revolutionaries argued that there are no distinctions among bourgeois groups and viewed governments and parliaments as merely "ruling committees" of the bourgeoisie. For that reason, revolutionaries believed that social legislation bettering working conditions would only reconcile workers and capitalists and advocated violent overthrow of the existing government.

But the social and economic crises of the late nineteenth century masked these divisions. By the early 1890s Anarchist influence had declined, and the socialists had clarified their social, economic, and political goals. Despite opposition by Marxist philosopher Antonio Labriola, in contact with Friedrich Engels, who argued that Italy had not developed to the point where a viable Socialist party was possible, Turati and Kuliscioff succeeded in founding one in October 1892. At a congress of working-class organizations held in Genoa, they achieved enough support from workers to defeat both the old POI leaders and the Anarchists. The victory over the POI meant that socialist intellectuals participated fully in the new party (although the worker-intellectual feud continued), and the Anarchists were expelled from the movement. Over the next three years, the party perfected its organization—making it the first centralized, disciplined modern Italian political party on the model of the German Socialist party—and adopted the name Partito Socialista Italiano (PSI).

The PSI bore Turati's stamp—a social and economic commitment to "the immediate improvement of working-class conditions (hours, salaries, factory rules, etc.)" and "a wider struggle having as its goal the conquest of the organs of public power (state, commune, public administrations, etc.)" to transform them from oppressive institutions "into instruments of economic and political expropriation of the dominating class." But divisions over political alliances remained, even if, as a compromise, the party did not immediately allow understandings with bourgeois parties, but the divisions remained. For Turati, alliances could not be admitted for the moment for practical purposes; for the revolutionaries, the reasons were ideological.

The Italian political situation seemed favorable for Socialist affirmation in 1892. A cabinet headed by Giolitti and friendlier to the workers than Crispi's took office in May. Giolitti's permissive attitude allowed the PSI to expand its membership and support but got the government into trouble with the Right and Crispi, especially alarmed at Socialist growth in Sicily. In 1893 several incidents combined to topple Giolitti: the bank scandals and resulting corruption charges against the prime minister; disturbances after the murder of several Italian workers in France; and finally, a revolt in Sicily headed by the *fasci siciliani*, peasant leagues considered to be under Socialist influence. Giolitti resigned and Crispi returned. He proclaimed martial law and established military tribunals on the island. Repression soon spread to the entire country as agitation increased, and Crispi received full powers. In June 1894 he secured passage of "exceptional" laws persecuting Anarchists and Socialists, and in October, he dissolved the PSI.

Crispi's policies set off an important debate within the PSI. As mentioned previously, his colonialism had already alienated northern industrialists. Should the Socialists modify their political intransigence and present a united antigovernment front with Crispi's bourgeois opponents? Turati and Kuliscioff had no ideological objection to alliances but had to move cautiously not to alienate their Socialist comrades. In January 1894 Kuliscioff wrote to Engels and secured his support for political alliances with the bourgeoisie. In July, Turati and Kuliscioff brought their group into the bourgeois-led anti-Crispi "League for the Defence of Liberty," and negotiated an alliance with non-Socialist radicals for the February 1895 local elections. This move completed the powerful alliance of Crispi opponents known as the "State of Milan," which took the lead in toppling Crispi after the Adowa defeat in 1896.

Turati's moves in Milan violated official party policy, and though the Milanese leader won modification of the strict electoral policy and an exception for Milan, he failed to secure an endorsement of political alliances in principle. He clearly believed in them, wished to make them a feature of Socialist policy, and remained ready to oppose his comrades if he believed alliances would further Socialist aims.

Government repression, which briefly paused after Crispi's fall, worsened in 1898 as the protective tariff, the country's poor social conditions, and international dislocations produced nationwide riots. This crisis developed into a political threat to the country's parliamentary system that lasted until 1901. Until then the Socialists remained unified to protect the basic liberties necessary for the party and the labor movement to survive. But when that threat receded, the fundamental division between Socialists who wished to improve the lot of peasants and workers through existing institutions and those who wanted an immediate overthrow of the state exploded with full force. As with the Catholics, a powerful wing threatened the existence of the liberal state; but unlike that movement, no Vatican kept a lid on the dispute.

12

The Rise of Socialism and the Giolittian Era

Depressed prices and poor economic conditions plagued Europe from the early 1870s to the 1890s, but higher prices and prosperity marked the years between 1896 and 1914, despite the sharp 1907–1908 recession. Protectionism increased prices for agricultural goods, industrialists created combinations to raise prices for their products, and gold discoveries in South Africa and the Klondike fueled expansion of the money supply. The demand for industrial products increased as a result of the arms race, growth of the middle class, the opening of colonial markets, higher wages, and governmental stimulation of the economy through increased spending. Most important, technological advances in electricity, chemicals, and the internal combustion engine created new industrial sectors and touched off the "second" industrial revolution.

These changes allowed Italy to become the first Mediterranean area to move into the advanced industrial arena, even if the country's development remained skewed by regional imbalances. Economic changes had drastic effects on the country's political and social life. Requiring more freedom and less friction, the growing and increasingly powerful northern bourgeoise displayed less tolerance for leaders like Crispi who failed to recognize the paramount importance of their goals, who favored foreign adventures, and whose recalcitrance stimulated the social unrest that interfered with the country's economic development. If necessary, during the early years of the twentieth century, industrialists could reach limited understandings with their enemies, and Socialists also were committed to liquidating the repressive mentality of late nineteenth-century government leaders; the previously mentioned Milanese alliance between radicals and business leaders against Crispi clearly demonstrated this tendency. Between 1901 and World War I, converging interests of bourgeoisie and proletariat outweighed ideology and had positive if limited effects. But in both camps the groups criticizing this practical "politics of things" gained strength, and as war exploded, the compromise responsible for Italy's political, social, and economic advances ruptured.

From End of Century Crisis to "Liberal Springtide"

Antonio Di Rudinì succeeded Crispi. A Sicilian leader of the Right, Di Rudinì had failed to live up to the promise he had demonstrated as a young man during the Risorgimento; he had been a boy wonder, one unkind critic commented, but then "the wonder disappeared but the boy remained."

The Milanese industrialists who had opposed Crispi supported Rudinì, but they felt ill at ease with his social and administrative reform projects. They favored drastic cuts in unproductive government expenses to stimulate northern industrial activity. To satisfy them, Di Rudinì retreated from Ethiopia into the existing East African colonies, but the funds saved by withdrawal satisfied no one. The war minister's plan to reduce the army's size while increasing its efficiency ran into King Humbert I's staunch opposition, and fearing for his government, Rudinì sabotaged it. The prime minister hoped to win support in the country by favoring agrarian interests, strengthening the executive power against Parliament, and meeting some of the workers' demands through social legislation. This "conservative decentralization" program included granting towns under 10,000 the right to elect their own mayors, permitting local referenda on tax matters, and creating a system of voluntary accident insurance.

Elements of this program resembled Bismarck's attempt to undercut the German Socialists by meeting some working-class demands, and it appealed to moderates on the left; but it alienated the extreme right, which advocated strong measures to meet the threat from the extreme left. The prime exponent of this course, Sidney Sonnino, published a famous article in 1897 arguing that the Statuto had not set up a parliamentary system in Italy and—condemning the system's democratic evolution over the past fifty years—suggested that political practice conform to the constitutional letter. Sonnino would have allowed the king to name and dismiss the ministers without Parliament's intervention. The dispute with the extreme right and the industrialists' uneasiness caused political instability.

Besides his troubles with the right, Rudinì alienated the Socialists, many of whose leaders imprisoned by Crispi remained in jail despite a partial amnesty. Turati denounced government repression of the Socialist press and associations as unconstitutional. The Socialists also warned that government tariff policy resulted in dramatic increases in the price of food and raised the specter of revolts. In the elections of March 1897 the Socialist parliamentary delegation increased from ten to fifteen, signalling the failure of the government campaign against them. Rudinì attempted to meet the twin threats to his faltering government by moving toward the moderate left, but in March 1898 the death in a duel of Radical Democratic leader Felice Cavallotti dashed this plan.

In February, food riots in Sicily had resulted in the death of ten demonstrators. After a two-month eerie calm, the disorders suddenly flared up again and spread with amazing rapidity throughout the country, fed by high prices, a bad harvest, and the disruption of trade caused by the Spanish-American War. The unrest culminated in Milan where demonstrators threw up barricades that the army destroyed with artillery fire. The indiscriminate shooting caused 80 civilian deaths and 500 wounded, according to official statistics, but unofficial estimates cite 400 dead and 1,000 wounded. After the firing stopped, the arrests began. The police detained leaders who had opposed the government—Socialists, Catholics, Radicals, and Republicans. Anna Kulsicioff and Filippo Turati ended up in jail, as did fellow Socialists Leonida Bissolati and Oddino Morgari, Catholic newspaper editor Don Davide Albertario, and Republican Luigi De Andreis. The government shut down the opposition press, somehow missing the Socialist daily *Avanti!*, and handed out long prison sentences. In seeking to explain the Milanese disorders, shocked conservatives ignored the harsh conditions in northern factories and blamed a conspiracy to destroy the state.

Rudinì's quick crackdown did not save his cabinet. In Parliament, Milanese industrialists and Sonnino attacked Rudinì's moderate policies for having encouraged the disorders. On June 18 Rudinì resigned. While opposition leaders were hauled before military courts General Luigi Pelloux headed up a new cabinet. Pelloux had liberal credentials, and a reactionary wave seemed to have been avoided when the government withdrew restrictive bills proposed by his predecessor. Pelloux, however, received emergency powers on a temporary basis and then asked for permanent legislation that would have severely restricted constitutionally guaranteed freedoms of the press, association, and assembly. He came under the influence of Sonnino, who led the floor fight for the bills. This development aroused the suspicion of the moderates, but they initially adopted a wait-and-see attitude.

The Socialists, however, reacted immediately to the Pelloux-Sonnino conjunction because Sonnino seemed positioned to implement his proposed constitutional revisions and end the country's democratic evolution. Convinced that socialism could not develop without democracy, the Socialists quickly changed from opponents of a Statuto they deemed too restrictive into defenders of the constitution "repudiated by the bourgeoisie." The party had officially rejected Turati's alliance policy even though it had made an exception for Milan; now it dropped its refusal to cooperate with all "bourgeois" groups and coordinated its political efforts in the country and in Parliament with the Radicals and Republicans. This action created a new parliamentary bloc, the *Estrema Sinistra* (Extreme Left).

In the Chamber of Deputies the Estrema could count on only about 67 deputies out of 508, but the rules and regulations of that body allowed a determined group to delay business indefinitely. Estrema deputies resorted to "obstruction"—long speeches, myriad amendments, numerous votes. As government supporters tired, Sonnino proposed limiting debate by changing the rules— against which the Estrema filibustered. The government then circumvented the Chamber by embodying the original bills in royal decrees issued by the king. Clearly unconstitutional, this procedure irritated moderates philosophically opposed to the Estrema's methods and contributed to an understanding between them and the *Estrema*. By July 1899 almost half of the deputies opposed Pelloux; in the country, jailed opposition leaders were elected to the Chamber and reelected when declared ineligible, and widespread agitation for an amnesty forced the government to grant several pardons. Tempers flared in Parliament and fistfights broke out on the Chamber floor.

Faced by an impossible situation, the king ended the session and attention focused on a court case appealing the government's enforcement of the royal decrees as law. In February 1900, Italy's highest court ruled against the government, forcing it to seek approval of the decrees in Parliament. Realizing that their majority had been slowly dissolving, Pelloux and Sonnino resorted to illegal procedures to limit debate, further alienating the moderate deputies. Although the rule changes were formally adopted as a result of these methods, the action failed to end the Estrema's resistance. The government had no choice but to appeal to the voters to reduce the opposition delegation.

But the government had already lost the battle in the country. The elections of June 3 and 10, 1900, spelled disaster for Pelloux. Despite government interference in the balloting, it lost the popular vote and could claim only a slim and uncertain majority in the Chamber. Instead of cutting down the opposition, the Socialist delegation doubled and the Estrema swelled to 95. Pelloux seized the first occasion to resign and effectively ended the reaction of 1898–1900.

As might be expected, the end-of-century crisis spurred debate among contemporaries and historians. Turati's Socialist opponent Arturo Labriola interpreted Pelloux as the front man in a royal plot to undermine parliamentary institutions, while in 1975 Umberto Levra viewed the crisis as a successful bourgeois coup d'etat against the proletariat because it resulted in the triumph of Turati's ideas within the Socialist party. Leaving aside Levra's ideological bias, the fact remains that by cooperating with other parties of the Extreme Left, the Socialists defeated the reaction of 1898–1900; in a similar situation during 1920 to 1924, they chose an isolationist course that contributed to the victory of fascism in Italy.

After Pelloux's resignation, the king asked the eighty-one-year-old president of the Senate, Giuseppe Saracco, to form a government. A wag commented: "When Italy most desperately feels the need for a lusty male to impregnate her, she consummates a union with an old man already betrothed to Death." At the end of July 1900, an Italian Anarchist returned from the United States to assassinate King Humbert. His twenty-nine-year-old son, Victor Emmanuel III, chose a conciliatory course over confrontation. The country rapidly returned to normal, but now it had less tolerance for government arbitrariness. Following a labor dispute in Genoa, Saracco authorized dissolution of the local Chamber of Labor. In response, a massive general strike paralyzed Italy's largest port city, while sympathy strikes occurred in other parts of the country. In February 1901, Saracco resigned.

United Italy's new king, Victor Emmanuel III, presented a different picture from the two monarchs who had preceded him. Physically he lacked the presence of his predecessors; his short stature caused him suffering and made him fair game for political cartoonists throughout his reign. In his personal life he was very cold, as his son frequently testified. Unlike Victor Emmanuel II and Humbert I, he eschewed relationships with women and became passionate only over his vast coin collection. Emotionally he was far less secure than his predecessors. He frequently seemed weak, tended to waver, to play his cards too close to his chest, and to follow the short-term path of least resistance. These qualities brought him and his country to grief, contributing to the coming of fascism to power, the country's confusion after the fall of fascism, and the end of his own dynasty in 1946.

Finding a replacement for Saracco presented unusual difficulties. Because of parliamentary maneuvering, the Chamber of Deputies gave no clear indication as to a successor. To the cheers of the left, the king appointed the liberal Zanardelli to form a government, despite indications that the Chamber preferred Sonnino. Although this solution pleased the left, it was fraught with long-term implications. Presented with an opportunity to designate the prime minister, the Chamber meekly relied on the monarch to make the choice. The king chose Zanardelli, who would come to power with Giolitti, because Zanardelli and Giolitti's ideas were popular in the country even though they had a doubtful majority in the Chamber. On the other hand, Giolitti advocated tax reforms; the king did not favor significant fiscal reform because it meant fewer funds for the army. The king handled the dilemma shrewdly: He opted for Zanardelli and Giolitti but made cuts in military expenses impossible by exercising his right to name the ministers for war and the navy and to influence the choice of foreign minister. In short, he presented Giolitti the option of joining the government or of fighting for tax reforms outside of it. Giolitti entered the cabinet believing that the need for a liberal government that would sponsor a dialogue between

Socialists and business outweighed meaningful fiscal reform—at least for the moment. A secret agreement committed Italy to ship six army corps to Germany in case of war, making it impossible to cut the existing force below the current twelve corps. Unable to alter this commitment, the Estrema had no choice but to support the Zanardelli-Giolitti cabinet out of fear of Sonnino. Under the circumstances, fiscal reform never came off the back burner.

For the Socialist delegation, Giolitti's presence as interior minister guaranteed the country protection against repression and compensated for the cabinet's imperfections. In a well-publicized speech in October 1899, Giolitti had announced the bankruptcy of reaction and outlined a program that included respect for civil rights, the overhaul of the judicial and administrative systems, and fiscal reform. He condemned fixed and indirect taxes and protective tariffs and advocated proportional taxation. It is true that the fiscal parts of his program remained unfulfilled, but, most important, Giolitti had argued that the government must no longer be at the service of "restricted cabals." How? It must cease intervening on the side of employers in labor disputes, grant labor's reasonable demands, and encourage higher wages as a sign of an advanced economy. As interior minister he ended the government's strike-breaking role. These developments encouraged strikes, especially on the land. Socialists formed agricultural leagues and unions and pressed for improved wages and working conditions. To cite one example of the labor unrest, in 1900 there were 27 agricultural strikes involving 12,517 participants, and in 1901 222,985 people participated in 629 strikes, almost all of them successful.

Not surprisingly, in April 1901 a conservative counterattack began in Parliament. Sonnino denounced the cabinet for its supposed subordination to the Socialists and called for a strong government to restore "discipline." Giolitti countered that the Chamber had to choose between liberty and repression. A dispute erupted among the Socialists, as to whether the deputies should vote confidence in the government or not; without a positive vote from the Socialist delegation, the cabinet would fall and be replaced by a Sonnino-led coalition. Consistent with official party policy, the Directorate ordered the deputies not to vote confidence in the government, but Turati persuaded the Socialist delegation to do otherwise. On June 22, 1901, the entire Estrema, including Socialists, voted in favor of the Zanardelli-Giolitti government, keeping it in power by a 264 to 184 margin—"The victory of liberty," Avanti! commented of the first Italian government to receive Socialist votes. The Socialists had saved "the Liberal Springtide."

Politics, Economics, and Society in the Giolittian Era

Between the turbulence of the reactionary movement that ended in 1901 and the forces set in motion by the Libyan War of 1911–1912, the Giolittian age appears as an oasis of political stabilization. A calm and collected Piedmontese nurtured in the bureaucracy, Giolitti consistently outmaneuvered his conservative enemies and seemed prepared to open negotiations with new forces previously excluded from the political process or from a reasonable share in the nation's growing wealth. His partial sympathy for the political and economic platforms of these groups stopped well short of agreeing with their ultimate aims, but his willingness to support some of their planks exposed him to attacks from the right.

Giolitti seemed to yield to the verdict of the 1900 elections, which had increased the representation of the Estrema and of the Socialists in particular. In 1903 he invited Turati to join his new cabinet, but, for the reason discussed below, the reformist leader refused. For the next decade, PSI leaders argued over whether cooperating with Giolitti would end with their "absorption" into the bourgeois political system. Weakened by their own divisions, as was the case in most European countries during the same period, Italy's Socialists won concessions but failed to enter the inner circle directing the country's policies.

Besides the Socialists, Radicals and Republicans debated "domestication" as well. The Radicals divided on the question, but some accepted cabinet posts at various times; the Republicans remained more adamant but, given the country's liberal direction, failed to make a convincing case to Italians as to why replacing the monarchy with a republic would make a substantial difference in the country's course.

In 1904 the country's first general strike occurred, but Giolitti correctly calculated that the movement would fall apart of its own weight after a few days and did not intervene. Although his conduct provoked criticism from disgruntled conservatives demanding strong action and contributed to his negative image among them, Giolitti shrewdly used the strike to bolster his position by calling new elections that produced a majority in the Chamber of Deputies that was more favorable to him.

In addition, the strike alarmed the Catholics, who were undergoing important changes. The election of politically moderate Pope Pius X in 1903, the dissolution of the Opera dei Congressi in 1904, and the influence of Lombard industrial and banking groups over Catholic economic organizations battered the Christian democrats, who opposed any accommodation with the state. Buffeted by the rise of anticlericalism in France because of the mistaken Catholic decision to support the anti-Drefusards (oppenents of Alfred Dreyfus, wrongly accused of treason) in that country and alarmed by the growth of socialism in Italy, the Vatican entered the Italian political fray on the moderate side, fulfilling the hope of Catholic banking and industrialist interests.

Although Catholics did not formally repudiate the *Non expedit* policy, they participated for the first time in national elections in an organized manner on the side of the government and in defense of the existing order. In the 1909 elections their participation increased, and in those of 1913, a pact by which the Catholics supported liberal candidates in return for a pledge to support the Church's position on Catholic education, religious instruction in public schools, and divorce was concluded with Count Ottorino Gentiloni, head of the Catholic organizations. When Gentiloni claimed that a majority of the Chamber had been elected under these conditions, a scandal broke out that provoked the resignation of Radical representatives from the cabinet and Giolitti's resignation.

But this situation was only the iceberg's tip. Counting on support from northern industrialists and southern landowners and electoral manipulation in the South, Giolitti had managed to stay in power from 1903 to 1913, a long stretch interrupted only by two Sonnino cabinets in 1906 and 1909, lasting three months each, and by governments headed by Alessandro Fortis and Luigi Luzzatti—stand-ins for the Piedmontese statesman. Under Socialist prodding, Giolitti moved toward quasi-universal manhood suffrage, which gave the vote to illiterate males at age twenty-one, if they had served in the army, and at age thirty if they had not. The reform strengthened both Catholics and Socialists. At the same time, Italy's maturing industrialization stimulated interest in colonies as sources of raw materials and markets, while a nascent and vocal Nationalist Association demanded colonies as an expression of national activism and prestige. The "Gentiloni Pact" represents Giolitti's attempt to accommodate the Catholics and draw upon their support in the first elections held under universal suffrage, while placating industrialists and Nationalists by undertaking the Libyan adventure.

The war signalled a defeat for Giolitti's domestic policy. Left-wing Socialists unhappy with Giolitti took over the party and expelled Leonida Bissolati, who was friendly to the prime minister. The Nationalists had advocated a heroic war and viewed Giolitti's military conduct as timid. Conservatives objected to Giolitti's leftward turn in domestic affairs, while industrialists discovered that they could not gain much from Libya and were drawn to economic penetration of the Balkans. The Gentiloni Pact alienated the Extreme Left, anticlericals, and anyone who believed that the Church should not have a privileged position in modern society. Although in 1915 Giolitti's majority in the Chamber might have served as the basis of a comeback if World War I had not erupted, his "system" seemed in shambles.

The political stabilization achieved by Giolitti until 1913 has been cited as the most important ingredient in the remarkable economic development that Italy achieved in the decade before World War I. The series of technical changes cited in the following discussion have as their premise the political advances made during the Giolittian era. According to economic historian Valerio Castronovo, Italy's industrial progress during this period "would be inconceivable without ... the maturation of new political orientations in the country. From here [one can understand] the ... centrality of the Giolittian age also for the nation's economic evolution to the extent that there occurred the most serious postunitary effort to widen the base of the bourgeois liberal state by reabsorbing, within the context of continuing national integration, the historic Catholic and Socialist oppositions."

In a political-economic sense, this process meant the liquidation in 1901 of the conservative desire for "strong governments." This crucial development had a number of important results and could not have occurred without reformist Socialist support. With the defeat of reaction, more progressive business forces bent on maximizing the economic changes then taking place came to the fore. More sympathetic to healing the fractures within Italian society, these forces supported government intervention to stimulate industry, spending for public works, social legislation, and reasonable labor demands. Both progressive bourgeoisie and reformist Socialists had their focus in the North, which brought about an unofficial but real loosening of the coalition between northern industrialists and reactionary southern landowners. The lopsided industrial development previously described continued apace as reformists consciously aided the more progressive northern bourgeoisie and neglected or misunderstood southern problems, contributing to tensions and strains within the Socialist movement. Whether within the Italian context the policy was the only or the best choice remains a matter of debate, but it contributed significantly to the country's political democratization, to its industrialization, to increased employment for workers and to better salaries, to greater unionization and to the freedom to negotiate contracts, to the diffusion of education, to the emancipation of day laborers from middlemen, and to universal suffrage. Furthermore, this "legalitarian" evolution of Italy's Socialists and their cooperation with a more liberal bourgeoisie until the Giolittian "system" fell apart coincides with a similar development in France and Germany.

It has been calculated that the percentage of net investment of Italian national income increased from 3.5 percent during 1896 to 1900, to 6.7 percent in 1901 to 1905, to 10.2 during 1906 to 1910. According to a conservative estimate, the average increase in industrial production, which had been 1.1 percent in the 1880s spurted to 4.3 percent. Manufacturing doubled in fifteen years, and from a Mediterranean backwater, Italy made its entrance into the western European industrial area.

Besides the political issues, a number of factors help explain this development. The international economic depression of the 1870s and 1880s had ended, creating an international boom in production and trade. More important, the depression and the introduction of new products, processes, and financial organization ended the industrial domination of Britain, giving greater space to the United States and Germany and, to a lesser extent, to countries such as Italy. New industries such as the electrical, chemical, and automobile sectors boomed, while radical reorganization of the credit industry by trusts, cartels, and banks contributed to this development.

In Italy the generation of hydroelectric power increased dramatically because the country had need of a source of cheap energy. In finance, the bank scandals of 1893–1894 resulted in reorganization of the banking industry and creation, for all intents and purposes, of a central bank; the Bank of Italy fostered discipline and an enormous growth of credit—essential for industrial development in old and new sectors of the economy. As previously discussed, despite its high cost for consumers and its other imperfections, the 1887 tariff spurred significant growth in the metallurgical and other industries. The mechanical, textile, automobile, and chemical industries acquired increased importance for their number of workers, capital investment, and production. Even though agriculture remained the economy's most important element and Italian industry did not reach world-class levels until World War I, the Giolittian period set the basis for that development.(See Table 12.1)

Prerequisite to this prodigious economic activity was the end of the agricultural crisis in the North after 1895. During the early twentieth-century, Lombard agriculture developed at a pace faster than at any time before and attained advanced European levels, producing more capital for investment. Energetic state activity in the economic sphere complemented this event. Increased taxes and spending cuts during the late nineteenth-century created budget surpluses that, in turn, allowed the government to stimulate the economy through spending for public works, the navy, and the merchant marine. The percentage of the budget devoted to public works went from 17.2 during 1897 to 1902 to 21 percent from 1903 to 1907 and military expenditures increased from 20.1 to 22.1 percent. In 1905 the government made another crucial contribution to economic development by resuming operation of the railways, improving service, and calming serious labor agitation in the vital transportation sector.

TABLE 12.1   Average Annual Growth Rate of Gross Domestic Product for Italy, France, Germany and the United Kingdom 1896–1913

Italy	2.8
France	1.9
Germany	3.2
United Kingdom	1.7

These economic developments made government and industrialists better able to meet the worker demands brought forward primarily by reformist Socialists. Even though Italy lagged behind the advanced industrial nations, in the north-western "industrial triangle" bounded by Milan, Turin, and Genoa, working conditions improved substantially. Unions protected workers' rights and work-ers' cooperatives competed for lucrative government contracts. In 1902, a law established a Labor Office and a Superior Council of Labor; consisting of rep-resentatives of all classes, this last institution collected statistics and proposed specific measures to alleviate working-class conditions. The Chamber also passed legislation providing for or extending old-age sickness and accident in-surance, and a measure to protect women and children from industrial hazards. Other legislation protected emigrants, aided malaria and pellagra-stricken areas of the country, promoted land reclamation, and instituted a medal honoring labor. The Chamber also responded to agitation demanding reduction of the work day and longer weekends. By 1913 most metal workers benefited from a shortened, ten-hour workday, and some worked shorter hours.

In the great northern cities and Rome, municipal administrations, with an eye to improving life for the community took over and ran essential services such as transportation and utilities. In Milan, a famous charitable institution, the Società Umanitaria, ministered to the spiritual and physical needs of the poor, and Socialists sponsored the establishment of free libraries (using the Boston Public Library as a model) and free educational programs. Progressive employ-ers interested in the welfare of their employees supported these activities, bring-ing them into frequent contact with Socialists and labor leaders with whom the owners cooperated.

All this activity brought the standard of living in the North close to that of industrialized Europe. In 1905 skilled workers with good earnings received three lire a day, and in exceptional cases five. Women earned from one lira to one and a half daily, and children less. These represented substantial wages compared with the South, where the peasant received less remuneration than either a northern industrial worker or a day laborer in the Po Valley. Between 1901 and 1914 real wages for industrial workers rose 26 percent compared to a national increase of 17 percent. In short, the struggle between the classes changed in nature during the Giolittian period because, whereas at the end of the previous century the oppressed southern peasant had been the protagonist of massive popular agitation, now "social conflict and political confrontation ... had as their epicenter the great cities and the countryside of the North, i.e., the structures of the Italian economy and capitalism which were the most ad-vanced or, at any rate, the least fragile."

Southerners shared little of this prosperity. The government did dramatize the South's plight and invested more in the region than it received from the area in taxes, but it continued to make political deals with large landowners and their supporters to ensure the government's majority in the Chamber and therefore had little incentive to alter existing social and political conditions. The government hoped that the expansive potential of northern capitalism could resolve the southern problem, and it did support sporadic industrial and agricultural projects in the area, but these attempts failed to alter conditions in the South. In fact, the gap between North and South increased in the early twentieth-century, representing a major failure of the Giolittian era. In the South, emigration accelerated and support grew for the conquest of African colonies where southern peasants might satisfy their land hunger under the Italian flag.

Even though the substantial and real legislative activity, accomplishments, and developments of the Giolittian age created "the first profile of an industrial society," many areas of the country did not participate in the progress. Southern illiteracy remained at 60 percent, elementary education was still deficient, and public spending stayed at late nineteenth-century levels. Despite his accomplishments, Giolitti missed a solid opportunity to knit the "two Italies" together.

Dilemmas of Italian Socialism

The previous sections illustrate the crucial importance that the Italian Socialist movement attained at the beginning of the twentieth-century and retained throughout the Giolittian era. The Socialist vote in favor of the Zanardelli-Giolitti cabinet in June 1901 firmly established the "liberal springtide" in the country. As if to mock the opening of a new era, however, shortly after the vote soldiers fired into a crowd of striking agricultural workers in a town near Ferrara, killing three and wounding thirty. In addition to touching off a parliamentary duel threatening the newly established cordial relations between Socialist deputies and the government, the incident made the reformists vulnerable to a violent onslaught by the Socialist revolutionary left wing.

The dispute illustrates the dilemmas faced by Italian Socialist leaders. Interclass alliances had been accepted during the 1898–1900 crisis, but whereas the revolutionaries considered them exceptions to the general rule of intransigence, Kuliscioff and Turati viewed alliances as a permanent feature of future Socialist policy. They maintained that Italy was a special case in Marxist terms. Given the country's industrial backwardness and the bourgeoisie's failure to transform the political and social structure, the Socialist party would have to assume, temporarily, the role of the democratic left and ensure the survival of democracy, socialism's prerequisite. Furthermore, in an intuition reminiscent of Eduard Bernstein's revisionism of the same period, Turati argued that the bourgeoisie was not a monolithic entity and that the Socialists could implement a policy of flexible alliances with advanced groups to win reforms for the proletariat. Turati had made this argument in Milan in 1894 and in November 1899 had identified Radical leader Ettore Sacchi and Giovanni Giolitti as national leaders with whom the Socialists could cooperate. Thus, after the crisis of 1898–1900, the reformists accentuated their alliance policy while leftist Socialists insisted it be dropped.

The contrasting positions found ideological expression in July 1901. Writing in his review *Critica Sociale,* Turati argued that the increasing industrialization of society was the basic cause of socialism, a gradual development about which parties could do very little. Socialists must spur the transformation of "the thinking, the habits, and the capacities of the proletarian masses" by training workers for political power through the gradual conquest of government institutions. Defense of basic freedoms necessary for the workers' development, in concert with liberal bourgeois groups, thus became the overriding consideration of Socialists. Political intransigence, the practical demand of the revolutionaries, meant rejecting reforms and weakening democracy; seizing power, their theoretical goal, would not advance socialism because it did not change society.

This position proved extremely difficult to sustain. If the Socialists had continued to win significantly higher wages and improved working conditions, and political and fiscal reforms, they might have resisted the onslaught of their revolutionary comrades. By late 1902, however, the vast strike movement spread to the public service industries, a development Giolitti could not sanction. Moreover, in response to higher wages, landowners brought in new machinery that cost the workers jobs. A rollback in salaries occurred and many agricultural leagues collapsed. These developments favored a new Socialist faction that challenged the reformists in their Milanese stronghold. Revolutionary syndicalism advocated an ever-escalating spiral of strikes which would culminate in a general strike mystically conceived as the "Revolution." The combination of the government's rightward drift and increased opposition within the PSI forced the Socialist deputies to withdraw their support from the Zanardelli-Giolitti government in 1903. Zanardelli's death and Giolitti's invitation to Turati to join his cabinet in the same year caught the Socialists in a quandary.

Turati's acceptance would have formally split the party, increasingly dominated by revolutionaries. Rebuffed by the left, Giolitti found support to his right, and the Socialist influence over his actions petered out. As mentioned, in 1904 a general strike exploded in response to more killings by soldiers; the strike both alienated public opinion and shattered the revolutionary syndicalist mystique. Giolitti seized the occasion to hold new elections that accelerated the entry of Catholics into national politics. The result was a significantly more conservative Chamber of Deputies. During the next several years, the reformists slowly reconquered the party, retook control of the labor movement, and founded the first national labor organization, the General Confederation of Labor (Confederazione Generale del Lavoro [CGL]). The defeated revolution-ary syndicalists abandoned the party while the traditional left wing remained in the PSI and planned a comeback. Its leaders took advantage of the reformists' inability to win spectacular political reforms while Giolitti switched allies and shifted across the political spectrum with great alacrity in his successful bid to stay in office. Though Socialists contributed to the passage of significant legis-lation, they remained seriously underrepresented because of the lack of pro-portional representation; this ensured that they would not achieve a a structural reorganization of Italian society and fueled revolutionary criticism of reformist action.

In addition to the schism between right and left wings, the reformists soon split among themselves. Historian and southern leader Gaetano Salvemini ar-gued that political corruption and the literacy requirement guaranteed that the government would always win an overwhelming number of seats in the South. When this was combined with the support which Giolitti enjoyed in the North, Socialist hopes of winning a majority in the Chamber and passing significant reforms were futile. Salvemini's solution: extending the suffrage to illiterates. Turati objected because he wished to retain the link between literacy and the vote as a means of eradicating illiteracy and because he believed that divorcing the two would benefit the Catholics. The dispute ballooned into a full-fledged war between the two reformist leaders, with Salvemini charging that a North-South split existed also in the Socialist party. Much to Salvemini's ire, Turati argued for northern economic investments and political guidance in leading the South out of its predicament. Salvemini condemned the reformists for allegedly sacrificing the South to Giolitti because they wished to protect the "workers' elites" that constituted their northern base and that received government con-tracts. In 1911 Salvemini left the party.

Besides the Salvemini-Turati argument, other cracks appeared in the reformist facade. Turati's public spat with his companion Anna Kuliscioff over immediate extension of the vote to women soon blew over, but a serious debate between Turati-Kuliscioff and their close friend Leonida Bissolati had portentous con-sequences. Bissolati wished to import the British Labour party model into Italy, according to which the PSI should deemphasize Marxist ideology and concen-trate on the immediate problems and demands of the labor movement—higher wages and better working conditions.

The two reformist factions also squabbled over escalating military expenses. European Socialists assumed that there could be no major wars in the future because workers composed the huge conscript armies—and workers would respond to their leaders' injunction to turn their guns on the officers in case of a "bourgeois" war. In 1905 Bissolati led an Italian Socialist delegation to Trieste to coordinate antiwar action with his Austrian counterparts in case of a conflict between Italy and Austria. The Italians pledged to take concrete measures to sabotage a conflict should one erupt, but the Austrians refused to make any commitments. Bissolati concluded that a war was both possible and likely. Moreover, he was concerned with the likelihood that a conflict ending in an Austro-German victory would destroy democracy in Europe. As a result, he quarreled with Turati and developed into a supporter of the government's military and diplomatic policies.

In the negotiations for his 1911 cabinet, Giolitti attempted to get Socialist support. He offered to extend the vote to illiterates, nationalize the life insurance industry, and take Bissolati into his government. Bissolati was tempted, but Turati dissuaded him from accepting the offer. Bissolati also seriously compromised the reformist image within the PSI because a war against Turkey for the conquest of Libya seemed likely. In fact, when the conflict began the same year, Bissolati did not oppose it because of his desire to strengthen the country against a future war with the Austro-Germans that he was certain would come. This made the reformists seem to support a colonial conflict despite Turati's principled stand against it. The revolutionaries had reorganized to seize control of the party and profited from popular revulsion against the war and the anger caused by a poorly organized general strike called to block the conflict. At the party's Congress of Reggio Emilia, July 1912, the left wing won a stunning victory.

Rage against the war had brought a new kind of Socialist leader to the fore—one who oversimplified issues, glorified violence, and polarized the political struggle. The Reggio Emilia congress starred Benito Mussolini, a revolutionary from the Romagna who had distinguished himself by his violent style and whose arrest because of antiwar activities had gained him national prominence. At the conclusion of a fiery antiwar speech, Mussolini successfully proposed the expulsion of Bissolati and his group for their support of the war.

Traditional revolutionaries distrusted this upstart, but Mussolini's performance thrust him into the forefront of Socialist politics and propelled him toward editorship of *Avanti!*, which he achieved in December 1912. Having failed to satisfy its base by engaging in the complex interplay of "bourgeois" parliamentary politics, the Socialist party, divided as ever, lurched toward violent confrontation with its enemies.

This change occurred just as the economic system turned down. The Libyan conflict produced credit restrictions, an interruption of Middle Eastern trade, price increases, and unemployment. Worsening economic conditions and political protest generated strikes, against which the authorities responded by firing upon the demonstrators. Mussolini utilized the Socialist party and the million members in its collateral organizations in a novel manner. He conceived of revolution as the violent overthrow of the ruling class, not political intransigence, as had traditional revolutionaries. Surviving in left-wing propaganda among the masses, this concept had been neatly sidetracked by the reformists, who had converted the party into an influential political force fighting for reforms within the system. Mussolini appealed directly to the Socialist masses through the newspaper, rather than depending on the party apparatus that opposed him.

In January 1913, at Rocca Gorga, a conflict between the police and demonstrators left seven dead and ignited a violent campaign by Mussolini's *Avanti!* against "proletarian massacres." Using language that foreshadowed that of the terrorists of the 1970s, Mussolini labeled the killings "state assassinations" and accused the government of "massacre politics." He advocated general strikes and claimed for the proletariat an innate right to revolt, to employ violence freely, and to kill anyone who murdered workers.

The reformists found themselves unable to dislodge Mussolini, who forced them to fight on emotional issues that negated their rational approach, their prestige, and their close links with organized labor. Neither the reformists nor Mussolini's traditional-leftist opponents could take effective action against him because Mussolini's demagogic approach achieved the powerful support of the party rank-and-file and of the masses, both of which considered him the premier Italian revolutionary personage. Indeed, at the next congress, Ancona, 1914, Mussolini strengthened himself primarily at the expense of his left wing antagonists. After that assembly, *Avanti!* wrote that Italian socialism had become "ever more class and ever less democracy." Mussolini remained consistent in proclaiming his disdain for democracy, the primary reformist concern.

In searching for deeply felt issues capable of galvanizing the masses, Mussolini assigned an extremely prominent role to antimilitarism. Military expenses had long drained the treasury, thus blocking reform, while the army aroused great hostility because it was the primary internal peacekeeper (a modern police force did not come into existence until after World War I when *Il Duce* created it). In 1914 *Avanti!* initiated a vigorous campaign against the army. In Ancona, a city in Emilia-Romagna, local Socialists, Republicans, and Anarchists mounted a strong protest over two soldiers who had been disciplined for political reasons. The authorities responded by prohibiting public meetings. A clash between soldiers and demonstrators left three dead and five wounded. The signal for "Red Week"—June 7–14, 1914—had been given.

Mussolini's *Avanti!* headlined "WORKERS OF ITALY, STRIKE!" The Socialist Directorate and the CGL duly agreed. Accustomed to strikes and violence, the nation did not at first comprehend the changed situation. In some areas, the strike followed a normal course, but in the Romagna it assumed an insurrectionary character. Socialists, Republicans, and Anarchists dropped their differences and organized action committees. All over the region, strikers attacked troops, invaded gun shops, sacked churches and government offices, and burned trains in the stations. Revolutionaries on bicycles and motorcycles linked rebel strongholds. A revolutionary roadblock netted a general on inspection who was forced to surrender his sword to the revolution. Strikers occupied sensitive points with military precision, raised barricades and roadblocks, isolated cities, and sealed off the region from the rest of the country.

Giolitti had been replaced in office by Antonio Salandra, a member of the Right. He denounced Red Week as a "criminal conspiracy," even though the movement clearly lacked planning and surprised the national working-class leaders. The railway workers, crucial elements in any revolutionary design, remained aloof, and CGL leaders called a halt to the strike, prompting Mussolini's denunciation. The army encountered little resistance when it moved into the Romagna to reestablish control. Mussolini exalted the strike's effectiveness but soon recognized reality. He admitted that the CGL had been correct in calling off the action because the insurrection had been doomed from the beginning. Salandra stated that the disorders had lasted as long as they had only because the government wished to avoid bloodshed and moved with extreme prudence.

In fact, the masses had surprised their own leaders, none of whom had come to terms with the concrete possibility of a revolution. No plan of action existed because the revolutionaries had not believed that the masses would revolt. As Mussolini realized that revolution was not imminent, he demanded ideological changes to work out the details of future revolutionary action. Even before Red Week, Mussolini had argued that the revolution needed the support of at least part of the army to succeed, a lesson he implemented during his later Fascist period. Red Week nevertheless revealed the masses' profoundly revolutionary mentality. "Italy needs a revolution," Mussolini wrote in his review *Utopia*, "and will have it." What kind of revolution would it be, he asked? Incredibly he answered: "It doesn't matter. Every political revolution, Karl Marx said, is also a social revolution." From then on, revolution in itself became the ultimate goal, and its objective receded into the background. Above all, revolutionaries must prepare for revolution. Revolutionary method had become paramount, and Mussolini worked to renew and strengthen the accords with the other revolutionary groups that had risen spontaneously during Red Week.

Thus Mussolini reduced revolution to a power struggle that the masses could win if they were united, organized, armed, and ruthless. Immediately after Red Week, he planned to strengthen the unity of groups dedicated to revolutionary action, but in August 1914, World War I erupted and completely altered the situation. Republicans and revolutionary syndicalists believed that the conflict would provoke a revolution and championed Italian intervention in the war, but the Socialist masses' deeply rooted pacifism forced Mussolini to adopt a neutralist course. Challenged by his revolutionary syndicalist friends to change his position in light of events, Mussolini recognized the war's revolutionary potential and switched to interventionism as the fastest means of achieving revolution.

In an emotionally charged gathering in Milan on November 24, 1914, the PSI expelled him, but the party and its aims had become irrelevant. Red Week had rooted in Mussolini and in influential Italian intellectuals the desire for action at any cost, the triumph of activism over ideology, the glorification of violence, the compulsion to greet revolution at any moment, the constant state of tension typical of revolutionary foot soldiers, the cynical use of ideology, ideological confusion, and a propensity for demagogy. The Giolittian Era's beginning had signalled a new political civility, but its twilight witnessed the metamorphosis of the debates among Socialists into fratricidal warfare.

"Minister of the Underworld" or "Italian Democracy in the Making"?

Once a neglected area of study, the historical interpretation of the Giolittian period increased in importance after establishment of the Fascist dictatorship in Italy (1922–1926). Seeking to bolster their regime, the Fascists argued that pre-Fascist Italy, exemplified by Giolitti, had done nothing to develop the country. This charge brought an immediate response from philsopher-historian Benedetto Croce who in his 1928 *History of Italy from 1871 to 1915* sought to demonstrate the progress made by the nation.

In their attacks on Giolitti, the Fascists utilized the many criticisms made by Giolitti's opponents during his long tenure. The most famous of these came in 1910, Gaetano Salvemini's *Il ministro della mala vita (The Minister of the Underworld)*. Salvemini condemned Giolitti because his "control" of southern elections ensured him a majority in the Chamber. Salvemini's pamphlet vividly described the stuffing of ballot boxes, the cooperation between police and criminals, and the terrorizing of political opponents undertaken during Giolitti's tenure. These tactics, Salvemini wrote, resulted in the South's returning 150 of Giolitti's 250 staunch parliamentary supporters. Giolitti refrained from using these methods in the North because the larger number of voters there made such techniques more difficult to apply than in the South, where the literacy requirement excluded most people from voting and where a change of a few hundred ballots could decide an election. Salvemini's remedy for the problem was to extend universal suffrage to the South.

Despite its appearance as part of the battle for universal suffrage, Salvemini's "Minister of the Underworld" epithet stuck. In historical memory, Giolitti's accomplishments receded and the unsavory methods described by Salvemini were remembered.

After the Fascist victory in Italy, Salvemini went into exile. He became a professor at Harvard University after spending time in France and England. In 1943 a young scholar, A. William Salomone, completed a manuscript on Giolittian Italy and asked Salvemini to comment. Salomone subtitled the work "Italian Democracy in the Making" and argued that "whatever the defects and limitations of his methods, Giolitti had represented a constructive moment in the development of pre-1914 Italy toward a genuine liberalization of the Italian national structure and conscience." The book contradicted Salvemini's well-known ideas and may have been expected to bring a violent reaction from him.

Two years later the book appeared sporting a surprising "Introductory Essay" written by Salvemini. In the essay, Salvemini accepted the author's conclusions. Allowing the imperfections of the Piedmontese statesman, Salvemini admitted that his experiences in foreign countries and with the regime that followed Giolitti had caused him to reassess his previous views. In comparing Giolitti with American and British politicians, he dismissed the charge that Giolitti had been a "dictator." He wrote: "My knowledge of the men who came after Giolitti in Italy as well as of countries in which I have lived during the last twenty years has convinced me that if Giolitti was not better, neither was he worse than many non-Italian politicians, and he was certainly less reprehensible than the Italian politicians who followed him. For while we Italian crusaders attacked him from the Left accusing him of being—and he was—a corrupter of Italian democracy in the making, others assailed him from the Right because he was even too democratic for their taste. Our criticism thus did not help to direct the evolution of Italian public life toward less imperfect forms of democracy, but rather toward the victory of those militarist, nationalist, and reactionary groups who had found even Giolitti's democracy too perfect."

Stung by rosy interpretations of Giolitti inspired by his so-called "recantation," Salvemini altered his vision of the Piedmontese statesman and described him as a "corrupter" of "Italian democracy in the making." Later historians such as Alberto Aquarone have attempted a more neutral assessment by delving into the details of Giolitti's policies, by seeking a more balanced view of his long tenure, and by examining the workings of Italian society of the time. To some extent these historians have reduced the passions that the calm and collected Giolitti stirred, and the historical debate seems to have settled somewhere between the two extremes.

PART FIVE

War and Fascism

13

The Culture of the New Italy

As already indicated, Italy after unification felt the influence of Europe more strongly. No longer obsessed by the fight for freedom and now masters of their own fate, the Italians created an economic infrastructure intimately linking the peninsula to the rest of Europe. In the North, this development stimulated industrialization and social conditions closely resembling the more-advanced European countries. In the cultural arena, the free circulation of ideas allowed the country's thinkers to participate vigorously in the constructive and the destructive intellectual currents of the age. In the South, industry did not develop to the degree it did in the North, but southern intellectuals had a notable role in cultural affairs. As might be expected, the intermixture of modern and ancient, a continuation of old traditions and the introduction of new trends characterized Italian society and thought during the late nineteenth and early twentieth centuries.

Private Lives

Before the 1848 revolutions, Italian family life was provincial, formal, and static. Children addressed their parents in the polite form (*Lei*). Parents decided which trade or profession their children would pursue and negotiations between families determined marriage partners. Girls typically married at sixteen, and boys were in danger of being drafted at nineteen. Young middle-class couples spent their marriage night not on a honeymoon but in the house of the bride's family. These generally large houses usually had a room with a double bed reserved for the bride and groom, an area that would later serve as their children's birthplace. On the morning following the wedding night, the relatives congregated to congratulate the newlyweds and bring gifts such as chocolate or snuffboxes. Poorer households usually lived together in one large room but sometimes had a bedroom that parents and children shared.

Families living together generally consisted of parents, children, grandchildren, and unmarried sisters. Women usually gave birth to eight or ten children. The father ran the household like a patriarch with complete authority over the family, but his wife had a great deal of unofficial influence.

The mid-nineteenth-century structures that housed these families lacked modern comforts. The fireplace predominated in the kitchen, a beautiful room lined by a great number of pots and pans, many made of gleaming copper. No running water existed, not even supplied by a pump, and water had to be drawn from wells with a pail. Some buildings had primitive bathrooms consisting of a hole that led to a cesspool, usually one toilet every three floors. Specially designed chairs supplemented the bathrooms. The furniture was varied and generally lasted a lifetime. Interestingly enough, households owned recently built ornate furniture, but, often, beautiful antique Renaissance pieces might be mixed in with the middle- or lower-class household's possessions. Since laundry had to be handwashed in public fountains, household furniture included huge closets to hold the large number of linens, which allowed women to delay washing as long as possible.

The inhabitants of these houses found it difficult to get comfortable. Although romantic, fireplaces produced insufficient warmth. Before 1856, paper lit by an oil lamp served to light the fire, but after then matches came into use. Since they were very expensive, the father kept them under lock and key; when he was ready to use them the children would gather round to enjoy the spectacle. To heat their hands, women used *scaldini*, commonly called "husbands"—terra cotta or copper vases containing lighted charcoal. Charcoal also filled braziers that the gathered family placed under tables. Before retiring, family members used special kinds of braziers, called "priests," to heat cold beds.

Women worked a hard and domestic life. They spent long hours in the kitchen where they cooked three- and four-course meals for eighteen or twenty, not counting children. They prepared the sauces, the bread, the preserves, and the liquors. Frequently they even made the soap. Families frequently possessed large numbers of homemade bed, kitchen, and personal items, making it possible to do the laundry only once every three months. Although middle-class families had maids to help them, all women ironed, sewed, and folded. Before the invention of irons in which lighted coals could be inserted, these instruments had to be heated in a fire while ironing. Hoop skirts and related paraphernalia might take a full day to iron. At night the women gathered around the light of an oil lamp till midnight to "relax"—talking, sewing, or knitting clothes for the children or for a trousseau. Women would continue this activity during pregnancy and nursing of children, which generally continued up to age one.

Generally women went out only on Sundays, when they dressed as elegantly as possible. On rare occasions, and only when accompanied, they went for a walk or shopped. Stores, which were long, narrow warehouses, had no display windows. Middle-class women still wore hoop skirts, crinoline, ribbons, lace, and hats. Fur coats had not yet been widely imported from northern Europe, so mantles served as protection against the cold. Fashion for men dictated tight suits, long tails, light-colored pants, striped vests, starched collars, big ties, and either a felt hat or a tophat. Beards and sideburns were de rigeur, and around 1880 waxed moustaches became popular.

Before midcentury, middle-class males seldom led a more exciting life than their female counterparts. Their usually authoritarian fathers might send them away to boarding school at age seven or eight. When male offspring were at the university, to avoid spoiling them, fathers would not give them generous allowances. The father of a young male would typically arrange a marriage for his son, without consultation, and keep him economically dependent as long as possible. Males also engaged in little or no physical activity, except fencing; this was an essential skill because the typical university student would fight several duels before he graduated. If he entered politics, continued practice would stand him in good stead. Dashing Radical leader Felice Cavallotti dueled routinely, dying in an 1898 encounter, and Turati and Socialist leader Claudio Treves as well as Mussolini faced challenges.

The wars of the Risorgimento, 1848 to 1870, brought changes in the social situation. Fired by the fight for independence, many young men and women ran off to join the struggle, frequently ending in exile. Their participation in the cause exposed them to new countries, conditions, and attitudes. This altered mentality, combined with improving economic conditions in the 1860s, 1870s, and especially the 1890s, spurred many couples to move out on their own and caused extended families to break up.

Salaries were still low, but so were expenses. In 1869 a typical professional such as a university professor earned 2,000 lire a year (a lira was about 20 cents). A four-room apartment plus kitchen cost 200 to 300 lire a year. At that salary maids were affordable; mostly peasant women who preferred this form of work to the heavy labor in the fields, maids earned 3 to 4 lire a month. Middle-class women still had many children, but this cheap labor supply enabled them to go out more often. Newly installed street lighting (gas illumination at midcentury, electric lighting later) made evening excursions safer, and the increased number of coffeehouses and the introduction of lower-priced theater seats made them more pleasant. In Milan, the city government subsidized its famous La Scala opera house, making performances more affordable. Couples customarily took a stroll (*passegiata*), exploiting the nightly occasion to comment on the outfits other people wore and to gawk at the rich returning from the races. Afterward, a couple could rent a chair (four *centesimi* or cents) to sit in the piazza, buy a sherbet (one cent) or ice cream from the carts (two or four cents), and enjoy the free band music supplied by the municipality. In Bologna, with the change from a ten-cent piece, one could buy a newspaper for two cents (*Il Resto del Carlino*—"the change from the dime"—still publishing).

Under the circumstances, the common people mingled with the day's famous personalities more often than today. In Rome, philosopher Antonio Labriola gave impromptu harangues on Marxist philosophy at the Caffè Aragno. Prime Minister Giovanni Giolitti strolled to his office past the train station escorted only by his friends and engaging in lively conversation. In Milan, Socialist leaders planned their moves in popular restaurants and shops where they gathered with workers to drink wine and discuss politics. A lowly factory worker could show up at a local party meeting and argue policy with the most famous chieftain—and did. On the midnight trams, Turati and Kuliscioff rode home, hand in hand, after those meetings or a rally. A citizen wishing to ensure that his or her letter reached Rome the next morning would deposit it in a mailbox carried by the same tram. In the city's "parlor," the *Galleria*, politicians animatedly discussed pressing issues. A few steps away under the portico at Number 23, the "Signora" of Italian socialism, Anna Kuliscioff, sat on a green couch before a magnificent window overlooking the *Duomo* and presided over the country's most famous salon. To attend Kuliscioff's salon, Benito Mussolini, newcomer to Milan, had to walk only a short distance from his lodgings in the shadow of the Sforza Castle, but his rejection there rankled him for the rest of his life. On his visits to Naples, Gabriele D'Annunzio frequented the same *pizzerie* as the common folk. The poet appeared in the company of the most famous journalist couple of the day, Matilde Serao and Edoardo Scarfoglio, soon the object of popular curiosity owing to their clamorous breakup. Contemporaries report D'Annunzio as always elegant, his outfit complemented by a fashionable straw hat, canary yellow gloves, a walking stick made from precious wood, and a fresh flower in his buttonhole. The royal family also enjoyed the city's most famous dish. In 1889, on royal stationery, Queen Margherita wrote to pizza maker Raffaele Esposito that "the three kinds of pizza which you made for His Majesty were found to be excellent." The Queen herself especially appreciated the kind with tomatoes, mozzarella, and basil, which Esposito personally created for her and that is still served as "pizza margherita."

During the same period, the increasing ease of travel within and outside cities sweetened life. Electric trams replaced horse-drawn ones and ran to the suburbs, where one could get away for the weekend. In 1885 there were as yet no fixed stops and trams would wait patiently for passengers who had hailed them from their windows. Still, the need for independent travel stimulated the bicycle's development from a crude to a comfortable instrument. With the application of rubber wheels and other innovations, this vehicle evolved into the major means of private transportation before diffusion of the automobile. For long-distance travel, nothing could beat the railway, with its reduced fares for special occasions, smoking and nonsmoking compartments, compartments for women only, and good food. The construction of a railway network and the improving economy enabled the middle class, especially mothers and children, to take summer vacations. During the same period, the cult for sports invaded Italy from England. People engaged in swimming and canoeing and, spurred by the example of famous finance minister Quintino Sella, mountain climbing.

Other inventions had a great impact as the new century opened. In the North, new houses featured central heating, flush toilets, and, sometimes, elevators. A telephone network fostered efficient communication and, along with it, police wiretapping. Economical stoves using a variety of fuels, the vacuum cleaner, the icebox, and the electric iron all appeared. Frozen meat arriving from Argentina and exotic fruits such as bananas, coconuts, dates, and pineapples reached the market, stimulating dietary variety. The typewriter came from the United States, making it easier for women to get jobs outside the home.

By the 1890s the position of women underwent important changes. In the North they went out alone to shop in modern stores featuring display windows and ready-to-wear merchandise. They also enjoyed their own magazines. By 1900 "hundreds" had earned university degrees in the same fields as men, including medicine. Fashion reflected this newfound mobility as skirts shortened, up to the ankle, and clothes became more practical for both sexes. Many practical obstacles still hindered the professional life of women, and most remained geared to the family; but women rebelled against chaperones, objected to arranged marriages, married much later, practiced birth control, and had fewer children.

Despite this real progress, however, women still suffered from an inferior economic, legal, and social status. They were denied the vote, despite the existence of a radical feminist movement and of women's associations of various political shades. (In 1909–1910, Turati and Kuliscioff quarrelled publicly over whether the Socialist party should demand the vote for women.) Courts annulled marriages in which the bridegroom discovered that his bride was not a virgin. Only women could be punished for adultery—a legal provision that lasted until after World War II. Women needed their husband's permission to open a bank account or administer their property. Socialists, Radicals, and some Liberals (Zanardelli) supported divorce, but bills which would have instituted divorce were regularly defeated by politicians, who argued that divorce would destabilize society, and by the Church, acting in concert. As late as 1913 a female law professor at the University of Rome was denied admission to the Bar. During the early twentieth century, the main choices for an occupation open to women were becoming schoolteachers or telephone operators. Working conditions in the elementary and secondary schools were so bad that Gaetano Salvemini felt compelled to take the leadership for improvement of the schoolteachers' lot, and the telephone operators' plight served as the subject of one of Matilde Serao's most famous novels.

As might be expected, changes came more slowly in the South. In 1905 in Sardinia, for example, men and women staying together at a hotel—even if married—still gave scandal. In parts of the South, men had to do the shopping because people frowned at women leaving the house alone. But despite uneven progress, Italian life generally improved during the early twentieth Century, even for the poor. Age-old diseases such as pellagra and malaria diminished and wealth increased. Along with the rest of Europe, Italy lived the "Belle Époque"—the continent's last self-confident moment.

Arts and Sciences

Although modern trends in society entered Italy with a vengeance during this period, traditional values continued in the arts. The peninsula's different dialects had developed a robust literature which continued to be produced, read, and performed. The most startling and recent examples of this rich legacy are the Neapolitan plays of Edoardo De Filippo, which achieved international prominence after World War II. The same might be said of folk or regional music, a rich source of social and religious commentary, which also had an important development during this period.

Since Italian opera continued to dominate Europe, it is not surprising that the art form attracted the most talented musicians. Of the four great nineteenth-century composers, Vincenzo Bellini and Gaetano Donizetti died before unification. Gioacchino Rossini, best known for his brilliant and iconoclastic *Barber of Seville* and his patriotic *William Tell*, had stopped writing and had dedicated himself to cooking. Giuseppe Verdi had fully participated in the patriotic cause by his actions and his music; besides the previously mentioned *Nabucco*, *The Battle of Legnano* told about the victory of Italian city-states over the German Holy Roman Emperor Frederick Barbarossa in 1176, while *Rigoletto* ridiculed the aristocracy to such a degree that Austrian censors intervened. After unification, however, Verdi wrote his three greatest works, *Aida*, *Otello*, and *Falstaff; Aida* was still concerned with patriotic themes, whereas the last two, based on Shakespearian plays, helped import the German "music drama" into Italy. Appointed a life senator, Verdi died in 1901.

Verdi's refinement of the music drama illustrates the vitality of opera composition in Italy. Arrigo Boito served as the vocal champion of this music form through his activities and through a brilliant concrete example, *Mefistofele*. Boito quarreled with Verdi over the music drama question, but later collaborated with him as the librettist for Verdi's last two operas. Boito also wrote the libretto for Amilcare Ponchielli's *La Gioconda*, which remains an extremely popular work thanks to such music as the "dance of the hours," used in Walt Disney's *Fantasia*. The dire suffering of Ponchielli's heroine seemed to signal a trend in opera as it incorporated a concern with social problems, known as realism in France and *verismo* in its Italian version. Pietro Mascagni appropriated *Cavalleria Rusticana*, a work of the most famous practitioner of this art, Giovanni Verga, and turned it into an operatic masterpiece, while Ruggiero Leoncavallo produced *I Pagliacci*, another tragic story of everyday people. The most famous opera composer after Verdi, however, was Giacomo Puccini, who, like Verdi, made both successful music and business. Puccini continued the "realistic" trend in such works as *La Bohème* and *Madama Butterfly* but also ranged into the historical and the fantastic with *Tosca* and *Turandot*. Presented posthumously at La Scala in 1926, this last opera illustrates Puccini's incorporation of "modern music" into his work.

Although operatic music dominated the Italian scene, the late nineteenth and early twentieth centuries also produced greater interest in symphonic music. Important societies and reviews promoted this art form, and by the 1880s the major cities had symphonic orchestras. This activity produced important conductors such as Giuseppe Martucci and Ottorino Respighi, perhaps the country's most famous symphonic composer. In addition, Ferruccio Busoni pioneered polyphonic music and has been called the first modern composer.

Literature during this period seemed especially attuned to modern concerns. In the 1870s in Milan, a movement of Bohemian writers, poets, and artists known as the *scapigliatura* favored the importation of trends important in other countries. Perhaps because of the Church's role in contrasting unification, Pius IX's condemnation of modern civilization in the *Syllabus of Errors*, and the Vatican's continued opposition to the Italian state, writers seemed preoccupied with antireligious themes. The country's best poet, Nobel Prize winner Giosuè Carducci, scandalized Italy with his *Inno a Satana (Hymn to Satan)*, an attack on the Church at a time when it opposed unification. His reputation rests on such works as *Odi Barbare* and *Rime Nuove*. After the death of this "poetic dictator," a "Triumvirate" dominated the Italian poetic world: Antonio Fogazzaro, Gabriele D'Annunzio, and Giovanni Pascoli. The poetry of the first two is still read, but their reputations rest on their novels and plays. Pascoli's best work makes the point that the poet has a special sensibility and understands life better than the philosopher or the scientist. The nation's most famous woman poet, Ada Negri, was influenced by the Socialist atmosphere of Milan and wrote poetry calling for social justice for the proletariat.

A new movement called futurism influenced poetry, although it had a more profound effect on painting and sculpture. Determined to bring Italian culture into the industrial age affecting Italian society, the Futurists glorified technology, hailed speed, and designed modernistic cities. They were especially taken with fast cars and composed hymns to coal and electricity. Founding father poet Filippo Tommaso Marinetti was the best-known spokesman for this iconoclastic movement. The Futurist manifesto, first published in Paris in 1909, declared that futurism was anti-everything and believed only in violence because energy and dynamism were born out of struggle, a principle that led them to favor war: "We want to glorify war," their manifesto said, "sole hygiene of the world." They demanded a "cynical, astute, and aggressive" foreign policy. They called for the rejuvenation of Italy by destroying its values and traditions, its monuments, its museums, and its libraries. Their "futurist evenings," which usually degenerated into chaos and fistfights, have remained famous.

The Futurist penchant for dangerous living, modernity, and violence made them precursors of the later Fascists. Writer Piero Gobetti believed that fascism was no more than "social continuation" of futurism. The Futurists were the Italian version of destructive artistic and intellectual forces sweeping Europe during the early twentieth century and had a major impact on Italian cultural life through their publications and the journal *Lacerba* (1913). They produced echoes as far away as Russia.

At the opposite pole from the Futurists were the "crepuscolari," best represented by Guido Gozzano. This school took its name from the Italian word for "twilight" because they believed the world to be at an end. Tired and pessimistic, these poets pictured life in somber tones. Instead of fading out, however, Italian poetry renewed itself in a remarkable burst of new life. The years between 1880 and 1901 witnessed the birth of four poets whose work during and after World War I would be hailed by critics as among the best in the world: Giuseppe Ungaretti, Umberto Saba, Eugenio Montale, and Salvatore Quasimodo.

Besides poetry, the Italian novel also underwent a profound period of renewal after unification. Influenced by French realism and English positivism, novelists in the 1870s and 1880s attempted to portray life as it really was; they concentrated on small areas and described the life of ordinary people in every detail.

Verismo or the social novel counted several distinguished practitioners. These included Luigi Capuana, a Sicilian who wrote about theory and produced a splendid example in his *Marchese di Roccaverdina*. Another Sicilian, Giovanni

Verga, produced this school's best novels. *I Malavoglia* and *Mastro-Don Ges-ualdo* are magnificent descriptions of social conditions in Sicily. The novels of the country's first important woman journalist, Matilde Serao, also provide an excellent social history of the time. She applied her journalistic talents to describing the life and foibles of the people—from gambling to the plight of early telephone operators, from political corruption to the miserable life of a nun no longer sheltered by the convent. One of her most famous books, *Il ventre di Napoli*, describes the life of Neapolitan poor during the cholera epidemic of 1883. According to persistent rumors, her last, anti-fascist, novel provoked Mussolini to veto her nomination for the Nobel Prize. Another woman did win the Nobel Prize. Grazia Deledda's novels are also concerned with social conditions, particularly in her native Sardinia. Counterpointing these women, Emilio De Marchi has remained famous for his description of Milanese life. His masterpiece, *Demetrio Pianelli*, graphically examines the exploitation of public workers.

Antonio Fogazzaro, previously mentioned as a poet, has remained famous for *Piccolo mondo antico*, whose action takes place during the Risorgimento, and *Piccolo mondo moderno*. His most controversial novel, *Il Santo*, supported the religious reform movement known as modernism, later condemned by Pope Pius X, and was placed on the Index. Gabriele D'Annunzio, also a poet and playwright, found fame as a writer of sensuous and decadent novels, such as *Il Piacere* and *Il trionfo della morte*. In addition to his writings, his private and political life electrified Italy and Europe.

As the nineteenth century closed, the psychological novel made its entrance, culminating in the work of Italo Svevo. *Senilità* (1898) was a novel so far ahead of its time that critical condemnation caused the author to quit writing. Later, encouraged by James Joyce, who taught English in Trieste, Svevo produced a second masterpiece, *The Conscience of Zeno*.

Another important genre during this period was the children's novel. The most famous novels in this tradition are Carlo Collodi's *Le avventure di Pinocchio* and *Cuore*, Edmondo De Amicis's story about schoolchildren.

In the drama field, D'Annunzio treated the most sensational topics, but the best dramatist was Luigi Pirandello, winner of a Nobel prize. Married to a woman who suffered from psychological disorders, his pessimistic plays investigate the question, What is reality? His most famous plays are still performed in many languages—*Six Characters in Search of an Author*, *Henry IV*, and *Right You Are, If You Think You Are*.

Literary trends also provide a clue to the philosophical concerns of the age. In the 1880s English positivism dominated Italian philosophical circles, greatly influencing young students who later became the leaders of Italian socialism. During the 1890s German philosophy, especially Hegelianism, became more important. In Naples, Benedetto Croce made the country a leading center of Hegelian philosophy. A leading philosopher and historian of his time, Croce's influence was felt throughout the Western world. In Italy he dominated Italian culture to such an extent that Italian thinkers have been revolting against him ever since.

Two areas once the province of Italian artists seemed to languish during this period. Antonio Canova, the last European-class sculptor, died in 1821. The best sculptors between unification and the 1890s were the Neapolitan Vincenzo Gemito and Medardo Rosso, the latter known particularly for his innovative impressionist style. The country did not produce first-class sculptors such as Marino Marini and Giacomo Manzù until the 1920s.

Immediately following unification, a school called the "Macchiaoli" (from "macchia," spot, a technique that employed patches of color) dominated Italian painting. Concerned with picturing the world as it really was, critics consider these painters interesting rather than important, although the best representatives, such as Giovanni Fattori, have recently enjoyed a revival. At the same time, the "Posillipo school" flourished in Naples, and Ferrara produced a great portraitist in Giovanni Boldini, noted for his painting of Verdi but who achieved his greatest fame in Paris.

Futurism had its greatest impact on painting between 1900 and 1914. Affected by the accelerating industrialization of society, Futurist painters were concerned with speed and energy and attempted to portray their concrete "decomposition" on canvas. Some of the most important Italian painters of this school produced works that had an impact on European painting. Giacomo Balla, an older painter, inspired the Futurists and showed the way. The best Futurist painters include Umberto Boccioni, whose devotion to action got him killed in World War I, Carlo Carrà, and Gino Severini. The works of this school are amply represented in the Museum of Modern Art in New York, but the most brilliant paintings are to be found in Milan's Villa Palestro.

Futurism had a major impact on Italian artists before and after World War I, although it is difficult to group them into "schools." Carrà, for example, later became a prime exponent of "metaphysical" painting along with Giorgio De Chirico. The list of avant-garde painters affected in different ways by futurist principles and techniques includes Amedeo Modigliani, Giorgio Morandi, Ottone Rosai, Filippo De Pisis, Mario Sironi, Scipione (a pseudonym for Gino Bonichi), and Massimo Campigli.

The period before World War I witnessed the beginning of a new art form influenced by scientific developments: motion pictures. With the French and Americans, Italians pioneered in this new endeavor. In 1896 the first documentary appeared for which admission was charged. These early films experimented with methods that went beyond still photography, which characterized early cinematic development. Italians produced different types of film genre, but the most popular and profitable were historical and costume dramas. In 1905 Vittorio Calcina produced *The Conquest of Rome,* which portrayed the Risorgimento's last episode. The most famous of these historical epics, however, were Mario Caserini's *The Last Days of Pompeii* (1913), Enrico Guazzoni's *Quo Vadis?,* and Giovanni Pastrone's *Cabiria* (1914). Memorable for its enormous cost of one million lire and for D'Annunzio's collaboration, the extravaganza *Cabiria* remained unsurpassed during the silent film era for its historical accuracy and craftsmanship. To give a sense of wide space and to move from long to short shots, Pastrone invented the dolly, which became fundamental for modern filmmaking. His lighting opened a new era, and his hand coloring of scenes gave the effect of a color motion picture. As might be expected, the Futurists also produced a manifesto on film and made actual movies.

Concentrated in Rome and Turin, the film industry formed a major production company in 1906 that briefly brought Italy domination of the world market. Film historian Pierre Lephrohon has called the years between 1909 and 1916 Italy's "golden age" with respect to the cinema. The film industry declined in the 1920s, primarily because of American competition, but would enjoy an artistic renaissance following World War II.

Besides the arts, the activity in the sciences was also notable. The peninsula had lost the preeminent position it had held during the seventeenth century as the cradle of the scientific revolution, but it maintained an important position in science. Mathematicians made important contributions to their field, but carrying on the tradition of Galileo and Alessandro Volta, Italian physicists excelled. Volta, who died in 1823, concentrated on the practical applications of electromagnetism—along with classical mechanics, the pillar of pre-twentieth century physics—inventing the "voltaic pile." Antonio Pacinotti also investigated electromagnetism and the application of electricity to motors. Besides Pacinotti's research on continuous current, Galileo Ferraris contributed to the understanding of alternating current. In a related field, Augusto Righi's work on electromagnetic waves stimulated the research of Guglielmo Marconi, who shared a Nobel Prize in 1909 for his accomplishments in the field of "wireless telegraphy." Marconi had successfully sent the world's first wireless transmission at Sasso Marconi, near Bologna. In the 1920s Marconi experimented with short waves, successfully sending radio signals over vast distances and linking the entire world together. In the culmination of the work on electromagnetism begun by Volta, Marconi made fundamental contributions that had great practical and theoretical significance for modern applications such as radar.

Biology as well was an active field for inquiry on the peninsula. Carlo Matteucci's research on the connection between electrical and biological phenomena proved important for the later invention of such diagnostic tools as the electrocardiogram and the electroencephalogram. At the same time, biologists conducted studies contributing to the understanding of the agents that caused deadly diseases such as pneumonia, meningitis, syphilis, malaria, and African sleeping sickness.

Political Culture

In addition to the arts and physical sciences, social sciences such as sociology received wide attention. This interest had its greatest impact on rightist intellectuals who did not enjoy a wide following. Nevertheless, these intellectuals propagated ideas that had important political effects in Italy and Europe before and after World War I and on modern political and social concepts.

The failure of great expectations of a "Third Rome," aroused during the Risorgimento, seems to be at the root of this rightist political culture. Undeterred by the realities facing the newly unified nation, intellectuals denounced the inability of their leaders to create another ancient Rome or Renaissance Italy. The death of Victor Emmanuel II and the monarchy's declining prestige under his son Humbert I quickly inspired acid criticism of Italy's "unheroic" status and touched off, in Richard Drake's felicitous phrase, "the politics of nostalgia."

Poet, dramatist, novelist, great lover, and European celebrity, Gabriele D'Annunzio symbolized these restless intellectuals' desire to perform great deeds. Crashing upon the literary scene at age sixteen, abandoning the right for the left in the Chamber during the parliamentary crisis of 1898, proclaiming "I go toward life!," hero of the army, navy, and air force during World War I, a Fascist precursor afterward, D'Annunzio moved in the tradition of a European school that drew strength from the mystical, irrational, and unexplainable sources of life. Consequently, in his art he attempted no elevation of human dignity or deep analysis of moral values. Only pure power and a love of action at any cost stimulated him. "D'Annunzio declaimed upon the beauty of fire and destruction, the voluptuous attractions of power and glory, he sang of the Nietzschian superman," A. William Salomone has written. A line from D'Annunzio's 1908 play, *La Nave*, succinctly epitomizes his philosophy: "Arm the prow and set sail toward the world!"

Socialism could only briefly attract D'Annunzio and other writers drunk with the desire for violence. They resented the patient work advocated by the party's reformist leaders but, above all, hated Giovanni Giolitti, the prosaic leader who understood that the country could not be immediately transformed by bombast and who blocked the ascent of brilliant intellectuals to the power they craved. D'Annunzio and his friends prodded the country to act heroically to take its rightful place among the great powers not only in name but in deed. In condemning the Italian government, these intellectuals denounced the parliamentary system, the source of Giolitti's power. From Sonnino's influential 1897 article "Let's Return to the Constitution" and before, there had been a long tradition of parliamentary criticism in Italy. In the late nineteenth and early twentieth centuries, sociologists Gaetano Mosca, Vilfredo Pareto, and Robert Michels (a German Socialist influenced by Italian politics, who taught at Turin and later turned to the right) modernized these beliefs. No matter what the political system, they wrote, the organized minority—the political class or "elite"—always rules over the disorganized majority. Regardless of the scientific value of their studies or their own views, extreme rightists incorporated these sociologists into their ideologies first to delegitimize the parliamentary regime and, after World War I, to justify the wielding of power by Fascists who considered their minority status a badge of pride.

Action at any cost, delegitimization of the liberal regime as a national representative, and justification of elites—these were the elements that underpinned the Italian nationalism of the early twentieth century, a movement radically different from the one that had produced unification. Influenced by these currents, Enrico Corradini, Giuseppe Prezzolini, and Giovanni Papini established the influential review *Il Regno* (1903–1905), dedicated to fighting Giolitti, democracy, socialism, liberalism, and pacifism and to reestablishing authority. They glorified war, power, and imperialism as ends in themselves.

In 1908 Prezzolini and Papini modified their ideas in a new journal, *La Voce*. Prezzolini believed that the country's moral life could be reformed by joining culture and politics. The journal aimed to purge politics of the rhetoric that Prezzolini claimed contaminated the country's political life and hoped to end what he considered Italian provincialism. The review brought together in its pages the most influential Italian and European intellectuals.

La Voce opposed the Nationalist movement in the name of a "true" nationalism, but it had little influence beyond restricted intellectual circles. Corradini established in 1910 the Nationalist Association, an organization that reasserted the themes expressed in *Il Regno*. Nationalists and Futurists linked up to emphasize the principles of power connected to the "beauty" of war. The Futurists had declared: "We exalt aggressiveness . . . and the fist." For Nationalists, war had become the chief instrument of national policy and, as for the Futurists, necessary for the health of nations, a kind of national Darwinianism and a means of maintaining eternal youth. Furthermore, Corradini had evolved a view of Marxism that both criticized and coopted it in a manner that produced profound effects.

Corradini believed in the class struggle, but among classes of nations, not social classes. Rich nations dominate "proletarian" ones both in an economic and a cultural sense. Rich countries possess colonies, essential for markets and raw materials. They export capital, whereas the proletarian nations, bereft of economic resources and colonies, must export labor to survive. This labor is exploited in third countries by exported capital. Thus British capital making a profit for its owners in New York exploited Italian labor necessary to build the subways. A revolution was necessary and would come in the form of a revolutionary war of the proletarian nations against the capitalist ones. Italy, the proletarian nation par excellence, would lead the other proletarian countries on this modern-day crusade for justice.

To prepare for this war, Italy needed colonies and had to reach a new level of unity. Corradini and the Nationalists demanded that Giolitti seize Libya; Nationalist propagandists pictured Libya as a grand oasis filled with raw materials, a perfect alternative to America as a goal for emigration, recalled Rome's heritage there, and exploited the fear that other countries might soon take it over. Although they were not solely responsible for pushing Giolitti into war in 1911, their campaign created great pressure forcing the government to act. To reach internal unity, Corradini criticized Marxism as the great dividing force: It split Italian workers and employers. Socialists emphasized the commonality of interests of Italian and foreign workers against Italian and foreign employers, but Corradini argued that workers in the rich nations made only a show of opposing their capitalists. They could have stopped imperialism but allowed it to continue because they benefited from it; French workers opposed social security for Italian emigrants in France, and Belgian workers attacked their Italian counterparts forced to toil in their country. Marxism for Corradini was a kind of capitalist plot. Italian workers should cooperate with their employers to prepare for the coming revolutionary war. Out of this unity would emerge fresh pride, a new culture based on ancient Rome, and a new efficiency; the trains would run on time, he said, and a new architecture based on Rome's rounded arch would flourish.

The Libyan War was too limited to qualify as the overarching conflict dreamed of by Nationalists. When World War I erupted, they demanded Italian intervention in the conflict despite the opposition of Parliament. Nationalists viewed the struggle at once as a revolutionary war that would redeem Italian honor and get rid of Giolitti. Afterward their ideology dovetailed nicely with Fascist practice and style. Unlike the Nationalists, Mussolini hailed from the revolutionary left, but as discussed in Chapter 12, after Red Week he too exalted violence for its own sake. By severing the revolution from its Marxist goal of redeeming the proletariat, his antidemocratic ideals, his taste for action, Mussolini's authoritarian tendencies, and his "will to power" became ends in themselves. By the time Mussolini came to power, the Nationalists had already worked these elements into an ideology that he could and did accept. In this manner, Nationalist antidemocratic ideals won out.

14

World War I and the Red Biennium

AFTER 1870 the European diplomatic scene changed dramatically. Italian and German unification ended the balance created by the Vienna settlement of 1815 and destabilized the continent in two ways. Austria's losses in Italy heartened minorities within the empire hoping to create their own nation-states. An independent Serbia serving as a pole of attraction for Slavs living in Bosnia-Herzegovina and Croatia seemed to fit the Piedmontese-Italian "model." The steady decline of Turkey in the Balkans polarized the Austro-Serbian conflict by eliminating a power that had been present in the area for centuries, leaving a rich inheritance for an eventual victor. On the other hand, the Austrians not only had never accepted their Italian defeat but also well understood the threat to their empire if all the national groups within it followed the Italian example. As a matter of self-defense, they determined never to allow other secessions but vowed to keep power in the hands of Austrians and Hungarians. In the ensuing struggle on this issue, the Risorgimento proved a harbinger of things to come.

At the same time, German unification also radicalized the diplomatic situation. Germany replaced France as the strongest continental power, its productive capacity outstripped Britain, and the new country marched toward world-power status. Convinced of enduring French hostility, Bismarck isolated France. Geographical and cultural considerations dictated an agreement with Austria-Hungary, but Bismarck also secured treaties with Russia (the Three Emperors' League) and Italy (the Triple Alliance) and achieved a friendly relationship with England.

Bismarck's brilliant diplomacy aimed at preventing a conjunction of France and Russia, which could trap Germany between them in case of war. Cracks appeared in Bismarck's diplomatic edifice because of Austro-Russian competition in the Balkans, with Germany certain to choose Austria should a conflict erupt. Bismarck attempted various expedients to keep Russia satisfied, but even before Emperor William II forced him to retire in 1890, the Bismarckian system had already begun to unravel. The diplomatic recovery of France, the struggle in the Balkans, and the German drive for world influence marked European diplomacy during the early twentieth century.

Diplomacy

Italian diplomacy after 1896 fits into this general scheme. Although in the pursuit of their national interests Italian diplomats could make independent moves that irritated European statesmen, they responded to diplomatic maneuvers rather than initiate them.

The circumstances that caused the Italians to enter the Triple Alliance in 1882 have previously been recounted. The Italians never conceived of the alliance to be exclusive, however, and quickly made clear their desire to maintain good relations with other countries. Upon signing the treaty, they publicly stated that their participation in the alliance could never be construed as unfriendly toward Britain. The British controlled the Mediterranean and the long Italian coastline made the peninsula vulnerable, but cultural considerations came into play in addition to power. Relations with France improved when tensions over Tunisia cooled down and when Crispi resigned in 1896. Under the expert guidance especially of Foreign Minister Emilio Visconti Venosta, the Italians remained friendly to the Germans but settled their problems with the French over Tunis (1896) and ended the "tariff war" with a commercial agreement (1898). In 1900, an Italo-Ethiopian accord liquidated Crispi's colonial heritage.

In their effort to escape the diplomatic isolation imposed by Bismarck, the French also began to cultivate their southern neighbor, through their skilled ambassador to Italy, Camille Barrère. In 1902, Italy and France agreed to remain neutral in case either was attacked by other powers, even if they should be provoked into declaring war (Barrère-Prinetti Accord). France also recognized Italy's freedom of action in Libya, and Italy did the same for France in Morocco—a prelude to both powers' move to take over the North African territories.

This understanding may have violated Italy's obligations under the Triple Alliance, and, in fact, the Germans objected. The Triple Alliance, however, was defensive and nothing obligated Italy to aid Germany and Austria-Hungary should they provoke a conflict. Furthermore, diplomatic uncertainty of this kind existed in the agreements of other countries at the time, as the secret Reinsurance Treaty between Germany and Russia (1887–1890) makes clear. In response to German concerns, Foreign Minister Giulio Prinetti offered an early renewal of the Triple Alliance; during the talks, he sought but failed to receive official guarantees on the defensive nature of the alliance, support for Italian interests in Libya and the Balkans, and commercial concessions. Luigi Albertini, who knew Prinetti, "several times asked himself whether the man would have concluded the agreement of 30 June 1902 with France, had Berlin and Vienna allowed him to boast of having his proposals, more formal than substantial as they were, accepted in the renewal of the alliance."

Important as personalities were, however, this diplomatic activity occurred within a context of significant power realignment. In fact, Russia and France had already come to an agreement while France and Britain had settled their colonial problems. England had emerged from its "splendid isolation" and the Triple Entente (France, Britain, and Russia) was being forged to counter the German threat. This altered power situation, in addition to cultural considerations, hostility to the Central Powers on the part of the Italian democratic left, and persistently poor relations with Austria, sapped Italian loyalty toward the Triplice. In fact, the Italian minority in the "unredeemed lands" (the Irredenta, Trent, the Trentino, and Trieste) remained subject to physical attack and abuse; and Franz Conrad von Hotzendorf, chief of the Austrian General Staff, missed no occasion to advocate a preventive war on Italy, as will be seen in the following discussion.

In addition, as full participants in the diplomatic initiatives of the period, the Italians followed the expansionistic policies common to European powers of this era, even if wisely proportioned by Visconti Venosta to their status as the weakest of the great powers. As in the rest of Europe, Italy's industrial development spurred this activity, especially in the Balkans. In this arena they came into conflict with Austria-Hungary. In 1903 during one of the many Balkan crises, Prinetti sought guarantees that Italian interests would be protected, since Article VII of the alliance, negotiated in 1887, promised Italy compensation for any Austrian changes in the Balkans. Instead of responding to the concerns of its ally, however, Austria reacted by concluding a secret agreement with the Russians directed against Italy. In 1909, during a crisis over Bosnia that had begun the year before, the Russians informed Italy of the accord because they believed that the crisis demonstrated that Italy had more in common with Russia than with Austria.

Austrian disregard for Article VII caused continuous problems for the Triple Alliance, producing strains with Germany as well that contrasted sharply with good Italian relations with France and Britain. During the Moroccan crisis of 1905–1906, for example, Germany asked for diplomatic support at an international conference but was irritated when the Italian representative, Visconti Venosta, failed to provide it. On the other hand, Morocco did not come within the purview of the Triple Alliance, and blundering German policy alienated the powers and isolated Germany itself. Shortly afterward, the intemperate German Kaiser William II told the Austrians that, "in case Italy should show hostility to Austria-Hungary," he would "seize with real enthusiasm" the opportunity to join in a military attack on the kingdom. Under the circumstances, the Italians were not about to go beyond their formal commitments under the alliance.

During the next year the Italians and Austrians tried to patch up their precarious relationship, but in late 1908 the situation deteriorated. Reacting to events in Turkey that threatened their military occupation of Bosnia-Herzegovina, dating from 1878, the Austrians formally annexed the area. This action produced the European crisis mentioned previously. The Italians asked for compensation under Article VII. The Austrians refused but promised concessions—pledges that went unfulfilled—to the empire's Italian minority. Not only did the Italians receive nothing significant from their ally, but when an earthquake killed more than 100,000 people in Sicily, General Conrad advocated an attack while the Italians were absorbed in massive relief operations. The public flap over Conrad's behavior caused more bad blood between the allies, and in 1909 the Italians reached the secret Racconigi agreement with Russia—rounding out their friendly relationship with the last of the entente powers and achieving Russian support for Italian interests in the Balkans and Libya. The Italians did not inform Austria of the Racconigi understanding when, later in the year, they apparently patched up their poor relations with Austria resulting from the Bosnian affair. In this accord, the Austrians promised that if they occupied a Balkan area known as the Sanjak of Novibazar, they would consult Italy. This settlement did not compensate Italy for the Bosnian annexation, and Italian diplomats reasoned that in promising to consult them over the Sanjak, the Austrians were merely fulfilling their future obligations under Article VII. Austrian refusal to compensate Italy under Article VII encouraged the Italians to comply to the letter of the Triple Alliance but alienated them from the spirit of the treaty.

With all these difficulties, the question might be asked as to why Italy did not simply abandon the Triple Alliance. The primary reason seems to have been fear of a war between Austria and Italy if the ancient enemies did not remain linked in an alliance. Even the pro-German Foreign Minister Antonino di San Giuliano admitted in 1914 that Italy would probably leave the alliance in a few years. The prognostication of an earlier foreign minister, however, proved more accurate. Answering a Russian diplomat who wondered why Italy did not denounce the Triple Alliance, Tommaso Tittoni replied: "We shall come out some day, but it will be to go to war."

The Libyan War, 1911–1912, briefly halted the Italian drift away from the Triplice. Although for years Italy had been making agreements with the other European powers, giving it a free hand to take Libya (actually Tripolitania and Cyrenaica), the Italian attack came abruptly and irritated European diplomats because it heightened tensions in the Balkans. As Turkish military resistance waned the Arabs organized guerrilla warfare, forcing the Italians to press for quick Turkish recognition of their sovereignty by bringing the war to the Turkish homeland. The other powers vetoed this action out of fear that Turkey would collapse, thrusting upon an unprepared Europe the explosive issues of how to divide the Turkish Empire and and how to satisfy Russian lusting after the Straits (the Bosporus and the Dardanelles).

Italy's allies provided no help. Germany and Austria had long recognized Italy's freedom of action in Libya, but Germany was wooing Turkey and hoped that Italy would become bogged down so that its attention would be diverted away from Europe and would become embroiled with France over colonial issues. The Italians occupied the Dodecanese Islands off the Turkish coasts, but great-power opposition to decisive military action against their homeland allowed the Turks to continue the conflict longer than otherwise would have been possible. Taking advantage of the conflict, however, Russian diplomats put together a coalition of small Balkan states that prepared to attack Turkey. This imminent threat caused the Turks to end the war.

The Balkan Wars that followed the Libyan conflict in 1912 and 1913 resulted in an aggrandizement of Serbia at Turkey's expense. In July 1913, the Austrians considered what to do in case the settlement after the Second Balkan War transformed Serbia into an irresistible pole of attraction for Slavs living in the empire, as Piedmont had become a model for Italians in the 1850s. To protect the integrity of their state, Austrian officials concluded that they must absolutely eliminate such a threat. The Germans cooled the Austrians down momentarily, but the Austrian attitude alarmed the Italians, who argued that an Austrian attack on Serbia would set off a European conflagration. Prime Minister Giolitti pointedly warned his allies that Italy would never follow them into an offensive war against Serbia under the terms of the Triple Alliance, the consequences of which would fall squarely on the Austrians. San Giuliano insisted: "It would be impossible in this eventuality to want to invoke the Triple Alliance which is purely defensive in character and has been so interpreted by all the statesmen of the three allied countries ever since it has existed." The foreign minister assured his allies that Italy would loyally fulfill its duty should they be attacked, but "no Italian Government could recognize the *casus foederis* in an Austrian war of aggression on Serbia."

San Giuliano's lucid reasoning found no interlocutor among Italy's allies, who took advantage of his clarity to cut the Italians out of the alliance's decision-making mechanism, another violation of the treaty's letter and spirit. When at the end of the Second Balkan War Serbia occupied Albania, giving it access to the sea and increasing its prestige enormously, the Austrians sent an ultimatum demanding Serbian evacuation of Albania. Aware of San Giuliano's position, the Austrians informed Italy only after sending the ultimatum, an action they would repeat in June 1914. Determined to crush the Serbian threat and accepting the risk—even desirability—of war, and contrary to the canons of diplomacy, the Austrians expected Italy to join them without having been informed or having consented. In 1914, fearing that Italy would either veto action or demand compensation, Germany and Austria-Hungary kept the Italians in the dark about their moves—which touched off World War I. As a result, when the war broke out, Italy concluded that the terms obligating it to join Germany and Austria-Hungary had not arisen because its allies had taken the offensive. Italy thus declared its neutrality and, under Article VII, requested compensation for Austrian gains in the Balkans.

Given their stormy diplomatic relationship, the violation of the Triple Alliance's terms, the popular hostility to Austria, and the absurdity of rendering aid to the Central Powers that, if successful, would only strengthen their hereditary enemy, the Italians followed the only rational course: neutrality. Furthermore, while the Allies sought to woo the Italians into the conflict on their side, San Giuliano opened negotiations to compensate Italy for Austrian changes in the Balkans. The empire's Italian-speaking areas became the chief focus of the talks, which the Germans encouraged the Austrians to undertake. Unfortunately, San Giuliano died in October 1914, depriving Italian diplomacy of a sophisticated practitioner. Negotiations continued under Prime Minister Antonio Salandra and Foreign Minister Sidney Sonnino according to the guidelines set down by San Giuliano. The manner in which they conducted these negotiations, however, amounted to a public relations disaster.

Neutralists and Interventionists

The domestic context of these foreign policy developments should be reviewed for a full understanding of the debate between the forces that wished to keep Italy out of the war and those that demanded intervention.

In 1914 Italy seemed over the worst of an economic recession begun two years earlier. Politically, however, the country was still in turmoil because of changes brought about by institution of universal manhood suffrage. The Extreme Left emerged strengthened but more split than usual. To win a majority, Giolitti had had to cooperate with the Catholics by stipulating the so-called "Gentiloni Pact." When news of the "Pact" emerged, Giolitti resigned, indicating he would allow the rightist liberals the opportunity to rule. On March 21, 1914, Antonio Salandra formed a new government with the support of the Giolittian majority. Undoubtedly Giolitti planned to return at the appropriate moment, as he had in the past, but four months later World War I erupted.

The Italian people favored keeping the country out of the conflict, but well-organized political minorities and industrial groups that would profit from intervention advocated entrance into the war. How did the battle shape up?

Although the Socialists and their organizations had grown significantly in numbers, the war found the Socialist movement greatly weakened: The reformists had been unable to win back control of the party and Mussolini's revolutionary platform proved unobtainable. The Socialists greeted the declaration of neutrality with relief. Although the party did not budge from its "absolute neutrality" policy, many Socialists came to believe that this position would isolate them and cut socialism off from the country's intellectual mainstream in the midst of great events. Moreover, after reports of German atrocities in Belgium and France, "absolute neutrality" came under attack as effectively favoring the Central Powers—a devastating charge because Italian leftists sympathized with the Triple Entente.

In addition, influential party members converted to interventionism. After some hesitation, the most important of these, Benito Mussolini, publicly advocated a change in the party's stated policy. Aside from Mussolini's personal views, he tackled some relevant issues that the PSI refused to deal with and that later damaged it. The party's inflexible neutralism isolated it from the "democratic interventionists"—Republicans, Radicals, and independent Socialists—"Wilsonian" precursors, who like most Socialists believed that the Central Powers had to be defeated to save democracy and produce a peaceful world free of militarism and authoritarianism. One of these democractic interventionists, Gaetano Salvemini, wrote: "It is necessary that *this* war kill *all* war." By defining the war as a bourgeois conflict which did not concern them, the Socialists cut themselves off from a vital issue dominating Italian and world concern not only in 1914 but in the future.

The Socialists expelled Mussolini and, under the slogan "Neither support nor sabotage," refused to endorse the country's choice even after it joined the conflict. Party discipline prevented many Socialists from supporting interventionism, but at the cost of leaving them open to the charge that they had betrayed their country.

The interventionists, though representing fewer people, were more active. Mussolini agreed with revolutionary syndicalist leader Alceste De Ambris that the war would lead to revolution. Nationalists and Futurists first advocated intervention on the German side against the French but then, realizing that this policy had little chance of succeeding, demanded war against Austria because it would make Italy supreme in the Adriatic—a line allowing them to link up with Salandra. Although they were small in membership, it is impossible to overestimate the activity and influence of groups such as these; they included all the live intellectual forces that had produced the country's most avant-garde reviews and its most visible artists such as Gabriele D'Annunzio.

Unlike the interventionist intellectuals, the country's liberal establishment initially agreed on keeping the country neutral and, because of the international situation, avoiding instability by retaining the present government. This broad liberal "party" consisted of two groups, left liberals, Giolitti followers, and right liberals, Sonnino-Salandra supporters—and contained within itself the seeds of division. Giolitti believed a war would be long and costly and that Italy could attain the Italian-speaking parts of Austria under Article VII of the Triple Alliance in return for its neutrality. He had the votes to become prime minister, but as a known neutralist, he felt that he would have less credibility if he threatened war in the event that Austria did not give up the territories.

By early 1915 Salandra and Sonnino became convinced that Italy could not remain neutral and be a player in the postwar European equilibrium. Preoccupied primarily with the Adriatic and the Balkans, they reasoned that if Italy did not intervene and Austria won, supremacy in those areas would devolve upon the Hapsburg Empire; in case of an Austrian defeat without Italian participation, an enlarged Serbia backed by a pan-Slavist Russia would dominate and perhaps even receive the Italian-speaking areas of Austria. In March 1915 Foreign Minister Sonnino negotiated the Pact of London with the Triple Entente, pledging Italian intervention within one month. In the negotiations, the entente had the advantage because Italian desires would be fulfilled primarily at Austria's expense. Within Italy, the the rightist liberal group of Salandra and Sonnino was backed by Luigi Albertini's *Corriere della Sera,* the country's most influential newspaper, and the liberal press. Behind this press were industrialists who stood to gain from war. Finally, as Giolitti's neutralist stance hardened, the liberals of the right, along with the revolutionaries and Nationalists who had chafed under Giolitti, seized the opportunity to get rid of him by defeating his line on the war.

A strong neutralist bloc that might have blunted these forces and helped keep the country out of the war never materialized. Different sympathies toward the warring sides marked Catholics. Some favored Austria as a Catholic bulwark against the Orthodox Slavs, others supported the entente as the hope of European democracy, and some saw the conflict as God's punishment. In practice Italian Catholics agreed with Pope Benedict XV's opposition to the conflict and favored staying out of it. Politically, however, Catholics remained subordinate to the liberals and did not take the initiative. Despite their pro-Giolitti role in the 1913 elections, Catholics did not choose sides in the struggle and stood ready to follow their government's decision, whatever it might be. As in other countries, when Italy intervened, the Catholics supported the war effort.

Before Italy could enter the war, the Pact of London had to be ratified by Parliament. This was no easy task. Parliament had not been informed and Giolitti commanded a majority. Including the Socialists, war opponents numbered about 400 out of 508 and could have refused to accept the agreement. However, "spontaneous" demonstrations took place against Giolitti, the Socialists, and a "decrepit" Parliament. In May 1915 handfuls of demonstrators rushed through the piazzas shouting for war and cheering the oratory of Italy's poet-warrior, D'Annunzio. The interventionist press magnified the size of the demonstrations, and the police suppressed Socialist organization of counterdemonstrations. When Giolitti learned of the Pact's existence, he believed that honor committed the country to adhere to it, ratified or not, and he exited the scene. His majority then went over to Salandra.

The "giolittiani" had no heart to make a stand. On May 20, 1915, the Chamber convened to ratify war against Austria, officially because of the Italian minority's mistreatment. Clearly the manner in which the Chamber had been maneuvered by Salandra, Sonnino, and the king into declaring war against the sentiments of the majority of the population debilitated democracy, confirmed the disdain of Parliament's critics, and produced terrible fruits.

World War I

The conflict with Turkey two years before had left Italy militarily unprepared. Nonetheless, the country mounted a massive war offensive against Austria in very difficult mountain terrain. In addition, the lack of coordination between the supreme commander and the cabinet hampered the war effort. Intervention also came at a crucial time when the war turned in favor of the Central Powers. As a result, Italy failed to deliver Austria a swift knockout punch, and the Italians bogged down in the trenches as had their French and British allies on the Western front. In 1916 the Italians survived a concentrated offensive of crack troops designed by Conrad to drive them out of the war—the Strafexpedition. Numerous battles exacting a tremendous toll from both Austrians and Italians occurred, but until 1917 neither side made much headway. Nevertheless, by summer 1917, the Austro-Hungarian army appeared worn down and unable to withstand another Italian offensive, planned for the next spring. To prevent such a defeat, the Austrians turned to their German allies and proposed a great offensive before the winter to knock Italy out of the conflict. The Germans consented, transferring experienced troops and generals to the Italian front.

Despite evidence that reached him, Italian commander Luigi Cadorna refused to believe that such an offensive was in the works. He failed to take adequate defensive measures and kept his forces in an offensive posture. The well-thought-out Austro-German plan thus had surprise on its side when the battle known as Caporetto began on October 24, 1917. Rapidity of movement and great local military superiority allowed the Austro-Germans to wipe out important units, while bad communications contributed to the false impression of a rout. Believing the war to be over, many soldiers threw down their weapons and streamed home. This information, combined with the well-known Socialist opposition to the war, caused Cadorna and interventionists to blame the defeat on Socialist propaganda. Even though the Socialists came out in favor of defending the country during this battle, the supposed Socialist "betrayal" of the war effort caused many Italians later to sympathize with the Fascists. Moreover, a distorted impression of the Italian war effort created by Cadorna himself led the Allies to denigrate Italy's contribution to the victory over the Central Powers. This view contributed to a peace settlement regarding Italy that the Italians resented; this resentment was partially responsible for the rise of fascism.

In the domestic arena, the fight between neutralists and interventionists, although muted, continued throughout the war. The Socialist slogan "Neither adhesion nor sabotage" meant that they continued to criticize the war. Italian Socialists participated prominently in the international Socialist conferences of Zimmerwald (1915) and Kienthal (1916) designed to bring peace. When these failed and military fortunes seesawed, some Italians favored efforts by Giolitti's followers to negotiate a separate peace on the basis of their leader's original suggestion that the Italians could get "a lot" ("*parecchio*") for their neutrality. The Catholics declared that they would do their duty, but the pope's constant attempts to end the war caused many to question their support for the conflict. These opinions, which the fairly mild censorship allowed to circulate freely, sapped enthusiasm among large strata of the population and, consequently, the soldiers, and drew interventionist fulminations.

Economic and social developments as a result of the war also had important consequences. Aided by new production techniques, war-related heavy industry expanded tremendously, and Italy acquired the capacity to make a major contribution to the Allied war effort. Production of electric power doubled and steel production increased 50 percent. The development of a modern engineering industry had implications for the country's industrial advance after the war, and the sector's percentage share of manufacturing went from 21.6 to 31.8. This expansion stimulated the growth of giant firms such as Ilva, Fiat, and, especially, Ansaldo. These companies tightened their relationship with big banks and presented the government with a major problem because they were in a position to dominate large sectors of the economy. On the other hand, the government felt obliged to support these giant industrial complexes because of their primary necessity for the war effort. Since they profited from the war, the owners of these firms also presented their activities and attempts to expand into the banking sector as patriotic endeavors. Anyone who put obstacles in their path was branded as unpatriotic. Besides these problems, the distortion of the Italian economy caused major disruption after the conflict ended and war materiel was no longer needed.

These and other war-related developments provoked dissatisfaction and disorder among the population. Industrial workers toiled sixteen hours a day, but the government favored the employers in order to keep production high. Consequently, workers had to put up with strict discipline, compulsory arbitration, and close surveillance. Real wages of industrial workers dropped with inflation by 27 percent from 1913 to 1917 while average profits of the industrial companies increased from 4.26 percent to 7.7 percent. Wartime inflation also cut the incomes of the middle class, but war profiteers flourished. Despite tax increases, the government was reluctant to crack down on them. The ostentation with which these profiteers exhibited their newfound wealth caused resentment among all sectors of the population. The worst-off sector was the peasantry. Exemptions from military service were much more freely given for industrial workers than for peasants. Women took the place of men in the fields, keeping production high, but real agricultural wages fell further than industrial salaries. The obvious shift of wealth from the countryside to the city further dampened enthusiasm for the war.

These resentments, fanned by shortages, overcrowding, and the Russian Revolution of March 1917, brought disorders beginning in the spring of 1917. Disturbances frequently led by women hit parts of northern Italy, but the explosion hit in Turin in August. Because of the increase in their bargaining power during the war, workers in the engineering sector there had achieved unofficial recognition of elected factory committees by the state. Some of these institutions had come to be dominated by intransigent Socialists, who, spurred by Russian events, intensified their antiwar campaign. Antiwar demonstrations erupted during a visit by a Russian delegation in August 13. On August 22 temporary bread shortages touched off protests that quickly developed into massive demonstrations against the war. The rioters attacked stores and police stations, burned churches, and threw up barricades. The army appeared the next day, bringing in tanks and machine guns. Socialist leaders called for calm and refused demands for a nationwide strike. By August 28 Turin returned to normal.

These wartime events had important effects on the government. Salandra's cabinet had fallen on June 10, 1916, because of discord with the high command over conduct of the war, interventionist dissatisfaction with his performance, and neutralist resentment over his outmaneuvering of Giolitti to get Italy into the conflict. Seventy-eight year old Paolo Boselli replaced him. Boselli was chosen because of his supposed ability to bring concord among the country's leaders. In fact, his cabinet represented a wide coalition, including liberals of the right and left, democratic interventionists, Radicals, a Republican, a Catholic, and a Giolittian representative. The Boselli government was criticized by the interventionists for its lack of energy, inefficiency, and reluctance to crack down on political activity of the kind that led to the Turin disorders. Demonstrations demanded a new and efficient war cabinet and better coordination between the home and fighting fronts. Better control of antiwar activity was instituted, but on October 25, 1917, the Boselli cabinet was brought down.

Vittorio Emmanuele Orlando replaced Boselli. Orlando had been criticized by the interventionists for being too lenient toward "defeatists," but he defended himself by arguing that a country fighting for liberty had to be sensitive toward civil rights. To Parliament's credit, Orlando was confirmed because of his pledge to combine a more efficient war effort with concern for civil rights.

With the Orlando government, Italy finally found the organization to pursue the war with great vigor. Orlando created a war council consisting of military and naval leaders and civilian ministers. This council directed the war effort with greater efficiency, created harmony between government and high command, and created effective political supervision of the army. The high command itself was reconstituted to remove the weaknesses from which it had previously suffered. Special units known as the *Arditi* were created to infuse a greater war spirit into the fighting forces. Recruited from young volunteers, usually middle class and university graduates, these pampered units had special privileges and distinctive uniforms—black shirts and special insignia. They were given special training and were employed for the most dangerous and visible military operations. Unlike the rest of the infantry, primarily interested in staying alive, the Arditi came to love fighting for its own sake and lived for war. After the war, these shock troops could not forget conflict and supplied the Fascists with their most warlike squads.

The Italian military effort in the war's most difficult sector eventually proved that the Caporetto defeat had military, not political, roots and that it was a temporary, although serious, setback. Caporetto was similar to the defeats suffered by all sides during the war. The battle's real significance is that the Austro-German objective failed; the enemy captured no major city, and the Italian army stopped it on the Piave line. Under its new commander, Armando Diaz, the army reorganized and within a year unleashed a great offensive of its own that broke the Austro-Hungarian army at Vittorio Veneto. The only Allied forces to end the war on enemy soil, the Italians signed an armistice on November 3, 1918. A week later, an armistice on the Western front ended all hostilities, but not the consequences of the war.

MAP 5   Italy after World War I

Aftermath: The "Red Biennium"

According to official statistics, 571,000 Italian soldiers died in combat during World War I, to which must be added 57,000 prisoners of war who died and 60,000 missing in action who never returned; the disabled totaled almost 452,000. This was a lower proportion of the population of the major European combatants but extremely heavy considering that the country entered the war ten months after it began.

The results of the war led Italians to conclude that their Herculean effort went unappreciated and uncompensated by their allies. The conflict's enormous cost had led the government to raise expectations; it claimed Fiume, an Italian-speaking city in the Austrian Empire not included in the Pact of London. The postwar settlement gave Italy Trent, the Trentino, Trieste, and, because of strategic considerations, the Austrian-populated South Tyrol (Alto Adige) up to the Brenner Pass, but a dispute broke out regarding the Adriatic coast of what became Yugoslavia. Italians had settled the area centuries before, but while they lived in the cities, the Austrians had encouraged Slavic immigration into the hinterland. After having given in to British and French demands to modify his Fourteen Points in their favor, President Woodrow Wilson resisted Italian requests for territory such as Fiume, which would have put Slavic minorities in Italy. In fact, there was a basic contradiction in the Italian position at the Paris Peace Conference. Foreign Minister Sonnino claimed fulfillment of the Pact of London on strategic grounds, even though it put German-speaking minorities in Italy, while Prime Minister Vittorio Emmanuele Orlando claimed Fiume on the basis of self-determination. The Italians believed that Wilson was pro-Yugoslavia and biased against them. A dispute broke out on this issue, and the Italian representatives withdrew from the Paris Peace Conference.

This break heightened the resentment, snaking through Italy, toward the war. The country also failed to reap the other rewards promised by the entente in 1915. The root of this situation was the inability of Italian diplomacy to exploit the traditional balance of power that the war had eliminated by prostrating Germany and making France supreme on the continent. The French and the British divided the German and Turkish colonial holdings among themselves using a method that galled the Italians—League of Nations "mandates," given to advanced countries capable of training the natives for democracy. Italian statesmen scoffed at this new system as an effort to refurbish the old colonialism in response to a war whose magnitude had made it necessary to justify imperialism in idealistic terms, but the lack of mandates impugned the country's democratic credentials and denigrated its role in fighting "to make the world safe for democracy."

Domestically, the resentment transformed the postwar Paris settlement into the "mutilated victory." Powerless to alter the international situation, the forces that had supported intervention blamed the Socialists for having scuttled the country's efforts to reap the rewards of its sacrifices. Lumped in with the Socialists were the democratic interventionists, who advocated a just rather than a harsh peace as the only means of avoiding a future conflict and who repudiated colonialism and nationalism and who wished to give up claims to Adriatic areas inhabited by Slavs. Interventionists responded that the neutralists had "sabotaged" the war effort and now wished to renounce the rightful fruits of the country's sacrifices. This extremist and simplistic argument produced a debate on the war similar to the "stab in the back" debate in Germany and would justify the later violent Fascist campaign to dismantle the Italian left.

The war's tremendous economic, social, and political dislocation, however, initially caused a reaction that favored former neutralist forces rather than the right. It has been estimated that the war effort cost Italy 157 billion lire (1962 values). As in other countries, this enormous expense fueled inflation, which reached spectacular proportions by 1919. Total note circulation, under 3.6 billion lire in 1914, hit almost 18.6 billion (values are in lire of the period). The lira collapsed, its exchange rate with the dollar dropping to to 4.97 cents in 1920 from 19.30 cents in 1913. The cost of living soared from a base of 100 in 1913 to 268.1 in 1919, and the wholesale price index reached 366. Real wages dove. The budget went wildly out of kilter. In 1919–1920, the state took in 15,207 million lire and spent 23,093 million, with the situation worsening the next year.

As in the other nations engaged in World War I, the conflict had brought a shift away from peacetime industry to a concentration on heavy industry and weapons production. At war's end the trend abruptly ended, throwing major industries into crisis and fueling massive unemployment. As in the other belligerent countries, hasty demobilization of the army worsened the unemployment problem.

These conditions created chaos in the country. On the land, man-days lost to strikes increased from 3,270 in the last year of the war to more than 3.4 million in 1919 and to 14.1 million in 1920. Promised land if they continued fighting, returning peasant soldiers invaded the large estates when the government failed to fulfill its pledge. Because of the political conditions next outlined, the left-liberal cabinets proposed compromises but did not decisively halt the movement—thus alienating the landowners and making them susceptible to paramilitary groups promising to defend their property.

In the cities a similar situation existed. Membership in the Socialist labor union, the largest, exploded from 249,000 in 1918 to 1,159,000 in 1919 and to 2,320,000 in 1920. Man-days lost to strikes increased dramatically from 906,000 in 1918 to 14.2 million in 1919. The most militant strikers, the metalworkers, won the eight-hour day in February 1919. To the consternation of industrialists, "Factory Councils" of workers demanded a dominant voice in management. Strikes turned into disorders and attacks on citizens and former soldiers. In major cities, workers established "Soviets" on the Russian model and sacked shops. Future Communist party founder Antonio Gramsci compared Italy to Kerensky's Russia—the last regime before the Communist Revolution.

Influenced by the Communist Revolution, the Socialist party seemed poised to overthrow the government. Turati argued that a revolution in Italy alone was impossible, but at its 1919 Bologna Congress, the party denounced the reformists, now reduced to a small minority, repudiated its 1892 program, and adopted one advocating violence on the Soviet model. Regardless of whether revolutionary conditions existed in postwar Italy or not, the new majority led by Giacinto Menotti Serrati was revolutionary in rhetoric only. It denounced existing institutions but turned down the left wing's argument that the party should abstain from elections and organize a revolution. Serrati's "maximalists" never attempted to organize a revolution and followed no consistent policy. At the same time, they antagonized reformist politicians and labor leaders, paralyzed the party's political action, frightened the middle class, and drove it to seeking salvation on the right.

The effect of this confused situation was tragic. In the parliamentary elections of 1919, the Socialists tripled their vote to become the largest party in the Chamber with 156 seats. The Catholics had formed their own independent Italian Popular Party (PPI), led by the left-leaning sociologist-priest Don Luigi Sturzo, and won 100 seats. These forces combined would have commanded a majority, but the Catholics would not cooperate with the PSI, and the radicalized Socialists, determined to destroy parliamentary institutions, collaborated with no one. The liberals were split, and implementation of proportional representation during these elections also fractionalized the Chamber. These conditions made it extremely difficult to put together a majority, which during this period depended on Catholic support, and produced continual cabinet reshufflings. For about a year, economist and historian Francesco Saverio Nitti headed governments brought to their knees by the labor agitation and civil disorders. On June 9, 1920, Nitti definitively resigned on the issue of reducing the expensive state subsidy for bread.

To many deputies it appeared that only the country's senior statesman, Giovanni Giolitti, could resolve the political crisis. On October 12, 1919, Giolitti had already proposed a leftist program but had modified it to gain support on the right. Giolitti aimed to restore parliamentary prestige and power by not resorting to decree laws. In the economic sphere, he proposed legislation that would have increased taxes on the rich—including a war-profits tax and registration of stocks and bonds in owners' names so they could be taxed. By having the rich pay more, he prepared the ground for reducing subsidies, ending inflation, and balancing the budget, thus reestablishing the liberal state's fiscal soundness and ending its agony. The strenuous opposition of the bourgeoisie and the Catholic party—alienated especially by the proposal to tax stocks and bonds—combined with Socialist lack of support caused his project to fail. Domestic and foreign problems intertwined as well to weaken Giolitti. In late June 1920 army units under orders to leave for Albania to consolidate Italian control there mutinied and consigned their weapons to the people, forcing the government to abandon that country. This development increased the hostility to Giolitti on the right.

But the culmination of Giolitti's tenure and of the "Red Years" occurred in August and September 1920: the factory occupations. This crisis had its origins in the demand for salary increases by workers in the metallurgical industry. This sector had been hard-hit by the postwar decline in demand for its products and its spokesmen refused all raises. Despite the economic crisis, however, the industry could afford to increase benefits and refused to provide documentary proof of its position when requested by the Labor Ministry. The adamant stance of the industrialists appears to have been politically motivated and formed part of a industrial counteroffensive begun several months before. By provoking a strike, the metal industry hoped to defeat the metalworkers' union, FIOM (Federazione Italiana Operai Metallugici), one of the country's most aggressive, and take the steam out of the workers' movement. The owners aimed to weaken Giolitti by forcing his government to intervene in case of violence, as seemed probable. At the same time, they hoped to bargain with the government, exchanging some salary increases for an increase in tariff protection for their hard-hit products. Finally, in the heat of the crisis, the owners hoped to obtain significant concessions from Giolitti on his fiscal policy of increased taxation for the rich.

As the workers implemented a slowdown, their leaders and government officials worked to avert a strike, but the industrialists remained inflexible on wage increases. FIOM had already announced that in case of lockouts the workers would remain in the factories. On August 30 the Alfa Romeo automobile factory in Milan implemented a lockout. Since Alfa Romeo belonged to Ilva, among the most intransigent industrial groups, the industrialists probably wished to provoke government intervention on the emotional ground of property rights violations. A FIOM order to occupy three hundred factories followed. The workers formed Red Guards to protect against police intervention and attempted to continue production in an orderly manner, but lack of technicians, supplies, capital, and markets made continued production unfeasible. As in his dealings with the 1904 general strike, Giolitti wisely did not use force, limiting the police to patrolling outside the factories. In defending himself from criticism denouncing his nonintervention, Giolitti stated that he had warned the industrialists not to provoke the occupations, that all the country's police would have been necessary to occupy the factories before the workers did so, and that then there would have been no one to safeguard public order against the hundreds of thousands of enraged workers left outside. Giolitti also noted the union leaders' declaration that the factory occupations had economic and not political significance. Furthermore, Giolitti believed that once the workers realized that they could not run the factories, the affair would be settled without bloodshed, as in fact happened in September.

The factory occupations had incalculable and ironic results. Probably conditions during the Red Biennium did not amount to a revolutionary situation, but if they had, after September 1920, the danger of revolution no longer existed. The maximalist leadership of the Socialist party had continually proclaimed its desire to effect a revolution in Italy, in emulation of Russia, but its failure to take any concrete action in this direction while abandoning the struggle within the existing political system at a time when it could have seriously pushed that system in a progressive direction resulted in paralysis. The maximalists squandered the Socialist party's reformist heritage, built upon patient work over two decades, and replaced it with nothing. Their rhetoric and lack of action also alienated the communistic left wing, which approached secession. Their support of continuous strikes and disorder without any apparent positive result alienated the lower middle classes, former Socialist sympathizers, depressed the workers, and provoked a strong bourgeois reaction.

Even though the factory occupations involved 600,000 workers and produced better working conditions, disillusion over the lack of political results spread like wildfire and killed worker militancy. In 1921 man-days lost because of strikes dropped by more than half in industry and by more than 90 percent on the land. The Fascist counterattack had begun by then, but this decline is only in part attributable to Fascist violence.

Furthermore, the change of mood caused by the occupations may be traced in the disappointing results for the Socialists in the local elections of November 1920 and by the definitive turn by industrialists and landowners to the paramilitary Fascist movement to protect their interests just when the improbable danger of a Socialist-Communist revolution had vanished. Socialists won a majority in 2,022 communes (out of 8,346) and in 26 provincial councils (out of 69 but lost clamorous battles in big cities such as Turin, Genoa, Rome, Florence, Naples, and Palermo to "national" and "patriotic blocs" formed by liberals, democrats, Nationalists, and Fascists. The Socialists won big against the national bloc in Bologna, which, because of that reason, became the flash point for Fascist violence against the left. In Milan, the Socialists squeaked to a narrow victory which boded ill for the future because Catholics supported the national bloc without a formal alliance. On its own, the PPI won a majority in 1,613 communes and 10 councils, while varied coalitions of liberals and democrats controlled 4,665 communes and 33 provincial councils.

So the reaction began in late 1920. The maximalists had wasted a unique opportunity to steer the country in a progressive direction and had helped foster conditions that destroyed Italian democracy.

15

The Rise of Fascism

IN DESCRIBING THE events of 1921–22 in Italy, *The Daily Mail*'s special correspondent and Fascist apologist Sir Percival Phillips wrote: "The Fascisti went about their grim work with a scornful calm. . . . They meted out punishment with the inexorable demeanour of an executioner."

During 1919 and 1920 the left's influence in Italy contrasted starkly with the conservative wave in Britain and France. Alarmed by what seemed the likelihood of domination by the left, the Italian middle classes and political right struck back with a ferocity unknown in western Europe up to that time.

Early Fascism

Who were the Fascists? Fascism had its start with leftist Socialist leader Benito Mussolini. The son of a poor schoolteacher and a Socialist blacksmith, Mussolini was born on July 29, 1883, in the village of Predappio in the Romagna region. He exhibited violent tendencies from his youth, and, in an attempt to calm down her unruly son, his mother had sent him to a Catholic boarding school. The harsh discipline there made things worse and he got into trouble for fighting and stabbing a fellow student. Mussolini had already declared himself a Socialist while in school. Thanks to his Socialist contacts, he was able to find a position teaching elementary school after graduation but could not hold onto his job because of a clamorous love affair. In 1902 he expatriated to Switzerland. He tried working at construction, but the work was too hard. He ran out of money and linked up with Italian Socialists and began writing for Socialist newspapers, including the revolutionary syndicalist organ *Avanguardia Socialista*. He got into trouble with the Swiss authorities because he advocated strikes and violence. In 1903 he was expelled, but the Italian police had no reason to hold him and he slipped back into Switzerland. There he continued his political activities, fell in love, claimed to engage in intellectual pursuits, and, he said, attended the lectures of Italian sociologist Vilfredo Pareto. Mussolini was due to report for the draft in 1904 but changed the date on his passport to show that it expired in 1905. In January 1905, perhaps suffering from homesickness, Mussolini returned to Italy, taking advantage of an amnesty, and began serving his term in the army. After 1906, his army time up, he spent several years teaching, engaging in political agitation, and writing for an Italian newspaper in Trent, then part of the Austrian Empire.

By 1910 he was back in Italy organizing the local Socialists of Forlì and editing their newspaper *Lotta di classe* (*Class Struggle*). He continued to advocate violent revolution and to denounce parliamentarianism, as he had in the past. He condemned war and joined his revolutionary comrades in attempting to dislodge the Socialist party's reformist leadership. The outbreak of the Libyan War in 1911 and his arrest for antiwar activities brought him a prison term and national attention. At the Congress of Reggio Emilia in 1912, he successfully presented a motion demanding expulsion of reformist leaders who had not denounced the conflict. Four months later he became editor of the Socialist daily newspaper *Avanti!*

When World War I broke out, Mussolini accepted the Socialist view of the conflict as a "bourgeois" war but, influenced by his revolutionary syndicalist friends, came to believe that it had revolutionary potential; at any rate, he argued, the Socialists were becoming isolated from the country's vital cultural currents by their intransigent position in favor of absolute neutrality. He attempted to alter Socialist party policy from his newspaper pulpit but failed. As a result, Mussolini not only lost his position as editor but also was expelled from the PSI for advocating Italian intervention. To implement his ideas, Mussolini accepted financial support from industrialists, who stood to make money from the war, to found a newspaper, *Il Popolo d'Italia.* His former colleagues then accused him of betrayal, charges that historians still debate. A consummate newspaperman, Mussolini kept his publication alive with industrialist help even after the war, when its function of helping prepare public opinion for intervention had ended.

The periodical established Mussolini as a leading interventionist and solidified his reputation among groups that resented Socialist party opposition to the conflict and then the PSI's later, lukewarm support as "defeatist." These associations shared a nationalistic, anti-Socialist, antiparliamentarian, and authoritarian outlook—and a propensity for violence. The groups included the Nationalist Association, already mentioned, and new organizations such as the "futurist fasci [bands]," the first to incorporate a military arm composed of war veterans from special combat units—the "Arditi" or storm troops devoted to violence. Under the leadership of Mussolini and poet Filippo Marinetti, these bands set a dangerous precedent by rioting to prevent Leonida Bissolati from delivering a foreign policy speech in Milan on January 11, 1919. At this time, Allied and Yugoslav opposition to demands for Dalmatian territory that the Italians claimed as a result of the war infuriated these small violent groups. Since they had fought in the war, they believed that they had earned the right to determine Italy's future and denounced anyone advocating "renunciation" of Italian claims after the country's victory.

Linked to these groups by his newfound nationalism, Mussolini claimed to remain a Socialist and attempted to found a labor party. This effort fizzled, but he insisted on creating a movement that was both "national" and "socialist." Responding to his call in *Il Popolo d'Italia*, on March 23, 1919, about three hundred journalists, war veterans, former revolutionary interventionists, and some Republicans and dissident Socialists accepted his invitation to meet in Milan's Piazza San Sepolcro. There the "Fascists of the first hour" organized themselves in the "fasci di combattimento" (combat groups).

These "fasci" (a member of which was a "fascista") fit the pattern of the nationalist, violent groups previously described, except that the fasci incorporated a leftist program that would appeal to the masses and claimed that they were not elitist. Mussolini's rhetoric was nationalist and anti-Socialist, and his methods violent, but the Fascist program published in June 1919 exhibited Mussolini's leftist heritage. Its demands included: universal suffrage, lowering of the voting age to eighteen, the right of women to vote and to hold office, abolition of the conservative Senate, election of a National Assembly to determine Italy's future constitutional makeup, an eight-hour day, a minimum wage, worker participation in industrial management, lowering of the retirement age from sixty-five to fifty-five, nationalization of all arms factories, a heavy graduated income tax "which will take the form of a true partial expropriation of wealth," the confiscation of all property belonging to religious congregations, and the sequestration of 85 percent of war profits.

Even though it aimed at gathering votes, this platform cannot be dismissed as demagogy. Mussolini later realized that he could never come to power if he pressed these demands, and he dropped them. In 1919 this program represented his views, but even after then the "leftist" Italian Fascist strain remained strong. In later years Fascist hierarchs such as Italo Balbo referred to Italy as "the Great Proletariat," and at least claimed to be acting on behalf of the masses, while others urged Mussolini to unleash the "second wave" of the "Fascist revolution" to destroy the bourgeoisie after the necessary compromises to achieve power.

In the 1919 elections, it became clear to Mussolini that he could not compete with the Socialists for votes on the basis of a leftist program. No Fascist won election to the Chamber of Deputies, and at the end of the year all the fasci together counted only 870 members. Mussolini found it imperative to change or become politically irrelevant.

In the early days, Mussolini also faced more prominent rivals, most important of whom was Gabriele D'Annunzio, poet and war hero. After the Allies had denied Fiume to Italy, D'Annunzio headed an expedition of volunteers to take the city in September 1919. From Fiume, D'Annunzio invented much of the symbolism later used by fascism, conspired against the Italian government, and, also having mass appeal, attempted to absorb the nascent Fascist movement. Mussolini avoided this peril until Giolitti dislodged D'Annunzio by military means in December 1920. Mussolini ably deserted D'Annunzio, going along with this operation, which damaged the poet's status while maintaining Mussolini's own reputation. More important, however, the incident prompted an informal accord with Mussolini, whose neutrality Giolitti considered necessary to avoid domestic repercussions of his attack on D'Annunzio. The Fascists were allowed to participate with the Liberals in the national blocs for the 1920 local elections, gaining important advantages from this alliance. Furthermore, the simultaneous failure of the factory occupations convinced Mussolini of the impossibility of a Socialist revolution. He aimed to absorb D'Annunzio's followers and intensified his violent attacks on the leftists in conjunction with rightist forces.

Agrarian Fascism

Politicians in postwar Italy knew that the country faced a severe political, social, and economic crisis but believed it could be overcome. In the struggle for normality, Giolitti achieved some important victories, such as defusing D'Annunzio and settling the factory occupations. But in confronting for the first time a radically militant new movement blending right and left that was bent on achieving power and headed by a brilliant, unprincipled tactician-opportunist, Liberal statesmen committed the error of conducting politics as usual. For example, Giolitti frequently cooperated with politically unruly forces to teach them responsibility by giving them a taste of power, as he did with Mussolini in 1920 and later. Unfortunately, his policy bears a major responsibility for fascism's explosive growth in 1920–1921 and its eventual triumph.

The economic crisis following World War I reached an acute phase in late 1920–1921, when the failed factory occupations had already taken the steam out of the labor movement. Industrial giants like Ilva, Perrone-Ansaldo, and big banks either crashed or slumped dangerously. Faced by dropping investments, skyrocketing business failures, and growing unemployment, Giolitti delayed implementation of his previously described fiscal policy to mollify the business community. Combined with the decline in power of the unions, the economic crisis favored rampant reaction, especially on the land.

One of the most dramatic scenes in Bernardo Bertolucci's film *1900* occurs when a Fascist passes around the hat for landowner contributions to finance violence against the peasants. Indeed, the reaction began in the Emilia (around Bologna), a rich agricultural area in which the Socialists had founded the modern peasant movement in the 1890s. In 1919–1920, the disciplined Socialist-led leagues achieved control of labor and of the local political institutions. This economic and political domination allowed the leagues both to set wages and impose lower prices. This policy angered the large landowners, who found willing allies among small landowners and the petit bourgeoisie who had supported intervention and who had been alienated by Socialist antiwar ideology, violence, and intimidation favoring the poorest peasants.

These nationalist, anti-Socialist, and antiworker sentiments fueled the spread of fascism on the land in the fall of 1920, as the agrarian bourgeoisie financed the reaction and supported it politically. In contrast with the movement's slower urban development, the number of rural fasci mushroomed, flanked by armed "action squads" composed of Arditi, former military officers, young people, students, former legionaire followers of D'Annunzio, and mercenaries who joined from the ranks of the unemployed and shiftless. The squads unleashed a campaign of violence against Socialists, Communists, and Anarchists, destroying property belonging to the leagues, leftist parties, and working-class institutions—Chambers of Labor, cooperatives, meeting halls, newspapers. They beat and killed Socialists and their sympathizers; they forced opponents to drink large quantities of castor oil. (Federico Fellini's film *Amarcord* includes a scene that illustrates the debilitating physical and psychological effects of this novel tactic.)

With many unemployed workers returning to the countryside because of the economic crisis, dispirited by the fate of the factory occupations, divided, lacking central direction, and not organized to respond to violence, the agrarian leagues could not hold on to their former economic gains and began to succumb to the Fascist offensive. Local authorities—prefects, police, magistracy, carabinieri and army—sympathized with the anti-Socialist forces and either turned a blind eye to the violence, supplied arms and transportation for Fascist "punitive expeditions," repressed the unsystematic efforts of the left to react, or arrested the victims.

One particular incident illustrates Fascist tactics, the level of agitation, and the attitude of local authorities. To protest the escalating violence, on November 21, 1920, the Bologna Socialists called for a great demonstration on the occasion of the swearing in of the newly elected Socialist mayor and city government.

The Fascists had vowed to take action, and when the day came, several hundred of them opened fire when the mayor spoke; instead of stopping the Fascists, the police joined in firing at city hall. From inside the building, a Socialist responded by hurling hand grenades, increasing the panic. Shots struck a minority member of the city council—a nationalist and war hero. The press blamed the "Bolsheviks" for his death and for the entire incident. The national government dissolved the city administration, and Fascist squads attacked their opponents in and out of the city. Fascist violence spread like wildfire from Bologna to other provinces, increasing in intensity in areas with strong peasant movements, Socialist or Catholic. Fascists conducted "punitive expeditions" with ever greater boldness, terrorizing entire towns, destroying property belonging to leftist organizations, invading homes to beat and kill their enemies, and implanting new fasci to keep control of the conquered areas. Hundreds of dead and wounded remained in the squads' wake.

Although these raids were primarily conducted on the local level and financed by the local bourgeoisie in cooperation with the local authorities, the national government indirectly supported the Fascist hordes. Although Giolitti condemned the violence and told authorities to be evenhanded in dealing with it, he took little practical action against the Fascist movement that directed the campaign. According to Arturo Labriola, a member of the governments of this period, with the Socialist party still powerful but uncooperative in Parliament, Giolitti hoped to exploit fascism to weaken the Socialists, after which he would have presumably offered them a deal. Tragically, he misunderstood the nature of the Fascists, who, as Alexander De Grand has written, "did not gain support because they promised subversion, but because they promised revenge against the Reds and restored social discipline."

In accordance with his plan and with the argument that the country's political mood had changed since 1919, in April 1921 Giolitti dissolved the Chamber of Deputies and called new elections. In preparation for the vote, which he hoped would diminish PSI and PPI strength, he fostered creation of national blocs consisting of Liberals, democrats, and Fascists. Because of the developments discussed, the Fascists had indeed become a force to be reckoned with. Between March and May 1921, the fasci had grown from 317 to 1,001, and their adherents from 80,500 to 187,100.

The Communist Split

The bourgeois counteroffensive had important effects within the Socialist movement. As violence escalated, the reformists became more convinced that the PSI must cooperate with political forces willing to preserve Italian democracy and support a national government that promised to enforce the law against Fascist atrocities. As we have seen, Giolitti ultimately aimed at Socialist collaboration; given the intransigence of the majority, he expected a PSI split on the right, after which he could reach an agreement with a new reformist party. The reformists, however, aimed at maintaining the party's contractual power intact by altering the PSI's policy and bringing the entire organization into a coalition. Such a task would be difficult. Taking note of the weakened Socialist position, the maximalist majority modified its view on the imminence of revolution, recognized the necessity for unity, but shunned collaboration with non-Socialist forces.

At the same time, the PSI's left wing (Communist) pressed for expulsion of the reformists. In July and August 1920, the Second Congress of the Third International (also called the Communist International or Comintern) established a centralized structure. Parties wishing to join the International had to accept the so-called Twenty-One Conditions subjecting the national organizations to the control of an executive committee. These demands included expulsion of "social democrats" such as Turati, a change of party name to "Communist," and a new party directorate to have a two-thirds majority of people who were Communists before formulation of the Twenty-One Conditions.

Maximalist leader Giacino Menotti Serrati objected to the mechanical implementation of these demands on the ground that each country had different traditions and conditions. He believed Italy needed unity both in the event of a revolution or to fight reaction. He also objected to the name change because it would disorient the masses, familiar with the PSI's glorious tradition. Serrati's objections were based on his knowledge that a PSI majority adamantly opposed the expulsions and the name change.

The disillusion caused by the factory occupations and the reaction's effects convinced maximalist leaders that a split would be fatal. Between September and November 1920, a series of meetings established that Serrati's viewpoint had majority support. There were two communist factions, one led by Antonio Gramsci, who headed Turin's *Ordine Nuovo* group, more flexible; the other, headed by Neapolitan engineer Amedeo Bordiga, advocated a disciplined Leninist revolutionary party on the Soviet model and unconditional acceptance of the Twenty-One Conditions. In a meeting of the Communist current on November 28–29, Bordiga won out.

Contrary to earlier expectations, the setting had been prepared for a split that would exclude the Communists and leave the squabbling reformist and maximalist wings in the same organization—the worst possible solution. This is what occurred at the Congress of Livorno on January 15, 1921. The communist motion mandating rigid implementation of the Twenty-One Conditions went down to defeat against a maximalist proposal allowing them to be applied with "autonomy." The Communists walked out and founded the Communist Party of Italy (PCdI, later PCI, Italian Communist Party).

Although if it may be argued that the split was a long time coming, resulted in an ideologically pure organization, and created a party that had a crucial role in Italian history, the immediate effects were disastrous. The schism divided the Italian working-class movement at the reaction's height, damaging even further its capacity to resist fascism. The PCI attracted fewer adherents than its founders anticipated and was less compact than it appeared; forced to compete with the larger PSI for the same political space, Communists targeted Socialists, not Fascists, as the primary enemies.

Furthermore, neither Communist nor Socialist party could contest the Fascist drive toward power. The schism did not clarify the ideological situation in the PSI, which meant that the reformists failed to alter intransigent party policy in favor of one supporting a government pledged to defend democracy, a fight that made for continuing paralysis and a fresh split in 1922. Nor was the new Communist party any more effective. Under Bordiga's leadership, it remained rigidly extremist, and Gramsci's view that revolution was the only possible answer to Fascist reaction delayed an appropriate analysis of fascism and consequently "of the means to combat it efficiently."

From Giolitti's Fall to the Fascist Coup d'Etat

The general elections of May 1921, designed by Giolitti to bolster his cabinet, doomed it instead. Of the two parties whose representation Giolitti had hoped to reduce, the Socialists declined only slightly and the Catholics picked up eight seats. At the same time, the Communists won fifteen seats and the Fascists thirty-five. Despite their limited representation, the Fascists could count on aid from Nationalists and right-liberal groups. Giolitti had hoped that the elections would provide him a stable majority based on center and center-right Liberals, but his rule remained dependent on the lukewarm support of the PPI and heterogeneous factions in the Chamber. As a result of this unstable situation, he resigned on June 27, 1921.

Ivanoe Bonomi replaced him. Bonomi, a moderate Socialist expelled from the PSI in 1912 with Bissolati, had links with the right and non-Socialist left thanks to his past as a democratic interventionist. He hoped to end the country's turmoil through a "Pact of Pacification" negotiated between Fascists and Socialists. Mussolini, concerned with the growing reputation of fascism as a violent movement, which he feared might isolate it and block its acceptance as a legitimate mass political movement, favored the pact because it demonstrated Fascist good-will. Negotiations proved difficult, but in July the police and population fired on a Fascist column in Sarzana bent on freeing jailed comrades. This incident showed that, sufficiently provoked, the police would attack Fascists and that workers and peasants could unite against fascism. Mussolini pressed his people to reopen talks and the pact was signed on August 2, 1921.

The pacification pact brought to the surface divisions between Mussolini and agrarian fascism—the political and military strains. Mussolini hoped to gain political advantage by inserting fascism into parliamentary maneuvers, by distinguishing it from the extreme conservative right, and even by considering agreements with leftists and the labor movement; reflecting their alliance with large landholders, agrarian Fascists aimed at the complete destruction of peasant leagues and organizations, not only Socialist, Communist, and Anarchist but Catholic and republican as well. Agrarian Fascists used violence less subtly than Mussolini and admired D'Annunzio too much, but they represented the movement's major force. As a result, a regional congress of Fascists from Emilia-Romagna rejected the pact and advocated calling a national congress. Since Fascist leaders Italo Balbo, Roberto Farinacci, and Dino Grandi were present at the gathering, Mussolini responded to the challenge by resigning as a member of the Fascist Executive Commission.

But since none of the leaders wished to weaken fascism by splitting it, the leadership buried its differences. Mussolini emphasized transforming the movement into a party, more easily subject to control, while the Fascist National Council rejected Mussolini's resignation. Meanwhile the pact had proved inapplicable, rendering the difference of opinion over it moot. Over the next few months, Mussolini concluded that it was inopportune to continue challenging agrarian fascism, gave it free rein, and formally denounced the dead pacification pact.

In return, the third Fascist Congress (November 7–11, 1921) formally established the Fascist party (PNF). This congress revealed the major changes that had occurred since fascism's birth in 1919. According to statistics unveiled at the meeting, the party consisted of 2,200 fasci composed of 320,000 members. Unlike early fascism, this membership hailed primarily from the landowning and middle classes; farm workers in the party were probably forced to join, but the organization counted numerous tradesmen, civil servants, and professionals. Reflecting this shift in membership, the congress abandoned the 1919 platform and adopted a "new program" emphasizing laissez-faire and nationalist principles instead of the "socialistic" ones of 1919. The 1921 program demanded the end of taxes on inheritances and bondholders, the abolition of public service strikes, a large standing army, freedom for the Catholic Church to perform its spiritual duties, and, paralleling Parliament, National Technical Councils with legislative powers.

While Fascist leaders demonstrated flexibility in submerging their differences, their enemies persisted in misinterpreting and undervaluing fascism. The Socialists erred in signing the pact, misjudging the government's commitment to crack down on fascism should its leaders violate its terms. The agreement provided an excuse for the authorities to dismantle the Arditi del Popolo, a leftist military organization created to defend against the squads. The reformists, strong supporters of the pact, drew the logical consequences of its failure by seriously posing the question of Socialist collaboration in a cabinet committed to defend democracy against the Fascist onslaught, but the maximalists remained inflexible. Encouraged by the divisions among Fascists, they interpreted fascism as an extreme bourgeois reaction that would simplify the class struggle and lead to the dictatorship of the proletariat. The PSI Directorate saw collaboration with governments, not fascism, as the major threat to socialism and declared "incompatible the presence within the party of those who affirm the collaborationist principle." Serrati opposed expelling the reformists, but his refusal to consider governmental collaboration, the agreement of Socialist representatives at the Moscow Congress of the Communist International (June 22 to July 12, 1921) to press for expulsion against Serrati's wishes, the consequent creation of a new "third internationalist" faction within the PSI bent on ejecting the reformists, and the maximalist victory at the Eighteenth PSI National Congress, October 10–15, 1921, all set the stage for a new split in 1922.

The Catholic PPI, another potentially powerful Fascist opponent, also made a series of errors during this crucial period. Like the Socialists, this organization also suffered from a left-right division. Represented by sociologist Don Luigi Sturzo and Guido Miglioli, a northern peasant organizer, the Catholic left staunchly opposed fascism but found itself weakened by Pope Pius XI's support of the right wing. Despite the left's desire for a strong statement against fascism, the PPI congress of October 20–23 avoided condemning it and delivered a weak statement on the possibility of collaborating with the Socialists in a governmental coalition. Noted for his staunch antifascism, Sturzo seemed not to comprehend how close fascism was to achieving power and had no practical plan for thwarting it. Even more serious and for reasons still hotly debated, Sturzo adamantly opposed the return of Giolitti to power after Bonomi's fall. Since even Mussolini believed that Giolitti would have used the army to defeat any Fascist attempt at a coup d'etat had he been at the government's helm in 1922, and given the PPI's lynchpin status for cabinets during this era, Sturzo's "veto" of the Piedmontese statesman was crucial to fascism's success.

Although Giolitti's past anticlericalism and his advocacy of registering securities in the names of their owners irritated Sturzo, a different conception of politics probably accounts for the PPI's opposition. Sturzo favored negotiating with the other political forces to achieve agreement on a cabinet's program and composition before its installation, whereas Giolitti insisted upon making the major decisions himself. The Catholic conception reflected the evolving mass party basis of Italian politics; although bargaining became standard operating procedure after World War II, in 1922 half the deputies belonged to ill-defined "parties" with vague programs and slight ideological commitment better represented by Giolitti's style. Furthermore, as events would demonstrate, the PPI lacked alternatives to a Giolitti cabinet, made impossible by its policy. Along with the other parties, the Catholics underestimated Mussolini's impending threat to democracy.

On February 2, 1922, Bonomi resigned, done in by the pacification pact's failure and his refusal to bail out the Banca Italiana di Sconto, a large bank linked to the Perrone industrial group. Although Bonomi acted to prevent major economic repercussions, and although other measures taken by his and the previous Giolitti government eventually reversed the dismal economic situation, rightist groups that supported Perrone and that had clamored for government intervention to save the Bank turned against Bonomi. Democrats representing irate depositors and moderate-liberal groups pressing for Giolitti's return joined them.

A drawn-out crisis followed Bonomi's fall, with a long string of prominent politicians failing to win support that would permit them to govern. Socialist reformist parliamentarians proposed a cabinet that would pursue an anti-Fascist policy but received no response from the PPI or democratic groups and a dressing-down from their own party. The Catholics vetoed Giolitti and refused to take the helm themselves. Finally on February 25, a temporary solution allowed formation of a government under Giolitti lieutenant Luigi Facta, who tacitly agreed to resign when a more permanent agreement could be reached. An unsteady coalition of Catholics and liberal democratic groups supplied the majority, despite Sturzo's displeasure.

Facta's manifest weakness encouraged a great Fascist offensive in the spring and summer of 1922, coinciding, oddly enough, with the burgeoning of the Fascist labor movement. In January 1922 previously autonomous Fascist labor organizations organized in a centralized federation linked to the PNF. A former revolutionary syndicalist and organizer of Italian workers in the United States, Edmondo Rossoni, took charge of the movement, which, for reasons that will be discussed, grew to an amazing 458,000 members by June 1922. Despite Rossoni's sincerity and skill in mobilizing workers, the labor movement contradicted fascism's real nature. In fact, Fascist labor leaders faced constant embarrassment, especially on the land where they had the most support, by the propensity of owners to violate agreements even after workers had taken cuts because of the economic situation. Fascist leaders shrewdly resolved their problem by organizing vast actions to wring concessions from an increasingly weak state. September 1921 had witnessed a "march" on Ravenna in imitation of D'Annunzio's Fiume exploit; organized by Italo Balbo, *Ras* (leader) of Ferrara Province, as a pilot project the march proved that Fascists could solve the logistical problem connected with moving large masses of people. In May 1922, 60,000 peasants protected by Fascist squads occupied Ferrara and forced the government to make appropriations for public works. Later the same month, 20,000 Fascists occupied Bologna for five days in a move against a prefect who had instituted measures prohibiting the importation of workers competing with Socialist leagues; giving in to Fascist demands, the government transferred the official, Cesare Mori. By moves of this kind, Fascists cleverly protected landowner interests by focusing worker demands against an enfeebled government.

Fascist inroads on the labor movement did not depend solely on these tactics. Besides the respect that the experienced Rossoni commanded, Fascist labor leaders enunciated a series of progressive demands, including an eight-hour day, a worker share in management, and worker representation in personnel decisions. Fascist labor leaders emphasized balancing the interests of workers and the nation; this concept appealed to peasants who rejected the Marxist emphasis on the class struggle and who favored practical means to increase production, opposed public service strikes, and trusted in the capitalists to lead the way out of the economic crisis. Fascist labor organizations took the name of "corporations" from D'Annunzio, which conveyed the idea of solidarity. Reflecting fascism's split personality, in September 1922 Mussolini's newspaper stated that it could do without the proletariat's support, but the idea of a partnership to rescue the country appealed to many workers.

Facta's failure to act against Fascist violence, and the de facto complicity of local officials, encouraged local Fascist leaders to escalate the violence. Punitive raids struck many cities but culminated on July 13. Squads led by Roberto Farinacci occupied the Cremona city hall, terrorized their opponents, and destroyed the homes of prominent Socialist and Catholic leaders. This event produced a PPI backlash against Facta, and his government fell without the solution it had been created to encourage. For a brief time it seemed Parliament would install a center-left government committed to curbing Fascist excesses. This hope evaporated amid the specter of civil war threatened by Mussolini and the divisions among his enemies. The reformists resolved to support an anti-Fascist cabinet and, in a clamorous development, Turati consulted with the king. Nothing came of these efforts. PSI executive organs denounced the reformist parliamentarians, and the Catholic right wing rejected cooperating with the Socialists, as did Sturzo. Consultations revealed that no agreement on resolving the crisis by naming an authoritative prime minister existed. As a result, Facta headed a new cabinet and again awaited a more permanent solution.

The failure to craft an anti-Fascist compromise strengthened Mussolini. This truth became clear during the July 31 to August 2, 1922, "legalitarian" general strike. Originally conceived as pressure in favor of a Giolitti-Turati cabinet, a "labor alliance" of anti-fascist unions formed the previous February called the strike to demonstrate against Fascist terror. Badly organized, the strikers were no match for armed *squadristi* who attacked them in the name of national solidarity, frequently in the company of police. The Fascists broke the strike and exploited the occasion to destroy labor organizations, burn their enemies' property, and expel Socialist city administrations.

The disastrous legalitarian strike and Facta's reconfirmation opened the road to power for Mussolini. The labor alliance crumbled, and in October the CGL severed its ties with the Socialist party. To their control of the land, the Fascists now added political domination of all the major cities in the North and Center. More important, the political establishment concluded that there could be no solution to the country's turmoil without Fascist participation in a governmental coalition. Giolitti and other liberal leaders agreed; in the PPI tensions between the pro-Fascist right and the anti-Fascist left wing increased. In response to these developments and to its intensified internal debate on collaboration, the PSI ripped itself in half at its Nineteenth Congress, October 1–4, 1922. With the help of the "third internationalists," the maximalists barely managed to expel the reformists, who formed the Unitary Socialist party (PSU) under the leadership of Turati and Giacomo Matteotti. The Marxist movement was now split into three competing parties, with the intransigent PSI and PCI viewing fascism as really signalling the approach of the dictatorship of the proletariat and the PSU advocating collaboration with democratic groups to defeat Mussolini. If PSI and PCI policy continued to be suicidal, however, the PSU had arrived at its governmental appointment too late because the PPI and the Liberals were now primarily interested in cooperating with Mussolini and not the Socialists. Defeated in the field, split, and shorn of their labor support, the Socialists no longer presented an effective opposition to fascism.

Mussolini's success, however, meant that he had to act quickly. With the "bolshevik" threat clearly smashed, his bourgeois allies might soon tire of supporting an expensive and now unnecessary repressive organization and would favor maintaining order by means of a strengthened traditional government. During the next two months Mussolini skillfully balanced military moves and the desire of establishment politicians to cooperate with him. At the same time he cleverly combined the differences of fascism's two wings; one, led by Dino Grandi, pressed him to come to power legally by taking advantage of a governmental coalition; the other, headed by Balbo, Farinacci, and Michele Bianchi, preferred the "insurrectional" approach, that is, a "March on Rome" from the provinces as perfected by the marches of local leaders on various Italian cities. Mussolini understood that only a mixture of these methods would work, since the army could easily defeat a Fascist coup attempt; he intensified the delicate task of convincing the army and its leader, the king, not to intervene against a coup that would be in their own interest.

In a complex series of maneuvers, Mussolini dangled both the "legal" and "military" solutions before friend and foe. He negotiated with Liberal leaders clamoring to form a governing coalition with him but remained unwilling to accept a subordinate position and stalled agreement. This was particularly true about the most discussed solution, a Giolitti-led cabinet; Mussolini considered Giolitti the Liberal statesman most likely to order the military to stop a Fascist coup d'etat. Mussolini also played up to the king by attenuating fascism's republican propensities, but he suggested that, by accepting only the monarchy, if Victor Emmanuel opposed him he would replace the king with his more glamorous cousin the Duke of Aosta. Counterbalancing these political maneuvers, in October Fascist leaders implemented an August decision of their Central Committee to form a unified military command of Fascist forces. This move amounted to formal creation of an illegal private army, whose organizational criteria Mussolini's newspaper published on October 3 and 12, 1922. The government did not react.

Mussolini masterfully managed the complicated and confused situation that now ensued. Gabriele D'Annunzio still rivaled him and had a strong following even among Fascists. In the course of talks with Liberal politicians, the poet agreed with Facta that a large demonstration of war veterans would take place in Rome on November 4, anniversary of the Italian victory in World War I. Rumor had it that D'Annunzio planned a ceremony to reconcile the country's opposing forces, close the continuing dispute over the war, and create the basis for a new government, perhaps headed by Giolitti. After an unsuccessful attempt to work out his differences with D'Annunzio, Mussolini decided to hold a march on Rome a week before the scheduled "reconciliation."

On October 16 Mussolini met in Rome with the military heads of fascism— Balbo, Bianchi, Cesare Maria De Vecchi, Emilio De Bono, and others. Mussolini declared a parliamentary solution to the country's crisis imminent and that the resolution would damage fascism; he insisted the time for a military takeover of the capital had arrived. He proposed moving immediately following a Fascist congress scheduled for Naples on October 24, which would both give the Fascists momentum and create a diversion. De Vecchi, head of the Turinese Fascists and a captain, and De Bono, a retired general, objected that Fascist forces were not ready, but Mussolini insisted. According to De Vecchi, Mussolini said that D'Annunzio and Giolitti planned a clamorous act of reconciliation on November 4—an embrace at the Tomb of the Unknown Soldier. Mussolini believed that this theatrical gesture would work and produce a Giolitti cabinet, "and you know that with Giolitti it is better to think of other things." Insisting that the government was "rotten" and that the time had come to act, Mussolini won out. Over the next two days, the Fascist leaders made military plans for the March on Rome.

At the Naples congress, the exact date of the march and other details were ironed out. Mussolini and the "quadrumvirs" who led the military action understood that they would be defeated if the army were called out. They moved to obviate that possibility. On October 25 Mussolini took the train for Milan, stopping at Rome to consult with pro-Fascist Masonic army elements with influence on the king. The next few days were marked by a series of intense consultations, which have not yet been fully reconstructed, with influential personages.

Writing to the king at his vacation retreat, Facta first expressed doubt about a Fascist insurrection, then said that the government was ready to meet it. He tried desperately to reach a political solution that would bring the Fascists into a ruling coalition. Mussolini played along, indirectly helped by Giolitti's refusal to be rushed; some influential Fascists believed that the best that could be achieved was a cabinet consisting of Fascists and Nationalists and headed by Salandra, but Mussolini preferred the weaker Facta and dragged out the negotiations. There are indications that on October 26 Mussolini agreed to a new Facta government with Fascist participation (the documents have not been found), but later the same day Bianchi stated that only a Mussolini-led cabinet could resolve the crisis.

Perhaps convinced that he had an agreement with Mussolini, Facta sent a soothing telegram to the king at 12:10 A.M. on October 27 but asked him to come to Rome. As Victor Emmanuel boarded a train to the capital, the first signs of Fascist military activity appeared, along with army preparations to meet it. During the day, negotiations with Mussolini for a new government broke down definitively; at the Rome station, Facta briefed the king on the day's developments and Victor Emmanuel expressed irritation that he had to make decisions under the pressure of Fascist rifles. Between nine and ten P.M., at the king's Roman villa, Facta pointed out that the king could declare martial law but apparently did not make a strong case. Facta then went to his hotel to sleep.

At midnight the prime minister was awakened and told of further Fascist military action. At 5:30 A.M., October 28, the cabinet convened. That night at the war ministry, some cabinet members complained of Fascist occupations of strategic sites as a result of the army's failure to act, while an army representative lamented the lack of orders. The cabinet proceeded to draft a proclamation of martial law; Facta consulted with the king, who agreed to sign the declaration the next morning. The cabinet voted unanimously to declare a state of siege, informed the police and military commanders of the decision, and revised the text. At 8:30 A.M. posters plastered in Rome announced martial law. At 9:00 Facta presented the decree to Victor Emmanuel for his signature; surprisingly, Victor Emmanuel refused to sign. There is some dispute as to whether a second meeting took place, but at 11:30, Facta resigned and telegrams went out countermanding the orders to institute martial law.

What accounts for the king's refusal? Much later he would argue that he feared civil war would result, but this explanation seems to have been concocted to justify the king during a referendum on the monarchy after World War II. Other accounts tell of secret meetings with his advisers and supposed doubts that the army, infiltrated by Fascist sympathizers, would fight; but no evidence exists that the military—fiercely loyal to the Savoys—would have refused to follow orders. Most probably, the king concluded that had he employed the army to stop the Fascists he would have prolonged the chaotic situation in Italy and encouraged a vacuum on the right that would have favored a leftist revival. Even though irritated by Fascist military action, Victor Emmanuel knew that the political establishment believed some form of Fascist participation in government to be inevitable, and he himself considered it a stabilizing force. Given these factors, he opted for the solution he believed would stabilize the political situation for a while.

More important, the monarch's refusal to sign the martial law decree in the face of a unanimous vote by the government reveals a fatal flaw in the Italian Constitution. In the West, constitutional development tended to weaken the executive. Italy participated in this trend, but it had not developed as fully as in Britain and France. Furthermore, the postwar political instability exacerbated this defect. It seems likely that Giolitti, more authoritative than Facta, or a prime minister with a strong parliamentary majority would have been successful in securing the king's assent to martial law. As in 1915 when he supported Italian entrance into the war, the king sided with conservative coteries against the legally constituted order.

Victor Emmanuel preferred Salandra to Mussolini as the head of a cabinet, even if such a government would have included Fascists in important positions. As indicated, some Fascists such as De Vecchi did not believe a Mussolini-led cabinet possible. More politically astute than they, Mussolini remained adamant, holding out for an official mandate to form a government. Given the circumstances, the king gave in. On the evening of October 29, 1922, Mussolini took a sleeper train for Rome. His cabinet, supported by Nationalists, PPI (against Sturzo's wishes), and Liberals, included five Fascists in the most important posts (Mussolini headed the cabinet and the powerful interior and foreign ministries), three pro-Fascists (War, Navy, and Education), and seven Fascist undersecretaries; Liberals, democrats, and Catholics completed the picture.

Fascist power in the government was out of all proportion to the PNF's representation in the Chamber of Deputies, but the cabinet was presented as the victory of the young generation that had fought and died for the country in war over the decrepit politicians. From this point on, the discredited Parliament steadily lost power and ceased being the center of political decision making. Many deputies voted for the Mussolini government because they believed that they retained the power to vote the cabinet out of office should they wish to do so—but this possibility became increasingly theoretical and the country no longer had a fully functioning parliamentary regime. "In this sense, on October 29–30, 1922, in Italy a coup d'etat occurred which broke the continuity of the parliamentary-constitutional tradition, even if it did not formally violate the letter of the *Statuto* issued by Charles Albert."

On October 30 the squads flooded into Rome and other cities, terrorizing and killing their enemies, sacking their meeting places, devastating their homes, and dismembering their organizations. With the government in Mussolini's hands, they became the country's real rulers. In doing so, they created a new style and began an era not only in Italy but in Europe.

16

Mussolini's Italy

D ESPITE SERIOUS PROBLEMS before World War I, the Italian constitutional system evolved in the same direction of the most advanced European countries, making notable progress toward democracy. By the 1850s Piedmontese ministers were responsible to Parliament, and this was also the case after unification, even though the king retained an important voice in governmental affairs. In France, this ministerial responsibility was won definitively only in 1877, although the executive power was much weaker. In addition, the Senate appointed by the king under the 1848 Statuto never had more than gadfly status, in contrast to Britain's House of Lords, which lost its power only in 1911 but before then hampered the country's democratic evolution. Unlike Italy, France, and Great Britain, Germany, Austria-Hungary, and Russia failed to develop ministerial responsibility before World War I. Indeed, immediately after the war, Italians probably enjoyed greater civil liberties than the citizens of most European countries and the United States. Indeed, perhaps this situation and the economic and social effects of the war help explain the reaction of 1921–1922 and the rise of fascism. These developments reversed the country's steady progress toward a parliamentary democracy and greater economic fairness and thus represented a radical departure from the recent past.

Consolidating the Regime

On November 16, 1922, Mussolini asked the Chamber of Deputies for a vote of confidence. This request and the Duce's creation of a coalition cabinet convinced traditional politicians anxious to ignore reality that the March on Rome signified only the installation of a cabinet capable of restoring order, which they could vote out of office any time they wished. But while right-wing Liberals such as Salandra saw Mussolini as heading a restoration government, and left Liberal leaders advocated patience until Fascist mistakes encouraged parliament to vote against Mussolini and recall Giolitti, the Duce presented the March on

Rome as a revolution and his request for confirmation only a courtesy. He remarked that he could have turned the Chamber into a bivouac for his Black Shirts and stated: "I could have bolted parliament shut and constituted a government made up exclusively of Fascists. I could have: but I did not, at least for now, choose to do so."

Liberal and Catholic deputies ignored these words in the confidence debate, choosing to emphasize Mussolini's promise to restore law and order. PSU leader Filippo Turati denounced Mussolini, but Communists and PSI Socialists continued to underestimate him and muted their response. On November 17, Liberals, Catholics, and small democratic groups joined Fascists and Nationalists to give Mussolini a 306 to 116 majority.

For the next year and a half, Mussolini maneuvered to outwit his opponents, who had considerable support in the country, in order to consolidate his rule. On December 3, 1922, the Chamber gave the government full powers for a year to confront the economic crisis and to reduce the bloated bureaucracy. Ironically, Mussolini's Liberal allies consented to the legislation despite its weakening of parliamentary prerogatives. The Fascists exploited the law to reorganize the state administration, fire their opponents, and gain control of the bureaucracy.

In addition to operating in the traditional governing sectors, Mussolini established institutions foreshadowing the one-party state Italy would become. On December 15, 1922, a meeting of Fascist chiefs gave origin to the Fascist Grand Council, which met on that date to solve the diverse problems represented by the squads. Their wanton violence had long threatened fascism's respectability, and their independence challenged Mussolini's control of the movement. With socialism's political defeat removing the excuse for violence, the Duce, heading a government supposedly pledged to restore law and order, could hardly afford to become the symbol of disorder. On January 11, 1923, the *Popolo d'Italia* announced who had the right to sit on the Grand Council; these persons included Fascist party Directorate members, Fascist ministers and other officials, and governmental functionaries such as the head of the police (pubblica sicurezza). Besides those specifically mentioned as sitting on the Council by right, there was no set rule as to who could participate in the deliberations, and Mussolini reserved the right to summon others whose presence he might find useful on an ad hoc basis. Thus the Grand Council assumed both party and state functions; it strengthened Mussolini's control over an unruly Fascist party, enunciated principles, and drafted legislation consolidating his power and organizing the regime. Other changes in membership occurred before the Council's existence was formalized in law in 1928, but after then it lost power, for the reason soon to be discussed.

Furthermore, hoping to assert control over an irregular (and rival) armed force, the army and non-Fascist conservatives pressured Mussolini to "normalize" the squads. Mussolini had his own problems with them, but he still needed an independent military force to continue intimidating his opponents and consolidate his power. The Fascist Grand Council resolved these issues by formally dissolving the squads and instituting the Voluntary Militia for National Security (MVSN), a decision adopted by the government and ratified by royal decree. Composed of former squad members and conserving Fascist symbols, the MVSN was officially entrusted with the mission of protecting the "October Revolution." This restructuring permitted fierce attacks against fascism's enemies, which intensified in 1923 and 1924 and forced many of them underground or into exile.

Used to their independence, local Fascist *Ras*—a term taken from Ethiopian chieftains referring to Fascist bosses in the provinces—resisted Mussolini's "normalization" attempts. Along with amalgamation of the Nationalist Association beginning in March 1923, these contrasts caused a crisis in the Fascist party. Mussolini supported the "revisionist" current led by Giuseppe Bottai and Massimo Rocca. These leaders argued that fascism must be transformed from a combat organization into a movement capable of renewing the nation. This task implied formation of a new ruling class that would accept into its bosom and make use of competent people from all sectors of Italian society. Opposing the country's normalization, the "intransigent" wing led by *Ras* such as Roberto Farinacci advocated a "second wave" of the Fascist revolution that would destroy by violence what was left of Liberal Italy, including the remnants of Socialist, Communist, and Catholic organizations. As was his wont, Mussolini switched his support to this second movement when he needed its military might.

The instability caused by adoption of proportional representation in 1919 produced widespread demands for its modification by Fascists and Liberal politicians. After lengthy debate, the government presented a bill drafted by Mussolini's undersecretary, Giacomo Acerbo, that would give two-thirds of the seats in the Chamber to the electoral coalition achieving a plurality, provided the coalition received 25 percent of the total votes cast; the remaining one-third would be distributed proportionately among the other parties. As expected, the left-wing parties opposed passage while conservatives supported it, but the real struggle occurred within the pivotal PPI. In fact, most of the PPI supported proportional representation, including Sturzo and others who wished to continue collaboration with Mussolini's government. Since Catholic defection on this issue would cause the bill to fail, Mussolini enlisted the Vatican's aid to block the PPI from voting against the Acerbo bill or at least to split the organization. By making important concessions to the Church, he hoped to convince the Vatican that it did not need a Catholic party or at least to encourage the PPI's right wing to support him. On January 20, 1923, the Duce and Vatican secretary of state Cardinal Pietro Gasparri met secretly; Mussolini agreed to continue the bailout of the Catholic Banco di Roma and the Vatican replaced the bank's directors, strong supporters of the Sturzo wing.

Shortly afterward, the PPI right wing, with Vatican support, called for continued collaboration with the Mussolini government and sought expulsion of Mussolini's enemies within the organization on the grounds that they sympathized with subversive parties. After a heated debate at its April congress in Turin, the delegates approved "conditional collaboration," meaning continued support for the government but defense of full proportional representation. Mussolini responded by dropping Catholic representatives from his cabinet, intensifying Fascist violence against Catholic organizations, and initiating an anti-Catholic press campaign. Supported by the Vatican, right-wing Catholic periodicals attacked the party leadership and pressured Sturzo to resign as secretary. Mussolini hoped to obtain Sturzo's resignation before debate on the Acerbo bill, an objective that he achieved on July 10, 1923. Five days later, the Chamber accepted the Acerbo bill; a number of right-wing PPI deputies bolted discipline, voted in favor of the bill, and were later expelled. Their close links with the pope, however, further alienated the Vatican; Mussolini had skillfully prepared the ground for the pope's abandonment of the Catholic party.

The political forces now faced new elections, called for April 1924. In addition to controlling the government apparatus, the Fascists had a great advantage because of the economy's rebound and Mussolini's diplomatic success in negotiating the cession of Fiume to Italy. The Fascists also agreed with prominent Liberals, such as Salandra and former Prime Minister Orlando, former PPI politicians, and other non-Fascist politicians on a single electoral list. These allies attracted many votes to the "listone" ("big list") and gave the Fascists respectability. On the other hand, Fascist opponents failed to present a united front. The PSI, racked by an internal dispute on whether to fuse with the PCI, underwent a fresh split in 1923; the PCI offered to join a united list, but the PSU, pushing for a coalition of all democratic forces and reunion with the PSI, branded the Communists "unwitting" accomplices of fascism and rejected collaboration.

These factors, heavy doses of Fascist violence, Mussolini's control of the voting machinery, and state intervention facilitated a Fascist victory. The Fascist-led electoral coalition won 64.9 percent of the votes and two-thirds of the seats in the Chamber. Despite Fascist terror, the elections revealed strong opposition to fascism; in the industrialized areas of North Italy not completely subjugated by the squads, the opposition lists outpolled the Fascist-led coalition.

Even the large Fascist majority achieved in the elections failed to assure Mussolini a docile Chamber of Deputies. As Fascist intimidation continued unabated and Mussolini alternated conciliatory words with threatening speeches, his enemies exhibited a growing combativeness. The PSU secretary, Giacomo Matteotti, gave a well-researched and effective speech contending that Fascist violence had invalidated the recent elections and demanding new ones. Republicans, Catholics, and Liberal monarchists took up Matteotti's cry. To throw the opposition off balance, Mussolini made overtures to the left, but this technique ended when Matteotti disappeared on June 10, 1924.

Despite apparent attempts by Mussolini to stall the investigation, the facts of Matteotti's disappearance soon became known. The concierge of a nearby apartment house noticed five men waiting in a car; suspecting that the men were thieves, he jotted down the license plate number. The police traced the car to the editor of a Fascist newspaper with links to the secretary of state for the interior ministry. Leader of the special squad was Amerigo Dumini, a Tuscan Fascist with a criminal record and a salary paid by Cesare Rossi, a Fascist party official and head of Mussolini's press office. The squad members belonged to the "Fascist checka," a term borrowed from the Soviet secret police and organized by Fascist party administrative secretary Giovanni Marinelli. Marinelli probably issued the order to kidnap Matteotti, but questions immediately arose as to the kidnappers' intent and Mussolini's responsibility.

Dumini and his cohorts later argued that they did not intend to murder Matteotti but to "teach him a lesson" by administering a beating, which, however, got out of hand. The crime's circumstances, including a premeditated attempt to cover up the disappearance by Mussolini's office, contradicted this explanation. Indeed, Matteotti's vigorous resistance apparently made plans to hide the body go awry so that it was eventually discovered. As to Mussolini's involvement, the Duce later contended that the affair caused him so much trouble that only his "worst enemy" could have conceived it. Attempts to find documents showing Mussolini's direct order to kill Matteotti have been unsuccessful and probably will be in the future; most historians agree that Mussolini created the conditions in which such a crime could occur, but others believe that the Duce ordered the murder and cite circumstantial evidence and his cover-up attempt to make their case.

Although it threatened his tenure, the Matteotti affair ended by consolidating Mussolini's power. If the Duce ordered Matteotti killed, he underestimated the reaction. A wave of revulsion swept Italy, affecting significant numbers of Fascists as well as non-Fascists. The police made arrests, and when details of the case emerged, most people assumed that Matteotti's outspoken opposition to fascism had gotten him killed, even though his body was not discovered until August. Hoping to prevent his non-Fascist allies from deserting his coalition, Mussolini denied any involvement in Matteotti's disappearance, said he had given strict orders for a thorough investigation that would punish all the culprits, promised that he would purge fascism's unruly elements, dropped all officials implicated in the case from his government, and expressed the hope that a national reconciliation would emerge from the affair. At the apparent behest of the king and his non-Fascist partners, Mussolini also relinquished the interior ministry to Luigi Federzoni, a Nationalist leader and the monarch's confidant. On June 30 the Chamber and Senate accorded Mussolini a vote of confidence.

Encouraged by the turn of public opinion against the government, the opposition took its case to the country. In what became known as the "Aventine Secession," Mussolini's enemies hoped to focus the nation's moral condemnation of Mussolini by boycotting the Chamber. There followed an intense press campaign by the opposition's remaining periodicals that kept the Matteotti affair before the public, which for a time promised to be effective. This technique was doomed to fail because its success depended on the king to dismiss Mussolini as prime minister, but the monarch refused because the Duce had won a vote of confidence and because Victor Emmanuel feared that removal of the cabinet would revive leftist fortunes. In the meantime, despite his conciliatory words, Mussolini swung his support to the intransigents within the PNF and a new wave of violence began. Given Fascist military domination of the country, an attempt at insurrection would have been suicidal, and the labor movement even refused Gramsci's proposal for a general strike because of the certainty of defeat. On the other hand, the opposition's absence from the Chamber made Mussolini's task easier when he introduced repressive legislation and established his dictatorship.

The struggle entered a new phase after discovery of Matteotti's body on August 16. The protracted crisis raised the possibility of a union of Mussolini's enemies and defection by his Liberal allies. Turati offered to coordinate action with the Catholics, a proposal PPI Secretary Alcide De Gasperi and Luigi Sturzo seriously considered. The Vatican vetoed the alliance, but Mussolini vowed to eliminate his old enemy. He pressured the Vatican to force Sturzo to leave Italy. Eager to rid itself of an embarrassing figure, the Vatican ordered Sturzo to leave the country. Sturzo departed for England on October 25, 1924, in what was the first stop of a twenty-two year exile in the United States. Mussolini's more radical opponents fared no better. Gramsci proposed transforming the Aventine into an "antiparliament" from which a revolutionary appeal would be made to the nation. The other anti-Fascist forces rejected the proposal as dangerous, and the Communists reentered the Chamber in 1925.

Although opposition tactics caused Mussolini trouble, they failed to shake loose his Liberal allies. In the wake of the Matteotti affair, the manufacturer's association, the Confindustria, which had financed the Fascist coalition's list in the 1924 elections, switched to an attitude of prudent reserve. Luigi Albertini, longtime editor of Milan's great *Il Corriere della Sera,* and Giovanni Amendola, monarchist opponent of Mussolini, had attempted to convince the industrialists to take a position against fascism. Albertini commissioned an article by respected economist Luigi Einaudi exhorting the *Confindustria* to condemn fascism. In September a *Confindustria* delegation presented a memorandum to Mussolini asking him to refrain from repressing the labor movement, allow freedom of organization, and eliminate political interference in the economic sphere. This attitude indicated a possible shift against the Duce if moderate political forces moved in the same direction, but despite favorable indications this change did not occur. In October a Liberal party (actually a loose collection of factions) congress voted for the return to legality, respect for the division of powers, maintenance of the constitutional order, the end of private armies, and respect for labor organizations. But no concrete action followed this strong statement, and Salandra's followers remained in Mussolini's cabinet.

Mussolini's more-determined Liberal opponents joined together in a "National Union" headed by Giovanni Amendola, later beaten to death by the Fascists. On December 27, 1924, the National Union's newspaper *Il Mondo* began publishing a memorandum by Cesare Rossi, who had been involved in the Matteotti affair, accusing Mussolini of personally having ordered many acts of violence and, by implication, of having done the same in Matteotti's murder. Coming on the heels of uncertainty within the Fascist-led coalition, the resignation of Italo Balbo as interim head of the MVSN following proof that he had ordered beatings, the attempt of a group of moderate Fascists to present a motion requesting the country's normalization, and rumors that Victor Emmanuel planned either a return to a Liberal government or institution of a military one, publication of Rossi's document created an enormous impression. Albertini demanded that Mussolini turn himself in to the police, while Salandra finally withdrew his support and his friends resigned from the cabinet. Had other non-Fascist government members done the same, the ensuing full-fledged crisis would probably have induced the monarch to dismiss Mussolini. Confronted by the military ministers' support for Mussolini and cowed by the Duce's promise to employ force against an eventual successor, the cabinet stuck by him at a meeting on December 30.

These events illustrate how Mussolini's ability to stay in power depended on his military control of the country. Only his fear that Victor Emmanuel and the army might turn against him had made Mussolini cautious. By the end of 1924, however, the violent wing of fascism had grown impatient with Mussolini's maneuvers. The political aftermath of the Matteotti murder had made Mussolini more dependent on the squads, whose leaders also feared that indecisive action might lead to his downfall and to their own trial. Fascist leaders intensified their violence and organized rallies demanding that Mussolini drop his "weak" policies and finish off the opposition once and for all. Whether Mussolini instigated this ultimatum or whether he merely agreed to it is still a matter of dispute, but he promised to silence the opposition when the Chamber reopened on January 3, 1925.

On that day, Mussolini made a famous speech accepting moral responsibility for Matteotti's murder. He challenged the opposition to move against him, threatened to use force, and added that the government could crush the Aventine "sedition." With most of Mussolini's opponents still boycotting the Chamber, no one responded to the Duce's challenge.

Between January 1925 and the end of 1926, the regime consolidated itself. Within days of his speech, Mussolini reshuffled his cabinet, making it all Fascist. The new ministers were Fascists, such as the ex-Nationalist Alfredo Rocco, known for their support of the monarchy and closeness to the king. In this manner, Mussolini gained the confidence of Victor Emmanuel, rumored to be lukewarm toward the Duce. In a series of shrewd concessions, Mussolini also gained the support of the army and industrialists. At the same time he balanced this policy of concessions with concessions to fascism's intransigent wing. Farinacci—proponent of the Fascist Revolution's "second wave"—was elevated to head the PNF and a new period of violence against fascism's enemies ensued. These actions prepared the way for measures that changed the country's constitutional structure and reversed the course of its democratic evolution since the Risorgimento.

Administration, Economics, Labor, 1925 to 1929

In 1925 and 1926, four attempts on Mussolini's life occurred, one probably staged, which the Duce exploited to pass and systematize repressive legislation. Culminating a process initiated in 1923, Luigi Albertini was removed as editor of the *Corriere della Sera* in November 1925. This Liberal organ passed under Fascist control along with the rest of the independent press. In 1925 and 1926 the government suppressed all opposition parties and associations, including the Masons, and excluded the Aventine deputies from the Chamber. In September 1926 Mussolini appointed the super-efficient Arturo Bocchini as national police chief, a position he held until his death in 1940. Bocchini wielded new repressive instruments against the regime's opponents. In November and December, the government was given wide power to confine persons who subverted the political and social order or who allegedly conspired to do so. To meet the growing exile opposition, government officials gained the right to review and annul passports, to fire on persons attempting to leave the country illegally, and to deprive Italians abroad publicly opposing the regime of their citizenship and property. The government also instituted the death penalty for assassination attempts against government and royal family members and established a special tribunal to try persons committing or contemplating political crimes against the Fascist regime.

Going hand in hand with these changes, new legislation modified the constitutional order and strengthened Mussolini's personal position. In December 1925 parliamentary control over cabinets evaporated with the transformation of the prime minister into the "Head of the Government," responsible to the king and no longer to Parliament. In addition to losing the right to determine who would become prime minister, the Chamber also lost its power to influence the choice of individual ministers, now nominated by Mussolini and appointed by the king. Mussolini also eliminated Parliament's legislative initiative by gaining control of its agenda. In January 1926 a measure ended Parliament's power over the state administration as well, by authorizing the government to implement decisions after consultation with the Council of State. In February a law replaced local elected administrations with appointed officials subordinated to the prefects—the *podestà*. In 1928 provincial administration came under similar control and local autonomy disappeared.

Mussolini also triumphed over the Fascist intransigents who aimed at destroying all pre-fascist institutions. Mussolini preferred to employ the police against his enemies, rather than the squads that besmirched his image at home and abroad, and unlike his enemies, Mussolini favored compromise with existing groups that he felt were necessary to maintain him in power. As a result, in 1926 the Duce forced intransigent leader Farinacci to resign and replaced him as secretary general with the more malleable *Ras* from Brescia, Augusto Turati (not to be confused with Socialist leader Filippo Turati). Turati eliminated all elected party officials, replacing them with appointees, purged the PNF of old *squadristi* who periodically embarrassed the Duce with their violent habits, and transformed the party into a highly centralized and pliable instrument of Mussolini's will. The organization lost its unruly character, the percentage of workers and peasants declined, and it became more middle class.

Mussolini also pursued a middle-class policy in economics, the touchstone of his regime's success. Between 1922 and 1925, Alberto De Stefani, a free-trader, ran Fascist economic policy as minister of finance. The European economy turned up during this period, due primarily to recovery from the war; in Italy, previous economic policy, the temporary disappearance of German competition, the low value of the lira, and low wages stimulated exports and contributed to an impressive increase in production. De Stefani immediately took steps that pleased large industrialists and the Church, including repealing the obligation to register stock, putting the telephone system and other industries into private hands, adjusting the tariff to help industry, giving up the state monopoly in life insurance, and abandoning an inquiry on war profits. These steps identified De Stefani's tenure with laissez-faire economic policy and won praise at home and abroad. But De Stefani also continued previous policies aimed at salvaging banks and industrial concerns most hit by the earlier economic crisis. Combining interventionist with laissez-faire principles proved a powerful combination that revived the economy and allowed the finance minister to balance the budget.

In 1925 the relatively stable lira began a precipitous decline. International speculation against currencies not backed by the gold standard, rather than Italian conditions, determined this fall. Within the country, the decline produced inflation, a drop in real wages, labor agitation, and a stock market boom. De Stefani attempted to stem the crisis by restricting credit and choking off speculation in stocks. As a result, the Confindustria asked for his replacement with a person in whom they had greater confidence. On July 8 Count Giuseppe Volpi di Misurata—a successful businessman who had held a series of government posts—replaced De Stefani.

Volpi unblocked negotiations with the United States over the war debt question. This agreement provided Italy with short-term favorable conditions for repayment and opened the spigot of American loans that the Fascists used to achieve stabilization of the lira. The lull proved temporary. A fresh international monetary crisis touched off a new spiral of decline beginning in April 1926. As the exchange rate fell to 155 against the pound and 30.54 against the dollar, Mussolini feared that the lira's collapse would threaten the regime. This political reason, international pressure, and the apparent desire of the middle class to end monetary uncertainty undoubtedly account for Il Duce's resolution to stabilize the lira at 90 to the pound, its rate when he took office in 1922.

On August 18 Mussolini declared that he would take strong action to defend the currency. Measures mobilizing public opinion, strengthening the central banking system, and instituting credit restrictions quickly followed. This deflationary policy and a hefty loan from the Morgan Bank caused the lira to rise to 92.46 to the pound and 19 to the dollar on December 21, 1927, at which point the lira returned to the gold standard and its exchange rate was fixed.

The lira's revaluation at such a high rate made Italian products expensive when international prices were declining and aggravated the economic situation. Export industries suffered most for this reason, and the credit restrictions hurt agriculture and commerce. Because of their conviction that the government would never let large industries dealing with the domestic market go under, banks tended to invest in them, and these firms weathered the crisis much better.

The government also helped these industries by placing orders, granting tax breaks and favorable contracts, and increasing protective tariffs. Foreshadowing future developments, the government also directly intervened in the economic sector by facilitating mergers, favoring rationalization, and cutting producer costs by reducing worker salaries. In 1927, for example, a 20 percent reduction in salaries was decided upon. The government argued that lower prices compensated the workers for these cuts, but this was only partially true. By 1929 real wages had fallen substantially. (See Table 16.1)

The revaluation crisis proved decisive for the Fascist labor movement, which had made a sincere effort to improve working conditions and wages under its leader, former revolutionary syndicalist Edmondo Rossoni. Rossoni aimed at strengthening the workers' position by absorbing the CGL and the Catholic labor unions into his organization (the Confederazione Generale dei Sindacati Fascisti) and to win employer recognition for it as the sole representative of

TABLE 16.1   Real Wage Indices for Interwar Italy,
              1919–1940 (1913 = 100)

1919	93.1
1920	114.4
1921	127.0
1922	123.6
1923	116.0
1924	112.6
1925	111.8
1926	111.5
1927	120.8
1928	120.7
1929	116.0
1930	119.0
1931	121.6
1932	118.4
1933	120.8
1934	124.2
1935	117.8
1936	108.8
1937	103.8
1938	100.5
1939	105.7
1940	107.8

labor. His ultimate goal was a "corporate" system that would enhance national unity by including workers and employers in the same union. This project faced stiff opposition from employers, who preferred to keep workers divided among different labor organizations. Mussolini, who blew hot and cold toward the workers, gradually came to favor the employers in order to consolidate his power. On December 19, 1923, the employers scored a victory against Rossoni in the Palazzo Chigi Pact, in which they successfully put off Rossoni's goal of a single employer-employee organization by establishing a privileged but not an exclusive relationship between employers and Fascist unions.

The tensions between the Fascist labor movement and the industrialists culminated in March 1925. The monetary crisis had already lowered the standard of living for workers and had stimulated labor agitation among the metal workers. During talks for a new contract, the industrialists, encouraged by rivalry between the non-Fascist metalworkers union (FIOM) and Fascist unions, resisted worker demands. On March 12, in the northern industrial city of Brescia, Fascist leader Augusto Turati initiated a strike that rapidly spread to Milan and Turin, where Communist labor leaders received strong backing. Alarmed at the strength of the labor movement, Mussolini halted the strike by ordering wage increases but resolved to break what was left of the non-Fascist labor movement and to tame the Fascist labor organizations.

On October 2 representatives of the Confindustria and of Fascist unions signed the Palazzo Vidoni Pact, which provided for their reciprocal recognition as representatives of employers and employees. Over the next two years, enabling legislation implemented this apparently favorable decision but defanged the labor movement. Only Fascist unions could legally negotiate and enforce contracts, and previous contracts were voided. These measures forced the Catholic labor unions and the CGL to dissolve in 1926 and 1927. The Confindustria became formally Fascist and its president and secretary entered the Fascist Grand Council, thus sealing the alliance with the government. In 1926 laws drafted by former Nationalist and "right" Fascist theoretician Alfredo Rocco prohibited both strikes and lockouts and mentioned "corporations" for the first time. Formally instituted only in 1934, corporations were defined as central organs linking workers' and employers' organizations with the aim of increasing production and of facilitating dispute resolution. A "Labor Magistracy" was also established as a court of appeal in case of deadlock. The Fascist party had a direct mediating role in helping resolve labor disputes. These offices were little used because of direct government intervention in labor disputes, but Fascist labor legislation had a lasting imprint by accentuating the trend transferring jurisdiction over the complex area of labor relations from private to public law.

These changes nailed down strong business support for the government during the revaluation crisis and the worldwide Great Depression, but at the cost of further reducing the standard of living for employees.

In agriculture, relations between Rossoni and the employers' organization, the Confagricoltura, were difficult to the point that the Fascists established their own employers' association. As the disagreements in industry were resolved, however, government pressure produced similar patterns on the land, and the attempts of Rossoni and other "left" Fascists to win gains for small landholders and for workers faded at a crucial time. In 1925 Il Duce announced the "Battle of the Grain," one of the regime's more spectacular and successful propaganda efforts. For reasons of prestige and self-defense in case of war, Mussolini aimed to make the country self-sufficient in foodstuffs. The government encouraged investment and improvements in a campaign to increase grain production. It hoped to achieve this goal by increasing yield per acre without reducing production of other crops. The campaign cut Italy's grain imports substantially, allowing Mussolini to claim "victory." But bringing more land into production and shifting away from other crops, not increased yield per unit, accounted for the greater production of grain. Exportation of more-lucrative products suffered, and the collapse of international food prices forced producers to become more efficient by killing off their animals and introducing tractors and modern chemical fertilizers. Small landholders who had contracted debts to pay for their land fell behind and lost their possessions, reversing the previous trend toward small landholding. In contrast, large landholders—better able to adapt to the changes and allied with the government—consolidated their position.

On April 21, 1927, the government published the "Labor Charter" with great fanfare. This document stated the right of labor to good working conditions, equitable wages, and social security; it also proclaimed private initiative the most efficient way of serving the country's interests but promised state intervention in the economy when necessary for the good of the nation. This last statement was an important one on which the regime acted during the Depression, but the charter remained primarily a statement of principle, which hardly compensated workers for their decreased economic position. Indeed, tensions continued and in 1928 the Fascists further weakened Rossoni's labor movement by splitting up his single national confederation of unions—which had given him some countervailing power in negotiating with the separate employers' associations—into six organizations corresponding to those of the employers.

The same year also witnessed fundamental constitutional changes to deal with the country's new political reality. The Fascist Grand Council altered the method of electing the Chamber of Deputies. The number of deputies was reduced to four hundred, no longer individually elected. The Council drew up a national list of four hundred persons recommended by the employer, employee, and other associations. The entire list was then presented to the voters, who either accepted or rejected it. Also inspired by former Nationalist thinker Alfredo Rocco, this law looked forward to changing the basis of representation from an individual one to one based on a person's economic role in society. It formally transformed Parliament into a rubber stamp.

The Grand Council also merged Fascist and state institutions by formalizing its own role in government. This recognition coincided with the Council's own decline because, unwilling to surrender any power, Mussolini ensured his control over the institution. Nonetheless, this measure had important results because the Grand Council gained a voice, however theoretical, in the succession to the throne, in naming an eventual successor to Mussolini, and in other prerogatives hitherto reserved to the monarchy. Rumored to be either a concession to intransigent Fascists or an expression of Mussolini's innate republicanism, this move damaged the king's prestige and strained relations between fascism and the monarchy. In the long term, during the wartime conditions of 1943 the Grand Council had an important role in securing Mussolini's ouster.

Completing the construction of the Fascist state, on February 11, 1929, Mussolini signed the Lateran Accords with the Vatican. These agreements formally ended the dispute with the papacy that resulted from annexation of the Papal State during the Risorgimento. The accords created the independent state of Vatican City in Rome, paid the pope a large sum to compensate it for the annexed territories, and regulated the religious affairs of the country.

The Lateran Accords had vast implications. Among the Italian masses and in the international community, the Duce received the credit for having settled the annexation dispute, a development that cemented his regime both at home and abroad. The pope announced that Mussolini was a man sent by Providence. The Holy Father's blessing prompted the leading scholar of Italian Catholicism, Arturo Carlo Jemolo, to interpret the agreements as "the last nail in the coffin of Italian liberty." In addition, the concordat reversed the lay character that the Italian state had inherited from the Risorgimento. By surrendering control over matrimony, allowing religious instruction in secondary public schools, giving the Church censorship powers over free expression in the Holy City, and renouncing other rights, the Fascists created major problems for the Italian state and colored its future character.

In 1929, however, this long-range result would have seemed paradoxical. Mussolini believed that he had relinquished nothing and, having signed the concordat, attacked the Church in an attempt to curb its political and social power and influence over the country's youth. This campaign ended in 1931 with an apparent victory for Mussolini, and, at least until the anti-semitic laws of 1938, the Church supported the regime in domestic and foreign affairs. Seven years after coming to power, openly opposed by no one but an increasingly isolated group of exiles, Mussolini had achieved unparalleled stability at home and a new respect abroad.

The Great Depression

The great world economic crisis struck when the effects of revaluation had not been completely absorbed by the Italian economy. As in other countries, the Depression hit industry hard, increasing unemployment and decreasing working hours. The government responded by encouraging a new round of salary decreases, but the price drop and the institution of additional compensation for large families cushioned the blow. Real salaries for industrial workers who remained employed—already cut during the revaluation crisis—consequently did not fall significantly as a result of the Depression. For the unemployed, receiving support for only ninety days, however, conditions were bleak. To increase employment and production, the government reduced the work week to forty hours and instituted new tariff measures to help industry. To cushion the Depression's social impact, the government expanded and rationalized a system of social security that had originated in the 1880s. This system included accident, old age, and health insurance, as well as maternity benefits. Following fascism's fall, the republic preserved and extended its social security system.

The regime also undertook a vast public-works program, a showpiece of the regime much ballyhooed abroad. This policy included building housing and roads, bringing electricity into areas that lacked it, and, above all, reclaiming land. This ambitious program failed to produce the desired results because the regime concentrated its resources on helping industry weather the Depression and, later, on rearmament. As a consequence, the government reduced its public-works funds, reclaiming only about 10 percent of the land that needed to be drained, irrigated, or otherwise reclaimed.

On the land the Depression had less impact than in industry, but it worsened chronically poor conditions caused by underemployment, the Battle for the Grain, government favoritism toward industry, and the collapse of international trade. These economic developments created tensions that caused serious strikes and tumults despite strong police repression. One of the responses to this disorder, or threat of it, was the "ruralization" policy. Justified ideologically in the name of a high rural ideal, the government instituted laws to stem the movement of people from the land and smaller cities into large urban centers. In this manner, Fascist officials hoped to decrease the concentration of the disaffected poor and unemployed in the cities, a source of opposition and in the past a reservoir for the Socialist and Communist parties. This population movement, however, was a long-term trend that preceded fascism and affected other countries as well. Despite harsh laws, the Fascists failed to reverse the trend. The cities continued swelling during the Fascist period, a phenomenon that continued into the time of the republic.

The economic crisis produced particularly interesting developments in the fields of industry and commerce and their relationship with the government. At first government economists misinterpreted the Depression's seriousness, but intensification of the international crisis with the bankruptcy of Austria's Kredit Anstalt Bank in 1931 laid bare a major problem. Italian banks were of the "mixed" variety, collecting deposits and investing them in commercial endeavors. Unlike in the United States, Italy's stock market did not collapse but continued the steady decline initiated during the deflation crisis. Unwilling to sustain major losses, the banks stepped in to buy up shares and maintain prices. By 1931 large banks held one-third of large and medium Italian firms, but as the crisis deepened, they could no longer obtain sufficient credit and a greater proportion of their loans to the firms became nonperforming. These conditions prompted the largest banks, especially the Credito Italiano and the Banca Commerciale, to call for government help.

The banks hoped for government aid while maintaining their holdings, but Mussolini turned for advice to Alberto Beneduce. A banker and a non-Fascist immune to pressure from Fascist hierarchs with links to bankers, Beneduce opposed the mixed banking system but proved unable to make his views prevail. An October 31, 1931, agreement resulted in the shifting of the banks' commercial holdings to companies controlled by the banks themselves—with the costs transferred to the Bank of Italy. The next month witnessed creation of an agency empowered to make loans to ailing companies (Istituto Mobiliare Italiano [IMI]). In 1932, however, the economic crisis worsened substantially, revealing the inadequacy of these measures.

In January 1933 Beneduce and the new finance minister, Guido Jung, founded a new state agency with Mussolini's approval: the Istituto per la Ricostruzione Industriale (IRI). Originally conceived to arrange long-term financing of industries in major difficulty and as a means of stimulating economic recovery, IRI was supposed to buy up the depressed companies in the banks' portfolios and liquidate them. Instead, IRI developed into a major new departure in Italian economic development with far-reaching future significance. IRI acquired the commercial holdings of the major banks and in the process achieved control of the banks themselves and of other companies. Although it sold some of the holdings, IRI discovered that many of its new acquisitions could not be disposed of. In addition, as Il Duce embarked on a series of wars, the state wished to keep in its hands basic industries, such as steel, necessary for the rearmament effort. These considerations led to the development and rational organization of IRI companies in important sectors of the economy such as steelmaking, shipbuilding, and communications. By the time of its establishment on a permanent basis in 1937, IRI had evolved into a modern holding company under public control employing the most-advanced private enterprise techniques.

IRI's ownership of about one-fifth of the outstanding stock in Italian companies led historian Rosario Romeo to remark that after 1936 the state in Italy managed a greater proportion of industry than did the states in any European country except the Soviet Union. Whether this fact made Italy effectively "Socialist" is a matter of debate; the state had always had a strong economic role in Italy, but now it had clearly entered the economic sector as a major player financing industry, creating new firms, owning companies, and operating like a private entrepreneur. The taxpayer bore the cost of absorbing companies battered by the Great Depression, but public intervention through IRI stimulated industry in northern Italy to improve production methods to such an extent that Italian industry in some areas at least matched the most-advanced European industrial standards. This development created a strong base that greatly contributed to the "economic miracle" that occurred following fascism's fall.

In 1935 preparations for the Ethiopian War forced adjustments in the economy. The government floated a series of loans to finance the conflict. The costs of economic intervention, increased interest payments, and war expenditures produced large budget deficits. In October 1936 Mussolini devalued the lira to bring the currency into line with the pound and the dollar. Prices rose despite attempts to control them, and unions obtained salary increases in 1936, 1937, and 1939. Since inflation remained relatively modest between 1935 and 1939 despite mounting government expenses, a general economic recovery accompanied by increased industrial production occurred during these years. The nation's gross national product rose, in 1938 lire, from 140 billion in 1936 to 162 billion, and national income went from 126 billion to almost 148 billion lire.

TABLE 16.2   Average Yearly Production of Electrical
Energy in Giolittian and Fascist Italy (in
millions of kilowatt hours)

1901–1910	752
1911–1920	3192
1921–1930	7640
1931–1940	14158

TABLE 16.3   Average Annual Capital Formation in the
Industrial Sector (Plant, Equipment, etc.)
during the Giolittian and Fascist Periods
(in millions of 1938 lire)

1901–1910	7,945
1911–1920	8,312
1921–1930	14,634
1931–1940	17,968

Although agriculture remained static, unemployment in the industrial sector fell and real salaries rose slightly.

Institution of the "autarchy" policy in 1936 contributed to this development. Announced by Mussolini as a response to League of Nations sanctions over Ethiopia and accompanied by a great propaganda campaign, this policy had its origins in the Great Depression. The free trading system that had collapsed because of that crisis had not been reinstituted, and countries continued to erect barriers to international trade with the aim of importing as little as possible and stimulating exports. Under the pressure of war, Mussolini sought to transform the system into a kind of economic plan for the country. This plan involved currency controls, an austerity program, the substitution of Italian products for imported ones where possible, the control of imported raw materials by large firms and state agencies, government involvement in the development of new products and processes, control of manufacturing from start to finish, and an intensified search for new sources of energy by state agencies such the Azienda Generale Italiana Petroli (AGIP).

In the light of later statistics, Fascist economic policies had their failures, particularly in agriculture and in the field of real wages. But those policies also stimulated important modern industries such as electricity, steel, engineering, chemicals, and artificial fibers. Italy's profile began to resemble that of the modern European countries to a greater degree than in the past. Between the end of the Ethiopian conflict and World War II, autarchy seemed to be a success as well, and in 1939 exports exceeded imports for the first time since 1871. Before Il Duce embarked on his warlike adventures, fascism's policies and ideology appeared brilliant and, for many Depression-era Europeans and Americans, a model to emulate.

Society, Ideology, and Culture, 1930 to 1940

From the beginning, Fascist ideology was described as a hodgepodge of ideas by its opponents, a view that occasioned public debates among Fascist and anti-

Fascist intellectuals in the 1920s and among historians afterward. The view of fascism as a bogus ideology unworthy of consideration as a thought system prevailed after World War II. In the 1960s, however, Italian historian Renzo De Felice began publication of his massive biography of Mussolini. In this and other writings, De Felice argued that fascism was a product of the Enlightenment and the French Revolution in that it looked forward rather than backward. This concept, according to De Felice, put fascism at odds with Nazism, the movement to which it was compared by historians. In examining Mussolini's life, De Felice explained the development of Mussolini's ideology as a subject worthy of serious consideration. More important, because of De Felice's work, fascism could be viewed as a "leftist" movement, or, at least, a movement with leftist roots. This analysis contradicted the one-sided interpretation of fascism as a reactionary rightist movement. As a result, De Felice ran into serious criticism from leftist Italian historians, who attacked his thesis in the popular and scholarly press

The attempt to dismiss De Felice's views failed, and they have given rise to an interesting historical debate. Israeli scholar Zeev Sternhell, for example, rejects De Felice's interpretation of fascism as issuing from the Enlightenment. According to Sternhell, fascism was derived from a late nineteenth- and twentieth-century European rejection of the rationalistic and materialistic aspects of Marxism and individualistic liberalism ultimately derived from the Enlightenment. Because of reformist domination of socialism the proletariat accepted the existing political system and tried to make gains within it. In short, the proletariat renounced revolution. But some Socialists remained revolutionary, namely the revolutionary syndicalists, while the proletariat ceased to be so. The syndicalists then discovered the nation as a revolutionary agent: "Having to choose between a proletarian but moderate socialism and a nonproletarian but revolutionary and national socialism, they opted for the nonproletarian revolution, the national revolution."

Sternhell thus sees fascism as grounded in European civilization and in leftist thought. In his opinion, fascism emerged from the process just outlined—specifically, the melding of revolutionary revision of Marxism, as operated by French and Italian revolutionary syndicalists, with Enrico Corradini's Nationalism and with Futurist aesthetics. This combination gave fascism its character of cultural and political revolt, which Sternhell believes was the essence of fascism already by 1910 before the movement adopted its name. As for the argument that it was not a coherent ideology, he writes: "Let there be no doubt about it: fascism's intellectual baggage enabled it to travel alone, and its theoretical content was neither less homogeneous nor more homogeneous than that of liberalism or socialism. Nor were the incoherences and contradictions greater in number or more profound than those which had existed in liberal or socialist thought for a hundred years." In addition, Sternhell insists, fascism, unlike Nazism, was not based upon racism. He concludes that fascism was an alternative to both socialism and liberalism. Ironically, this is also the way the Fascists saw themselves.

By the 1930s fascism had been in power for ten years and felt the need for a more systematic statement of Fascist ideology with which to explain itself to the outside world, a task undertaken by sophisticated thinkers such as philosopher Giovanni Gentile and Nationalist theoretician Alfredo Rocco. Judging from the regime's actions, this ideological framework functioned primarily as window dressing for conservative economic and social policies, but the ideas expressed during frequently passionate debates, and their links to other ideologies of this troubled period, help to understand the inner mechanisms of the movement.

In a comprehensive statement published in 1932, Mussolini himself described fascism's early doctrine simply as "action." He condemned economic materialism—the basis for the fundamental Marxist conception of the class struggle—as "an absurd delusion." He denounced liberalism and democracy, which he and other Fascist theoreticians lumped together with socialism, because they emphasized the individual over the community. According to these doctrines, Fascists argued, society "is merely a sum total of individuals." Paradoxically, they generated communism, which submerges the individual within the community. Fascism instead represented a "third way," because while it recognized the community as supreme, it left ample space to individual initiative. Unlike the other ideologies, fascism believed in the objective inequality of individuals and therefore emphasized "heroism" and "sentiment." Fascism combined state superiority and individual enhancement without the false freedom found in the liberal and communist countries.

These last elements ultimately derived from Nationalist ideology, but the Fascists also adopted other Nationalist principles that had a major impact on their movement: Italy as a "proletarian nation," the "class struggle" among nations, and the inevitability of war. As noted in Chapter 13, the Nationalists projected the Marxist class struggle onto the international plane as the struggle between rich and poor nations. The Fascists updated this idea into the fight between the "have-nots" and the "plutocratic" countries, but the concept also had internal repercussions. The Nationalists believed that internal unity had to be achieved to prepare Italy for the coming "revolutionary" war against the rich nations. This vision prompted formation of institutions to bolster the government by mobilizing the masses, to be discussed later. But the quest for unity could also be discerned in Rocco's successful prohibition of strikes and lockouts and in the concrete formalization of this concept in the Corporate State.

As previously mentioned, a 1926 law alluded to "corporations" but did not institute them because of the employers' satisfaction with the legislation. With the Great Depression, however, Fascist unionists pressed for formal institution of the much-heralded corporations and a clear definition of their structure and functions. Between 1930 and 1934 a vigorous debate on the issue took place among Fascist intellectuals, with many interpreting the corporations as the concrete embodiment of the Fascist third way. To the conservative view that the corporations be simple coordinating bodies, philosopher Ugo Spirito countered that corporations set up by the state should take over ownership of firms, integrate the workers as full-scale partners in production, and leave entrepreneurs in a managerial capacity. Spirito argued that this solution would mark the real end of the class struggle and fulfill fascism's promises, but he was roundly denounced as a "Bolshevik." Spirito's "left Fascist" colleague Giuseppe Bottai adopted a middle position between these "conservative" and "radical" conceptions.

The law of February 5, 1934, which set up the corporations, ended debate and produced a conservative win. Twenty-two corporations were created to cover all sectors of production—agriculture, commerce, services, and industry. In the end, the corporations turned out to be councils in which employer and employee organizations had equal representation despite the numerical superiority of workers. Theoretically, in each corporation employers and employees sat down together to determine production and settle differences between workers and capitalists, with government representatives present to protect state interests. The Fascists claimed that in this manner they had officially ended the class struggle. In effect, however, the corporations had little power and normally ratified government proposals generated by the employers' associations. Completing this Corporate State, a 1938 law abolished the Chamber of Deputies and created the Chamber of Fasces and Corporations composed of Fascist party officials and members of the National Council of the Corporations. Members of the Chamber became so by virtue of their office, eliminating the need for elections to a national representative body. In theory, the Corporate State altered the basis of representation from the individual to productive members of society and fulfilled the Fascist view of economic self-government and national unity. In practice, a PNF-business alliance ran the country.

Besides setting up the Corporate State, the Fascists sought support by creating a number of institutions in the 1920s, organizations that became more important in the 1930s as Mussolini sought to mobilize public opinion in favor of his wars and to transform the Italians into militant Fascists. The Opera Nazionale Balilla (ONB) regimented boys and girls from six to twenty-one in seven youth organizations. These young people wore uniforms, marched in a military manner, and participated in highly organized group activities. Mussolini considered the ONB the training ground of the Fascist of the future. To control future intellectuals, university students were obliged to join the Gioventù Universitaria Fascista (GUF). This organization in particular provided scarce results for "fascistization" because, even though Mussolini forced university professors to sign an oath of allegiance to the regime, higher education remained relatively free from political interference.

Despite the emphasis on "fascistizing" education, the inability to make education Fascist substantially held true for the secondary schools, reformed by Giovanni Gentile in 1923. Gentile's major innovations were a more rigorous selection process for the best schools, institution of a stiff national examination for graduation, and establishment of the scientific lycée alongside the *liceo classico*. Gentile's reform applied principles that had been discussed during the liberal era and was not specifically Fascist, even though the regime exercised greater control. Primary schools were more heavily propagandized than higher education, with the inculcation of Fascist and Nationalist principles and the overt glorification of Il Duce. The Opera Nazionale Dopolavoro (OND) rounded out the Fascist socialization network. This leisure-time organization arranged discounts for theaters and cinema and provided vacations, tours, and sports events at reduced prices. The OND had precursors in Italy, came into contact with millions of workers, and was the regime's most successful institution of this kind. Nazi Germany imitated these institutions, projecting a picture of similarity between the Italian and German regimes.

By the 1930s the Fascist party could also be classified as an organization primarily devoted to socialization. In 1930 Mussolini demoted Augusto Turati and put in Achille Starace as secretary. An unintelligent and obsequious tool of Mussolini, he implemented Il Duce's policy of reducing the once-obstreperous PNF to a bland and unthreatening body. At the same time Starace attempted to impose on the Italians the spirit and "discipline" of ancient Rome by, in the words of Philip Cannistraro, "substituting the handshake with the Roman salute, by adopting the *passo romano* [goose step], by introducing mass marches and parades, and by [implementing] a host of minute and frequently ridiculous details. . . ." On October 29, 1932, Fascist party membership, which had been closed, was reopened and greatly expanded. Unlike Nazi Germany and Communist Russia, membership in the PNF came to mean nothing. Indeed, as if to emphasize the party's social function, the ONB was put under an umbrella organization, the Gioventù Italiana del Littorio (GIL), and absorbed by the party in 1937. Along with the OND and other organizations, the party secretary ruled over a large social organization with scant political significance. This transformation of the party helps explain why the PNF was not a factor in the struggle to save Mussolini when he fell in 1943.

The ambivalence of fascism's social policies may also be seen in its treatment of women. In general, attitudes toward women did not differ to a great degree from those of the democratic countries during the same period. Conflict existed because of a desire to use women workers in building up the nation's economic base while suppressing the liberating aspects that greater economic security implied. During the 1920s fascism praised women and argued for recognizing their rights and duties within the nation, just as it did for men. It attempted to "nationalize" women, as it had men, by creating special organizations and by expanding maternity leave and other social security benefits specific to women. During the 1930s, however, the Depression and the country's foreign adventures made policy on this issue more consonant with Fascist style, which glorified virile and warlike masculinity. Since the Duce required more soldiers and a larger population to claim more territory, he encouraged women to stay home and have bal ies. The state gave medals to mothers who had a large number of children. To increase productivity and profits, the government tolerated young women working at low wages but discriminated against them as they got older to force them back into the home. Fascist propaganda discouraged viewing work or the professions as a means of liberation for women. Furthermore, since male unemployment—at a high point during the Depression—could cause the regime more problems, it took measures to reduce the number of women in the more remunerative jobs, encouraging them to return to the home or to enter the traditional low-paying women's jobs that men refused to do. In accomplishing this objective, the regime passed laws such as that of September 1938, which mandated a cutback of women workers in both state and private offices to 10 percent of their total staff. Despite these measures, however, "in the 1930s, over one-quarter of Italy's work force was female, and one woman out of every four between the ages of fourteen and sixty-five was economically active."

The 1930s also witnessed greater use of technological innovations for propaganda, although to a lesser degree than one might imagine. The radio, favored by the regime but of slow diffusion in the 1920s, profited from government intervention in the 1930s, but the number of sets still trailed far behind the number in Britain, the United States, and Germany. The cinema, a field in which the country had once led, languished behind foreign and especially American films, which dominated at the box office. In 1931 a new law encouraged domestic production under government supervision, and later the Cinecittà studios were built. These events aided the Italian film industry and set the conditions for future development, but it still remained behind in its own market. Ironically, censorship seemed to have little effect, and this period was the seedtime of the postwar flowering of Italian directors. In addition, although the question of using film for propaganda was raised, few such films were made. The regime preferred to use as its primary propaganda vehicle the weekly newsreel, in whose editing Mussolini personally participated, which private theaters were obliged to show. In 1935, press and propaganda affairs, radio, cinema, and other means of communication were brought under the umbrella of a new Ministry for Press and Propaganda, later renamed the Ministry of Popular Culture (Minculpop). In this manner, the regime hoped to rationalize the instruments discussed for the purpose of creating the "new Fascist man."

In the more classic field of literature, the regime also exercised a weak censorship. Prominent intellectuals exhibited their resistance by translating American novels dealing with social issues, and publishing houses became frequent hotbeds of opposition. Officials discouraged such translations but did not crack down except in cases of overt political opposition. Until the anti-Semitic campaigns of the 1930s, Mussolini's Jewish mistress Margherita Sarfatti—"a vigorous champion of modern, international currents in cultural life"—served as the regime's unofficial "dictator of culture," according to Philip Cannistraro and Brian Sullivan. The regime never adopted an official artistic style, exercising indirect control over artists through a combination of labor unions, government purchases, and a network of regional and national exhibitions. Mussolini considered architecture, which was heavily dependent on public construction projects, the most important of the arts, but building design ranged from classical to the most modern, international styles.

Whether as a result of personality characteristics, the pressure of war, or the way in which he increasingly isolated himself from those around him, in the 1930s Il Duce accentuated his personal power. Slogans like "Mussolini is always right" and "Believe, Obey, Fight" covered Italian buildings. Mussolini chafed at the king's formal supremacy, conferred by the constitution, and talked about seizing the first occasion to abolish the monarchy. He eliminated potential rivals such as the popular Italo Balbo, chief of the air force famous for conducting mass flights across the Atlantic, by giving them honorable jobs without real power. In 1933 and later, he reshuffled the cabinet several times, taking the military ministries for himself. Despite this apparent control, Mussolini failed to achieve operational direction of the armed forces, which remained in the hands of military undersecretaries. He also became more narrowly nationalistic and chauvinistic, attempting to rid Italy of foreign influences. This policy culminated in the anti-Semitic campaign and the racial laws of 1938.

Fascist anti-Semitism has remained a matter of debate. On the one hand, anti-Semitism had no deep roots in Italian society or in the Fascist movement; there were many Jewish Fascists and the idea of racial superiority seems to have been based on "spirit" rather than biology. Mussolini himself had had a Jewish mistress, condemned Nazi anti-Semitic policies in a famous interview, and allowed fleeing German Jews to use Italy as a transit point into Palestine; even during World War II, Italian occupying armies protected Jews from the Germans. On the other hand, through no fault of their own, Italian Jews lost basic rights and suffered because of the racial laws, even if not on a scale approaching Germany or the German-occupied areas of Europe.

In 1937 and 1938, an anti-Semitic faction emerged within Italian fascism, but Mussolini refused to sanction a campaign against the Jews, who only numbered around 50,000 in the entire country. This current formed primarily because Fascist hierarchs wished to cement Italian-German relations and "left" Fascists such as Bottai identified Jews with a "bourgeois" spirit; as in other countries, the anti-Semitic faction also associated Jews variously with liberalism, socialism, and communism. After May 1938, perhaps influenced by Hitler's visit to Italy, Mussolini gave the go-ahead for an anti-Semitic campaign. Besides the reasons mentioned, he may have been motivated by a desire to increase his power by decisively influencing the Italian character. Il Duce was currently railing against the bourgeoisie and particularly taken with the idea of transforming the Italians into a "warrior" race, a concept that had prompted prohibition of racial interaction in Italian East Africa. A racist journal was founded, *La difesa della razza*, and, in September 1938, laws prohibiting foreign Jews from entering Italy, banning Jews from the teaching profession, and excluding them from receiving an education in public secondary schools were passed. More serious provisions, including a ban on intermarriage, exclusion from the army and public jobs, and a limit on Jewish economic activities, followed in November. A host of confusing exceptions accompanied these laws, allowing many individuals to escape their effect.

Contrary to Il Duce's expectations, a wave of disgust and passive resistance followed enactment of the anti-Semitic laws, despite their acceptance by party hacks and some intellectuals. Anti-Semitism had entered the Fascist movement and remained part of it until the end because Mussolini strangely seemed to consider it a means of enhancing his stature. In general, the anti-Semitic campaign caused surprise in the country and prompted many people to turn against fascism. As such, it was a symptom of the growing disenchantment of the country with the movement that had been in power for almost twenty years. Even though the opposition was primarily passive at this point, by 1940 increasing isolation from the nation characterized fascism.

Resistance

Mussolini's victory in the 1920s ushered in various types of resistance. Opponents who chose to remain in Italy and who dropped out of political activity were closely watched and occasionally jailed but relatively undisturbed. A significant number of these opponents would participate in the Resistance and return to political prominence after Mussolini's fall. Many political leaders, however, chose to emigrate and carry on the fight from foreign soil. The center of this exile community was Paris, although Communist leaders such as Palmiro Togliatti fled to Moscow, and other European and American cities counted active exile communities. The exile leaders reorganized their movements abroad and in Paris established the Concentrazione Antifascista, an umbrella organization of the exiles, to fight Mussolini and to warn other countries against the spread of fascism. Until Hitler's rise, these warnings were ignored by foreigners, including leftists, who interpreted fascism as a purely Italian phenomenon. The exiles became increasingly isolated in their host countries through the activities of the Italian consulates and by the host governments, who wooed Mussolini and were embarrassed by the exiles' presence. In addition, exile groups were infiltrated by the secret Fascist police, the OVRA*, who stimulated disagreements to keep the exiles ineffectual.

At first the exile organizations operated outside Italy primarily by disseminating information, but later they physically attacked prominent Italian figures traveling abroad. Among the leftists, the Socialists were loath to create an underground organization in Italy, while the Communists established the first and most robust clandestine network. This activity increased Communist influence among the Italian masses and helps explain Communist strength when Mussolini was overthrown. The Socialists soon followed the Communists' example, but a new organization, *Giustizia e Libertà* (GL, Justice and Liberty), led by Carlo Rosselli demanded greater aggressiveness in fighting fascism within the country. Operatives of these organizations, including future Socialist presidents Giuseppe Saragat and Sandro Pertini, infiltrated Italy, usually to be apprehended by the efficient Italian police, which also periodically delivered heavy blows to the underground organizations. These defeats failed to break the spirit of the vigorous anti-Fascist movement, which was in a poor position to overthrow Il Duce despite the growing disenchantment of Italians with fascism.

International events altered this perspective. German Nazism spurred Soviet-backed Communist parties to cooperate with their former Socialist rivals. Italian Communists and Socialists formed a Popular Front on the French model, and the exiles were less isolated as a result of Mussolini's growing cooperation with Hitler and his more aggressive foreign policy. With the occurrence of the Spanish Civil War, Carlo Rosselli spearheaded an Italian exile force to combat Mus-

---

* This acronym had the purpose of terrifying opponents. Some experts believe the term to be meaningless while others consider it ultimately derived from [Pi]ovra, Octopus, supposedly to signify that the secret police was omnipresent. Still others think it stands for Opera Vigilanza Repressione Antifascista, or some variant thereof.

solini's intervention there. Rosselli's view of Spain as a training ground for fighters who would later overthrow fascism in Italy so irritated the Italian authorities that they plotted his assassination, which occurred in France along with that of his brother Nello on June 10, 1937.

Although the chances of overthrowing fascism seemed better thanks to international developments in the late 1930s, only war could dislodge Mussolini. Given this reality, fascism's opponents could only maneuver within the shadows of international politics, rearranging their alliances and alignments in preparation for the day when the fall of Mussolini's Italy at the hands of foreign armies would permit them to return to their homeland and implement their visions of a post-Fascist Italy.

17

World War II and the Resistance

THE CHANGES WROUGHT BY fascism had important repercussions not only for Italians but also on international developments, and thus the world. In discussing Fascist foreign policy, historians debate whether the aims and policies of fascism represented an essential continuation of pre-Fascist Italy's foreign policy or a radical departure.

The Radicalization of Foreign Policy

Surface similarities exist between Fascist and pre-Fascist foreign policy. The country had previously embarked on colonial adventures, nationalism had been a potent force, and to some extent inconsistency had marked Italian diplomacy before Mussolini; but imperialism characterized all the great powers, exasperated nationalism was comprehensible after centuries of foreign control, and Italy's internal weakness made it particularly sensitive to alterations in the balance of power. The peculiarities of Italian foreign policy before fascism could be rationally explained by history or the international situation, and Italian foreign policy operated within the mainstream of European diplomacy.

With Mussolini's advent, this essential characteristic would change. It would be surprising if fascism's nature and ideology had not affected foreign policy. Extremist nationalism—once the province of the small Nationalist Association and now absorbed by fascism—became official policy, favoring expansionism and generating unreasonable demands on other nations to boost Italy's prestige. Fascism's exploitation of nationalism as a means of mobilizing the masses increasingly fed on itself, for failure to make touted gains could destabilize the regime. For its own internal reasons, the regime heightened existing resentments—for example, that Italy had been cheated of the fruits of victory in World War I and that the country should have colonies because it was overpopulated—and further exasperated the diplomatic situation. More properly ideological considerations also complicated the foreign policy picture, especially Mussolini's antibolshevism and his disdain of democracy. These views led him to support and help install reactionary and philo-Fascist movements all over Europe, a policy that continually created tensions. To these elements should be added objective ones that affected international relations, such as rising unemployment during the 1930s and the closing of immigration by the United States. Furthermore, Mussolini's personal style, including threats, bombast, and quick mood changes, also shocked European diplomats. Before World War I, liberal democrats who more or less shared common viewpoints determined Europe's diplomacy, but fascism radically altered this consensus. As in domestic affairs, Benito Mussolini was prepared to do anything to achieve his ends.

To this new force that revolutionized Italian foreign policy must be added the Fascist desire to revise the Paris settlement following World War I, a necessity that would probably have been strongly felt even by non-Fascist governments. Not only had the Versailles settlement left Italy unsatisfied territorially but also from Rome's perspective, by prostrating Germany, it made France supreme on the continent. With Britain on the French side, there was no possibility of constituting a second camp that Italy might join to accomplish its aim of redressing the "mutilated victory." This anomalous situation, combined with a Fascist regime that glorified war and violence, proved fatal to the European system, because although Italy lacked the strength to alter the status quo unilaterally, a resurgent and vengeful Germany bent upon doing so would find a willing ally in a Fascist Italy.

Between 1922 and 1925 Fascist foreign policy followed pre-Fascist lines, and Mussolini achieved the consensus of the traditional diplomats. Despite his tough talk, only the Corfu incident in 1923 caused an acute problem. Mussolini ordered the navy to take the Greek island after several Italians helping mark the Albanian border were assassinated, but he evacuated Corfu after Greece met his conditions for reparations. As previously mentioned, in 1924 Mussolini also signed an agreement with Yugoslavia that gave Fiume to Italy. This initial "good behavior," however, did not mean that the Duce's aggressiveness in domestic affairs would not prevail in foreign questions.

The consolidation of Mussolini's rule into an open dictatorship in 1925 and 1926 had external effects. The transformation of Paris into a hotbed of exile antifascism strained relations with France. Exacerbating this situation was France's dominance in the Danube region of eastern Europe and Italy's attempts to compete. In practice, this meant opposing France's allies—the "Little Entente" of Yugoslavia, Czechoslovakia, and Rumania. Italy supported the claims of another revisionist power, Hungary, against the Little Entente by signing a Hungarian pact in 1927 and supplying arms and other aid to Hungarian pro-Fascist groups. At the same time, Italy aimed at the dismemberment of Yugoslavia, especially by financing and arming anti-Serb Croatian separatist elements who wished to break up the country. In addition, Italy and Yugoslavia competed in Albania, prompting Mussolini to transform the small Balkan state into an Italian protectorate.

Italy had traditionally been active in those areas, even though it had not acted as aggressively, so its moves did not attract much attention. Besides, the international situation in the 1920s remained relatively stable, and since Italy lacked the power to alter it, Italian policy oscillated from revisionism to conciliation. During the tenure of Fascist hierarch Dino Grandi as foreign minister from 1929 to 1932, Italian diplomacy emphasized stabilization over revisionism. At the Geneva disarmament conference in 1932, Grandi proposed an "arms moratorium" that would reduce Germany's military inferiority and eventually produce parity among the major powers. In effect, this step would have reestablished two European "camps," a more normal diplomatic situation, and would have enhanced Italy's position.

The Italians hoped eventually to barter their support for France vis-à-vis Germany for colonial concessions, but Grandi ran into internal opposition because the Fascists were too impatient to wait for his policy to yield results. Mussolini took over the foreign ministry in 1932, appointing Fulvio Suvich as his undersecretary. Up to this point, Fascist policy had alternated from demanding change by violent means to presenting itself as the champion of a just and negotiated alteration in the European *status quo* as defined by the Paris Peace Conference and social conservatism, exhibiting in foreign as in domestic affairs its fundamentally dualistic nature. This characteristic explains why the Western powers downplayed Fascist rhetoric, considering it for internal consumption only, and adopted a friendly attitude toward Mussolini. But Hitler's rise and the Depression's economic effects allowed fascism to pursue its destabilizing foreign policy aims.

Mussolini viewed Hitler with a combination of apprehension and hope. On the one hand, the similarities between Nazism and fascism and Hitler's friendliness flattered him, but on the other, Germany was a powerful force to be reckoned with. German resurgence presented Italy with a familiar choice: either with Germany or Britain and France. In judging which option would pay the most, Mussolini by no means made his selection quickly or, initially, on ideological grounds. In fact, Italo-German relations started off badly. The Allies accepted the Italian proposal for eventual parity among the powers, signing a four-power pact in 1933, but Hitler pulled Germany out of the disarmament conference and the League of Nations without any regard for the feelings of his supposed mentor.

In 1934 relations deteriorated further with Hitler's attempt to absorb Austria (*Anschluss*). Austrian opponents of "union" tried in vain to get Franco-British support against Hitler. They turned to Italy, understandably anxious to keep

Germany far from its northeastern border. The Italians encouraged Austrian leader Engelbert Dollfuss to cooperate with the paramilitary Heimwehr to eliminate the Social Democrats, who preferred the democracies to Fascist Italy. Dollfuss complied in February 1934, when he proceeded with the suppression of the Austro-Marxists. On March 17, at the signing of the Rome Protocols among Italy, Austria, and Hungary, Italy publicly declared that it would defend Austria from invasion. A meeting between Hitler and Mussolini followed, which left the Italian unimpressed. On July 25 a Nazi *putsch* occurred in Vienna and Dollfuss was assassinated. In the face of Franco-British inaction, Mussolini mobilized four divisions and sent them to the Austrian border. Hitler immediately retreated.

As relations with Germany cooled, those with France improved. Italy and France had argued over their respective influence over eastern Europe, naval parity, and colonial concessions promised in the Pact of London, but anxiety over Hitler's rise made the French more conciliatory in an attempt to gain Italian support against Germany. Jean-Louis Barthou, the hard-line French foreign minister, initiated the move for a Franco-Italian rapprochement over Yugoslavia, which was carried forward after his assassination by his successor Pierre Laval. A convinced partisan of Italo-French cooperation in the face of Hitler's rising bellicosity, Laval was particularly anxious to secure Italian cooperation. On a Rome visit from January 4 to 7, 1935, Laval signed a series of accords with Mussolini that resolved several outstanding problems between the two countries. These written accords reveal that Italy made a number of concessions and accepted some worthless African territory to settle its claims against France. The mystery of why Mussolini would accept such a bad deal is explained by his contention that Laval orally assured him that France granted Italy a free hand in Ethiopia, which the Italians were preparing to invade. Laval later denied the contention, but in this dispute the evidence favors Mussolini.

Convinced that he had a French agreement not to oppose a conquest of Ethiopia, Mussolini sought British acquiescence. This enterprise proved more difficult, since the British, safe behind the Channel, feared Hitler less than the French. In April 1935, Italian, French, and British representatives met at Stresa in hopes of reinvigorating the old wartime alliance after Hitler's attempt to seize Austria and his declaration, in further violation of the Versailles Treaty, that Germany would reinstitute compulsory military service. At this meeting, lower-level diplomats discussed the Ethiopian crisis; citing unfavorable public opinion, the British refused to sanction an Italian takeover. Their answer did not discourage Mussolini for a number of reasons. The British possessed the largest colonial empire, and this fact combined with exaggerated fears that the Italians might deprive Egypt and the Sudan of water by damming up Lake Tana in

Ethiopia made British objections seem like sour grapes. Furthermore, by failing to make clear their actions if the Italians went ahead anyway, the British encouraged Mussolini to think that they would not act decisively. Moreover, the British soon afterward signed a naval pact with Hitler that sanctioned violations of the Versailles Treaty, thus killing the "Stresa Front."

As talks continued, diplomatic tensions between Italy and Britain escalated. The "Peace Ballot" and approaching elections made the British more resolved to obstruct Mussolini. In June 1935 Anthony Eden carried to Rome a plan for settlement of the Ethiopian question that had already been rejected by the Italians and ridiculed by the French. A Fascist propaganda campaign against the British followed. Both Italians and British planned for a possible war, with the British transferring significant naval units to the Mediterranean. Although the British navy was confident, it calculated that it would take heavy losses in any confrontation with the Italian fleet. Mussolini found himself in a perilous situation, since he had sent a strong force to East Africa that could easily be cut off by British naval power.

Given this difficult position, why did Mussolini persist? Three reasons seem to have been paramount in the Duce's mind. These were the perceived economic advantages for Italy in taking over a land rich in natural resources, the domestic prestige which would accrue to him from conquering a land adaptable to Italian colonization (unlike the other Italian colonies), and the belief that the new international situation provided him with a unique opportunity because the British Admiralty was distracted by the Japanese in the Far East. In addition, fascism had always emphasized nationalism and glorified war and violence, and Ethiopia presented it with the opportunity to implement its theories. Mussolini correctly calculated that mobilizing the masses and bringing them to a fever pitch without any concrete result would jeopardize the regime. Indeed, the war would represent the high point of his regime's popularity. Finally, the effects of the Depression lingered and war would increase employment and stimulate the economy.

Following several border incidents in 1934, Italian military preparations commenced in earnest. The Italians invaded Ethiopia in October 1935, provoking imposition of economic sanctions by the League of Nations. These sanctions were serious, but the failure to add petroleum to the list and Italy's continuing ability to trade with nations not belonging to the League, especially the United States, encouraged the Italians. In the meantime, the military effort went well, despite widespread predictions to the contrary because of the difficult terrain and logistical concerns. The use of modern weapons and the extensive employment of mustard gas and terror turned out to be effective, though expensive. Only guerrilla tactics would have helped the outgunned Ethiopians, but Emperor Haile Sallasie avoided them. In December 1935 there was an attempt to end the conflict by granting Italy ample concessions—the Hoare-Laval proposals; Mussolini agreed to consider them, but the political backlash in Britain caused their quick withdrawal. By May 1936 the Italians took the Ethiopian capital and the emperor fled. On May 9 Mussolini proclaimed the empire.

Although thoroughly condemned outside the country, the Ethiopian victory affair enormously increased Mussolini's prestige in Italy because he had stared down the British and won an important military success. But Ethiopia also had wide-ranging negative effects—it worsened Europe's international crisis, destroyed the League's influence, encouraged new adventures, increased the Duce's contempt for the democracies, made him turn against the Western powers, and pushed him into Hitler's arms.

Italo-German relations had improved during the conflict because of Mussolini's worsening relations with Britain and France. Furthermore, with Europe's attention riveted on Ethiopia and fearing that a quick Italian victory would deprive him of the opportunity, Hitler had announced remilitarization of the Rhineland in March. This move took some pressure off Mussolini and marks the beginning of de facto collaboration between the two dictators. Trying to assuage the Western powers, Hitler declared his readiness to provide guarantees of peace and rejoin the League; but this move would have obligated Germany to institute sanctions against Italy. Responding to Italian protestations, Hitler promised to delay reentering the League, should he do so, until after the war, and in return Italy refused to approve a motion condemning Germany's action. Shortly thereafter and in response to the Communist Popular Front policy, the Italian and German police officially began cooperating against their Socialist and Communist enemies. This agreement signalled the beginning of a common policy eventually focused upon anticommunism, antidemocracy, and, finally, anti-Semitism.

In June 1936 Mussolini appointed his notoriously pro-German son-in-law Galeazzo Ciano as foreign minister. In the summer, Italy and Germany independently decided to intervene in the Spanish Civil War on the rebel side against the Popular Front Republican government. Mussolini was originally opposed to intervention but gave way to Ciano, since both calculated that the war would be short and handily won by Francisco Franco. Intervention brought Italy and Germany closer together. As an indication of their new friendliness, the German foreign minister visited Rome in the fall and signed several accords with the Italians. During the conversations the Germans agreed that the Mediterranean basin was to be considered an Italian sphere. The Duce defined this new collaboration as the "Axis." With German strength apparently behind him, Mussolini publicly challenged the British, who had dominated the Mediterranean since the eighteenth century, claiming that Italians would fight if the British tried to "suffocate" them in their own sea.

This preoccupation, unexpected Republican resistance in Spain, and mounting evidence of Soviet activity in the Mediterranean stimulated massive Italian intervention in Spain in 1937, which further cemented relations with Nazi Germany. Italian participation in that conflict had been limited before that date but, spurred by a willingness to commit more troops in an area that Italy was supposed to dominate and motivated by fear that the Popular Front French and Spanish governments would collaborate against fascism, the Duce poured men and equipment into Spain. This large force, he believed, would soon produce victory, but it failed to do so. The Italians met an embarrassing defeat at Guadalajara, exceeded only by the battle's political significance. News travelled all over the world that for the first time Mussolini's Fascist armies had been stopped, partly at the hands of Italian anti-fascists. Furthermore, rebel commander Franco turned the conflict into a war of attrition, against the Italians' protests, bogging them down in a long drawn-out fight that ended only in 1939. Mussolini weighed pulling out of the Spanish Civil War but his pride would not let him do so. Beyond torpedoing ships supplying the republic, the Italians could take little independent action, but Il Duce's continued involvement heightened tensions with Britain and France, with whom Mussolini considered reconciliation. As a result, any chance at rapprochement with those two powers vanished as he became friendlier to Germany. Hitler had written in *Mein Kampf* that Germany should divide the World War I coalition by separating Italy from it, and he was succeeding despite Il Duce's wariness. In 1937 Hitler proposed a military alliance with Italy, but although Mussolini adhered to the German-Japanese Anticomintern Pact—a move of little significance—he hesitated to take the radical step of linking up militarily with Nazi Germany and stalled.

In March 1938 Nazi Germany absorbed Austria. This action nullified Italy's greatest gain in World War I—elimination of a major power on its northeastern border—and created the potential for trouble in the South Tyrol, predominantly populated by German-speaking peoples. Unlike Mussolini's response to Hitler's move against Austria in 1934, friendliness between the two dictators and Italian isolation produced by the Ethiopian War now prevented Mussolini from opposing Hitler's move. Hitler guaranteed the Brenner Pass as Italy's border, but the Italians recognized *Anschluss* as a defeat for them, despite Mussolini's attempt to put a good face on the affair. His popularity plunged.

Preoccupied with Italy's accelerating drift toward Germany, Britain and France hoped to avoid a break and attempted a rapprochement, but it was too little too late. The League had already lifted sanctions on July 15, 1936, and in January 1937, Britain and Italy had reached a "Gentlemen's Agreement" on maintaining the status quo in the Mediterranean. Mussolini hoped to win Franco-British recognition of the empire. On the heels of Anschluss, Mussolini authorized Dino Grandi, the Italian ambassador in London, to open negotiations aiming at a general understanding. On April 16, 1938 the two countries resolved several important problems affecting their relations. British recognition of the empire followed, but, as will be explained, this success could not be duplicated with France.

In September 1938 Mussolini played an important role at the Munich Conference, which resolved the Czechoslovak crisis of that year. Hitler's demands for immediate cession of German-speaking areas of Czechoslovakia made war seem likely, but Mussolini played a key part in a compromise solution. Widely perceived as a peacemaker, the Duce received general applause. But the weakness demonstrated by the democracies during the crisis—by allowing Hitler to gobble up the Sudetenland—apparently encouraged Mussolini to act tough to achieve a French agreement. In November, staged demonstrations demanded the former Italian territories of Corsica, Nice, and Savoy, and the French colony of Tunisia where many Italians had settled. Apparently Il Duce meant to prepare the ground for settlement of outstanding questions with France in Africa, but his unorthodox methods quickly backfired. Anti-Italian demonstrations shook France, making it difficult for French diplomats to respond to Italian requests. Mussolini realized that if France resorted to military action (unlikely, but something to be considered), Italy would face the attack alone, since the British would not support him and no military pact with Germany existed. The choice that Mussolini's foreign policy presented Italy stood out in all its striking clarity: Either the Duce would have to sign an alliance with Hitler or he would have to abandon Hitler and become friendlier to Britain and France. This second selection, however, was highly improbable for several reasons. It would contrast glaringly with his recent policies and damage his personal prestige. It would also put him in the anomalous position of allying with countries whose internal composition conflicted with his own; because of fascism's evolution, by 1938 this consideration, though not insuperable, had become significant. Politics, past behavior, and the internal contrasts between his regime and the democracies made the second selection highly improbable.

As a result, Mussolini moved toward a German military alliance even though the Germans made it difficult for him. In March 1939 the Germans irritated the Duce by occupying Bohemia and Moravia. Clearly Mussolini's risky foreign policy had so far benefited only Germany, with the galling corollary that the Duce appeared unable to duplicate the spectacular gains of his one-time disciple. In April, Mussolini ordered his army to occupy Albania, which had been an Italian protectorate, ironically as a response to possible German expansion in the Balkans. The British, who had rushed to guarantee Poland's boundaries in the wake of Hitler's occupation of Bohemia and Moravia, now guaranteed Greece against an Italian attack and opened talks with Turkey. These moves convinced Mussolini that he urgently needed a military pact with Germany to protect himself.

In the Italo-German talks concerning this alliance, Mussolini and Ciano made it abundantly clear that Italy would not be prepared for a major war for at least three or four years. The Germans readily agreed to such a condition and on May 22, 1939, the two countries signed the "Pact of Steel." Unlike traditional alliances, this pact did not limit mutual aid only in case of attack by a third power. Il Duce had foolishly committed Italy to go to war on Germany's side even if Germany initiated a conflict and naively believed Hitler's assurances that he would not precipitate a war for at least three years.

By signing the German pact, Mussolini reversed traditional Italian foreign policy and threw elementary caution to the wind by abandoning his country's freedom of action, by committing Italy to follow another power into a war, by disregarding the British navy, long dominant in the Mediterranean and capable of striking the long and vulnerable Italian coastline (in the 1880s, Italian diplomats had publicly declared that Italy's participation in the Triple Alliance could not be construed as an anti-British act), and by turning against the French, who, despite their stormy relationship, shared powerful cultural traditions with Italians.

Furthermore, Hitler's word meant little, even to the people he professed to admire. As the Polish crisis heated up, Mussolini repeatedly tried to convince Hitler to back off. When World War II broke out on September 1, 1939, over the issue of the German minority living in the "Polish corridor," the Italians reacted with consternation over the German action. Foreign Minister Ciano, formerly pro-German, accused the Germans of lying and tricking the Italians. He argued that since Italy had made it clear that it would be several years before it could be prepared for war, German provocations had absolved Italy from its obligations under the Pact of Steel. Fearing for the country and the regime, important Fascist hierarchs, including Grandi, Bottai, Balbo, and De Bono, agreed and advocated disengaging from Hitler. Even pro-German hierarchs were prepared to follow the Duce's lead should he abandon Hitler. A struggle now began to win Mussolini over. Mussolini's mood shifted erratically from disengagement because of German betrayal to intervention on the grounds of "honor." Il Duce found it humiliating, after his own boasts and threats of war, not to follow Hitler, but events seemed to favor a German success from which he could draw advantages, and he never dreamt that Hitler would crush France. The Soviet-German nonaggression pact pointed to a probable British and

French accommodation with Hitler after these two powers had made a good show of not abandoning Poland. On the other hand, Italy's military unpreparedness made Mussolini cautious. He attempted to restrain Hitler, but if the Germans won a quick victory, he wanted a share of the spoils. As time went on, the Duce calculated that in the event of a short war Italian unpreparedness would matter little. The maximum gain at least cost would come by staying out of the conflict but keeping his German connection; in case of a fast and certain Nazi victory, he would intervene.

Mussolini accomplished the first part of his plan by reminding Hitler that their talks had contemplated war only after 1942. Consequently, the Duce would be willing to fulfill his obligations if the Germans supplied the war materiel Italy lacked. Hitler asked for a list detailing Italian needs, and Ciano drew up one that, he remarked in his diary, "would kill a bull, if he could read it." When Hitler received the request, he acknowledged that Germany could not meet the Italian requests and stated that he understood Italy's position. Mussolini then declared not neutrality but "non-belligerence."

Terrified that they might have to participate in the conflict on the side of the hated Germans, the Italian people rejoiced at the decision. The anti-German wing of Italian fascism campaigned to disengage Italy from the Nazis. The industrialists happily took advantage of the conflict's economic opportunities by doing business with both sides. Unless a German defeat loomed, however, all hope of keeping the country out of war was vain. The carefully crafted term nonbelligerence—as opposed to neutrality—signified continued adherence to the German alliance in view of further developments. As Hitler piled up victory after victory, Mussolini remained loyal to him—and none of the hierarchs could contest the Duce. Mussolini had hitched his star too closely to Hitler to pull away from him and he was determined to achieve spectacular gains by military means, according to Fascist doctrine. Furthermore, abandoning Germany would have meant altering the nature of fascism to effect a rapid rapprochement with the democracies; this policy not only implied a sudden reversal of his attitude condemning the "decadent" democracies but also suggested an implementation of domestic reforms transforming his dictatorship into a more conventional conservative regime. Finally, turning against Hitler would likely provoke German military retaliation. In the end, the Duce's own domestic and foreign policies combined to spur him to enter the war on the German side.

The Unprepared War

As impressive Nazi victories continued, Mussolini's reluctance to intervene dissolved. On May 10, 1940, the Germans launched a successful offensive that brought France to its knees within a month. At this point, the question of Italian military preparation became secondary for the Duce because he believed the war would soon end. By the time the deficiencies in the Italian armed forces could be repaired the opportunities offered by a German victory would have passed. In a meeting with military leaders on May 29, Mussolini is reported by Badoglio to have asserted that the war was over and that he needed only a few thousand dead to participate in the peace discussions. Mussolini's conviction that the war would end quickly is further substantiated by his demobilization of military units shortly after he entered the conflict on the grounds that he wanted the men to return to industrial pursuits to take advantage of the economic opportunities presented by the war's imminent end!

In his conviction that the war would be a short one for Italy, the Duce began discussing hypothetical dates for Italian intervention—each closer at hand. The ideal time would be late enough to be certain that Britain and France were really defeated but early enough to substantiate a claim that he had made an important contribution to victory. At this time and throughout the coming war, Mussolini's military advisers had serious misgivings about his decisions, which they expressed privately but not to the Duce. After rejecting appeals from the British, French, and Americans to keep out of the conflict, Mussolini declared war on Britain and France on June 10, 1940.

Italy's extreme unpreparedness, in addition to military errors made by the Duce or generated by Fascist ideology, explains the poor Italian performance in World War II. The previous wars in Ethiopia and Spain had consumed great quantities of war materiel, and other equipment had been handed over to Franco or remained in East Africa, out of the main war theater. Of the enormous amount of money spent for these wars, a large part had gone for the building of roads necessary to conquer the difficult Ethiopian terrain and for the transport of troops to the distant theater of operations. Thus a large proportion of the military expenditures did not go for equipment and materiel lost in fascism's wars and did not begin to be replaced in significant amounts until the 1938–1939 budget cycle; on the other hand, the other European belligerents rearmed more effectively after 1935. Moreover, Italian industrial potential could not match that of the other European powers, so Italy produced the needed arms at a much slower rate. Although Mussolini initially believed that Italy would be ready for war in 1943 and stepped up rearmament efforts during the non-belligerence period, it soon became clear that the country could not meet even that target. Finally, financial constraints remained severe. Faced with the major questions of financing arms acquisitions, of increasing production, and of paying for the great quantities of raw materials that had to be imported to sustain a first-class rearmament program, the government resolved only the first dilemma.

These problems, by no means new, placed a great burden on the armed forces. The army had modernization plans, but owing to financial considerations and the country's limited industrial capacity, they were never implemented. The land forces began the war with rifles designed in 1891, a lack of modern artillery, and with only light tankettes. The army's military doctrine was still dominated by World War I notions of a war of position. The modern idea of *blitzkreig* was discussed but only partially implemented by altering the division structure; without applying the doctrine's other elements, the change only increased the units' vulnerability to attack. In addition, the army suffered from "fascistization" attempts, which, though never completely successful, produced favoritism.

Because the air force was new, modern, romantic, and emphasized individual initiative, the Fascists considered it their particular preserve. Led by the dashing Italo Balbo, undertaking highly visible prestige flights under his command, and winning important competitions during the interwar years, the air force had great pretensions but even greater weaknesses. Even though the Italians possessed in Giulio Douhet perhaps the first theorist of the modern employment of air power, the air force stressed individual derring-do, failed to get modern projects into mass production, slacked off from a technical viewpoint in the years immediately preceding the war, and was characterized by a highly competitive spirit with regard to the other armed forces. During World War II, this last point contributed to a lack of coordination with the army and the navy which gravely hampered war operations. Furthermore, Balbo and his successor, Giuseppe Valle, were prone to exaggerate the numbers and quality of aircraft, leading to a false sense of security. For example, in 1939 the air force undersecretary claimed over 5,340 aircraft while his successor, Francesco Pricolo, stated that only 650 bombers and 190 fighters were in good fighting condition. When the war began, the Italian Air Force was probably comparable to France's, which had been unable to stand up to the Germans, and inferior to England's.

The navy had a claim to being the the most efficient fighting force. It had built itself up considerably during the interwar period and had most successfully resisted Fascist attempts to influence it. Despite these notable accomplishments, however, a heavy-handed rigidity hampered the navy's technical development. Its weaknesses included poor antiaircraft defenses, no air arm of its own and lack of coordination with the air force, deficient means of sighting the enemy (no radar), and a lack of fuel. Although the navy fought well and frequently imaginatively with new and effective weapons such as the midget submarine, its commanders realized that it faced a losing battle against its traditional ally, the British fleet, which was three times as large.

Mussolini's inept leadership compounded the armed forces' weaknesses. In March 1940 Mussolini had delineated an essentially defensive posture for an eventual Italian war effort, reflecting his desire to save his strength to take advantage of a German breakthrough. Since he and the Italian commanders did not trust their German allies, the Duce rejected coordination with the Germans and planned on an independent "parallel" war. The Italians opened hostilities with an attack on France, already reeling from the German offensive. Italian unpreparedness took its toll and the campaign failed. The Italians also attacked the British in the Mediterranean, North Africa, and East Africa, all with scarce results. From the beginning, Mussolini demonstrated a fatal propensity to scatter his forces. He held back badly needed men and equipment from North Africa—important for the capture of the Suez Canal, which would have allowed resupply of East Africa—because he wished to take over the Balkans. Hitler, however, vetoed Mussolini's plans because he feared giving the British an excuse for setting up bases there, providing the Soviets a pretext to get involved, and hampering the delivery of supplies to the Reich. Later Mussolini insisted on sending an Italian army to fight in Russia. Such a force could not make a decisive contribution there, but the men and equipment might have made a difference in North Africa, or at least given the British a harder time. Major theaters of operation soon included the Balkans, Russia, and North and East Africa, weakening the army's action everywhere and rendering it incapable of defending the homeland.

Soon after Hitler vetoed Mussolini's plans in the Balkans, he moved into Rumania. This action made the Duce furious and he vowed to retaliate by attacking Greece. He exclaimed: "Hitler always presents me with a fait accompli. This time, I'll do the same thing. He'll find out from the newspapers that I have occupied Greece."

The Greek attack turned out to be one of the war's gravest blunders. The invasion was not seriously planned because Mussolini pushed it forward in great haste to prevent Hitler from vetoing the operation. The chiefs of staff of all the services opposed the invasion, making their reasons known to chief of staff Pietro Badoglio, who agreed in private but who did not bring their opposition to Il Duce. Military disaster resulted. The Italian move meant that the British could set up Greek bases from which to bomb southern Italy and the vital Rumanian oil fields, prompting the Germans to intervene, which set the Balkans aflame and forced the Nazis to postpone the attack on Russia. With the Italians still reeling from the Greek debacle, the British unleashed a great North African offensive in January 1941 that inflicted dangerous defeats on the Italians. Italian East Africa, cut off from resupply, capitulated by November 1941 despite a heroic resistance. These developments spelled the end of Italy's "parallel war," and the Germans descended to rescue the Italians in North Africa as well. From now on, the conflict became a German-directed war. After American intervention, the tide of war began turning and on July 10, 1943, the Anglo-Americans landed in Sicily.

This development stunned a country already prostrate from war's effects. The conflict had reduced real salaries, already battered by the Depression and the revaluation crisis, to the subsistence level. Starvation threatened great numbers of people, especially city dwellers. Lengthy work shifts in war-related industries, the flourishing black market, and the extremely cold winter of 1942 caused mounting unrest and claimed many victims. Allied bombardments destroyed houses, killed and maimed citizens, and caused intolerable living conditions. Rising popular disaffection against Mussolini and the war alarmed government authorities, who made some economic concessions. These proved inadequate, however, and in March 1943, widespread strikes broke out in Turin, Milan, and other important centers—the only ones to affect Axis or occupied Europe during the war. Although economic distress was the major cause of these strikes, Communist, Socialist, and anti-Fascist activity in general during these actions alarmed Italian authorities and the Germans. Although the industrialists granted pay raises, disaffection remained widespread.

The strikes provided big business and other supporters of fascism with a good reason to back away from Mussolini. As the war had gone sour, important Fascist hierarchs became convinced that Mussolini's removal from power was essential to disengage Italy from Germany to prevent catastrophe. The Duce could only be dislodged with the king's support because the monarch retained supreme constitutional authority and the army's loyalty. Even though dispirited by defeat, the army was still formidable enough to carry off a coup d'etat against Mussolini. As a result, a bloc of Fascist hierarchs ready to appeal to the king to take control of the country formed. This group, which included Grandi, Ciano, Bottai, Federzoni, De Vecchi, and De Bono, communicated its disaffection to the king. In a report to SS commander Heinrich Himmler, SS Colonel Eugen Dollmann commented that in case of a conflict with the king, Mussolini "could only count on about 150 bodyguards armed with pistols."

The revolt against Mussolini occurred at a dramatic meeting of the Fascist Grand Council that lasted from 5:15 P.M. on July 24, 1943, to 2:40 A.M. the next day. In preparation for the meeting, Grandi drew up a motion that called upon the Duce to surrender his powers to the king for the country's good. Grandi hoped to secure Mussolini's acceptance of the motion's substance without convoking the the Grand Council, but the Duce refused on the grounds that the Germans possessed a "secret weapon" that would reverse the conflict's fortunes. The Council meeting produced heated debate and acceptance of Grandi's motion by a vote of 19 to 7.

Mussolini's behavior has puzzled observers because he could easily have refused to convoke the Fascist Grand Council as he had refused to do since December 1939 and because he seems to have been particularly passive during the the attempt to remove him. But the session seems to have had its origins in Mussolini's attempts to quell internal opposition following the defeat of his armies; as to his passiveness, he appears to have had no option, besides convincing his own men to retain him, except a humiliating appeal to his German allies for protection.

After the vote, Mussolini had no choice but to bring the motion to Victor Emmanuel III and to convince the sovereign to accept a compromise. He made an appointment to see the king at 5:00 P.M. on July 25. At 11:00 A.M. that morning, the king had already appointed Badoglio head of a military government without informing the Duce, and plans were drawn up for army units, the carabinieri, and the police to occupy key ministries, communication centers, and strategic locations in the capital. When Mussolini arrived for the appointment, a car with his bodyguards remained outside the gate as he drove in to talk with Victor Emmanuel. At the meeting the monarch informed the Duce that he had decided to replace him with Badoglio. As the shocked Mussolini walked out of the villa, two carabinieri requested that he follow them for his own protection. Il Duce was ushered into an ambulance and arrested.

Finding their communications cut, and feeling dispirited and disoriented, Mussolini's remaining Fascist supporters dispersed—fleeing to the German embassy, submitting to arrest, or surrendering. Neither the PNF nor the Fascist militia rose to defend the Duce during the ensuing uprisings and demonstrations that shook the country. Crowds destroyed Fascist party offices and symbols and demanded an end to the war. Workers walked off their jobs and listened to anti-Fascist orators released from the jails. The Badoglio government dissolved the PNF and repealed Fascist measures; but it feared that the demonstrations would develop into a Communist or a republican-led revolution and it ordered the armed forces to fire against the demonstrators.

Besides suppressing a possible revolution, Badoglio and the king faced the major problems of avoiding German retaliation and preserving the dynasty. Furious at Mussolini's overthrow, Hitler wished to order the immediate arrest of the "traitors," but his advisers persuaded him to wait until more German forces could move into Italy. To calm the Germans, Badoglio had already announced on July 25 that "the war continues." Badoglio rejected immediate abandonment of the German alliance—insistently demanded by newly reconstituted anti-Fascist associations and clearly the will of the people—on the grounds that such a move would provoke a harsh German military response. In fact, had the government quickly turned against the Germans while the Italians had military superiority in central and southern Italy, it probably would have succeeded in acquiring control of a least a large part of the country, sparing the Italians great suffering and the Allies a year's hard fighting. Instead, several high-level meetings between Italian and German officials took place at which they reciprocally attempted to deceive each other by agreeing that they were still allies.

Badoglio also initiated talks with the Anglo-Americans, stalling for time because of the feared German reaction, and irritating the Allies as well. Among other things, this delay produced cancellation of a coordinated attack with Allied airborne troops to save the capital from German occupation. At the same time, Badoglio and the king did nothing to stop German troops pouring into Italy or to prepare the army for a military confrontation with them. No orders went out to the forces in the field, and the government informed them that an armistice had been arranged with the Allies only when it was already too late to react. The announcement of an armistice with the Allies on September 8 provoked a German attack. Italian troops around Rome heroically resisted the Germans for a time, but the lack of orders made the fight futile. While the battle raged the king, the royal family, and Badoglio fled ignominiously to Allied-occupied Brindisi. The Germans also suddenly attacked their former allies in the various occupation areas, and the army dissolved. Some soldiers left for home, others fought the Germans until overwhelmed and taken prisoner or executed, and others joined the Resistance in Italy or in the countries where they were stationed. On the Greek island of Cephalonia, fierce fighting occurred between Italians and Germans, and the German army (not Nazis) brutally executed the survivors after they surrendered. These dramatic events set the stage for the Resistance, elimination of the monarchy, and establishment of the Republic.

The Resistance

On September 12, 1943, German commando Otto Skorzeny liberated Mussolini from his mountaintop prison in a daring rescue. Hitler then set up Il Duce in German-occupied Italy, transformed into the puppet Italian Social Republic (RSI), commonly called the Salò Republic. Here the dispirited Mussolini attempted to create a functioning state but failed to do so. His anger at the "bourgeoisie" for having overthrown him led to the reemergence of his youthful anticapitalism. The most rabid Fascists followed Mussolini to his truncated domain, zealously cooperating with the Nazis in their hunt for opponents, who were regularly executed. Among those Mussolini had killed were his former foreign minister and son-in-law Galeazzo Ciano and some of the others who had voted against him at the Grand Council meeting of July 25 who could be apprehended. In all of German-occupied Italy, the hunt for Jews and their deportation to German concentration camps began, along with non-Jewish Italians.

The disasters that fascism caused created perhaps the most widespread and powerful Resistance movement of occupied western Europe. This movement had its origins in the opposition that had built up against Fascism beginning in the 1920s. In October 1941, in Toulouse, an alliance between Socialists, Communists, and GL strengthened cooperation among the major anti-Fascist exile parties. The agreement not only appealed to political, social, religious, and cultural groups to unite against the Fascists but also created a policy implementation committee. As the war turned bad for the Axis, anti-Fascists set up committees representing Socialists, Communists, Liberals, Christian Democrats, "Demoliberali" (the old Radicals), and Actionists (the GL political party) in Italy. As Mussolini settled into the RSI, local Committees of National Liberation (CLNs) took charge of the Resistance and centralized themselves under more important committees in Rome—headed by the moderate Ivanoe Bonomi—and a radical Milanese body, the CLNAI, for North Italy. The Rome committee delegated the armed struggle to a military junta composed of Communist Luigi Longo, Socialist Sandro Pertini, and Actionist Riccardo Bauer. These committees operated under extreme danger and were distrusted by the British, who pursued an openly pro-monarchist policy, and the Americans, who were particularly suspicious of their communist or leftist orientation.

In January 1944 the Socialists, Communists, and Actionists proposed abolition of the monarchy but encountered predictable resistance from the Christian Democrats and other conservative CLN parties. Unable to secure endorsement of their policy, the left parties requested Victor Emmanuel's abdication and establishment of an openly anti-Fascist government; the king refused but responding to increasing pressure indicated that he would yield his powers to his son Humbert upon the liberation of Rome. On March 14, however, the Soviet Union formally recognized the Badoglio government. Following through on this policy, Communist leader Palmiro Togliatti returned from exile in Moscow and, in Salerno, announced postponement of the "institutional problem" and advocated a Badoglio-led unity cabinet to drive the Germans out of Italy. Togliatti also downplayed the PCI's revolutionary image and set the stage for a "new party" willing to compromise and come to power within a democratic context. This "svolta di Salerno" shocked the country and ignited a fierce debate among leftists, given Badoglio's long collaboration with fascism and his role in Italy's intervention in the war. With the "svolta" came a reshuffling of the Badoglio cabinet in April 1944 and promises by the weakened leftists that they would delay demands for major social reforms until war's end. These concessions were imposed by the Allies anxious to preserve the social order. Socialist leader Pietro Nenni feared that Togliatti had seriously compromised the chances for a republic.

With Rome's liberation in June 1944 and the transfer of powers from the king to his son (with the title of "lieutenant-general of the realm") came a Socialist decision to reverse the conservative tide by eliminating Badoglio and setting up a cabinet responsible to the CLN. The campaign culminated in a meeting between Badoglio and representatives of the six anti-Fascist parties on June 8 in which the Socialists demanded that ministers must swear allegiance to the CLN, not Humbert, that a law convening a Constituent Assembly be adopted immediately, and that an anti-fascist civilian take over the war ministry. This crisis culminated in replacement of Badoglio by Bonomi, but the Communists and conservatives united to thwart the other Socialist requests. For their pains, the Socialists were temporarily eased out of the government.

In the meantime, the military ranks of the Resistance swelled. The movement acquired a social aspect that raised the specter of class war by virtue of the contact it established with peasants and workers. For the moment the focus was on expelling the Germans, as Nazi-Fascist atrocities—including the slaughter of innocent civilians, deportation of Italian workers, and the rounding up of Jews—created mass revulsion. In conjunction with the victorious Allied march up the peninsula, an insurrection was touched off in northern Italy by the CLNAI on April 25, 1945. In the liberated cities, the partisans took over maintenance of law and order and named local officials from the ranks of anti-Fascists. On April 27, Mussolini and his mistress Claretta Petacci, previously captured by partisans while trying to escape Italy, were executed by partisan commander "Valerio" (Walter Audisio); their bodies were later exposed to the crowd's scorn on a site in Milan where fifteen hostages had been executed by the Fascists. The best estimates indicate that 40,000 Resistance fighters lost their lives in Italy and that between 12,000 and 15,000 Fascists died during and after the April insurrection that marked the end of hostilities.

In the euphoria of liberation, the CLNAI revived demands for a purge of Fascists and demanded the end of the Bonomi cabinet. Bonomi could not withstand this "wind from the North." Partisan commander Ferruccio Parri replaced him as prime minister, with Nenni as vice premier and minister for the Constituent Assembly, Togliatti as justice minister, and Christian Democrat Alcide De Gasperi as foreign minister. The government's program included punishing Fascist supporters, reconstructing the Italian economy, redistribution of the wealth, an exchange of the currency, a graduated income tax, a capital levy, and allocation of raw materials in a manner favoring small firms over large.

This program raised havoc among the conservatives. Communists and Socialists had a preeminent position within the Resistance movement, and they had achieved considerable local power; but the partisans were no match for the Allied armies, which controlled the peninsula militarily and politically and, despite the partisan contribution, had won the war. In addition, although personally respected, Parri belonged to the Action party, composed of intellectuals with scant popular support and on its way to extinction. Business interests not only opposed the government's program but also feared continued occupation of factories by workers and partisans, who claimed to have saved them from destruction by the Germans. This tense situation spelled the end of the Parri government, which fell under Allied and conservative pressure. On a visit to Italy, Italian-American banker A. P. Giannini criticized Parri and warned that American loans essential for the country's survival would not be forthcoming as long as partisans occupied the factories. Allied support aided the Liberals in bringing the cabinet down. In the succeeding cabinets headed by De Gasperi, the Liberals attained a stranglehold over economic policy.

Many Italians who fought in the Resistance believed it would be the starting point of a social revolution. Probably this hope was doomed from the start because Allied armies dominated the country, a reality the Communists rushed to recognize. Indirect Allied support allowed the conservatives to postpone indefinitely the economic provisions of the Parri government, end the purge of former Fascists and regular administrative officials tainted by fascism, and replace CLN-nominated local authorities by traditional officials. Whether or not a revolutionary situation—or even the conditions for radical reforms—ever existed, it ended with Parri's fall, which "marked the comeback of all the old conservative forces in Italian society."

PART SIX

The Republic

18

The Structure of Postwar Italy

FASCISM AND WORLD WAR II left Italy a troubled legacy. Not only had the war been lost in an inglorious manner, but the country's participation in the conflict had no moral or diplomatic justification. In addition, the Resistance confirmed the aspects of civil warfare initiated by the Fascist regime in 1922. The division of Italy into northern, German-controlled and southern, Allied-dominated regimes exacerbated existing confusion and increased animosity among Italians. Creation of an Italian army in the South to fight alongside the Allies, designed to refurbish Italy's image, helped perpetuate the stereotype of Italian "treachery," and the Resistance, even though it did much to save Italian honor, hardly reversed hostile Western opinion. Indeed, the Communist-dominated Resistance caused the Allied victors considerable worry.

The Resistance, however, allowed anti-fascists to claim credit for overthrowing Mussolini and the mission of ruling Italy. But twin fears threatened the future—a Fascist resurgence or a Soviet-style dictatorship. Right and left evaluated these threats and their implications differently, and their contrasting judgments determined the country's postwar destiny.

A Devastated Land—and the "Golden Age"

To contemporaries, Italy at war's end presented a desolate picture. Combat deaths were fewer than in World War I, but the bombings and fierce fighting on Italian territory more than made up the difference among civilians, and a million and half deportees and prisoners of war were not finally repatriated until 1947. Of the 31 million rooms available to the population before the conflict, 6.7 million had been either destroyed or damaged. In the North, electricity functioned 90 percent of the time but in the South less than 45 percent, and in parts of the Center, where the worst fighting had occurred, 3 percent. Another crucial economic sector, transport, had been hardest hit, with the once-proud merchant marine reduced to a tenth of its prewar size, the railway system working at 40 percent efficiency, and the trucking industry operating at 35 percent. The economic indexes reflected this situation. With 1938 equal to 100, in 1945 the index for industrial production stood at 29, with the corresponding figures for agriculture at 63 and national income at 51.9. The black market flourished and starvation stalked the civilian population.

In reality, statistics painted the country's portrait inaccurately. The pre-Fascist and Fascist periods had created a robust industrial infrastructure. The success of the Fascist regime in bringing industry and production methods up to the most-advanced European standards has already been noted. Northern industry had survived German plans to transfer or destroy it, thanks to the efforts first of the RSI economics minister, Angelo Tarchi, and then the Resistance. According to the minister of reconstruction, Meiuccio Ruini, lack of raw materials, transport, and other collateral elements accounted for the low index of industrial production, not destroyed plant; he estimated that production would be at 75 to 80 percent of the 1938 figure were it not for those factors, more easily corrected than rebuilding factories.

In addition to plant, the previous regime had bequeathed a rich legacy of ambitious projects, trained engineers, skilled workers, and a low-wage labor force. In the 1930s and 1940s the workers' depressed buying power and the wartime economy had handicapped industry's ability to expand to its potential. After World War II the new Western economic order imposed by the United States—which produced a sextupling of international trade based on commerce and manufacturing between 1950 and 1970—created the premise for removal of these limits. Italian success in achieving a moderate, pro-Western democratic regime allowed Italian industry to exploit its solid base and to become a leader in the Atlantic world's unprecedented economic development. The massive movement of low-wage workers from the South to the North, from less efficient enterprises to more modern ones, and from agriculture to industry also provided a great reserve of labor that enormously enhanced the competitiveness of Italian industry on the world market. In real terms, Italian GNP increased at a yearly average of about 5 percent between 1950 and 1980. This figure surpassed the United States and Britain, matched France and Germany, and built the country into the world's fifth-largest industrial power. A revolution half a century in the making, and based on the restoration of democracy, this "economic miracle" completely transformed the country's face.

The Anti-Fascist Alliance Breaks Up

The six anti-Fascist parties of the Committees of National Liberation collaborated in the government from the last two years of the war until May 1947. Two of them, the Action party and the Demoliberals, did not survive the immediate postwar era. The Liberal party inherited a great European tradition and through their most noted economist and future president of the republic, Luigi Einaudi, dominated economic policy in the immediate postwar period, but the Liberal party's influence remained minuscule.

The Christian Democrats (DC), heirs of Luigi Sturzo's *popolari*, emerged as the largest Italian party under the leadership of Alcide De Gasperi, last PPI secretary. Reborn in 1942, the Catholic party believed that Christian values could resolve modern society's tensions. It supported small propertyholders and small business and opposed big capitalists. It sank deep roots into Italian society by founding an association of peasant landowners, the Coldiretti (under Paolo Bonomi) and a Christian workers' association (Associazioni Cristiane Lavoratori Italiani [ACLI]). These institutions, soon joined by the two-million-strong Catholic Action organization, and the Vatican's support established the party's credentials as a mass organization. The DC's appeal to the poor, traditional Catholic concern for the disinherited, and the robust left-wing Catholic ideology of philosopher Giuseppe Dossetti, appealed also to Communists and Socialists, who theorized a working-class alliance regardless of party affiliation. The uncertain Communist attitude toward small propertyholders and Catholic hostility to the Soviet system, however, made Catholics the sworn enemies of Communists and their Socialist allies. An incalculable advantage for the DC was De Gasperi himself, a shrewd moderate standing between a Vatican hoping to impose its wishes and the DC left. De Gasperi's willingness to compromise with secular political groups, and the powerful Christian Democratic appeal within Italian society, induced industrialists to deemphasize their traditional Liberal connections and link up with the DC to combat communism.

Strong Marxist influence stemming from the Communist role in the Resistance represented the real novelty of postwar Italian politics and society. During the first postwar era, leftist Socialists and Communists had pursued a policy of intransigence and verbal revolution that had contributed to the rise of fascism. Now Communists and Socialists participated in the government and, dissuaded by the presence of Allied troops, Togliatti vetoed the Socialist idea of a revolution based on popular Resistance organizations. As previously mentioned, Togliatti advocated a new party capable of appealing to the masses, arguing that a revolution was impossible within Allied-controlled West Europe. Whether this principle was Togliatti's or imposed by Stalin, as argued by historian Sergio Bertelli, is a matter of dispute, but influential and rank-and-file hard-line Communists accepted the policy as a method of obtaining an electoral majority based on reform while adhering to a secret revolutionary agenda. Communist officials denied this "double-track" policy, but even Togliatti's attitude appeared ambivalent, as illustrated by a speech to the Constituent Assembly during which he renounced violence, but only for "today." At any rate, in 1948 it seemed to friend and foe alike that the Marxist parties indeed had an excellent shot at winning a majority in free elections.

The Socialist party regenerated itself after fascism's fall, despite the heavy burden it carried of having failed to stop Mussolini's rise. As minister for the Constituent Assembly in the De Gasperi cabinet, Pietro Nenni was instrumental in setting a date for national elections and securing a referendum on whether the monarchy should be eliminated. Another Socialist, interior minister Giuseppe Romita, reduced the banditry and political violence that plagued postwar Italy, ensuring peaceful conditions for elections and countering a powerful argument for their possible postponement or nullification. On June 2, 1946, the referendum and national elections for a Constituent Assembly took place; they instituted a republic and established the Socialist party as the country's most popular leftist organization.

The Socialists proved unable to maintain their position for three major reasons: the Communist connection, the Socialists' divisions, and the inability to match the financial support that the big powers funneled to their Catholic and Communist rivals. Led by Giuseppe Saragat, the Socialist right wing believed the Socialist party should sever its alliance with the PCI and become explicitly social democratic as had the parties in other Western European countries. Nenni rejected this idea, convinced that there would be a resurgence of fascism if Communists and Socialists were divided, and advocated instead a Popular Front alliance as had been constituted in France in 1935. This debate produced a disastrous split in January 1947 at a Socialist congress held in Rome. Saragat founded a Social Democratic party (the PSDI), which over the years became a splinter organization tied to the government. With his great rival out of the party, Nenni and his ally Rodolfo Morandi established the Popular Front alliance with the Communists and reversed Socialist tradition by reorganizing the PSI on the Communist party model—a dictatorial organization in which no one could question leadership decisions. The Communists quickly seized advantage of the divisions to wrest control of the leftist labor union, the Confederazione Generale Italiana di Lavoro (CGIL) and the League of Cooperatives and Mutual Aid Societies. With PCI domination of the PSI, hope for substantial middle-class support for the Socialists disappeared, and they lived on handouts from the well-heeled Communists subsidized by the Soviet Union. In Italy, contrary to what happened in the rest of Western Europe, the Communists achieved political and intellectual hegemony on the left.

These developments reflected the international situation, where the wartime alliance between the Western powers and the USSR had given way to the Cold

War. According to James Miller, after World War II U.S. policy focused on a postwar world based on stabilization and democracy. The Americans could not allow a Soviet-dominated force to come to power in Italy, a strategically placed country with historical ties to the United States and astride the Mediterranean with its close proximity to the oil-rich Middle East. Understanding that the Socialists were unavailable for dialogue and viewing imposition of an extremist government as a blow to their design for political stabilization and economic prosperity, the Americans turned to the Christian Democrats.

The superpowers' Italian struggle culminated in 1947 and 1948. In January 1947 the head of the Italian government, De Gasperi, visited the United States without Foreign Minister Nenni. There is a difference of opinion as to whether the decision to oust the Marxist parties from the government was made explicit during De Gasperi's trip, implicit in his talks with American officials, or an outright condition of further American financial aid. In May De Gasperi ousted the Communists and Socialists from the cabinet. In October the Soviets established the new Communist International, the Cominform, which chastised the Italian and the French parties for being too prone to compromise and initiated a period of greater confrontation. "The era of antifascist coalitions was over and that of the Cold War had begun."

In response to the virulent Popular Front electoral campaign against the United States, the American embassy in Rome estimated the Front's electoral strength at 40 percent and judged the Italian situation "extremely dangerous." Aware of massive Russian aid to the PCI—Ambassador James Dunn reported a Communist electoral budget of 3 billion lire in the three northern industrial provinces alone—and convinced that the Communists harbored insurrectionary designs, Secretary of Defense James Forrestal, supported by President Harry Truman, authorized clandestine action. Fitting within the Truman Doctrine's general framework, Italy became the major theater of American intervention. In November 1947 the National Security Council (NSC) recommended an interruption in the rate of American troop withdrawals if the Communists took power anywhere in Italy before December 15. The NSC also authorized Central Intelligence Agency (CIA) operations in Italy. An installment of ten million dollars secretly entered a fund for anti-Communist activities, bribes, and to influence elections. Aid arrived through other avenues as well. In view of the crucial national elections scheduled for April 18, 1948, American officials threatened a cutoff of aid should the Front win and stimulated a letter-writing campaign by Italian-Americans to their relatives in Italy.

Front leaders believed that they had an excellent chance for victory, but the campaign by the Christian Democrats and their American supporters proved extremely effective. Revulsion against Communist totalitarianism and the conviction of many voters that they risked putting another dictatorship in place worked against the Front, as did the threat of reduced aid. The same period witnessed the overthrow of the Czech government and the establishment of Communist regimes in East Europe by the Red Army, and this Soviet activity influenced the Italian elections. When the results came in, the Christian Democrats alone had won 48.4 percent of the vote, allowing them to rule without any allies if they wished. The Popular Front did much poorer than expected, capturing only 31 percent of the vote. The Socialist share of this figure came to only 10 percent, bringing it even more forcefully under PCI domination and cementing the "Italian anomaly": a Communist party that was much larger than the Socialist.

The 1948 elections ended the immediate postwar era. The anti-Fascist alliance had broken up and—given the fear of a Communist takeover and American opposition to a Communist presence in the government—the DC remained the fulcrum of politics in Italy for the next forty-five years.

The Structure of Postwar Italy

The Constituent Assembly elected on June 2, 1946, wrote a constitution for the new republic established at the same time. On December 22, 1947, the draft constitution passed by an overwhelming majority and went into force on January 1, 1948.

The major forces represented in the Constituent Assembly and their percentages were: DC, 35.2; PSI, 20.7; and PCI, 18.9. This split guaranteed that the new Constitution would be a product of compromise, which indeed proved the case. The document incorporated democratic and social principles being enunciated by other postwar European constitutions, reestablished where possible the governmental structure of pre-Fascist Italy, and instituted measures to prevent a possible relapse into dictatorship.

Since the leftist parties were unable to transmute the Resistance into the revolution to which they had constantly appealed, the Constituent Assembly allowed them to write the hope of future change into the constitution itself. For this reason, and because of the strong leftist affinity with Catholic social thought, social principles protecting less-advantaged citizens were written into the constitution. Theoretically this incorporation permitted the left to pass specific legislation making those principles real should it receive enough support in the country; practically, however, it embarrassed future cabinets, whose actions could never measure up to those principles.

The constitution declared Italy a democratic republic "founded on labor," gave sovereignty to the people, promised social equality, and proclaimed that citizens and groups possessed inviolable rights. In accordance with the evolution of Western political thought, it pledged to demolish economic and social obstacles that hindered effective participation by workers in the country's political and economic order, blocked development of the human personality, and prevented the attainment of true equality. To achieve these goals, the constitution refused to accord private property the status of an absolute right, recognizing it but emphasizing its social obligations and limitations. Furthermore, while favoring free initiative, it provided for nationalization of important industries on the grounds of utility and allowed for the possibility of a massive land reform program. Included also was a promise of full employment. In short, the constitution provided for a mixed economy with a large dose of public participation and the basis of a welfare state; in this it continued the work of previous regimes but went much beyond them.

Besides these principles dear to both Marxist and Catholic thinkers, the Constituent Assembly accepted provisions expressly designed to please the Catholics. The most important made the Lateran Accords of 1929 an integral part of the constitution. Besides the anomaly of incorporating a treaty with a foreign state into a country's constitution, this move created major problems for the future—blocking divorce until 1970–1974, permitting the continuing heavy interference of the Church in public education, violating the rights of former clergy, and discriminating against other religions. Fearing criticism and alienation of Catholic opinion, the Communists split with their Socialist allies and voted with the Christian Democrats in favor of instituting into law this most backward aspect of the constitution. Bowing to another Catholic concern, the Assembly also adopted provisions favoring the family.

In the political arena, the constitution followed the principles of restoring pre-Fascist institutions where possible, modernizing them where necessary, and attempting to create a governmental structure that would resist creation of a future dictatorship. Essentially this technique involved creating a weak governmental structure that no one group could dominate, thus opening the road to inefficiency. This principle is at the origin of the famous governmental instability of the republic, which, however, did not prevent the political longevity of certain individuals and the shifting of political power to external areas, particularly the parties.

To begin, the new constitution differed from the 1848 *Statuto* because it was a "closed" document that could no longer be modified by Parliament. It will be recalled that the Statuto had been altered by Fascist manipulation of the legislative process to build their dictatorship and was never repealed. The new republican instrument resembled the American Constitution rather than the British in that legislation had to be judged for its adherence to constitutional principles. This structure mandated a high court to make these decisions, the Constitutional Court—a totally new body consisting of fifteen judges sitting for a limited term and chosen separately by the president of the republic, Parliament, and high judicial groups. In effect, this provision weakened the Parliament when compared to the pre-Fascist period.

As before, Parliament consisted of two bodies. The Chamber of Deputies was reinstituted practically as it had existed before Mussolini and consisted of 630 members. The Chamber's usual term is five years, but it can be dissolved earlier and new elections held under certain conditions. The Senate, previously appointed by the king, now became elective and consisted of 315 senators. The Senate's functions parallel those of the Chamber; since there has never been a clear rationale for its existence, reform and even elimination of the Senate has been a constant theme of debate in the republic. Although the Senate is theoretically entitled to a longer term, it is dissolved along with the Chamber of Deputies. The powers of the Italian Parliament resemble those of the Third and Fourth French republics; the body is responsible for legislation, approves the budget, ratifies treaties, declares war, and conducts investigations into important matters. Its most important function, however, is to create a government and to vote confidence in it.

Officially the government or cabinet is known as the "Council of Ministers," and its head carries the title of "President" (referred to herein as the "Prime Minister" or "Premier" to avoid confusion with the president of the republic). In accordance with the principle of avoiding a future dictatorship, the constitutional framers reversed Fascist practice and made the cabinet completely dependent on parliamentary whim. The republican cabinet has thus been a weak institution. The prime minister-designate is nominated by the president of the republic after a wide round of consultations. Although the president is bound to nominate the person with the most obvious chance of success, the Italian political system and the constitution provide some leeway and confer more prominence on the Italian president than do the corresponding offices in Germany and in the Fourth French republic, which ended in 1958. Once chosen, the cabinet must obtain a vote of confidence (a majority vote) in both houses. Far from determining the cabinet's policy, the prime minister is the first among equals and rules by consensus; this is a difficult and frequently impossible task given the cabinet's usual composition of temporarily allied parties and/or factions continually jockeying for position. The government has no fixed term and can be formally overthrown at any time by a no-confidence vote in either house. Add to this factor "pure" proportional representation, which produces only slender majorities, factionalized parties and secret voting (which permits deputies to take cover while voting against major legislation without fear of political retribution), and the exclusion of a large bloc of representatives for the formation and support of governments (primarily Communist), and the premise was set for governmental instability throughout the Cold War. Once a government fell, the old government remained only as a caretaker unable to take major policy decisions while the interminable process of forming a new government, frequently with the prospect of only a brief life, began anew. Within this context, however, the parties were able to create a surprising measure of de facto stability, as will become clear in Chapter 19.

The voting system set up at the republic's beginning and undergoing a process of change only in 1992–1993 also encouraged the instability of national and local administrations. Concerned with giving all political views a voice in Parliament and in local government after twenty years of Fascist repression, the Italians established "pure" proportional representation—for example, by application of a complex formula, parties were represented according to the number of votes they received in the country as a whole, not just in a particular electoral district. No 5 percent barrier existed, as is the case in Germany. Citizens voted for lists presented by parties, not for candidates, although they could express preferences within those lists (limited to one in 1991). This procedure gave party establishments immense power because they determined who got onto the lists and the prominence of their positions within those lists. In addition, since no one party held a majority, with the exception of the DC from 1948 to 1953, coalition governments became the rule. Small parties wielded power disproportionate to their numbers because a shift of even a few votes could prevent a cabinet from coming to power, from maintaining it, or from fulfilling its legislative program.

To form a government, a prime minister-designate must negotiate with several parties large and small. Each of these parties has its own treasured items to insert into the government's program and its favorite ministries (government departments) to demand. The whole process is complicated because the large Communist party and, until the late 1950s, the Socialist party, and the neo-Fascist Movimento Sociale Italiano (MSI) were frozen out of the ruling coalitions because they were considered undemocratic. This factor enhanced the roles of parties with as small as 2 or 3 percent representation. Further complicating this already-complex procedure, the parties were divided into many disagreeing currents that might oppose their party's participation in a cabinet for various reasons. Frequently it was impossible to determine a party's position until after a congress that thrashed out competing principles—and often not even then, which meant another assembly. Even if a party agreed to vote for a government, that support might evaporate at any time and bring down a cabinet. Despite strong party discipline, parliamentary rules allowing secret votes on crucial issues provided cover for "snipers" in the ruling coalition wishing to shoot down a cabinet against their own party hierarchy's wishes.

At the local level, this procedure had to be repeated in electing the legislative councils, executive committees, and mayors of the provinces (equivalents of the French departments, but centering around a major capital) and the communes and introduced instability there as well. More characteristic of local government was the state's failure to fulfill the constitution's promise of decentralization. Moreover, the prefect, a central government representative dating back to Napoleonic times with wide powers to interfere with and dissolve local government institutions and to influence elections, hindered local autonomy. Although the prefect's powers tended to diminish over the years, he remains a powerful figure. Another unfulfilled promise was partially implemented in 1970, when equivalents of the American state government, regional governments, were instituted—but their powers have still not been finally defined. Promised in the constitution as a reaction to Fascist centralization, the government refused to establish regional governments because the Communists controlled strategic regions in Central Italy—the Red Belt—and their fate became a major issue during discussions that brought the Socialists into the governing coalition in August 1960.

The failure to institute regional autonomy illustrates a major problem with the 1948 constitution. The Constituent Assembly left many of the principles enunciated in the constitution to be implemented later by enabling legislation. As the long delay in establishing the regions shows, crucial parts of the document were implemented late or not at all. In addition to the delay in setting up regional government, the Constitutional Court began operations only in 1956, and the magistrates' self-governing body, the Consiglio Superiore della Magistratura (CSM), had to await 1958. A related but more serious issue in implementing the constitution's democratic principles was the failure to alter important laws adopted during fascism. Thus, Fascist legislation in criminal matters remained in effect, modified only piecemeal by specific Constitutional Court decisions before it was finally replaced in 1990; the case of the civil code, although better, was similar. Nonimplementation of solemnly declared principles continues to be a major problem of the Italian constitutional system.

The Constituent Assembly instituted the president of the republic as the head of state. Elected by a two-thirds majority on any of the first three ballots and a majority thereafter by the Chamber of Deputies and the Senate sitting together, the president rather resembles a constitutional monarch. His powers are ill defined and the office increases in prominence when Parliament is gridlocked or its prestige is low. The president's right to return legislation for reconsideration, to dissolve Parliament, and to influence the choice of a prime minister-designate is conditioned by the political situation. Furthermore, the constitution provides that to be valid the president's acts must be countersigned by the ministers or the premier. The president's real power stems from his long term of office (seven years), his irremovability (except by impeachment), his ability to persuade, his chairmanship of important bodies such as the CSM, and his supposed position above petty politics.

Rounding out republican Italy's governmental structure is the legal system. Based on career judges who advance on the basis of examinations and qualifications, the magistracy governs itself through the previously noted CSM. The legal system's organization makes the judiciary a more independent power than it is in other Western democracies, including the United States. The Constituent Assembly aimed in this way to create another roadblock to possible dictatorship. But although this feature has allowed magistrates to pursue investigations free from interference, it has also produced highly politicized judges who are responsible to no one outside their organization, not even the minister of justice. The judges have also created their own partisan groups, further compromising the justice system's impartiality.

The method of dispensing justice has exacerbated the tendency toward lack of impartiality, despite lip service to that ideal. There is a very close association between prosecuting attorneys (the *pubblico ministero*), who are magistrates serving in that capacity, and other judges. Furthermore, indictments are handed down not by grand juries but by an investigating judge known as the *giudice istruttore*. These magistrates investigate alleged criminal behavior in secret with the help of their favorite police force—competing police forces being another safeguard, at the cost of inefficiency, against a revival of dictatorship. Prosecutors selectively leak evidence against a defendant, whose guilt the press then publicly proclaims. Moreover, allegations of police brutality have been rife in postwar Italy. In addition to the cozy relationship among police, prosecutors, and judges, there is no real protection against being forced to testify against oneself, no habeas corpus, no guarantee of a speedy trial, and no hard exclusion of hearsay evidence. A favorite technique of investigators is to hold defendants in jail until they implicate others. A defendant's presumption of innocence is at best vague, and until lately, Italian law allowed the verdict of "acquitted for lack of proof," which subjected the accused to another trial on the same charge if frustrated prosecutors believed new proof establishing guilt had been gathered. Crimes punishing free speech, such as criticism of public officials, established institutions, and the pope, have only recently fallen into abeyance.

Although the legal system's insensitivity to civil rights symbolizes the contradiction between the constitution's promises and its reality, the republic has important gains to its credit. It has established a generous welfare system, a modern economy in most of the country, and a democratic environment that—despite occasionally sensational cases—has allowed the most diverse opinions to flourish. For interconnected international and domestic reasons, however, the republic has proved unable to correct its major deficiencies over time, and this failure threatens its viability.

19

Postwar Politics: "Imperfect Bipolarism"

GIVEN THE PCI'S EXCLUSION from the ruling coalition, the political arithmetic meant permanent control of the government by the other large party, the Christian Democratic. But steady electoral losses for the DC-led bloc, combined with PCI increases as time went on, rendered the governmental system even more unstable than provided for by the institutional makeup, despite addition of the Socialists to the ruling coalition in the 1960s. These conditions produced a gridlocked political situation labeled "imperfect bipolarism" by political scientist Giorgio Galli. This term means that—because of domestic and international fears the Communists and their supporters would establish a Soviet-style dictatorship and ally Italy with the USSR should they be entrusted with any degree of governmental participation—the alternation of power became impossible. Because Communists and not Socialists dominated the Italian left, Italy became a "blocked democracy." During the duration of the Cold War, DC-led coalitions could not be voted out of power; this long tenure in office favored the inefficiency and corruption that produced the republic's major crises.

Centrism

Following World War II, the major items of business for Italy were negotiation of a peace treaty, rebuilding a political system, and reconstruction of the economy. The first question found a relatively rapid resolution, while the second proved the thorniest; both will be the subject of this chapter. As will be discussed in Chapter 20, the republic completed the third task beyond everyone's wildest expectations.

Even though the peace treaty allowed the country to put the war behind it because most of the questions were settled, its terms deluded many anti-fascists because they had expected their opposition to Mussolini, their role in the Resistance, and Italian support of the Allies in the South to placate the antagonism of their country's former enemies.

The territorial provisions of the settlement signed on February 10, 1947, caused the most consternation. Italy lost all of its colonies, a bitter blow, although a blessing considering the money that the country had wasted on them. French border rectifications also hurt Italian pride but were minor—and French attempts to annex larger areas were thwarted. In the northeast, Italy retained its 1919 boundaries despite an Austrian claim. The area in dispute, the South Tyrol, included an ethnic Austrian majority, which had prompted Hitler to annex it during the war; later, Italians and Austrians worked out an agreement to respect *Sudtiroler* rights, which brought peace to the region despite tensions and periodic flare-ups. The Italian border with Yugoslavia—which, unlike Austria, was not handicapped by having fought on Hitler's side—was a different question. The Italian population had been expelled from the prewar boundary areas closest to Yugoslavia; even more menacing, however, the Russians and Togliatti supported Marshal Josip Broz Tito's exaggerated claims on the entire region of Venezia Giulia. The Allies drew various lines based on ethnicity; the Italians claimed the most favorable but were forced to accept the least favorable. This solution, exacerbated by an agreement to divide Trieste into Allied and Yugoslav occupation zones, outraged Italians. The emotional dispute occasioned several serious crises with the Americans and Yugoslavs before being finally resolved in October 1954.

The other peace provisions caused emotional pain but were less significant. The country had to pay reparations, and Italian assets in some countries were also lost. The Italian argument that they had made a substantial financial contribution to the Nazi defeat was rejected, and, in addition, the country's gold reserve stolen by the Germans and recovered by the Allies was not returned intact. The United States, Britain, and France renounced reparations in 1945, but the Soviet Union and the smaller countries with claims against Italy refused to do so. In the context of postwar economic recovery and American aid, however, the economic provisions of the peace had slight practical significance. The other volatile issue involved limits on the Italian military establishment and the breakup of the Italian fleet. Despite De Gasperi's contention that restrictions on fortifications and on military hardware and limiting the Italian army—including carabinieri—to 250,000, the navy to 25,000, and air force to 200 combat planes left the country defenseless, the Italians were forced to accept them. Again, the practical importance of the defense clauses were limited, given the change in the world's military configuration and extension of the American nuclear umbrella to protect the country.

Having disposed of World War II's diplomatic heredity, the country turned to ordinary administration. As mentioned, the DC won a majority of the seats in the Chamber of Deputies in the 1948 elections. De Gasperi could have formed a cabinet consisting exclusively of DC members as his party's right wing demanded. Wisely, De Gasperi resisted this temptation and created instead a center coalition including, besides the DC, the small secular parties—Liberals and the moderate leftist Republicans and Social Democrats.

This coalition faced a difficult political time. Excluded from power, Communists and Socialists attacked the government at every turn. They vigorously supported Soviet foreign policy, most notably by conducting a raucous campaign in the country and in Parliament against Italian entrance into the North Atlantic Treaty Organization (NATO) in 1949. Socialist leaders publicly approved of the Communist takeover in Czechoslovakia and, symbol of their subservience to the Communists and Soviet foreign policy, also criticized Marshall Plan aid as an instrument of American domination, called protest strikes, and attempted to stop the delivery of supplies. These policies illustrated Communist manipulation of the labor movement and produced strains in the CGIL, the union created in June 1944 to represent workers of all political shades. In July 1948 an attempt to assassinate PCI head Palmiro Togliatti occurred, and a general strike to protest the event ensued. Many Communist workers considered this action a call to revolution and the party had to pull them back. Non-Communist labor leaders decided to break with the Communists and their Socialist allies. Over the next year, a series of splits took place, and by 1950, the three unions that were to dominate the postwar era emerged: the Communist-controlled CGIL (which included the Socialists); the Catholic-influenced CISL (Confederazione Italiana dei Sindacati dei Lavoratori); and the smaller UIL (Unione Italiana del Lavoro) representing primarily Republicans and Social Democrats.

Communist stimulation of labor protest and escalating unrest caused by unemployment and peasant demands for land prompted a strong reaction. The Christian Democrat interior minister, Mario Scelba, forbade propaganda in the workplace and organized special police squads that specialized in beating up recalcitrant workers. Although these policies further alienated the left, they brought De Gasperi no peace from conservatives, including Christian Democrats, who demanded he put down the agitation with even greater firmness and that he outlaw the Communist party. Conservatives also denounced the prime minister's attempt to address peasant demands through land reform, and their opposition greatly limited its scope. These developments estranged the moderate leftists in the coalition, who also resented the manner in which Christian Democrats assumed a near-monopoly in appointing members of their party to head public corporations and other agencies under government control; this policy initiated a perverse tradition that, over the life of the republic, parceled out crucial public sector jobs to people not according to merit but on the basis of party affiliation and influence in governing coalitions (*lottizzazione*).

The small parties generally voted for the cabinets even though, given DC control of Parliament, the Christian Democrats could have managed without these votes, but as the 1950s progressed, by-elections indicated that the Catholic majority was threatened. The Vatican and Catholic Action—led by Pope Pius XII and Luigi Gedda—intensified their intervention in secular affairs. The Church rightly claimed a great deal of credit for the DC victory of 1948; given the weak DC organization, the party depended on parish priests and Catholic Action committees to organize the voters and get them to the polls. Because of their role, bishops and other clergy felt authorized to influence the choice of important state managers and public policy. This activity further alienated the DC's lay allies and embarrassed De Gasperi, who favored state independence from the Church and in the words of political scientist Norman Kogan, "fought a hard battle against the clericalization of Italian life."

This struggle culminated after the local elections of 1951–1952, in which the DC share of the vote dropped to 35.1 percent (compared with 48.5 in 1948). On the right, the neo-Fascist MSI had absorbed the votes of the *Uomo Qualunque* (*Any Man*)—a Fascist-oriented movement opposing all politicians—and along with the Monarchist party (PNM) tripled its votes. At the same time, the Socialists had also had obtained more electoral support. These developments led Gedda to propose an alliance with the extreme right in Rome and the South. De Gasperi bitterly fought the deal, realizing that a victory in local Rome elections on that basis would produce a powerful demand for a similar coalition on the national level; De Gasperi believed that the DC had a future only if it pursued a progressive social policy. De Gasperi won the struggle and the center coalition formula prevailed, but the fight greatly weakened both De Gasperi and the DC.

The decline in DC support in the 1951–1952 elections indicated that the stable majority possessed by the center parties would disappear during the 1953 parliamentary contest, creating governmental instability. To forestall this development, the centrist coalition proposed to alter the electoral system so that any alliance of parties receiving one vote more than 50 percent would receive an "electoral bonus" bringing their seats in the Chamber up to two-thirds of the total. Because of the resemblance of this provision to the Acerbo law, instrumental in consolidating Mussolini's power in 1924, the proposal touched off a bitter brawl in the country and Parliament. Baptizing the bill the "swindle law," the left initiated a major campaign against it, but influential moderates such as lawyer Piero Calamandrei also opposed it. The law passed in Parliament after an animated debate, but moderate opponents blocked its implementation by forming an independent group that attracted just enough support during the elections to keep the center coalition's share of the vote to 49.85 percent.

The predictions of those who forecast instability came true. Although the center coalition received a slight majority of seats in Parliament, it lacked a viable majority. All the government parties lost support, and divisions within the individual parties and disputes among them increased in the postelectoral attempt to fix blame. Combined with the increased votes for the Communists and the extreme right, these conflicts guaranteed the formation of unstable governments. Even Alcide De Gasperi failed to put a cabinet together and retired from politics. A year later he died.

Despite the similarity of the electoral bonus and the Acerbo law, the persons who suggested the 1953 proposal had personally suffered from Fascist repression and, despite leftist accusations, did not plan a return to fascism. Given the instability to which the country has been subject since 1953, electoral mechanisms similar to the swindle law have been put forward many times since. The loud voice that the Italian system gave to political minorities encouraged extreme fragmentation, a tendency that—except for the call of history—might have been eliminated in 1953.

The Long Travail of the Center-Left

The instability generated by the 1953 elections made it urgent to widen the governing coalition. Two solutions existed—either bringing in the extreme right or the Socialists. Christian Democrats were divided on this issue. As indicated, Gedda wished to ally with the MSI and the Monarchists, but the DC left wing, influenced by the long tradition of Catholic social thought, favored an "opening to the left" with the Socialists. This solution, however, faced many serious obstacles. The social thinkers of the Catholic left did not control the DC. Could they win the backing of the party, and if they did, would the conservatives go along? DC conservatives adamantly opposed the Socialists because of their affiliation with the Communists and would never trust them. Along with the Liberals—who would be ousted if the Socialists joined the coalition—the conservatives argued that the PSI would not renounce the Communist alliance, and if they did, Socialist party members would not go along. Worse, they regarded Nenni as a "Trojan Horse" for PCI influence and eventual membership in the government.

In their struggle, the DC conservatives had powerful allies: the Vatican and the United States. Pope Pius XII had attempted to help Gedda; for fear that Communists and Socialists would take Italy out of NATO, the United States officially opposed the opening to the left even though the American embassy first secretary, George Lister, quietly made contact with Socialist representatives with the approval of Ambassador James Zellerbach. Liberal party leader Giovanni Malagodi's contacts in the Rome embassy, however, stiffened the back of American diplomats, and the Republican administration of President Dwight Eisenhower seemed unlikely to lift the American "veto."

Pietro Nenni had believed that the Popular Front of which he was a part would win in 1948. The defeat of that year damaged his party much more than the Front as a whole. Because of superior Communist organization and the manner in which seats were distributed, PSI representation in Parliament declined drastically. Nenni recognized the election as a disaster and contemplated getting out of the alliance, but he had to move gradually; his party had become subordinate within the labor movement, depended on the Communists for financial support, and, in effect, had become a PCI satellite.

The elections of 1953 brought Nenni an opportunity to resolve his dilemma. If he withdrew from the Communist alliance, not only would his party regain its independence but also he would strengthen Italian democracy by increasing governmental stability and widen its base by bringing part of the working class to the republic's support. As a condition of this operation's success, however, he required domestic reforms that would reduce the gap between rich and poor and regional imbalances, implement land reform, industrialize the South, institute rational economic planning, make electoral modifications, create regional governments, and nationalize the electric industry (a conservative fortress). In foreign affairs, Nenni needed a more "defensive" interpretation of NATO to garner party support.

The Socialist leader launched these principles in March 1955 at the Congress of Turin. His party apparently accepted his new policy, but, controlled by the apparatus, the PSI greeted it without understanding its implications. But the death of Rodolfo Morandi, who ruled the party bureaucracy with an iron hand and seemingly supported Nenni during this phase, spelled trouble. In April, Nenni shrewdly maneuvered to attain election of a Christian Democrat friendly to the Center-Left, Giovanni Gronchi, to the presidency of the republic. Between 1955 and 1956 Socialist prestige grew remarkably with successes in local elections, attainment of several important Socialist-sponsored measures, moves to loosen ties with the Communists, and, most important, a meeting with Giuseppe Saragat during which Saragat and Nenni agreed to merge their respective organizations. In 1956 came the Khruschev report on Stalin's crimes at the Twentieth Congress of the Communist Party of the Soviet Union (CPSU), the

Hungarian Revolution, and the Soviet repression. These events caused great consternation among Italian leftists, which Nenni hoped to harness to his cause. Nenni swiftly denounced the invasion and wrote a series of articles maintaining that the dictatorial aspects of communism could not be attributed to a person but to the system.

From this high point, however, Nenni's problems began. Togliatti feared isolation and fought back. Talks to implement the PSI-PSDI merger stalled. The PSI's pro-Communist left wing mobilized against Nenni. At the Congress of Venice, February 1957, the PSI left wing dramatically demonstrated its power by electing a Central Committee opposed to the opening to the left even though the delegates approved Nenni's Center-Left policy. Two years of complex maneuvering ensued while Nenni attempted to secure control of his own party. At the Naples congress, January 1959, he received a 58.3 percent vote of support. Though this majority seemed comfortable, his opponents were far from out.

These developments allowed conservative Christian Democrats and American diplomats resisting the Center-Left to argue that even if Nenni had dropped his philo-communism, his party would not follow him. The DC left had won the position of secretary in the person of Amintore Fanfani; both the left and Fanfani sympathized with the Socialist aims previously mentioned and hoped to transform the DC into a modern mass party with a progressive program. But conservatives blocked attempts at dialogue with the Socialists and favored maintenance of the party's traditional policies and structure, based on financial contributions from private industrialists and an organization rooted in the parishes and Catholic Action. A struggle paralleling the one in the PSI raged within the DC. Hampered by disappointments in the 1958 elections, a feeble majority in the party, and a scandal, Fanfani was forced to resign as prime minister and secretary. His faction, based on the ideas of progressive Catholic thinker Giuseppe Dossetti, dissolved and was replaced by a looser coalition of DC leaders, known as the "Dorotei," headed by Aldo Moro.

This confused infighting reflected itself in Parliament and the country. The cabinet Fanfani had headed sympathized with the Center-Left, and his resignation made it extremely difficult to find agreement. President Gronchi gave Fernando Tambroni a mandate to form a government. Tambroni had recently defended Fanfani, but anxious to achieve a majority on his own, he haggled both with the left and, secretly, with the right. Astoundingly, on April 3, 1960, he accepted MSI support in a confidence vote in the Chamber. Ten cabinet ministers resigned, but since no other majority existed, Tambroni survived for the moment.

Although Tambroni said that his government would handle only routine administrative matters until a more permanent solution could be found, his actions spoke differently. He pledged strong government and took steps to increase his popularity with the business community and middle classes. During the delicate international period following the downing of a United States U2 spy plane and the resulting clamorous breakup of the Geneva Summit, Tambroni projected the image of a strong leader. Rumors flew that he had established a secret police and awaited radicalization of the political situation to "save" the country. Furthermore, Tambroni's dependence on MSI votes conditioned his action toward the neo-Fascists, who in June scheduled a congress for Genoa. The city, a major Resistance center against the Fascists, considered this development a provocation. Spontaneous strikes and riots protesting the congress began in the port city on June 30 and spread all over the country. Tambroni mobilized massive police forces, but the resulting street battles ended his experiment. The riots allowed Moro to press the DC for immediate truncation of Tambroni's tenure and his substitution by Fanfani. The emergency situation allowed Moro to secure parliamentary support from Social Democrats, Liberals, and Republicans (PRI) and the abstention of Socialists and Monarchists. The DC directorate asked Tambroni to resign, and he did so on July 19, 1960.

The new Fanfani cabinet—called that of the "parallel convergences"—produced several important Socialist-inspired reforms, but these did not result in PSI gains. Local elections witnessed instead a PSI decline and a PCI increase, attributed to leftist Socialist voters crossing over to help the Communists. Lack of an electoral breakthrough complicated the next step toward a Center-Left coalition—establishment of local four-party Center-Left administrations (DC, PSI, PRI, PSDI) foreshadowing a national coalition. As the price of cooperation, Christian Democrats demanded an immediate end to local Socialist coalitions with the Communists while political realities dictated gradual disengagement. The Church intervened when Cardinal Giuseppe Siri brutally informed Moro that the bishops could not condone DC collaboration with the PSI until the Socialists had guaranteed their independence from the Communists.

At this point, two elections—of liberal Pope John XXIII in 1958 and President John F. Kennedy in 1960—influenced the struggle for the Center-Left. The pope imposed a pro-Center-Left policy on the Church and silenced anti-Socialist conservatives in the DC. The American position was more complex. Given the many crises that the new administration had to resolve, it did not immediately stifle anti-Center-Left opponents in the Rome embassy, the State Department, and the CIA. Kennedy, however, gave carte blanche to presidential adviser Arthur M. Schlesinger, Jr., to support the Center-Left. A well-known historian of the United States, Schlesinger had learned to love Italy through contact at Harvard University with anti-fascist exile Gaetano Salvemini. The next three years witnessed a complicated struggle within the American administrative and diplomatic establishment between forces—flanked by their respective Italian allies—that favored or opposed the opening to the left.

A continuing fight in Italy paralleled this maneuvering. The attraction of communism for left-wing PSI leaders and voters allowed the PCI to whittle away at the Socialist electorate, and DC leader Moro had trouble keeping his right wing in check. In February 1962, the Socialists agreed on an advanced program to be implemented by Fanfani and supported him in Parliament by abstaining in the vote on his cabinet. With decisive Socialist encouragement, this cabinet nationalized the electric power companies, imposed a new withholding tax on stock dividends, implemented obligatory school attendance until age fourteen, and passed a host of other potentially significant reforms. This activity, however, alienated conservatives and did not satisfy leftist Socialists, who were especially upset because nationalization of electric companies provided compensation for the owners and did not organize the industry in a way that clearly represented an attack on the capitalist system. The withholding tax closed an important tax loophole but frightened investors, prompting a massive flight of capital abroad. In addition, the Communists moved to sabotage the Socialist-DC agreement by stimulating massive strikes by the unions. The resulting wage increases fueled inflation, which caused more disorder and further weakened the government.

The unrest exacerbated the political situation as well. Discussions that were to have led to the entrance of Socialist representatives in the cabinet increased the infighting, which continued up to November 22, 1963. Only the shock of Kennedy's assassination induced the last Socialist holdout, Riccardo Lombardi, to give in, and an agreement was reached to form a cabinet including Socialists. This action caused the PSI left wing to split off and form a new, pro-Communist party, the PSIUP (Partito Socialista di Unità Proletaria). In this dangerous situation, DC secretary Moro negotiated with the unions to moderate their demands and thus soften the economic crisis, but they refused. On May 27, 1964, a Rome newspaper published a letter in which the treasury minister predicted economic collapse if the government did not drop its Socialist-inspired reform program. The divisions prompted the government to resign in order to review the political agreements.

During the discussions, Moro pleaded with Nenni to slow down the pace of reforms, but the party refused. Negotiations dragged until July 17, when the Socialists suddenly agreed to a new cabinet that would put less emphasis on reform.

What accounts for this strange capitulation? Nenni indicated at the time that if the Socialists had not given in, there would have been a rightist coup d'etat. During the crisis, president Antonio Segni took the highly unusual step of consulting with military commanders and Senate president Cesare Merzagora, vocal advocate of an emergency government. In 1971 a parliamentary investigation confirmed existence of a plan drawn up in 1964 by General Giovanni De Lorenzo, the commander of SIFAR (Servizio Informazione Forze Armate, the se-cret service), to provoke disorders that would serve as an excuse to gain military control of the country. This plan, of which American military commanders were informed, included setting up detention camps and arresting prominent leftist politicians in and out of the government. According to some scholars, such as Giuseppe Tamburrano, fear of a coup forced Nenni to jettison his reform pro-gram to save Italian democracy.

Did a serious possibility of a coup exist, or did Center-Left opponents merely exploit the threat? The answer is still debated, but one thing seems clear: Op-position to the Center-Left from both extreme right and extreme left helped degrade a program of reforms from a plan to correct the country's social ills into a political deal.

This development had dire consequences for the future. Despite notable leg-islative achievements, especially in the labor field, between 1964 and 1968, the Socialists no longer had any countervailing power with which to convince their Center-Left allies to implement significant reforms and failed to renew the basis of Italian politics. Disappointment among the electorate followed. Hammered by Communist charges of Socialist betrayal, the Socialist share of votes nose-dived in the May 1968 general elections, causing recently reunited Socialists and Social Democrats to redivide and the PSI to adopt, once more, a politically disastrous philo-Communist policy. These developments foreshadowed a new, tumultuous era.

Years of Lead

With the breakdown of political cooperation came the intense turmoil that char-acterized Italian life in the 1970s. The unrest affected the entire Western world, but Italy more so. The student protests that struck France and Germany in May 1968 had a long prelude in Italy in 1967 and lasted longer. The students went from criticism of the failure to reform education—an unfulfilled Center-Left plank—to a virulent attack on the political system and society. Riots also shook the South, whose problems the gridlocked Center-Left had also left unresolved. In October 1969—the "Hot Autumn"—the three major unions initiated a long series of rancorous strikes for higher wages, better working conditions, and reforms. Parliament prepared to adopt reforms in response to the agitation when the reaction arrived. On December 12, 1969, terrorists planted four bombs in Milan and Rome, killing thirteen people. Thus began the so-called "strategy of tension," supposedly implemented by occult rightist forces that aimed to create the impression of leftist violence, which would justify a takeover by conserva-tive forces. Political violence, armed confrontations, and conspiracies to overthrow the republic continued unabated over the next years. Combined with hot political battles over divorce and a number of important scandals, Italy seemed to fall apart.

In 1973 two foreign occurrences profoundly influenced the country: the Yom Kippur War with its resulting oil embargo and Salvador Allende's overthrow in Chile. The oil embargo occasioned draconian conservation measures that shut down recreation facilities at night, restricted automobile circulation, and set off fifteen years of drastic inflation, jeopardizing the energy-short country's economy. Chilean events provoked an important rethinking of PCI strategy by its secretary, Enrico Berlinguer. To defeat the reactionary forces threatening Italian democracy, to cure Italy's ancient ills, and to ensure Italian economic development, Berlinguer offered a "historic compromise" among the progressive forces that represented the majority of Italy's population—Catholics included.

This proposal capped a long Communist evolution away from Soviet control and toward Westernization. Berlinguer indicated that he was willing to play by democratic rules, favor pluralism, and accept NATO; thus began "Eurocommunism," a democratic "Western" communism. This policy made the PCI attractive to Westerners and increased Communist votes in Italy. At the same time, extreme leftists, influenced by mythical revolutionary leaders Mao Tse-tung and Che Guevara, viewed the PCI as having been absorbed by the capitalist political structure and had no where to go; convinced as well that the country had to be rescued by military means from the regressive forces behind the strategy of tension, they turned to terrorism.

Fueled by the failure to reform Italian society during the late 1960s, terrorists found sympathy in Italian society, and their movement achieved proportions unseen in other modern Western democracies. The incidence of violence, knee-cappings, and murder escalated by the mid-1970s. By 1977 terrorism, labor agitation, economic distress, social unrest, and the appearance of a raucous "extraparliamentary left" had created a national emergency. Political instability worsened. As Communist votes approached the DC total it seemed necessary to "unfreeze" the Communist electorate, excluded from the ruling coalition and now necessary for governmental stability, and to convince workers to accept economic sacrifices. The Communists agreed because Italian democracy seemed to be in danger. Thus was born the "national solidarity" coalition whose immediate manifestation was a PCI commitment not to vote against a cabinet headed by DC leader Giulio Andreotti. This was the culmination of "consensus" politics—in which Communists and Catholics had unofficially cooperated. Reflecting its enhanced role and supported by DC secretary Moro, in late 1977 and 1978 the PCI negotiated for full equality within the coalition and eventual membership in the cabinet. Despite an official rebuke from the United States on January 12, 1978, these discussions culminated in agreement that an Andreotti cabinet would be supported by a parliamentary array openly including the Communists.

At the same time, in Turin, the trial of Red Brigades founder Renato Curcio and his colleagues opened a new round of attacks on the state by leftist guerrillas. In a textbook-perfect military operation, Red Brigades terrorists kidnapped Moro in Rome on March 16, 1978, killing his five-man escort. The suspicious timing of this operation on the eve of the official Communist entrance into the governing coalition fueled speculation about the real motives of the kidnappers. If they meant to block the operation, however, they failed, because the Andreotti cabinet attained confirmation as agreed. After "interrogating" him, the Red Brigades offered to exchange Moro for thirteen jailed terrorists, but the government refused. When talks broke down, the terrorists killed Moro and symbolically left his body midway between DC and PCI headquarters in Rome.

The Communist experiment as an open member of the governing coalition damaged the party. The government undertook unpopular austerity measures, but the economy worsened, as did unemployment and crime. The PCI, locked in the coalition, could not avoid its share of blame, but when it asked for representation in the cabinet to have some control over policy, the request was rejected. Despite declared PCI autonomy from Moscow, many Italians were still unwilling to entrust PCI members with power. Finally, in January 1979, the PCI officially withdrew from the ruling coalition—although under-the-counter collaboration continued—badly bruised by the experience.

Political Revival—and False Dawn

Had the historic compromise succeeded, the Socialists would have been damaged the most. Their pro-Communist policies had already cost them support, since the PSI was no longer the balance of power and the leftist electorate preferred to vote directly for the stronger PCI if no policy differences existed. In both the 1972 and 1976 national elections, the PSI vote share remained stuck at its historic low of 9.6 percent. In July 1976 a revolt occurred at a Central Committee meeting at the Midas Hotel in Rome; younger leaders removed their older brethren from power and installed Bettino Craxi as PSI secretary. Craxi was not expected to last long, but by 1980 he had defeated his numerous internal enemies and had established an iron control over the party. He ended the policy of cooperation with the Communists. In both the intellectual and popular press, Socialist intellectuals argued against the democratic credentials of the PCI by demolishing the idea that Antonio Gramsci had established a democratic brand of communism, as the Communists maintained. On the contrary, the Socialists claimed that only the PSI had inherited the Italian social democratic tradition. Proclaiming Socialist independence from the Communists represented the first step in Craxi's goal of ending Communist hegemony of the left and reversing the "Italian anomaly," that is, a large Communist and a small Socialist party.

Craxi hoped to achieve these results by increasing Socialist prominence and importance in governmental affairs. He put forward his own candidacy for prime minister and pushed Socialist candidates for key institutional positions. In 1978, after the resignation of scandal-ridden Giovanni Leone, Craxi intervened decisively to secure Sandro Pertini's election as president of the republic. Pertini, an old freedom fighter, turned out to be an enormously popular choice and enhanced the Socialist image. But attaining the premiership seemed an insurmountable task. Since the DC, as the largest party, had a permanent claim on the office, Craxi put forward the theory of "alternation" of the premiership within the coalition. In the ensuing political maneuvering, the Socialist secretary demonstrated himself to be a brilliant tactician and took on the Christian Democrats as well as the Communists. Craxi was stymied in his drive to become prime minister in June 1981, when Republican Giovanni Spadolini became the first non-DC premier in thirty-five years. Despite the achievements of Spadolini's government, his party proved too small to retain the office for long. In the 1983 elections, the Socialists increased their votes slightly, but the DC suffered an electoral defeat by dropping 5.4 percent. This set the stage for a Craxi-led cabinet.

Despite his abrasive personality, Craxi proved himself a excellent governmental leader. He presented a well-articulated, broad, and specific program reinforcing the issues with which his party had gone to the polls. Beginning with crucial economic questions, his government proposed lowering the inflation rate from 15 percent in 1983 to 10 percent in 1984. The government hoped to accomplish this goal by reducing the deficit from 16 percent of GNP to 15 percent. Two-thirds of the deficit reduction would come from less public spending while increased revenues would account for the rest. Acting on another inflation factor, the government proposed limiting salary increases to the inflation rate, slowing wage indexation, and discouraging price rises.

To avoid labor trouble, previous governments had sought agreement with the PCI before instituting economic policy, making it impossible to alter the system that produced the double-digit inflation threatening the country. Craxi's "decisionism" ended this consensus politics, causing a harsh reaction from the Communists who resented their displacement at the center of Italian politics by their erstwhile subordinates. The Communists rejected out of hand a proposal to slow the automatic cost of living increases that economists had long identified as a major contributor to spiraling inflation. They set out to topple the cabinet

MAP 6   Italian regional divisions, 1985

through strikes and stiff parliamentary opposition. The government stood its ground and the PCI discovered itself politically isolated; the law was applied, and the inflation rate fell dramatically. Refusing to accept its defeat, the PCI forced a national referendum on the *scala mobile* (automatic cost of living increases) question. On June 11, 1984, Berlinguer died suddenly, and later in the month a sympathy vote for the PCI during the European elections resulted in the Communists receiving a higher share of the vote than did the DC. Communist leaders mistook this development for the long-awaited *sorpasso* (overtaking) of the DC, but their party lost both the ensuing referendum and local elections by significant margins. Their opposition appeared as pique toward effective government and their electoral slide, begun during the "national solidarity" period, accelerated.

Combined with the defeat of leftist terrorism—exemplified by the brilliant rescue of American general James Lee Dozier during the previous administration of Giovanni Spadolini—Craxi's stunning victory on economic policy signaled a change in the country's style. Absenteeism, strikes, low productivity, tax evasion, bloated state industry, and incredible deficits attached to social services had become legendary during the previous fifteen years. These problems could not suddenly disappear, but the nation altered its work habits and seriously discussed the more difficult issues confronting it. Between 1985 and 1986 abstenteeism declined greatly, and time lost because of strikes diminished to among the lowest in Europe. At the same time, the government successfully encouraged industrial reconversion, productivity increased, industry registered higher profits, and progress was made on privatization. In another amazing shift, employers seemed to be achieving their long-desired linkage of salary and productivity increases. These developments, combined with the drop in oil prices, led Bank of Italy chairman Carlo Azeglio Ciampi to declare that the back of inflation had been broken. Italy's economic reflowering resulted in a sustained stock market boom that doubled the value of shares in four months and attracted heavy foreign investment.

In addition to its activity in the economic sphere, the government put institutional reform on the table. Although the legislative process was streamlined, however, fighting among the parties blocked all serious reform—a mistake that would debilitate them in the 1990s. The government also signed a new concordat with the Vatican that, although it enhanced the Church's position in religious education, ended state salaries for the clergy. Craxi also pursued a more active foreign policy than had previously been the case. The sending of an Italian contingent in 1983 to Lebanon had signalled a willingness to shoulder greater international responsibility in areas close to the country. Now Craxi made frequent trips to foreign capitals and regularly corresponded with President Ronald Reagan, demonstrating a tendency to negotiate with the Americans on more equal terms than his predecessors. Although the Socialists were instrumental in the acceptance of American cruise missiles on Italian soil, Craxi adopted a more independent policy in the Middle East. He called for talks with PLO chairman Yasser Arafat who, he argued, stood ready to renounce terrorism and formally recognize Israel, a Craxi attitude the Americans disliked. Craxi also promoted an active Mediterranean policy and established an informal entente with Spain, ruled by his Socialist counterpart Filipe Gonzalez. Craxi's insistence on Italian jurisdiction in the *Achille Lauro* affair and a standoff with American troops who, he claimed, violated Italian sovereignty by landing in Sicily to capture the terrorists greatly increased his popularity in Italy even among Communists. At the Tokyo Economic Summit in May 1986, Craxi insisted on Italy's entrance into the "Club of Five, " which made the world's most important economic decisions, and won his case. The new course in foreign policy met with general approval and renewed Italian pride.

When the Craxi government resigned in 1987 after a record tenure in office, the Socialist leader seemed dominant in Italian politics. He chastised the Vatican for its interference in Italian affairs, attacked judges for their easy arrest propensities, successfully pushed for the sending of Italian warships to the Persian Gulf to protect the shipping lanes, and sponsored a series of victorious national referendums. Despite this activity, the 1987 national elections failed to reward Craxi with the electoral breakthough he always predicted, but the PSI vote share did increase and the party seemed more attractive for women and young people. The PCI, on the other hand, continued its electoral slide, failed to appeal to the youth, and seemed to be falling apart. An influential segment of the leadership wished to link up with the Socialist leader and reach an agreement with him. A fierce battle within the PCI leadership sanctioned the existence of two official factions and shattered the antique Leninist principle of "democratic centralism" that imposed unity by suffocating debate. Reversal of the Italian anomaly appeared within reach as Communist vote share declined.

At this point, however, Craxi began making a series of bad mistakes. He left office with the promise to reform the PSI—his Achilles' heel—by strengthening its structure, promoting internal dialogue, and weeding out the persistent corruption problem that seriously compromised its image and proved his eventual undoing. Instead he left the party as it was. Believing the Communists dead, Craxi attempted to cannibalize the party instead of reaching agreement with the leaders who believed in his policies but made the mistake of refusing to force early elections to take advantage of the collapse of international communism. This failure allowed the Italian Communists to regroup, cut themselves free of association with the USSR, and to change their name; they emerged seriously damaged but not destroyed as a political force. In an egregious and useless statement, Craxi opposed a 1991 referendum designed to reduce corruption in elections. Correctly predicting that the change itself would probably make things worse, his denigration of the referendum backfired because of his arrogant invitation to Italian citizens not to vote but to "go to the beach." This statement not only made him extremely unpopular but also turned the vote into a referendum against him.

Craxi's major strategic error, however, proved to be his deal with the Christian Democrats designed to ensure his return to the office in which he had proved so successful. He agreed with DC leaders that he would back them in keeping the premiership during the entire life of the legislature, 1987 to 1992, in exchange for their support of him for the five years of the legislature that would follow. As the world rapidly changed with the fall of the Berlin Wall and the end of the Soviet Union, Craxi openly adopted the old politics of wheeling and dealing he had, ironically, not accepted when he was weak. His support in the country rested on the belief that, despite his arrogance, he was the only politician capable of implementing a serious reform program that could renew the nation; but his shift to a cozy DC alliance destroyed that contention and revealed him as accepting "politics as usual," which Italians increasingly rejected.

The elections of April 5 and 6, 1992, produced a political upheaval. The Christian Democrats lost 5 percent of their vote; the Democratic Party of the Left (PDS), which had succeeded the PCI, received 16 percent, and the hard-line rump, Rifondazione Comunista, took 5.5 percent. The Socialist vote remained stable and the difference with the PDS was minimal. But the real story was that the four-party ruling coalition retained only a very slender majority and that the Lega Lombarda—an antigovernment force advocating drastic political changes and a federal Italy—received 9 percent nationwide, was the North's largest party, and continued to grow rapidly. The political basis for Craxi's deal was gone, and a major corruption scandal, which would deprive him of the office of premier and secretary and sweep away all the old parties, was on the horizon. With the Cold War over, the postwar politics of imperfect bipolarism came to an end.

20

The Economic Miracle and Its Effects

Italy's stunning economic performance contrasted with and counterbalanced the negative politics of imperfect bipolarism. The industrial base constructed during the Fascist period and a large labor reserve, which meant low wages for workers, allowed the Italians to take advantage of the high degree of international economic cooperation that produced a boom of unprecedented proportions after World War II, primarily in the vital industrial sector. This "economic miracle" and its benefits fostered the view at home and abroad that, in contrast to the Communists, Christian Democratic leadership guaranteed democracy, participation in Western multilateral organizations, and continued economic development. Italians complained about the government's imperviousness to reform but the economic miracle kept the DC in power.

Reconstruction, Economic Growth, Miracle

The end of hostilities allowed the first postwar governments to tackle the problem of reconstruction. The presence of Communist and Socialist representatives in those early cabinets had little influence on postwar economic policy, but their exclusion after May 1947 guaranteed resolution of the most pressing questions through classic economics. As previously mentioned, Luigi Einaudi, budget minister in the fourth De Gasperi cabinet, was primarily responsible for this policy.

Among the many urgent economic problems, inflation predominated. To fight the war, the Fascist government had frozen prices and wages in June 1940, but prices doubled by late 1942 anyway. After Mussolini's overthrow in 1943, German economic demands on the Salò Republic, the infusion by the Allies of "amlire" in the South to pay for their needs, and wartime hoarding caused inflation to explode. The price index (1938 = 100) rose from 273 in 1943 to 1215 in 1944 and 2392 in 1945, and real wages dropped 75 percent. In the North, the efficient German repressive apparatus controlled inflation better, but by war's end real wages had still fallen 50 percent from their 1938 level. In 1945–1946, prices stabilized as the government floated loans and confidence in the lira seemed restored.

Strong inflationary pressures on the lira soon resumed because of government spending, continued price supports for flour, the failure of a plan to replace the old currency with a new one, pressure from labor for cost-of-living increases, and sabotage of a proposed capital levy tax. The dollar rose to 900 lire (from an official rate of 225) by May 1947, setting off a new round of credit expansion, government deficits, and rising prices. By the spring of 1947 the annualized rate of inflation reached 50 percent, sending the wholesale price index to 6200 by September.

The government responded by instituting a deflationary policy, restricting credit, and encouraging repatriation of capital that had fled abroad. Companies that had hoarded goods in anticipation of rising prices brought them out for fear of losing money. The wholesale price index began a steady fall and in 1950 went down to 5000. Foreign reserves also increased dramatically because of the return of Italian capital and European Recovery Program (Marshall Plan) aid, which also stimulated foreign investment. In September 1949 the lira was stabilized at 625 to the dollar, where it remained until the 1970s.

By itself, the improved monetary situation did not resolve the nation's foreign trade problems because the war had practically destroyed Italy's gold and foreign currency reserves. As a result, the country lacked funds to replace destroyed plant, to purchase raw materials for industry, and to pay for foodstuffs to keep its population from starving. This situation, common to war-devastated Europe, necessitated American intervention. The United States initially provided aid to Italy through the United Nations Relief and Rehabilitation Administration (UNRRA) and the Foreign Economic Administration and, in 1947, provided credits with Argentina for buying food and ships. This assistance tided the country over until aid on a more systematic basis reached Italy through the Marshall Plan. American aid accounted for 1.75 billion of the total 2 billion dollars received by the Italians between 1943 and 1947. Seventy percent of this aid went to industry, railways, and public works and encouraged "a more rational development of the economy." All American loans were repaid by July 1962.

The Italians also helped their own recovery by reversing previous trade policy and by inserting their country into the international trading system created after World War II. Trade liberalization marked this new Western economic regime, which the major European countries adopted with American encouragement. As a result, Italy dropped quotas or loosened restrictions on imports from countries belonging to the Organization of European Economic Cooperation (OEEC), even though Italian tariffs remained higher than those of its European trading partners.

In addition to liberalizing trade regulations, the Italians made it a point to be among the founders of the key multinational organizations on which the new

European trading system was based. These included the European Coal and Steel Community (ECSC). This organization created free trade among member nations (Italy, West Germany, France, Belgium, Luxembourg, and the Netherlands) in coal and ferrous metals on February 10, 1953. An English participant at the sessions establishing the organization remarked that the noisiest representatives were the Italians "and they don't even have any coal or iron." The country was also a founding member of the European Economic Community (EEC, the Common Market, later called the European Community, the EC, and the European Union). Europe recognized Italy's importance in this initiative by selecting Rome as the site to sign the treaty establishing the EEC. Taking effect on January 1, 1958, the EEC successfully established free trade among its members and looked forward to complete economic integration and common political and foreign policies.

These measures and the advantages of a solid economic base and cheap labor transformed Italy from an agricultural country into a world industrial power. The index of industrial production tells this story. The index reached 102 in 1948 from a base of 100 in 1938; in 1953, it hit 164; from a new base of 1953 = 100, the index went to 196 in 1961. The mechanical industry (automobiles, railway stock, tractors, shipbuilding, airplanes, and electrical equipment, including appliances, calculating and office machines, and typewriters), ferrous metal production (at which the country became efficient despite the lack of raw materials), road building, electricity, chemicals, and, especially, the petrochemical industry all expanded at a tremendous rate. Private enterprises, such as Fiat and Olivetti, and the public companies changed the country's physiognomy. By 1960 industry accounted for 46.6 percent of national income, compared with 34.2 percent between 1936–1940. According to the census taken in 1961, industry employed 38 percent of the working population, while the service sector accounted for 32 percent; agricultural workers had declined to 30 percent.

Rounding out the "miracle," the Gross Domestic Product (GDP) increased at a yearly average of 6.5 percent between 1958 and 1963, while the comparable figure for industry was 8 percent, the highest rate since unification. Exports took off as well, increasing at an average of 14.5 percent a year; the percentage of Italian products exported to the EEC went from 23 percent in 1955 to 40.2 percent in 1965. By 1967 the country had become the world's third-largest producer of refrigerators and Europe's largest manufacturer of washing machines and dishwashers. With the remarkable jump in production and exports came wage increases that touched off a boom in private consumption, further stimulating the economy.

The negative effects of very rapid economic development could have been mitigated by economic planning, a concept widely discussed in all Europe following World War II. In Italy, however, economic planning had radical implications rejected by politicians. The Socialist minister for industry and commerce from July 1946 to May 1947, Rodolfo Morandi, conceived of economic planning as a transition to socialism, but he ran afoul of both the DC and PCI. In fact, because Communists labeled planning within a capitalist system useless, the DC had a greater influence in this area. Catholic economist Pasquale Saraceno argued that Church thinking sanctioned state intervention to correct social and other imbalances caused by the free market; the Christian Democrats accepted his premises but shied away from their implications: state enforcement of production levels and equitable income distribution. The issue came to the fore again in the late 1950s during the Center-Left period, pressed by Christian Democrat Ezio Vanoni and the Socialists, but political opposition ensured the nonimplementation of economic planning.

Planning objectives were instead loosely set by the powerful public companies established under fascism, which controlled a large part of the Italian economy under the republic and that determined where investments would be made. The South served as a prime example of this policy, which ultimately failed to redress the economic imbalance with the North. In 1957 the government mandated that IRI concentrate 40 percent of its total investment and 60 percent of its investment in industrial plant in the South; the idea was to kick off economic development in the region by greatly improving the infrastructure and building model industries in the region.

Nationwide, IRI had become an enormous holding company with major interests in all sectors of the economy—from shipbuilding to steelmaking, roads to airlines, banking to communications. Another public corporation established by the Fascists, the Azienda Generale Italiana Petroli (AGIP), was transformed in 1953 by its director, Enrico Mattei, into a gigantic company for the hydrocarbon sector. This Ente Nazionale Idrocarburi (ENI) aggressively developed Italian natural gas deposits and the petrochemical industry. It also became an international power by defending the economic interests of oil-rich Arab and African states and challenging the Western oil companies that, Mattei believed, exploited them. Mattei's activities—combined with creation of a state monopoly of electric power, Ente Nazionale per l'Energia Elettrica (ENEL), during the Center-Left—assured Italy cheap supplies of energy, which fueled its amazing postwar industrial development.

Besides its involvement in industry, the government also intervened in agriculture by pouring in considerable amounts to repair war damage done to plant, livestock, and machines and investing in land reclamation and improvements. To satisfy the traditional peasant land hunger, beginning in 1950 the government passed a series of reforms that applied to the regions where need was greatest.

The laws allowed expropriation of land from large landowners—who were paid by government bonds—and the sale of the land to peasants under favorable conditions. A series of other laws provided further economic benefits for peasants. Because of conservative opposition, these laws were not comprehensive nor did they eliminate all the problems, but by 1950 agriculture had recovered from the damage wrought by war, and exportation of agricultural products resumed. The Center-Left implemented further measures favoring peasants, but the great draw of industry and tertiary economic activities induced many of them to abandon the land.

The failure to stem this movement and the attempt of government planners to industrialize the South proved to be errors. Not only could the region not compete with the North in industry, but as national income rose to European levels the country ran an enormous deficit to import expensive agricultural items, which, with proper encouragement, could have been supplied by the South. The modernization of southern agriculture could have contributed to solving the southern problem and to reducing the enormous deficit that afflicted the country.

Insufficient attention to agricultural development was one aspect of the republic's inability to resolve the problem of the South despite great expenditure and some successes. Besides attempting to industrialize the region through public company intervention, on August 10, 1950, the state instituted a special fund to improve economic conditions there. The Cassa per il Mezzogiorno fund spent enormous sums on the development of a badly needed transportation system (including roads), land reclamation projects, and, most important, tourism. Though there were definite improvements, the return was not proportional to the amounts spent. The Cassa proved subject to political pressure and corruption, and the equipment and know-how for industrialization came from the North, ironically stimulating that region's economy. The North has continued to increase its economic development at a higher rate than the South. Not only did the South continue to lose its most active population to northern migration, but infrastructure problems, such as the lack of water, still hampered the South's growth.

Poor economic conditions, combined with the influx of government money, exacerbated the region's exploitation by organized crime. Criminal organizations such as the Mafia and the Camorra became more entrenched by siphoning off Cassa funds earmarked for economic development. Moreover, they expanded their activities to the North and to different economic sectors. The inefficiency and corruption of the state's southern operation produced resentment and rebellion in the North. Northerners had to put up with discriminatory economic policies favoring the South; the wealth they produced was grabbed by the central government through heavy taxation. This wealth has gone to help organized crime and to create a vast welfare network (*stato assistenzialista*) based on clientelistic relationships and controlled by criminal elements and corrupt politicians. Organized crime used its gains to finance corrupt organizations and the traditional parties, whose vote-getting capabilities were strengthened by their unholy alliance with organized crime and by their ability to dole out government jobs and welfare benefits. In this way, politicians beholden to criminals increased their influence over the country and procured more funds for the South to keep the process going. As a result, many northerners believe that the South is dragging the entire country down and favor breaking the cycle. The Lega Lombarda, discussed in the next chapter, has advocated a "federalism" bordering on separatism to cure these ills and has revolutionized Italian politics.

Indeed, the spread of criminal associations to the most-advanced parts of the country to take advantage of the spectacularly greater economic advantages in those areas presented uniquely modern problems. Easier communications and Italy's participation in international trade organizations facilitated worldwide cooperation of Italian and foreign crime syndicates. The world narcotics trade enriched the Mafia and created a grave drug problem; this development produced an explosion of petty crimes throughout the entire country and contributed to the spread of AIDS in the North. Thus development further strained the overburdened and national health system. Furthermore, as discussed in the next section, organized crime seriously affected the political and business climate as well. These are some ways in which Italy's amazing economic development, which has brought great advantages, has also produced novel and very serious problems.

Social Transformation

There are more traditionally negative sides to Italy's unprecedented expansion. It has been estimated that between 1951 and 1971, interregional migration totaled over 9 million, outpacing emigration to Germany and Switzerland, which had been the earliest destinations of southern workers. In fleeing, the emigrants abandoned agricultural land, overcrowded big cities and their hinterlands, and seriously polluted the environment. The automobile manufacturing city of Turin—a good example of the country's drastic urbanization—increased from about 719,000 in 1951 to 1.25 million inhabitants in 1967, and its immediate suburbs grew by 80 percent. Unhampered growth of this kind combined with new wealth pouring into the country set off an uncontrolled housing boom and real estate speculation that compromised the environment in urban and rural areas. Even though the law provided for planned development, bureaucratic inefficiency, corruption, and free rein for private initiative frequently resulted in wholesale violation of aesthetic principles and safety norms.

Facing low wages and discrimination, southern emigrants lived in shanty-towns and in drastically overcrowded and unhealthful conditions. Besides housing, their numbers also overwhelmed the social services of the North—including health services and education—that had been barely adequate for the native population.

As the economic miracle accelerated, however, successful trade union agitation won wage increases and raised cost-of-living adjustments to the point that raises for workers outstripped both the rate of inflation and increases for salaried professional workers. Inspired by the Center-Left, the "Brodolini reform" revolutionized relations in the workplace by mandating important rights for the worker, by vastly strengthening job security, and by watering down employer control. Italian workers also enjoyed long vacations and maternity leaves, generous severance packages, and a low retirement age. Outside the workplace, new working-class housing went up in large numbers, and, despite great strains, the educational system gradually integrated emigrant children into northern society. In the 1970s social services were greatly extended and the Italian welfare state became one of the most generous in Europe. Despite serious inefficiencies and long delays in securing services, the system supplied a safety net that provided basic care from cradle to grave. By the 1980s and 1990s, extended benefits and poor administration of this system represented a major item in the state's escalating public debt, and governments took action to control costs; but for southern workers, "the terrible period of uprooting and transition seemed to have been worth it; a new life had begun."

Postwar social transformation affected the entire population. The Italian business class, both public and private, underwent a major overhaul, implementing modern business techniques learned in American universities. Highly efficient and profitable small firms in such areas as shoe manufacturing brought a flood of wealth even into the provinces. White-collar employment increased from 9.8 to 17.1 percent between 1951 and 1971, at a par with other advanced countries. By the same year, the percentage of industrial and building workers taken together exceeded that of Britain or France. This prodigious activity greatly increased per capita income; with a base of 100 in 1950, it reached 234 in 1970, compared with 136 for France and 134 for Britain; starting from a lower level, this faster increase brought Italy up to the most-advanced European standards. Thanks to the economic miracle, greater numbers of Italians than ever before could afford washing machines, dishwashers, telephones, television sets, cars, long vacations, and expensive foods. The famous Fiat 600 motorized the country as the number of automobiles rose from 342,000 in 1950 to 4.67 million in 1964.

In terms of durable goods, Italy became a "saturated" country by the 1980s. (See Table 20.1)

This injection of new wealth had profound social effects. The increase in leisure time created a greater demand for periodical literature and books, even if the nation still lagged behind other European countries. Daily newspapers such as *La Repubblica*, established in 1976, and weeklies such as *L'Espresso* and *Panorama* joined the older *Corriere della Sera* in replacing the party press in the formation of public opinion because the best writers preferred to write for them, regardless of their own political affiliation. In the 1970s, the revolutionary press flourished, contributing to the radical climate of the age, only to disappear rapidly, with the notable exception of *Il Manifesto*. *Rotocalchi* (illustrated magazines) for women, such as *Annabella* and *Amica*, proliferated and greatly increased in circulation.

Television was also instrumental in forming popular opinion, in altering existing values, and in uniting the country linguistically. Introduced in the late 1950s, limited to evening hours and to one official station, the medium had an explosive development as private sets became common and private stations invaded the airways. "Tribuna Politica" provided equal time for politicians during elections to explain their ideas. Quiz shows taken from American models and providing fabulous prizes became extremely popular and helped spread a consumeristic mentality. Advertising was an integral part of this process, even though the government tried to control it by setting standards; this effort gave rise to "Carosello," an advertising program that became the most popular TV show in Italy, after which Italian children went to bed. But the state gave up its attempts at regulation, and consumerism triumphed.

Along with the development of a consumer society came a reduction in religiosity. A 1988 survey found that only 35 percent of Italians went to Church. In the early 1960s Church attendance was more characteristic of women than

TABLE 20.1 Annual Production of Selected Consumer Goods, 1987–1992

	Automobiles*	Refrigerators (Non-commercial)	Washing machines (Non-commercial)	Dishwashers (Non-commercial)	Color Televisions
1987	1,912,232	3,767,006	4,140,481	614,597	2,054,887
1988	2,114,108	3,942,495	4,368,157	783,279	2,262,058
1989	2,224,602	4,082,478	4,337,681	746,193	2,380,702
1990	2,120,879	3,971,645	4,339,188	742,906	2,332,602
1991	1,878,561	4,155,481	5,028,676	893,279	2,433,607
1992	1,681,555	4,010,639	5,132,477	883,106	2,149,854

* For civilian use only; excludes motor scooters, motorcycles, trucks, and buses

men, but in later years the number of women going to Church declined drastically. While in the 1950s Catholic teaching had repressed sexual behavior, by the 1980s Italian women appeared as free as their European sisters in this area. With increasing wealth, the size of the Italian family shrank, as did the number of extended families. This change helped elevate the status of women, who had long been relegated to an inferior social and economic position. For example, the infidelities of husbands were winked at while those of wives were legally punishable. Relationships between men and women were graphically depicted in two classic Pietro Germi films, *Divorce Italian Style* (i.e., murder) and *Seduced and Abandoned*. Attitudes toward women during this period were also reflected in statistics showing that fewer Italian women worked outside the home than in other European countries, even during the early period of the economic miracle.

Feminist movements, however, had been present on the Italian political scene since the 1890s, and in the early republic the Communist-dominated Union of Italian Women (UDI) had been an important PCI flanking organization, while Christian Democratic women had decisively contributed to their party's earliest and most convincing electoral victories. Women's concerns, however, had been subordinated to those of men in both instances, even though abolition of legalized prostitution had been a victory for women during the early republic and a divorce law passed in 1970 was confirmed by a hard-fought 1974 referendum. The 1970s witnessed the birth of an aggressive feminist movement that brought women's issues forcefully to the nation's attention. Under feminist pressure, several major pieces of legislation passed. These included a reform of family law establishing equality of the sexes (1975), parity with men in the workplace (1977), and legalized abortion (1978); this last hotly debated measure provided free abortions through the national health care system, although a "conscientious objector" provision for doctors opposing abortions limited the law's effectiveness.

With birth control also legal, and with consumer values firmly entrenched, Italy's birth rate in the 1990s fell to the lowest of any country in the world. The lower birth rate, an educational system that mandates free preschool care and free obligatory schooling up to age fourteen, and a generous paid leave policy for pregnant women and mothers with young children have all enabled women to work outside the home in greater numbers. Compared to the United States, Italian higher education is also substantially free. Despite organizational and funding problems, this factor, combined with liberalized access, has brought about an enormous increase in the proportion of Italians, including women, holding advanced degrees. Once economically "visible" primarily as industrial workers and peasants, Italian women have now become a crucial presence in the professions and in politics.

A Maturing, but Anomalous, Economy

In the 1970s the Italian economy went through numerous crises that paralleled the political unrest. Labor agitation touched off by the 1969 Hot Autumn, the oil crisis, and a rapid rise in real wages touched off double-digit inflation that continued for fifteen years. Before 1969, for example, real wages increased in Italy at about the same rate as in other Organization for Economic Cooperation and Development (OECD) countries, 10 percent a year; in the 1970s the annual increase jumped to between 20 and 25 percent, double the OECD rate, and was no longer matched by increases in productivity. The resulting inflation outstripped that of the other advanced European countries and the United States, reaching a high of 21 percent in 1980, and remained substantially above the rate for the other highly industrialized countries. In 1983, when Craxi's Socialist-led government took office, inflation was still at 15 percent. At the same time, economic growth languished, scoring in the negative numbers in 1982 and 1983.

Craxi's tenure brought a return to prosperity. The Socialist leader was helped by a decline in oil prices and a worldwide recovery, but he came to office with the goal of preparing the country to share in this recovery, already foreshadowed on the horizon. Political stability, redressing the balance between business and labor by reducing worker excesses, measures encouraging business, and the scala mobile referendum mentioned in the previous chapter brought inflation down to 4.6 percent in 1987 and productivity into line once again with the increase in real wages. Growth rates also took off, averaging over 2.5 percent per year from 1983 to 1987 compared with under 1 percent during the previous four years. The stock market soared, allowing capitalization to quadruple, and major business restructuring occurred—industry became more efficient and profitability increased dramatically. Fiat engaged in a seesaw battle with Volkswagen for the position of largest European automobile manufacturing concern; clothing and shoes rode the reputation for Italian design to world prominence; and engineering firms prospered. Names such as Benetton, Armani, Valentino,

TABLE 20.2   Gross Production of Electrical Energy, 1986–1991 (in millions of kilowatt hours)

1986	193,330
1987	201,372
1988	203,561
1989	210,750
1990	216,891
1991	222,041

De Benedetti, Gardini, and Berlusconi became familiar throughout Europe and in the United States. Public industry also restructured itself under IRI's Romano Prodi and ENI's Franco Reviglio, became profitable once again, and undertook important privatization initiatives.

As a result of this "second" economic miracle, the Italians claimed to have surpassed the United Kingdom as the world's fifth-largest economy in 1987. Despite British denials, later figures confirmed the Italian contention, especially if the large underground economy was considered. Italy's statistical profile more closely resembled that of the advanced European countries—a sharp decline in agricultural employment, a slower one in industry, a rapid rise in the tertiary sector, and a massive increase in female employment (50 percent since 1972). (See Table 20.3) As in the rest of Europe, the country's economic development also resulted in a great influx of immigrants, especially from Africa, willing to take jobs that Italians no longer wished to perform.

The size of Italy's underground economy is one sign that the Italian economy remains anomalous with respect to the other economically developed countries, despite the country's accelerating modernization. Usually "black" economies have the purpose of circumventing not only taxes but also fringe benefits paid by employers, thus exploiting workers. The first intention is present in Italy, but the second—though it is certainly a factor—also served to increase worker income by ensuring an extra job (*doppio lavoro*). The phenomenon of the worker who gets off early or continually calls in sick to "moonlight" while receiving generous paid benefits from a first job is more widespread than in other countries. The tax revenue lost to the state is incalculable.

TABLE 20.3   Percentage Employment by Economic Sector

Year	Agriculture	Industry	Services
1971	20.1	39.5	40.4
1981	13.3	37.2	49.5
1982	12.3	36.7	51.0
1983	12.3	25.8	51.9
1984	11.8	34.1	54.1
1985	11.1	33.2	55.7
1986	10.7	32.7	56.6
1987	10.4	32.2	57.4
1988	9.8	32.2	58.1
1989	9.3	32.2	58.6
1990	8.7	32.4	58.8
1991	8.4	32.0	59.5
1992	8.1	32.0	59.9

The tax structure is another anomalous feature of the Italian economy. First, it provides a moral justification for evasion. There are more than two hundred taxes in Italy that, if paid according to law, would quickly bankrupt the ordinary citizen. Second, compounding this situation is the confusion and inefficiency of the tax collection system, which makes it difficult to know when and how taxes should be paid. Nevertheless, Italians do pay heavy taxes, and when governments have undertaken austerity measures, the extra revenues have usually exceeded their expectations.

One group, storekeepers, has successfully resisted paying its full share of taxes, usually by doing a cash business and woefully underestimating receipts. This situation has resulted in strong resentment on the part of salaried workers, who claim that they pay an unfair proportion of taxes. In an attempt to redress this situation, in 1983 the government mandated that shopkeepers install electronic cash registers and give receipts for purchases. Although these enforcement measures, some of which are questionable, undoubtedly helped, they have not resolved the problem. The ability to evade taxes and the protection that shopkeepers receive from their association has preserved small shops from the decline that has occurred in other parts of the industrialized world. As a result, Italy has the highest density of small shops in Europe, causing some critics to maintain that the country has an inefficient distribution system.

The phenomenon of the old and the new existing side by side characterizes the Italian economy, but the inefficiency of public services hampers the drive for modernization and contrasts starkly with sectors—such as computers, textiles, steel, automobiles—that are among the most advanced in the world. Most evident to the casual observer is the poor state of the mails and telephones. Italians adapt by making greater use of fax machines and private couriers, but Italy has not kept pace with the communications revolution on a level with

TABLE 20.4   GDP and Gross Wage per Full-Time Labor Unit (in thousands of current lire)

Year	GDP per F.T. Labor Unit	Gross Wages per F.T. Labor Unit
1986	39,494	18,865
1987	43,002	20,540
1988	47,321	22,296
1989	51,694	23,881
1990	56,382	26,475
1991	60,835	28,793
1992	64,842	30,214

other European countries. In addition to a horrifically slow bureaucracy, this lack has handicapped Italian ability to compete in an increasingly integrated world economy. Important legislation to reform the bureaucracy has gone unenforced, and basic services such as health care not only cost the taxpayer more but also become more degraded over time and threaten to break down. Myriad documents requiring great expenditure of time and effort are required for the simplest operations. This reality has encouraged corruption as private citizens, business people, and even public servants have attempted to get around regulations unanimously judged to be ridiculous and harmful. The corruption has increased costs so much that they have contributed significantly to the massive increase in the public debt and have damaged the efficiency of Italian enterprises.

The public debt, though always high, increased steeply during the Craxi years and has continued its rise. By 1985 it had reached almost 85 percent of GDP, compared to 48.5 percent for the United States, and by the 1990s it surpassed 100 percent. The resulting need for the state to borrow spurred it to offer very attractive yields, at first tax free and then taxed at a favorable rate. Investors earn more in absolute safety by buying bonds instead of investing in productive enterprises and risking their money. Public borrowing thus soaked up capital that might otherwise have been invested in the private sector and has bloated the debt even more.

The enormous debt has weakened the lira and hampered Italian efforts to become fully integrated into the EC, since Italy is unlikely to meet the prerequisites the Community set for creation of a common currency. Indeed, because of their economy's inefficiencies and the resulting need for economic protection, the Italians have dragged their feet the most in adhering to EC regulations designed to integrate Europe's economy. This has happened despite the Italian role in encouraging integration and the widespread support the EC enjoys among the Italian people. In fact, Italians hope that the EC will force them to adopt difficult measures they otherwise would be politically unable to take on their own, and entrepreneurs such as Olivetti's Carlo De Benedetti have been extremely aggressive in anticipating European integration by attempting to take over companies in other countries.

This activity has been centered in the North, which illustrates another enduring economic anomaly. As mentioned earlier, Italy's statistical profile approaches that of advanced Europe, but this is an average caused by great progress in the North. The South remains one of Europe's most backward areas economically, resembling Ireland and parts of Spain. Compared to the North and the Center, unemployment has remained high (surpassing 20 percent), more persons work without benefits, the workforce is still declining, fewer women are employed outside the home, family size is larger, more young people leave school for menial jobs or to seek low-paying state positions, demeaning public assistance is infinitely more widespread, and over 18 percent of the population subsists below the poverty line compared with under 7 percent for the other regions. Besides the psychological wounds this situation inflicts on southerners, it makes Italy less competitive in a more open Europe and has provoked the northern revolt against the *stato assistenzialista* discussed earlier.

In addition to the frustrations of the Italian South, the extent of organized criminal activity is also anomalous in a modern country with a thriving economy. In 1986 officals estimated that organized crime profits accounted for about 12.5 percent of GDP. To protect this investment from state offensives, criminal organizations committed a series of spectacular crimes, including the murders of Alberto Dalla Chiesa, who had defeated the terrorists, and Mafia-fighters Giovanni Falcone and Paolo Borsellino. The state has struck back by adopting laws making it easier to fight criminal activity, with maxi-trials, by exposing connections between politicians and criminals, and with successful captures of major leaders. Despite this activity, in 1986 an anti-Mafia official claimed that three southern provinces were no longer under the full control of the state. Whether this assessment was accurate or not, by the late 1980s the state had initiated a vigorous counterattack against the criminal organizations and had scored significant successes. Italian officials claimed that Italian organized crime was expanding its activity into eastern Europe and Russia as a result of its defeats in Italy. Nevertheless, there is concern that Italian criminal organizations will find it easier to penetrate other western European countries as a result of the EC's elimination of border controls.

Finally, the enormous Italian public sector itself constitutes an anomaly. Its size represents greater state intervention in the economy than other countries. Despite the crucial role that public companies have had in economic growth, they have frequently been inefficient. Furthermore, their size and importance have made them targets of political influence and corruption. The political scandal that erupted in 1992, which involved public activity, has brought insistent demands for privatization beyond that accomplished during the Craxi era. Italians have been struggling to achieve a proper balance between state intervention and private initiative, and it is unclear how or at what point an equilibrium will be attained.

A Style for the Republic

Sociologist Francesco Alberoni has written: "Italians do not have an ethical tradition, but an esthetic one.... They would be lost if they were not able to save themselves through good form and good taste."

In modern times, the republic has enabled this esthetic tradition to become supreme. Emerging from a detested dictatorship and devastated psychologically by participation in an immoral war, the country achieved a positive image despite its perennially troubled political atmosphere. The culture that the republic allowed to flourish—supported by the benefits of the economic miracle—made this possible.

Harking back to a notable tradition, cinema was the first area to incorporate a new cultural style. Immediately after the war, directors of the "neorealistic" school, such as Roberto Rossellini, Vittorio De Sica, and Luchino Visconti, focused on contemporary Italian problems and characters taken from ordinary life and made Italian film world famous. Historians have now discovered this movement's seeds in the Fascist period, but Rossellini's *Rome, Open City*, produced in 1944, signalled a new flowering of Italian cinema. The first neorealist masterpiece, however, was probably Visconti's 1942 *Obsession*, considered a "resistance" film made just before Mussolini's fall. Visconti, whose film was based on James Cain's novel *The Postman Always Rings Twice* and was influenced by French filmmakers, "achieved . . . a magnificent linkage between his tragic protagonists and their environment" and showed the importance international currents had in the movement. Stimulated by the artistic success of these two films and De Sica's masterpieces (*The Bicycle Thief, Shoeshine, Umberto D*), neorealist cinema had a greater commercial and artistic impact abroad than in Italy, which remained dominated by Hollywood productions. Even after 1951, when an Italian-American accord curbed imports and allowed more Italian films to be exported to the United States, American films predominated at the Italian box office; nevertheless, Italian neorealist works had a lasting cultural influence in the cinematic field.

The 1950s witnessed the emergence of a classic director, Federico Fellini. His films of this period—*The White Sheik, I Vitelloni, Variety Lights, The Nights of Cabiria*, and especially *La Strada*, which won an Oscar for best foreign film—established his reputation and sparked debate over the future course of Italian cinema. In the 1960s Fellini directed other masterpieces that received great play abroad, especially the semiautobiographical *8½, La Dolce Vita*, a criticism of contemporary society, and *Juliet of the Spirits*. His later movies include a haunting depiction of life under fascism, *Amarcord*, and movies on the cultural and political milieu of the 1970s and 1980s. The music for Fellini's films was written by Nino Rota, who became a world-renowned composer for film.

Spurred by this fame, the Italian film industry reorganized itself in the late 1950s. In the 1960s producers financed not only "art" films but also "serious" comedies such as Mario Monicelli's *The Organizer*, about the early Socialist and labor movements, the Germi films previously mentioned, and Sergio

Leone's "spaghetti" westerns that made Clint Eastwood's career. This success allowed Italian production companies to break into the middle-class market and to capture a wide international audience—and to increase their share of the home box office with respect to Hollywood's take, which declined to 15 percent.

In the 1970s the crisis that struck the country as a whole also affected the film industry. As the economic picture for Italian cinema became less rosy, the country was represented on the international scene by Marxist-influenced directors who explored alienation in modern life and political issues. These directors included Michelangelo Antonioni (*L'Avventura, Blow-Up, Red Desert*), Pier Paolo Pasolini (*Pigpen, Teorema, Salò*), Bernardo Bertolucci (*Last Tango in Paris, The Conformist, 1900*), and Visconti (*The Damned*). As in literature, fascism and the Resistance provided favored themes for Italian filmmakers, inspiring, among others, Lina Wertmuller's *Love and Anarchy*, Bernardo Bertolucci's *The Spider's Strategem, The Conformist,* and *1900,* and the Taviani brothers' *The Night of the Shooting Stars.* The current Italian political situation also came under scrutiny in the films of Elio Petri, *Investigation of a Citizen above Suspicion;* Ettore Scola (*We All Loved Each Other Very Much*); Francesco Rosi, *Three Brothers* and *Excellent Cadavers;* and Lina Wertmuller, *The Seduction of Mimi* and *Swept Away.*

Faced by renewed American domination in the motion picture field, the economic crisis of Italian cinema continued into the 1980s and 1990s, although there was some recovery. Filmmakers turned to television and international cooperation to continue making high-quality products such as Bertolucci's Oscar-winning *The Last Emperor.* Despite its inability to compete in the contemporary high-budget, action-oriented movie climate, Italian film retained a strong presence on the international cultural circuit in this best-known art form of contemporary Italy.

Besides cinema, literary endeavor brought a high profile to the Italy of the republic. Three world-class poets who had done a great deal of important work during the earlier period remained very active after the war. Widely regarded as deserving a Nobel Prize, Giuseppe Ungaretti did not receive that honor (possibly for political reasons) but collected a host of other awards. Noted for shearing Italian poetry of rhetoric and metaphor, his work translated into many languages, Ungaretti lectured in foreign countries, including the United States and was one of the strongest influences in modern poetry. The prestigious Nobel Prize that had eluded Ungaretti was awarded to two of his contemporaries. Salvatore Quasimodo, who won the prize in 1959, claimed to be the real founder of hermetic poetry in which the poet had to face himself without referring to conventional cultural standards. Eugenio Montale, Nobel Prize winner in 1975, "was probably the profoundest poetic interpreter of the drama of twentieth-century man, with his existential anguish and his victimization by events and movements." These three poets testify to the extraordinary presence of Italian poetry on the twentieth-century stage.

As in poetry, prominent novelists who wrote during the Fascist period continued publishing important works during the republic. Unlike the poets, however, their writings bore directly on the political situation. Fascism—opposition to it first, the Resistance after, and as an evil to be guarded against later—thus served as a prime stimulant to literary production. Indeed, publishing houses had served as centers of anti-Fascist activities and many of the writers associated with them were Communists, although some later turned against the movement. Ironically—given the writers' future anti-American stance—this "resistance" to fascism frequently took the form of translating into Italian the American novels of the 1930s that dealt with social issues (e.g., Steinbeck's *Grapes of Wrath*), and, as in cinema, exposed many Italian writers to international currents.

Among the novelists criticizing fascism and whose work had international repercussions was Alberto Moravia, who had burst onto the literary scene with a masterpiece that condemned Fascist values—*The Time of Indifference*. Moravia continued to publish into his eighties at the rate of about a novel a year, commenting on the ills of modern society. *The Conformist*, a book loosely based on the murder of the anti-Fascist Rosselli brothers by the secret police, and one of Moravia's later works, *Two Women*, became classic films. Carlo Levi, a left-wing painter condemned to "internal exile" in a poor southern region, profited from his experience to write *Christ Stopped at Eboli*, one of the most famous characterizations of the oppressive Fascist climate there. Ignazio Silone, a Communist who later repudiated the movement, also condemned Fascist oppression in *Fontamara* and gave a picture of the underground in *Bread and Wine*. This last novel also raised important moral issues and demonstrated increasing disillusionment with communism. In his later works, Silone was preoccupied with the relationship of Christianity and politics in society. Another world-class novelist had a continuing influence on the literary scene during the republic, Elio Vittorini. Vittorini's first novel, *Il garofano rosso* (The Red Carnation) had been condemned as subversive by the government. His *Conversazione in Sicilia* combines "the energy of political commitment with a strikingly effective technique."

With the war and censorship over by the late 1940s, Italy witnessed an "explosion" of novels about the Resistance. Vittorini's *Uomini e no*, a stark portrayal of Milanese partisans fighting the Nazis, heavily influenced by Hemingway's style, served as the prototype. The country's best writers—Vasco Pratolini, Cesare Pavese, Italo Calvino, Carlo Cassola, and Guido Piovene—wrote important works. Renata Viganò published *L'Agnese va a morire*, an examination of a woman's road to antifascism and the Resistance. The Resistance novel has had a continuing influence on the literary scene through the works of Beppe Fenoglio.

Fueled by an enduring tradition of high-level literary journals, Italian literature continued to demonstrate great vitality in the postwar decades. Its preoccupation with national, social, and political issues was illustrated in Giuseppe di Lampedusa's 1958 international literary sensation, *The Leopard*. Later transformed into a film by Visconti, this novel describes Sicily—caught between the old and the new—at the time of Garibaldi's landing in 1860. Vasco Pratolini, best known for his description of Florentine life, also dealt with a historical motif with contemporary implications in *Metello*, a novel of early socialism. The Sicilian novelist Leonardo Sciascia drew international acclaim for a series of brilliant novels which unmasked the Mafia's operations, as well as for his political novels. Giorgio Bassani examined the effects of the war on Italian Jews in Ferrara in works such as *The Garden of the Finzi-Contini*, popularized outside of Italy by a De Sica movie. On this same theme, two excellent nonfiction works—*Survival in Auschwitz* and *The Reawakening*—by a former concentration camp inmate, Primo Levi, have been translated and widely covered by the American press (interviews of Levi by American novelist Philip Roth had an important impact). Other prominent writers of the republican period who gained worldwide fame, this time for novels reflecting a less concrete and more fantastic world, include Carlo Emilio Gadda, Italo Calvino, and Umberto Eco. Pier Paolo Pasolini and especially Edoardo De Filippo illustrate another postwar literary trend, a preoccupation with literature written in dialect.

The republic's lively literary atmosphere also allowed women writers to come into their own, building on the tradition of female novelists discussed in Chapter 13. The best woman novelist to emerge in contemporary Italy was Elsa Morante. She produced a number of very important works, but probably her greatest is *History: A Novel*. Creating a literary sensation when it was first published in 1974, this work has been judged a masterpiece on the model of nineteenth-century Russian novels. The works of Oriana Fallaci, a prominent newspaperwoman, are regularly translated into English; her novels and other writings rely heavily on her journalism, as did those of Matilde Serao. More in the traditional mode of a novelist, but emphasizing memorialistic material, are the books of Natalia Ginsburg, a member of a prominent Turinese Jewish family. Other prominent women novelists include Dacia Maraini and Anna Banti, whose novels remain untranslated into English.

Besides literature and cinema, two related areas have spread Italy's fame during the republic: design and fashion. Attractive design of modern industrial products must be ranked among the major reasons why Italian products have had such great appeal on the world market. This activity includes everything, as the catalog of one exhibition put it, "from the spoon to the city." The products of large companies such as Olivetti and Fiat and design outfits such as Kartell (plastics), Artemide (lamps), and Brionvega (electronics) illustrate the reputation that the country has gained in this field, which has become an essential part of modern marketing.

In addition to advanced design, fashion became a byword for Italy during the republic. Names such as Armani, Versace, Krizia, Valentino, Fendi, Mila Schön and Ferré are known the world over, but it is not just in style that they are important. Thanks to the activities of firms such as these, in the 1980s Italy became the third-largest world manufacturer of apparel, with production amounting to 20 billion dollars. Much of this production was exported, making the sector into the industrialized world's largest export-oriented business. The clothing industry's development is a tribute not only to the country's esthetic sense but also to its adaptability and to its technological and organizational know-how. In the 1970s the industry began reorganizing to meet the demands of the "mass individualism of post-industrial society" by combining modern inventions with artisan techniques and imagination. This effort involved heavy industry application of CAD-CAM (Computer Aided Design-Computer Aided Manufacturing). In twelve years, CAD-CAM systems increased at an annual 48 percent rate so that by 1987 they accounted for 50 percent of market potential. As a result of this massive effort, apparel exports increased 700 percent from 1976 to 1987.

This advanced technology also indicated the country's position at the cutting edge of modern technology. An example of this increasingly close interconnection between science and technology has been the development of new materials. In this field, G. Natta of the Milan Polytechnic won the 1963 Nobel Prize in chemisty for his research on high polymers, essential for the production of plastic.

Another field in which Italy has distinguished itself is nuclear physics. As in the case of electromagnetism discussed in Chapter 13, research in this area cuts across political regimes and dates back to 1927, when physicist Orso Mario Corbino acted to transform the University of Rome's physics institute at Via Panisperna 89A into a world-class institution. Corbino approached Mussolini for financing and assembled a brilliant team of nuclear physicists who ranked among the best in the world—the "Via Panisperna Boys." Star of the institute was Enrico Fermi, winner of the 1938 Nobel Prize in physics, unusual among physicists because he excelled in both theory and experimentation. In 1933 he published a fundamental paper describing the "weak interactive force." His statistics were very important for quantum mechanics, and his research on "slow neutrons" culminated in the first controlled nuclear chain reaction at the University of Chicago after he left Italy and came to the United States in January 1939 in protest against Italian anti-Semitic legislation (his wife was Jewish). Continuing Italian research in the field of the weak interactive force resulted in another Nobel in physics for Carlo Rubbia in 1984.

By then the internationalization of nuclear research had occurred and, in addition to his Italian research, Rubbia worked at CERN (Conseil Européen pour Recherches Nucléaires), the European research center in Geneva. Paralleling Italian interest in multilateral economic organizations after World War II, physicist Edoardo Amaldi, youngest of the "Via Panisperna Boys," realized that modern nuclear physics was impossible without great economic resources. This reality dictated the pooling of European money and talent, he believed, if Europe was to be in a position to compete with the United States. Amaldi became a powerful advocate for a European nuclear research facility, which culminated in the foundation of CERN.

Indeed, during the years of the economic miracle, increasing internationalization became the hallmark of modern science. Scientists such as Rubbia and Riccardo Giacconi, a major pioneer in X-ray astronomy, moved comfortably from Italian posts to European and American ones and back again. Italy thus benefited greatly from the republic's openness, support, and encouragement of economic and cultural ties with other countries—and has made significant contributions in these crucial areas.

21

Conclusions: Where Is Italy Headed?

I<small>N</small> 1992 a drastic shakeup in Italy's political and economic system, labeled the "bloodless revolution," began. It caught commentators completely by surprise, but if imperfect bipolarism had been the hallmark of republican politics, international communism's collapse and the Cold War's end was bound to produce extreme consequences. Faced with the choice of losing their liberty or tolerating a "blocked" political system that encouraged corruption, Italians had selected the latter; with the threat to their freedom gone, this dismal choice faded as well.

The "Bloodless Revolution"

Several key developments preceding general elections in 1992 signalled important changes in the Italian political equilibrium. The first put intense pressure on the PCI. In 1989 the revolution against Soviet power in Eastern Europe and the Red Chinese massacre in Tienanmen Square forced the PCI to distance itself further from Moscow than it had in the past. PCI secretary Achille Occhetto decided to change his party's name and apply for admission into the Socialist International. Led by prestigious party founder Pietro Ingrao and former secretary Alessandro Natta, the hard-liners objected because, they argued, PCI tradition differed from those of the "People's Republics." The long debate over these issues and grave internal opposition to Occhetto's leadership—not only from hard-liners but also from Communist "reformists" (*miglioristi*)—presaged a split. With selection of a new name, the Democratic Party of the Left (PDS), the hard-liners broke off and formed Rifondazione Comunista.

International communism's fall caused a grave crisis for the Christian Democrats. Relying on their status as an anti-Communist bulwark, they had blocked progressive reforms advocated by their Socialist and smaller allies over the years. The odd contrast between a modern economy and inefficient public services, discussed in the previous chapter, and the brazen exploitation of state resources for political gain fueled the Lombard League's rise in the North. This new force spread like wildfire, in the beginning primarily at Christian Democratic expense.

The general elections of April 5 and 6, 1992, focused all these elements and produced a political earthquake. The DC dropped 5 percent, a big change in Italian elections. The League won over 9 percent of the vote, making it the largest party in Milan, the country's industrial and financial heartland, and later local elections would confirm it as the largest northern party. The PDS received 16 percent of the vote and the hard-line *Rifondazione*, 5.5 percent. The four-party coalition that ruled Italy before the elections no longer had a stable majority.

Given the bankruptcy of international communism, maintenance of PSI vote share, and Craxi's blank check from DC leaders who had promised to support him in the new legislature, Craxi claimed the prime minister's office. But Craxi soon faced a more serious crisis. In February 1992 a Milanese businessman had complained to the authorities that money had been extorted from him by a local Socialist. Officials conducted an investigation that eventually uncovered an incredible network of bribes paid by businesspeople to politicians to obtain public works contracts. Although further investigation revealed that all the parties were involved, the scandal's first wind affected the Socialists most. As the scandal spread implacably, in the summer of 1992 recently elected president Oscar Luigi Scalfaro refused to commission Craxi to form a government. His reason: If the scandal ever involved the Socialist leader personally, the republic itself would be endangered. After a long crisis, Craxi agreed to Giuliano Amato, his second-in-command, as prime minister.

While Amato implemented an austerity program and imposed new taxes to confront the nation's enormous deficit and the serious international recession, the corruption scandal assumed incredible dimensions. Arrests produced allegations of corruption at the highest political levels, implicating Secretary Bettino Craxi, several former DC secretaries and prime ministers—including Arnaldo Forlani and Giulio Andreotti, with whom Craxi had allied—and leaders of the smaller parties such as Republican Giorgio La Malfa. Before the scandal, there had been revelations that the Soviet Union had subsidized the PCI, but later investigations demonstrated that the PCI and PDS had also participated in the widespread system of payoffs and kickbacks. In Milan, "kickback city," payoffs were divided among all the traditional parties, including the PCI, according to a preset formula.

Besides the imperfect bipolarism blocking alternation in power and allowing the DC to dominate the government for forty-five years, other factors favored widespread corruption. The first was the financing of the PCI by the Soviet Union and of the DC and its allies by the United States throughout the Cold

War. Besides the direct subsidies Moscow provided, Moscow also required Italian companies doing business with Soviet-dominated Eastern Europe to contribute a percentage of the proceeds to firms controlled by the PCI, while American unions funneled money to anti-Communist forces. Exploiting their ability to influence public enterprise through the governing coalition, the non-Communist parties demanded kickbacks from private companies such as Olivetti seeking contracts in the vast public sector. A campaign-financing law failed to break this cycle because of the insufficient sums allocated to political activity. Unlike in the United States, for example, this legislation left only the antiquated system of membership dues as the other legal means of financing the party bureaucracies and activities, and illegal methods escalated during the 1980s. Furthermore, given the complexity of Italian law, contradictory legislation, and the government bureaucracy's inefficiency, it became essential to buy political influence to accomplish anything in the economic field—as some of Italy's most famous business leaders such as Olivetti's Carlo De Benedetti and Fiat's Cesare Romiti testified when they became enmeshed in the scandal. Bribes became necessary to conduct business even on the smallest scale; not surprisingly, the enormous sums of cash siphoned off from state coffers not only went to pay for political expenses and to grease contracts but also to increase funds in personal bank accounts. Payoffs thus became the glue linking political fund-raising and economic activity and generated personal wealth for politicians and business leaders as a by-product.

Rapid-fire and continuous revelations of the enormous funds involved and the personal profiteering inflamed public opinion. The most spectacular example is the Enimont affair. This scandal involved manipulation of ENI by private concerns in the formation and maneuvering of a gigantic chemical company, which produced great losses for the taxpayers. The resulting profits were reportedly split among the parties and the private company. As investigation into these clamorous allegations proceeded, Gabriele Cagliari, former ENI head, and Raul Gardini, chief of the Ferruzzi group, committed suicide.

Several important issues important for Italy's future arose out of the scandals: the deficit, privatization, civil rights, and political dislocation. Although there were payoffs in all countries, the scandals broke when corruption in Italy had reached the point of raising the cost of public works beyond that of other countries to the point that they contributed dramatically to the country's ballooning deficit and had a negative influence on the economy. Italians hoped that the greater stringency and oversight of public spending resulting from the scandals would reduce the excessive costs of public works. Publicity over corruption dampened the willingness of companies to bid on public works, but where bids did come in, they were about 40 percent below prescandal levels. Significantly lower costs may thus turn out to be a bright postscript to the scandal, while another plus may be creation of a much cleaner administration than in other Western countries, where corruption is handled on a case-to-case basis.

In addition, the scandals convinced many Italians that the government was too heavily involved in the economy and that public companies were particularly vulnerable to extortion by political forces. This attitude promoted an increased drive for privatization and a debate on the proper balance between the private and public sectors. On one side of the discussion are those Italians who believe that private business is more efficient than the public enterprise and that the government should reduce its influence on the economy. On the other side are those who point to the crucial role companies such as IRI and ENI have had in the country's spectacular development and who argue, although they admit the need for reform, that public companies still have an important part to play.

Another major issue that arose from the scandals was whether a highly politicized justice system traditionally insensitive to civil rights could resolve the questions raised by the scandals. The most prominent figures in the scandals were targeted through an instrument designed to protect their civil rights, the *avviso di garanzia*. This is notification that a person's name has come up during an investigation, allowing that person to obtain legal representation. Most of the politicians enmeshed in the scandals were not immediately indicted and would not be tried for years, but the press proclaimed them guilty and they were destroyed politically. Leaking allegations to the press was a favorite method that the magistrates used to "burn" political leaders and end their careers.

Moreover, in violation of basic Western legal norms, Italian magistrates continued arresting people and incarcerating them until they "named names." This procedure produced extraordinary numbers of names, a host of conspiracy theories, clamorous miscarriages of justice, little evidence, and few convictions. In the latest corruption scandal, it also prompted suicides such as that of the ex-head of ENI in July 1993, mentioned earlier, who was kept in prison because he would not "talk." This episode brought the ire of the justice minister, Giovanni Conso, against the investigating magistrates, but the Italian system gave him no control over their activities, and legislative proposals to guarantee the rights of the accused—such as the right not to testify against oneself and safeguarding against officials leaking material to the press—were drowned in a chorus of protests.

These events had rapid and dramatic political repercussions. So many members of Parliament came under investigation that there was a loss of confidence in that institution—which, in turn, prompted deputies and senators to yield to a seemingly irresistible popular consensus, formally expressed on April 18, 1993, in a series of referendums calling for fundamental changes in the electoral system. The proportional representation instituted following World War II was overhauled. Citizens could now elect mayors directly, and other provisions ensured that the winner would have majorities in the city councils. In the Senate, a winner-take-all system on one ballot was instituted, but there were fears that if many candidates ran in a district a person could get elected with an insignificant number of votes. A similar winner-take-all system was also adopted for 75 percent of the Chamber of Deputies, although 25 percent would continue to be elected by proportional representation; so out of favor was proportional representation that this last provision aroused loud protest. To discourage political fragmentation, the new legislation required that a party or an electoral coalition receive a minimum of 4 percent before it could be represented in Parliament. This provision did not allay fears that the splintering of political forces would worsen. Even before the first national elections under the new system were held, there were calls for changes.

In addition to overturning the electoral system, the bloodless revolution produced the indictments, arrests, or implication of more than 3,000 of Italy's most famous politicians and business leaders. The parties of the old ruling coalition have practically been destroyed. Hit hard by charges of corruption and Mafia collusion, and by the revolt of its own Mario Segni—who initiated the referendum movement to change the electoral system—the Christian Democratic party formally decided to "dissolve." With the aid of northern leader Rosy Bindi, the DC hoped to link up once again with Luigi Sturzo's tradition and took the name of his Popular party. It was unclear whether this delicate operation would succeed in maintaining the Catholics as a major political force. For the ex-Communists, luckily, their crisis had come earlier, and their severed ties with world communism were formalized by their new name and their oak-tree symbol (with a small hammer and sickle at its roots). Presenting itself as a moderate leftist party, the PDS hoped to create a coalition at the head of which it could come to power. The Socialist party had practically disappeared. It was unable, for example, to elect a single city councillor in Milan, its former stronghold, and its rank-and-file deserted in droves. New PSI secretaries struggled to revive the party but failed in a hostile political climate. At a congress held from November 11 to 13, 1994, the Socialist party formally dissolved itself, with a majority of Socialists moving toward a PDS-dominated coalition and a minority establishing a new reformist organization.

As the political crisis worsened and the Western recession hit full force, the Italians established a government of "technicians" under former Bank of Italy governor Carlo Azeglio Ciampi. Charged with remaining "above politics," providing stability, beginning the task of reforming the country's most serious ills, and presiding over elections to be held under the revamped voting system, Ciampi managed to govern during unruly times and to gain popularity. His government confronted the privatization issue directly, saw through the first local elections under the new voting law, carried on a renewed war against the Mafia, adopted economic austerity measures, cut government spending, and instituted a hiring freeze and other measures to gain control of the bloated bureaucracy. His government also did well in foreign policy, receiving widespread international approval when it criticized the American propensity to use force in Somalia.

The first national elections to be held under the electoral modifications already discussed loomed as a watershed in the republic's history. This balloting, scheduled for Spring 1994, seemed crucial because of the rapid decline of the traditional parties and the rise of the Lombard League. Local elections pointed to the League, once considered to be a political flash in the pan like the postwar Uomo Qualunque, as the largest vote-getter in northern Italy. This situation created several major problems for the country. The League's antisouthern rhetoric likely burned its bridges in the South, where the decline of the traditional parties was slower than in the North. This fact already indicates a political schism in the country. No matter how much support the League has in the North, it will not be able to achieve a majority in Parliament against a South solidly lined up against it. By 1993 indications were that the League had recognized this dilemma, had moderated its rhetoric, and had begun seeking support in the South. If it managed to become a nationwide political force, would the League become a conservative party on the European model, alternating power with leftist political forces? And if that happened, would Italy take on the physiognomy of northern European countries? Would the nation benefit from such a change?

But it is much more difficult to construct a new system than it is to tear the old one down. The League thrived on negative criticism of taxes, the South, and the central government, but can it develop a positive ideology? Its "federalism" is not linked to the Italian federalist thinkers of the Risorgimento but to a search for scapegoats holding back the North's further economic expansion. Although the League has tapped into a real issue regarding government incompetence, its leader Umberto Bossi's speeches are sprinkled with violent terms and contain elements bordering on racism. To an extent, Bossi did moderate his ideas, but Italians wondered whether he would be able to pull back from his most extreme positions to adopt a statesmanlike attitude if his movement won enough support to help govern the country.

Already the League has been criticized for exacerbating the southern problem by cutting off the dialogue between southerners struggling to modernize the region and the most-advanced part of Italian society, which is in a position to help resolve the complex southern question. In addition, though few people took seriously the League's contention that it aimed at splitting Italy into different states, representatives of the armed forces proclaimed this goal unconstitutional and indicated that they might intervene if League members were awarded delicate political positions. This aspect of the League's rise caused rumors of a coup in conjunction with the 1994 elections and contributed to the resignation of the army chief of staff in October 1993.

Coup rumors seemed exaggerated, but they reflected concerns with the coming changes. Would the politics of the new era cause more or less fragmentation? With the League's growing strength concentrated in heavily populated Lombardy, it threatened to elect a large bloc from this restricted geographical area. Would this bloc prove large enough to prevent formation of governments, should the League be so inclined? On the other hand, framers of the new voting system incorporated majoritarian principles into the voting system and encouraged electoral alliances to reduce political fragmentation. Would these alterations create more stability?

Indications of further complications in the political situation appeared in the local elections of November and December 1993. The League's political problems confined its power to the area north of Genoa and Venice. In the mayoral elections of important cities, the PDS participated in coalitions that received the largest number of votes, but not enough to gain a majority on the first ballot in any big city but Palermo. The big surprise was the MSI, which ran alone and did not win any mayors but emerged as the largest single party. Did these results point to political polarization? This seemed unlikely because voters appeared to reward political organizations that had not been part of the ruling coalition. Moreover, not only ex-Communists but also the neo-Fascists had dropped their extremist ideologies and had moved toward the political center formerly occupied by the governmental parties.

The evolution of the PCI into the PDS has already been described, but a similar tendency away from its Fascist roots emerged over the years within the MSI. That organization witnessed a long struggle between Pino Rauti, an unrepentant Fascist, and Gianfranco Fini, who acknowledged the MSI's origins but who pressed the party to distance itself from them. Fini, born in 1952 and too young to have experienced fascism, became MSI secretary and maintained that he wished to bring his organization into the Italian mainstream, but he had trouble with his rank-and-file.

Thus a picture of once-radical parties battling for Italy's center came into focus. Was it possible that the PDS might emerge as the mainstay of a moderate, left-leaning coalition while the MSI became the core of a respectable conservatism? Would the PDS and MSI share of the vote hold in the future, or did their performance represent only a protest? Would their need for electoral alliances stimulate them to compromise with other political forces? Both movements were aware of these issues and openly discussed them. If a moderate mass conservative movement eventually emerged in Italy, it would be the first time since unification—when conservativism was discredited because of its identification with the Austrians and the old states. This development would have a salutary effect on Italian politics—but could the MSI with its undemocratic origins create such a movement? Or would some factions of the former ruling coalition revive and succeed in capturing the political center? Would the Italian political system evolve to such a point that moderate leftists and conservatives presenting the country with meaningful choices alternate in power without threatening democracy?

The national elections of March 27–28, 1994, may have provided some answers to these questions. The new electoral law did indeed encourage the formation of electoral alliances. On the left, the "Progressive Pole," led by the PDS, confidently expected victory. This "pole" grouped together parties that traditionally identified themselves as leftist organizations, including Rifondazione Comunista, Socialists, and a loose federation of leftist groups called Alleanza Democratica (Democratic Alliance). The Christian Democrats, former lords of the political arena, ran as two formations in the center, the Popolari, their new name, and the Pattisti, a group of adherents to the so-called Pact for Italy drafted by Mario Segni, an early champion of altering the political system.

The major question was whether the right would succeed in forming an electoral bloc. Only three months before the elections, media magnate Silvio Berlusconi made his entrance into politics, primarily to contest the growing strength of the PDS. He named his political formation Forza Italia (Go Italy) and made use of a network of fan clubs organized to support a soccer team he owned. He also exploited three private television stations that he owned (although the traditional parties controlled the three public television stations). In tune with the themes that had lately shaken Italian politics, Berlusconi advocated greater privatization, drastically lower taxes, and a smaller governmental role in economic life. He promised that these measures would produce a great number of jobs and an end to the recession.

Berlusconi had to confront the opposing demands of the two groups with which he had to forge an alliance if he was to have any chance of beating the *progressisti*. The Northern League, whose base consisted of small businesspeople fed up with the state, demanded a "federal" Italy divided into three republics so it could dominate the rich North and leave the rest of the peninsula to its fate. The MSI, which ran as the focus of a new political organization, Alleanza Nazionale (National Alliance), traditionally believed in a centralized state. In addition, the gruff Bossi and the sophisticated Fini got along poorly. Despite serious unresolved differences, however, the election's approach forced Berlusconi, Bossi, and Fini to put together a bloc called the "Liberty Pole."

The results of the elections were astounding. The Liberty Pole won an absolute majority of seats in the Chamber of Deputies, 366 out of 630. The *progressisti* picked up only 213 seats in the Chamber and the Center, 46. In the Senate, the right fell only three votes short of an absolute majority (since the voting age in the Senate is 25, compared with 18 in the Chamber, this result suggested that the youth vote went for the Liberty Pole). The parties that had been the nucleus of the ruling coalitions since the end of World War II had disappeared, with only the former Communists surviving. After the elections, however, the disputes among the organizations of the Liberty Pole continued. The major questions were whether they they could resolve their differences, for how long, and whether they could provide a long-term stable government for the country. Berlusconi did become prime minister but, in addition to criticism from the opposition, had a particularly hard time with Bossi. The allegations of conflict-of-interest and bribery against Berlusconi with relation to his vast business holdings also heated the political atmosphere and threatened both his cabinet's and the coalition's survival. In December 1994, Bossi withdrew from the coalition presenting a no-confidence motion. In response, Berlusconi resigned and demanded new elections. Berlusconi and Fini argued that the voters had endorsed a specific coalition which no longer existed and that, therefore, the electorate's opinion must immediately be sounded on any new political alliance which would govern the country.

Thus, as the political and economic crises deepened, the nation's politicians came under great pressure to produce practical results on the local and national planes. From now on, if they won and performed poorly, the voters would have a specific party or coalition to blame and would vote it out; as in other countries, that party would have to reorganize itself in the opposition while its successors have the opportunity to prove themselves. With the Cold War's close and the virtual end of proportional representation, Italy is no longer a frontier area between the two great powers or a "blocked democracy," and Italians will be free to implement immediate changes if they believe that the persons governing them do a bad job or are corrupt. That newfound ability—in addition to the decimation of the old political elite—constitutes the real bloodless revolution.

The Course of Modern Italy

Insistent demands, such as those made by the Lombard League, for local autonomy based on regional diversity have emerged periodically not only in Italy but throughout Europe—from Brittany in France to the Spanish Basque country and Catalonia, from Wales in the United Kingdom, not to mention the Balkans, Eastern Europe, and the former Soviet Union. In Italy's case, the peninsula was divided after the Roman Empire's end and remained so until the nineteenth century, so it is hardly surprising that regionalism has deep roots and would spawn similarly powerful political movements. The Piedmontese who united the country feared such developments and centralized the country to prevent the new state from falling apart, which is exactly what the European powers expected to happen. Applied too rigidly, centralization had its defects, and Italian administrations up to and including the republic have witnessed tensions between centrifugal tendencies and centripetal forces. Thus, the renewed strength of parties that do not question unity may represent a reaction to the League's federalism.

Although the new structure of Europe may eventually make national histories and regional questions obsolete, historical reflection is still in order. From a cultural and economic viewpoint, Italy's political division had scarce significance in the politically divided Europe of the Middle Ages and the Renaissance, but when strong nation-states emerged in the sixteenth century and Italy failed to follow suit by unifying, the peninsula became subject to its powerful neighbors. There were other factors, but the invasions were a prime reason why Italy's cultural dominance and economic prosperity waned beginning in the same period.

Revival began during the Enlightenment, thanks to the peninsula's strengthened ties with the rest of Europe, which had been weakened by Spanish domination but never severed. At first the rebirth did not produce widespread hope for political unification but reflected a need to reform Italian culture and economics to bring the peninsula up to European standards. Italian history from the Enlightenment represents the peninsula's struggle for economic development and political aspirations that slowly evolved into a democratic vision along the lines of the eighteenth-century Atlantic revolutions, which included the American Revolution. The most significant of these revolutions occurred in France and had major repercussions in Europe, including Italy throughout the ensuing century.

Under the spur of French revolutionary ideas and Napoleonic reforms, Italian patriots came to understand that unity alone could combine the economic advantages of a larger trading area, social renovation, and the recovery of the nation's ancient prestige. Italian moderates initially resisted; unity was the left's demand, and conservatives feared, not unreasonably, that unity would lead to French-style Jacobinism. Later conservative models for altering the peninsula's makeup emerged to counterbalance the more extreme elements identified with unification. The moderates succeeded in taking over the movement because they alone could make the enormous diplomatic changes involved in unifying the peninsula acceptable to the European powers; they had the best chance of being successful. The accomplishment of the small Kingdom of Sardinia in unifying Italy against overwhelming odds should not be underestimated because it served as a model for other national elements chafing under Hapsburg domination and was the first major step in splitting up the Austrian Empire, as Mazzini had foreseen.

The newly unified state faced a staggering task in melding together highly diverse areas. That it tried to do so using the centralizing methods of the French Revolution may be criticized, but within the context of late nineteenth-century Europe, it is likely that the more "democratic" methods later emphasized by some critics—allowing the South to determine the modalities of its union with the North and Center—risked scuttling unification. The contention made famous by Antonio Gramsci—that the conditions for a social revolution existed during the unification movement and that the Risorgimento "failed"—seems motivated more by Marxist theory than fact.

Moreover, given the country's conditions, united Italy made impressive economic strides, especially during the Giolittian era, despite its inability to resolve the southern question and the limitation of industrialization to the North. The strides made during World War I greatly accelerated the country's industrial development, but they also intensified economic imbalances. Not surprisingly, the boom affected primarily war-related industry; the war also resulted in great political dislocation not only because of domestic reasons but also, and perhaps more important, because of external factors. The fallout from these developments, the desire of new economic interests to hold on to their power and the exasperation of nationalism, conflicted with the Socialist mania to imitate the Russian Revolution. This situation created the parameters for a titanic struggle between right and left.

The fight ended in the Fascist regime. But to label Italian fascism a rightist regime *tout court* seems simplistic; it began as a leftist movement under a revolutionary socialist leader, mobilized the masses as do leftist movements, and retained leftist elements until its end. Because of its interruption of the country's democratic development, fascism appears as a political hiatus in the country's history, but in the economic field, Fascist government involvement in economics, state-led stimulation of industrialization, and extension of social services represented continuity with earlier Italian history. Indeed, the Italian republic profited from Fascist industrial plans and continued similar policies.

The republic had the misfortune of being caught in a very delicate and dangerous political and strategic position during the Cold War. Socialist errors and abdication to the Communists resulted in the country's having the largest Communist party in the West, which also was the second-largest party in Italy. Given these circumstances, Italians feared Soviet dominance if the PCI entered the government and, with American collaboration, kept the Christian Democrats in power. The DC was thus able to rule uninterruptedly for forty-five years following World War II; alternation in power became impossible and fueled political patronage and corruption. Despite this handicap, the Italian economy took off thanks to the unprecedented economic boom in the West, Italian participation in the substantially free trade system established after World War II, and a strong economic base. Although much progress was made in transforming the economy, however, political factors obstructed the overcoming of serious liabilities such as the South's backwardness, bureaucratic and public sector inefficiencies, and political interference in the economy.

By 1992, with the Cold War over, it was possible to tackle the widespread corruption that had resulted from the blocked democracy. The old fear of communism and the loss of liberty disappeared and the bloodless revolution began. Although this development raised novel political issues, it also offered the hope that corruption and politics influenced by fear would end. This development would make possible replacement of the old political system by a flexible one more responsive to the people and would remove serious impediments holding back the country's difficult modernization.

Thus despite the turmoil of modern Italian history, Italy continues on its course characterized, according to Giorgio Candeloro, by "an extremely complex development process . . . , tending to make Italy into a modern country capable of confronting the exigencies of today's dynamic contemporary civilization, and of contributing to the civil progress of humanity without impoverishing itself."

Bibliographical Essay

Bibliographical Essay

SINCE CONVENIENT BIBLIOGRAPHIES on Italy from the eighteenth century to the present are not readily available, this bibliographical essay has been designed with several purposes in mind. For undergraduates writing papers and having little or no familiarity with Italian, the works cited in English will allow the students to find documentation on the major themes discussed in the various chapters. Both general and specific works have been included so a person interested in Italian history may first become familiar with the general history of a period or topic before proceeding to a more-detailed analysis of particular questions. This technique may also prove useful for general readers. For graduate students or scholars interested in different periods, the most useful works in Italian have been included.

Before considering works connected to specific chapters, several useful reference publications may be mentioned. There are two good historical dictionaries that provide brief biographies of major characters and discussions of minor personages, institutions, publications, and movements, and discussions of minor personages that would be otherwise be difficult to find, along with some indications for further reading. They are Frank J. Coppa, Editor-in-Chief, *Dictionary of Modern Italian History* (Westport, 1985), and Philip V. Cannistraro, Editor-in-Chief, *Historical Dictionary of Fascist Italy* (Westport, 1982).

Convenient short bibliographies worth noting are Frank J. Coppa and William Roberts, *Modern Italian History: An Annotated Bibliography* (New York, 1990), which begins in the eighteenth century; Charles F. Delzell, *Italy in the Twentieth Century* (Washington, D. C., 1980) (American Historical Association Pamplet, No. 428); and Clara Lovett, *Contemporary Italy: A Selective Bibliography* (Washington, D.C., 1985). Essays on recent American books on Italy and valuable memoirs of Americans involved in Italy are in Borden W. Painter, Jr., ed. *Perspectives on Italy* (Hartford, 1992), a special issue of *The Cesare Barbieri Courier*, based at Trinity College. Lists of works, including recent books, articles, papers, dissertations, and works in progress may be found in the annual *Newsletter of the Society for Italian Historical Studies* (edited by Alan Reinerman, Boston College). An equivalent publication discusses recent works primarily in political science: the *Newsletter of the Conference Group on*

Italian Politics and Society, published at Dickinson College, Carlisle, Pennsylvania.

INTRODUCTION: From "School of Europe" to Conquered Land

For the history of Italian heretics, see the classic work by Delio Cantimori, *Eretici italiani del Cinquecento* (Florence, 1967), and his short and brilliant *Prospettive di storia ereticale italiana del Cinquecento* (Bari, 1960). Eric Cochrane and John Tedeschi summarize Cantimori's work and its influence in "Delio Cantimori: Historian," *The Journal of Modern History* 39, no. 4 (December 1967): 438–45. In English, Barry Collett, *Italian Benedictine Scholars and the Reformation* (Oxford, 1985), tells of the failure of a congregation of monks to resolve the schism between Catholics and Protestants.

The pessimistic view of the post-Renaissance is represented mostly by Italians. See Benedetto Croce, *Storia dell'età barocca in Italia,* 5th ed. (Bari, 1967), Giorgio Candeloro, *Storia dell'Italia moderna,* Vol. I (Milan, 1956), and Guido Quazza, *La decadenza italiana nella storia europea* (Milan, 1971). A more-balanced view and rich detail is provided by Romolo Quazza, *Preponderanza Spagnuola (1559–1700)* (Milan, 1950). The revisionists are best represented by Eric Cochrane, *Florence in the Forgotten Centuries* (Chicago, 1973), an exciting voyage through the years under consideration, and more explicitly, in his *Italy 1530–1630* (London and New York, 1988), edited posthumously by Julius Kirshner. R. Burr Litchfield's *Emergence of a Bureaucracy. The Florentine Patricians 1530–1790* (Princeton, 1986) essentially concurs with Cochrane. Domenico Sella, *Crisis and Continuity: The Economy of Spanish Lombardy in the Seventeenth Century* (Cambridge, MA, 1979), provides a reasoned argument against "refeudalization" and a judicious interpretation of the economic crisis of the period. Antonio Calabria discusses decline in Naples in *The Cost of Empire: The Finances of the Kingdom of Naples in the Time of Spanish Rule* (New York, 1991). Richard Tilden Rapp examines the meaning of decline in his *Industry and Economic Decline in Seventeenth-Century Venice* (Cambridge, 1979), while the essays in Brian Pullan, ed., *Crisis and Change in the Venetian Economy in the Sixteenth and Seventeenth Centuries* (London, 1968), are fundamental for an understanding of the period. In *Shipbuilders of the Venetian Arsenal: Workers and Workplace in the Preindustrial City* (Baltimore, 1991), Robert C. Davis discusses the role of ordinary workers and their families in Venice. Finally, the Einaudi *Storia d'Italia,* Vol. 2, Pt. 2 (Turin, 1974), provides a comprehensive survey of the period and its antecedents, including a good economic overview.

Chapter 1: The Italian Enlightenment

Although English-language historians have not devoted much attention to the Italian Enlightenment, a host of works exist in Italian, only the most important of which can be listed here. Franco Venturi's multivolume *Settecento riformatore* (Turin, 1969) is the fundamental work on this period discussing in detail Enlightenment activity in the Italian states and tracing European connections. This work has only been partially translated, but students may get a taste of Venturi's style in the excellent *Italy and the Enlightenment* (London, 1972). Venturi's views have influenced all modern scholarship on the eighteenth century, as may be seen by Dino Carpanetto and Giuseppe Ricuperati, who present an exquisitely balanced survey, including a discussion of the historiographical problem in *Italy in the Age of Reason, 1685–1789* (London, 1987), and the early chapters of Stuart Woolf, *A History of Italy* (London, 1979), which provide an excellent introduction to the period. Woolf's *The Poor in Western Europe in the Eighteenth and Nineteenth Centuries* (London, 1986) also focuses on Italy. Giorgio Candeloro concentrates on the crisis of the Italian states in Volume I of his *Storia dell'Italia moderna* (Milan, 1966).

For particular areas, consult Eric Cochrane, *Tradition and Enlightenment in the Tuscan Academies, 1690–1800* (Chicago, 1961), for a peek at the intense Tuscan intellectual life. Benedetto Croce's insights in his classic *History of the Kingdom of Naples* (Chicago, 1970) have been modified but are still provocative. On intellectual women in this era, see Gabriella Berti Logan, "The Desire to Contribute: An Eighteenth-Century Italian Woman of Science," *The American Historical Review* 99, no. 3 (June 1994): 785–812. consult also Paul Oskar Kristeller, "Learned Women in Early Modern Italy: Humanists and University Scholars," in Patricia H. Labalme, ed., *Beyond Their Sex: Learned Women of the European Past* (New York, 1980).

Harold Acton's *The Bourbons of Naples* (London, 1956) includes an interesting, detailed, and sympathetic synopsis of the period. A good account of Sicilian society and the attempts at reform is in *A History of Sicily: Modern Sicily after 1713* by Denis Mack Smith (London, 1968). Franco Venturi gives an intimate look at life in Venice in his short but provocative *Venezia nel 700* (Turin, 1980). In English, Frederic C. Lane's *Venice: A Maritime Republic* (Baltimore, 1973) and William H. McNeill's *Venice: The Hinge of Europe* (Chicago, 1974) are concerned with the glory days but have short chapters on the eighteenth century. On the Lombard land survey and its implications, see Daniel Klang, *Tax Reform in Eighteenth-Century Lombardy* (New York, 1977); on the nobility, see J. M. Roberts, "Lombardy," in Albert Goodwin, ed., *The European Nobility in the Eighteenth Century* (London, 1953), pp. 60–82. Alexander I.

Grab argues that the Austrians in Lombardy were interested in reform only for the added power it might bring them and essentially failed. See his articles, "The Politics of Subsistence: The Liberalization of Grain Commerce in Austrian Lombardy under Enlightened Despotism," *The Journal of Modern History* 57 (June 1985): 185–210; "Enlightened Absolutism and Commonlands Enclosure: The Case of Austrian Lombardy," *Agricultural History* 63, no. 1 (Winter 1989): 49–72; and "Enlightened Despotism and State Building: The Case of Austrian Lombardy," in *Austrian History Yearbook* (Minneapolis, 1989), pp. 43–72. Further information on particular areas may be found in Venturi's *Italy and the Enlightenment*, already cited.

On daily life, the best book is the short, comprehensive, and insightful *Daily Life in Eighteenth Century Italy* (New York, 1963) by Maurice Vaussard. Though concerned primarily with the nineteenth century, Stuart Woolf's *The Poor in Western Europe in the Eighteenth and Nineteenth Centuries* (London, 1986), previously cited, discusses the eighteenth century and has an excellent introduction analyzing the parameters of the problem. Books by foreigners telling about their travels in Italy are prime sources for our knowledge of daily life during this period. These include Johann Wolfgang von Goethe, *Italian Journey* (New York, 1989), Arthur Young, *Travels during the Years 1787, 1788 and 1789* (London, 1794), and Frank Brady and Frederick A. Pottle, eds., *Boswell on the Grand Tour: Italy, Corsica, and France* (London, 1955).

On the question of growing national feeling, Emiliana Noether's *Seeds of Italian Nationalism, 1700–1815* (New York, 1951) makes the case for the importance of the eighteenth century. On Muratori's role, consult Comitato per le onoranze a L.A. Muratori nel bicentenario dalla morte, *Miscellanea di studi muratoriani* (Modena, 1951).

Chapter 2: Italy and the French Revolution

French revolutionary and Napoleonic Italy has suffered from a scarcity of works and research, and the period would reward any investigator who decides to dedicate time to the topic. The English-language literature is particularly thin, and though more has been done in Italian, considerable work is still needed on the social and economic implications of the reforms of this period, particularly in the South. The same could be said for the counterrevolutionary movements.

Some of the works cited for Chapter 1, including Croce, Woolf, Acton, and Candeloro, have good discussions of this period. R. M. Johnston, *The Napoleonic Empire in Southern Italy*, 2 vols. (London, 1904), is old but still useful, as is Guglielmo Ferrero, *Avventura. Bonaparte in Italia (1796–1797)* (Milan, 1947). Angus Heriot, *The French in Italy, 1796–1799* (London, 1957), is short on insights but good on gossip. Giorgio Vaccarino, *I patrioti "anarchistes" e l'idea dell'unità italiana* (Turin, 1955), is an excellent account on the beginning of the idea of Italian unity during the period. Georges Bourgin, *Italie et Napoléon, 1796–1814* (Paris, 1936), is an insightful short account. The economic life of this period is explored by Evgenij V. Tarle, *La vita economica dell'Italia nell'età napoleonica* (Turin, 1950). John A. Davis has published an interesting work on *Conflict and Control: Law and Order in Nineteenth Century Italy* (Atlantic Highlands, NJ, 1988), which considers the issue from 1790 to 1900. Pietro Colletta's, *Storia del reame di Napoli* (Florence, 1962) is a classic account, as is Vincenzo Cuoco's history of the Neapolitan counterrevolution of 1799, *Saggio storico sulla rivoluzione di Napoli* (Milan, 1806). On the Neapolitan counterrevolution, see also Benedetto Croce, *La rivoluzione napoletana del 1799* (Bari, 1961). The case of a Tuscan reformer through the Enlightenment and the Napoleonic periods is examined by Renato Pasta, *The Making of a Notable: Giovanni Fabbroni between Enlightened Absolutism and Napoleonic Administration* (Princeton, 1985).

Further literature on the historiographical question discussed at the beginning of this chapter may be found in Emiliana Noether, "The Transition from the Enlightenment to the Risorgimento: A Question of Historical Interpretation," in Frank J. Coppa, ed., *Studies in Modern Italian History from the Risorgimento to the Republic* (New York, 1986).

Chapter 3: The First War for Italian Unity

The events discussed in this chapter suffer even more from neglect than those of Chapter 2. Very little exists in English, and foreign language works are mostly old. The best work on Murat is Angela Valente, *Murat e l'Italia meridionale*, 2d ed. (Turin, 1965). Antonio Spinoza's *Murat* (Milan, 1984) is a biography that portrays the cavalry general as the most adventurous of the rulers set up by Napoleon. In French, see *Joachim Murat, Roi de Naples. La dernière année de règne*, 5 vols. (Paris 1909), and H. Weill, *Le prince Eugène et Murat*, 5 vols. (Paris, 1902). See Johnston and Colletta, cited previously. There is ample literature on the *carbonari*, but, again, it is usually old; see A. Ottolini, *La Carboneria dalle origini ai primi moti insurrezionali (1797–1817)* (Modena 1936); a more recent account is R. J. Rath, "The Carbonari: Their Origins, Initiation Rites and Aims," *American Historical Review*, LXIX, 1964. On events in the North, see D. Spadoni, *Milano e la congiura militare nel 1814 per l'indipendenza italiana*, 3 vols. (Modena, 1936); Spadoni is also the author of "Nel centenario del proclama di Rimini," in *Rassegna Storica del Risorgimento*, 1915. On British policy, see C. K. Webster, *The Foreign Policy of Castlereagh, 1812–1822*, 2 vols.

(London, 1931–34), H. M. Lackland, "The Failure of the Constitutional Experiment in Sicily, 1813–1814," and "Lord Bentinck in Sicily, 1811–1812," both in *The English Historical Review*, 1926 and 1927; and C. W. Crawley, "England and the Sicilian Constitution of 1812," in *The English Historical Review*, 1940.

Chapter 4: A "Geographical Expression"

On the diplomatic side of the Restoration, two older works are still useful: René Albrecht-Carrié, *A Diplomatic History of Europe Since the Congress of Vienna* (New York, 1973), and C. K. Webster, *The Congress of Vienna 1814–1815* (London, 1919). Giuliano Procacci, *Storia degli italiani*, gives a good account of this period. An interesting article on the diplomatic rivalry between Austria and Russia in Italy is Alan J. Reinerman's "Metternich, Alexander I, and the Russian Challenge in Italy," *The Journal of Modern History* 46, no. 2 (June 1974): 20–38. On the intellectual side, Ettore Alberoni's, *Storia delle dottrine politiche in Italia* (Milan, 1985) presents a succinct history of political theory during this time. Pietro Colletta's, *Storia del reame di Napoli* (Florence, 1962 reprint) is a classic with a chapter treating this period. On the early Restoration in the North, see R. J. Rath, *The Provisional Austrian Regime in Lombardy-Venetia, 1814–1815* (Austin, 1969); on Austrian relations with the papacy, see Alan Reinerman, *Austria and the Papacy in the Age of Metternich I. Between Conflict and Cooperation 1809–1830* (Washington, DC, 1979). John Tracy Ellis's, *Cardinal Consalvi and Anglo-Papal Relations 1814–1824* (Washington, DC, 1942) is an older but still excellent account of Consalvi's diplomacy. Good cultural insights may be found in Benedetto Croce, *Una famiglia di patrioti* (Bari, 1927) and *Storia della storiografia italiana nel secolo decimonono*, 2 vols. (Bari, 1921). In English, see Christopher Cairns, *Italian Literature* (London, 1977), a general work that includes good brief discussions of the dominant themes of the literature of this period. Useful information on Sicily is in M. I. Finley, Denis Mack Smith, and Christopher Duggan, *A History of Sicily* (New York, 1987).

Chapter 5: Failed Revolutions: The 1820s and 1830s

The most comprehensive work in English on the Neapolitan Revolution is still George T. Romani's *The Neapolitan Revolution of 1820–1821* (Evanston, IL, 1950). Chapters can be found in Harold Acton's *The Bourbons of Naples*, and in Croce's *History of the Kingdom of Naples*, previously cited. A discussion of Restoration culture, the secret societies, and the revolutions of this period is in Stuart Woolf, *A History of Italy, 1700–1860* (London, 1979), and Harry

Hearder, *Italy in the Age of the Risorgimento, 1790–1870* (New York, 1983). George Martin, *The Red Shirt and the Cross of Savoy* (New York, 1969), shows particular insight into the problems of the period. See the previously cited works also on the Piedmontese agitation of 1821 and on the 1831 revolutions, but Giorgio Candeloro, *Storia dell'Italia moderna*, Vol. II (Milan, 1962), is excellent, as is Nino Valeri, ed., *Storia d'Italia* Vol. III, (Turin, 1965), whereas great detail and an especially good section on the Italian exiles of this period may be found in Cesare Spellanzon, *Storia del Risorgimento e dell'unità d'Italia,* Vol. II (Milan, 1934), which covers Italy up to the eve of the 1848 revolutions. Alan Reinerman has studied how the first effort of the powers to reform the Papal State failed, "The Concert Baffles: The Roman Conference of 1831 and the Reform of the Papal States," *International History Review* 5, no. 1 (1983): 20–38. The standard works on Buonarroti are Armando Saitta, *Filippo Buonarroti,* 2 vols. (Rome, 1950), and Alessandro Galante Garrone, *Filippo Buonarroti e i rivoluzionari dell'Ottocento* (Turin, 1951). In English, see Arthur Lehning's articles, "Buonarroti and His Secret Societies," *International Review of Social History* I (1956): 112–40, and "Buonarroti's Ideas on Communism and Dictatorship," *International Review of Social History* II (1957): 266–87, and Elizabeth Eisenstein, *The First Professional Revolutionary: Filippo Michele Buonarroti* (Cambridge, 1959).

Chapter 6: Three Models for Unification

Mazzini was fortunate in finding English-language scholars who studied his work; although there is a lack of recent books, perhaps Denis Mack Smith's new work, *Mazzini* (Milan, 1993), signals a change. The classic work by Gaetano Salvemini, *Mazzini,* is an essential starting point for an understanding of Mazzini's thought. Gwilym O. Griffith, author of *Mazzini: Prophet of Modern Europe* (New York, 1970, but first published in 1932), quotes Lloyd George's statement about Mazzini—"How right he was!"—which summarizes the book's main thesis. E.E.Y. Hales, *Mazzini and the Secret Societies: The Making of a Myth* (London, 1956), rightly emphasizes Mazzini's "shock value" to the existing Italian order. An older but excellent treatment of Mazzini is Bolton King's *Mazzini* (London, 1903). The author was able to speak to persons who had known Mazzini intimately, yet succeeded in providing an objective study. It can be stated that Mazzini both accepted foreign influences and had an impact in other countries. An aspect of this interaction has been examined by Joseph Rossi, *The Image of America in Mazzini's Writings* (Madison, WI, 1954). Mazzini's writings have been collected and published, and a good, albeit brief, sampling may be found in N. Gangulee, ed., *Giuseppe Mazzini: Selected Writings*

(Westport, CT, 1974). On the central "religiosity" of Mazzini's thought, see the essay on Mazzini in John MacCunn, *Six Radical Thinkers* (New York, 1964). Italian counts many works on Mazzini. Emilia Morelli, *Giuseppe Mazzini: Quasi una biografia* (Rome, 1984), emphasizes the point that Mazzini's religiosity was both the force behind and the brake upon his entire activity. Salvo Mastellone's *Mazzini e la "Giovane Italia"*, 2 vols., (Pisa, 1960) is a particularly fertile work that discusses the modern revolutionary method found in Mazzini's thought. Franco Della Peruta, *Mazzini e i rivoluzionari italiani* (Milan, 1974), is another important work on the subject.

While Gioberti's works and numerous letters have been published, the biographies dedicated to him are good but old. A. Anzilotti's, *Gioberti* (Florence, 1922) is a positive work, and Adolfo Omodeo, *Vincenzo Gioberti e la sua evoluzione politica* (Turin, 1941), takes a more complex view, according to which Gioberti used neo-Guelphism as an instrument to impart movement to the Italian situation. Omodeo's argument that Gioberti was able to mobilize moderate public opinion, in addition to a discussion of Balbo, may be found in his far-reaching work *L'età del Risorgimento italiano* (Naples, 1946). Besides the works by Gioberti and Balbo mentioned in the text, see Gioberti's *Del Rinnovamento civile d'Italia*, 3 vols. (Bari, 1968), and Balbo's *Sommario della storia d'Italia* (Milan, 1927). The relevant portions of Stuart Woolf's previously cited *A History of Italy, 1700–1860* are excellent on the discussion of alternative plans for Italian unification.

Developments in the Papal State in the period before Pius IX are cogently discussed by Alan Reinerman, *Austria and the Papacy in the Age of Metternich. Vol. II: Revolution and Reaction, 1830–1838* (Washington, DC, 1989). G.F.H. Berkeley, *Italy in the Making. Vol I: 1815 to 1846* and *Vol. II: June 1846 to 1 January 1848* (Cambridge, reprint, 1968), provides an informative and interesting account of events of the period, as does the older work by William Roscoe Thayer, *The Dawn of Italian Independence, Vol I* (Boston, 1893). These last two works are also valuable for the views of English-language historiography during the periods in which they were written.

Books on Charles Albert are few and far between. On foreign policy, see F. Lemmi, *La politica estera di Carlo Alberto nei suoi primi anni di regno* (Florence, 1928), while N. Radolico, *Carlo Alberto negli anni di regno 1831–1843* (Florence, 1930), discusses most of his reign. The chapter on Charles Albert in Rosario Romeo, *Dal Piemonte sabauda all'Italia liberle* (Turin, 1964), gives the best insight on developments during this period.

Chapter 7: Revolutions of 1848: The Great Shakeout

Priscilla Robertson's *Revolutions of 1848: A Social History* (Princeton, 1971) is an excellent work that puts the Italian revolutions into the European context.

G.F.H. Berkeley, *Italy in the Making. Vol. III: January 1st 1848 to November 16, 1848* (Cambridge, 1940), covers the revolutions in great detail. William Roscoe Thayer, *The Dawn of Italian Independence, Vol. II* (Boston, 1893), gives a stirring account that may seem outmoded but, like Berkeley's work, conveys a real portrait of the passions of the period. Kent Roberts Greenfield presents long-term economic and political developments in *Economics and Liberalism in the Risorgimento: A Study in Nationalism in Lombardy, 1814–1848* (Baltimore, 1965). George Martin's previously cited *The Red Shirt and the Cross of Savoy* has several good chapters on events of the period. In Italian, Candeloro, *Storia d'Italia, Vol. III*, is entirely devoted to the revolutions and their implications, while another excellent account is in Nino Valeri, ed., *Storia d'Italia, Vol. III* (Turin, 1965). Luigi Salvatorelli, ed., *Prima e dopo il Quarantotto* (Turin, 1948), a collection of essays from different journals, is excellent on the implications of the revolutions.

On particular persons, besides D'Azeglio's *Ultimi casi*, mentioned in the text, see his extremely important memoirs: Massimo D'Azeglio, *I miei ricordi* (Turin, 1965). On Cattaneo's role, see Clara Lovett, *Carlo Cattaneo and the Politics of the Risorgimento, 1820–1860* (The Hague, 1972), and Cattaneo's own memoirs of this period, Carlo Cattaneo, *Dell'insurrezione di Milano nel 1848 e della successiva guerra. Memorie* (Milan, 1973). On Pius IX, see E.E.Y. Hales, *Pio Nono: A Study in Euopean Politics and Religion in the Nineteenth Century* (Garden City, 1954), a very sympathetic biography, and the more up-to-date biography by Frank Coppa, *Pope Pius IX: Crusader in a Secular Age* (Boston, 1979). George M. Trevelyan's older work is still useful, *Manin and the Venetian Revolution of 1848* (London, 1923), as is Paul Ginsborg's *Daniele Manin and the Venetian Revolution of 1848–49* (Cambridge, 1979), marred by its overtly Marxist viewpoint. On the exiles in England, see M. C. Wicks, *The Italian Exiles in London, 1816–1848* (Manchester, 1937).

Chapter 8: Cavour and the Piedmontese Solution

There are a number of good general histories of the Risorgimento that cover the events discussed in this chapter. Edgar Holt, *Risorgimento. The Making of Italy, 1815–1870* (New York, 1970), provides a detailed and well-organized story. Bolton King's *History of Italian Unity* (New York, 1967 reissue) is an old but still useful work. A more recent overview, Harry Hearder, *Italy in the Age of the Risorgimento, 1790–1870* (London and New York, 1983), is valuable for its discussion of varying interpretations and the culture of the movement. Derek Beales, *The Risorgimento and the Unification of Italy*, Vol. 2, (New York, 1971), has a stimulating and comprehensive introduction and reprints a number of important documents. Another excellent book of documents is Denis Mack

Smith, ed., *The Making of Italy, 1796–1870* (New York, 1968). A short work that may be profitably consulted is Massimo Salvadori, *Cavour and the Unification of Italy* (New York, 1961). The documents relevant to Plombières, along with an intelligent introductory essay, have been published by Mack Walker, ed., *Plombières: Secret Diplomacy and the Rebirth of Italy* (New York, 1968). Two brilliant works by A.J.P. Taylor explain both the Italian and European diplomatic context of the era. They are *The Italian Problem in European Diplomacy* (Manchester, 1934) and *The Struggle for Mastery in Europe, 1848–1918* (London, 1954). Other aspects of the diplomacy of the period as it relates to Italy may be found in Nello Rosselli, *Inghilterra e regno di Sardegna dal 1815 al 1847* (Turin, 1954), and the interesting book by Giuseppe Berti, *Russia e stati italiani nel Risorgimento* (Turin, 1957).

As might be expected, there are many works on the most important individuals of the Risorgimento that are fundamental to an understanding of the age. The best and most exhaustive biography of Cavour and his times is Rosario Romeo, *Cavour e il suo tempo*, 3 vols. (Bari, 1984). In English, the massive and sympathetic work by William R. Thayer, *The Life and Times of Cavour*, 2 vols. (New York, 1971 reprint), is still useful. Maurice Paleologue's *Cavour* (New York, 1927) provides a flattering portrait of Cavour as a statesman, while A. J. Whyte's *The Political Life and Letters of Cavour, 1848–1861* (Westport, CT, 1975 reprint) connects his parliamentary career to his diplomacy. Denis Mack Smith's *Cavour* (London, 1985) is unfriendly to the Piedmontese statesman. Frank J. Coppa has written a short biography, *Camillo di Cavour* (New York, 1973). By analyzing the relationship between *Cavour and Garibaldi 1860* (Cambridge, 1954), Denis Mack Smith has concluded that it could not be assumed in 1860 that a monarchist unitary state was the only solution that could emerge from the revolution. But Harry Hearder, *Cavour* (London and New York, 1994), presents the Piedmontese leader as a subtle statesman who, in practice, had "no alternative" to imposing a unitary state on Italy. J.A.R. Marriott's lectures on the three major figures of the period, *The Makers of Modern Italy* (London, 1889), are still valuable.

Besides Cavour, Garibaldi has attracted the attention of English-speaking historians. George MacCaulay Trevelyan has written three classic works: *Garibaldi's Defense of the Roman Republic* (London, 1907), *Garibaldi and the Thousand* (London, 1909), and *Garibaldi and the Making of Italy* (London, 1919). More recent biographies include Paul Frischauer, *Garibaldi: The Man and the Nation* (New York, 1935); David Larg, *Giuseppe Garibaldi* (New York, reissued 1970); Peter de Polnay, *Garibaldi: The Man and the Legend* (New York, 1961); Christopher Hibbert, *Garibaldi and His Enemies* (London, 1965), a readable account; and Jasper Ridley, *Garibaldi* (New York, 1974), which is perhaps the best. Denis Mack Smith has also written an excellent short biography, *Garibaldi. A Great Life in Brief* (New York, 1956). Garibaldi's memoirs have also been published as *The Memoirs of Garibaldi,* edited by Alexandre Dumas (New York, 1931). An idea of Garibaldi's military genius may be gleaned from Andrea Viotti, *Garibaldi: The Revolutionary and His Men* (Dorset, 1979). For Garibaldi in "art and history," see the reproductions in *Garibaldi, arte e storia* (Florence, 1982). On military aspects of the Risorgimento, Piero Pieri, *Storia militare del Risorgimento. Guerre e insurrezioni* (Turin, 1962), cogently argues that Risorgimento military history demonstrates heroism and illustrates the capacity of the Italian people for sacrifice; especially interesting is his contention that the Risorgimento was accompanied by a valuable theroretical literature on utilizing all vital forces of a nation in the struggle for freedom. In addition to Pieri, Frank Coppa has published a good account of *The Origins of the Italian Wars of Independence* (London and New York, 1992).

For some of the other characters in the story, see Denis Mack Smith, *Victor Emanuel, Cavour, and the Risorgimento* (London, 1971); Clara Lovett, *Giuseppe Ferrari and the Italian Revolution* (Chapel Hill, 1979); William Hancock, *Ricasoli and the Risorgimento in Tuscany* (New York, 1969 reprint); and Michael St. John Packe, *The Bombs of Orsini* (London, 1957). For views of Italian events outside of Italy, see Howard R. Marraro, *American Opinion on the Unification of Italy, 1846–1861* (New York, 1932); Harry W. Rudman, *Italian Nationalism and English Letters* (New York, 1940); and A. William Salomone, "The Nineteenth-Century Discovery of Italy: An Essay in American Cultural History. Prolegomena to a Historiographical Problem," *American Historical Review* 73, no. 5 (June 1968): 1359–91.

On the activity of the democrats in the South, see the fundamental work by Franco Della Peruta, *I democratici e la rivoluzione italiana* (Milan, 1958), and Giuseppe Berti, *I democratici e l'iniziativa meridionale nel Risorgimento* (Milan, 1962). Raymond Grew has written the definitive *A Sterner Plan for Italian Unity. The Italian National Society in the Risorgimento* (Princeton, 1963).

For more general interpretations of the Risorgimento, Luigi Salvatorelli argues that the Risorgimento was spiritual in addition to material and sought a "new" Italy—*The Risorgimento: Thought and Action* (New York, 1970). The fundamental Marxist interpretation of the Risorgimento as a "failed" revolution may be found in Antonio Gramsci, *Il Risorgimento* (Turin, 1955), while Rosario Romeo's *Risorgimento e capitalismo* (Bari, 1963) offers a brilliant rebuttal to the thesis. Good contributions to the historical debate may be found in A. William Salomone, "Statecraft and Ideology in the Risorgimento," now in Edward R. Tannenbaum and Emiliana Noether, *Modern Italy. A Topical History since 1861* (New York, 1974); and in Salomone, "The Risorgimento Between Ideology and

History: The Political Myth of *rivoluzione mancata*," H. Stuart Hughes, "The Aftermath of the Risorgimento in Four Successive Interpretations," and Raymond Grew, "How Success Spoiled the Risorgimento," now all conveniently grouped in A. William Salomone, *Italy from the Risorgimento to Fascism. An Inquiry into the Origins of the Totalitarian State* (New York, 1970). Walter Maturi's *Interpretazioni del Risorgimento. Lezioni di storia e storiografia* (Turin, 1962) is an excellent and detailed history of Risorgimento interpretations from thinkers of the period up to Mack Smith. The book edited by John A. Davis and Paul Ginsborg, *Society and Politics in the Age of the Risorgimento: Essays in Honour of Denis Mack Smith* (Cambridge, 1991), brings together the interpretations of British and Italian experts.

Chapter 9: Cavour's Heirs: The "Right" Reigns

Works in English on the period of the Right's rule are few. General works mentioned previously can be consulted. In keeping with the book's tone, Denis Mack Smith's *Italy. A Modern History* (Ann Arbor, 1959) provides a generally negative interpretation of the Right's tenure. On the economic problems and policies during this period, Shepard B. Clough's *The Economic History of Modern Italy* (New York, 1964) gives a balanced and impartial account. A more recent survey of economic history beginning from this period is Vera Zamagni, *The Economic History of Italy, 1860–1990* (New York, 1993). A series of well-connected (and difficult to find) documents in translation, readings, and comments on Italian developments from this era and others are in Shepard B. Clough and Salvatore Saladino, *A History of Modern Italy: Documents, Readings, and Commentary* (New York, 1968). A quantitative analysis of Italian democrats, the social context, and their significance and activities in the new kingdom can be found in Clara Lovett, *The Democratic Movement in Italy, 1830–1876* (Cambridge, MA, 1982). John Whittam's discussion of this period in *The Politics of the Italian Army, 1861–1918* (London, 1977) is a convincing description of the difficulties of establishing a national army. A wider discussion of the army and its role before World War I, relevant also for succeeding chapters, may be found in John Gooch, *Army, State and Society in Italy, 1870–1915* (New York, 1989). On the Papal State, Frank J. Coppa's *Cardinal Giacomo Antonelli and Papal Politics in European Affairs* argues that the policies for which Antonelli was condemned were really the pope's.

In Italian, the discussion on this period in Nino Valeri, ed., *Storia d'Italia*, Vol. 4 (Turin, 1965), is complete, balanced, and richly illustrated. Volumes 5 and 6 of Candeloro's *Storia d'Italia moderna* (Milan, 1968, 1970) also give a detailed and excellent account. Raffaella Gherardi, *L'arte del compromesso: La politica della mediazione nell'Italia liberale* (Bologna, 1993), argues that the statesmen of the Right such as Minghetti were practical rather than ideological and that liberals of Right and Left stood ready to compromise. On some of the economic issues, see G. Are, *Il problema dello sviluppo industriale nell'età della Destra* (Pisa, 1965), Luciano Cafagna, "Industrialismo e politica economica dopo l'unità d'Italia," in *Annali dell'Istituto Giangiacomo Feltrinelli,* (Milan, 1962), pp. 150–82, while Romeo's previously cited *Risorgimento e capitalismo* includes a section on this period. On Sicily during this era, see Paolo Alatri, *Lotte politiche in Sicilia sotto il governo della Destra (1866–1874)* (Turin, 1954). The most concise story of the "brigandage" phenomenon is Franco Molfese's *Storia del brigantaggio dopo d'Unità* (Milan, 1966).

Chapter 10: Two "Parliamentary Dictators"

The developments discussed in this chapter are, again, unfortunately not well covered in English, although a general discussion may be found in the relevant sections of Christopher Seton-Watson's excellent *Italy from Liberalism to Fascism, 1870–1925* (London, 1967). Another general work, Christopher Duggan's *A Concise History of Italy* (Cambridge, 1994), suffers from the attempt to impose on all of Italian history a single, overwhelming theme above all others: disunity. Besides the works cited in this section, more follow in the next section of this essay, which is devoted to a discussion of more specific problems during this rich and understudied period. Giampiero Carocci's *Agostino Depretis e la politica interna italiana dal 1876 al 1887* (Turin, 1956) is a detailed study not only of Depretis but of the Italian politics of the period. Carlo Vallauri discusses Zanardelli's activities in *La politica liberale di Giuseppe Zanardelli dal 1876 al 1878* (Milan, 1967), while the biography of the man who conducted the survey of southern social conditions may still be consulted with profit: Stefano Jacini, *Un conservatore rurale della nuova Italia,* 2 vols. (Bari, 1926).

On international affairs, Federico Chabod's classic *Storia della politica estera italiana dal 1870 al 1896,* 2 vols. (Bari, 1965) is notable for its documentation and fundamental for an understanding of the entire period. Luigi Salvatorelli's discussion of the Triple Alliance, *La Triplice Alleanza. Storia diplomatica, 1877–1912* (Milan, 1939), provides a clear view of the diplomatic issues involved.

The most detailed biography of Crispi is Massimo Grillandi, *Crispi* (Turin, 1969). Nicolò Inglese's short biography, *Crispi,* (Milan, 1961), is less satisfactory but still worth consulting. Earlier works include a balanced interpretation of the controversial statesman by the distinguished Arturo Carlo Jemolo, *Crispi* (Florence, 1921), and a favorable one by Gioacchino Volpe, *Francesco Crispi* (Venice, 1928). Much primary material relating to Crispi has been published, including speeches and memoirs. See in English translation his *Memoirs*, 3 vols. (London, 1912–14).

The fundamental work on the African venture and Italian imperialism of the Crispi period has been written by Roberto Battaglia, *La prima guerra d'Africa* (Turin, 1958), which includes a detailed account of the Battle of Adowa. For an English-language view of the international implications of Italian actions in Africa, consult Arthur Marsden, "Salisbury and the Italians in 1896," *The Journal of Modern History* 40, no. 1 (March 1968): 91–117. On Italian policy in the area after the Crispi period, see the well-documented Alberto Aquarone, *Dopo Adua. Politica e amministrazione coloniale* (Rome, 1989). Although more valuable for information on the later periods of his life, Giovanni Giolitti's *Memoirs of My Life* (London, 1923) can be consulted for his views of Crispi's involvement in East Africa. On the first Giolitti cabinet, the best source is Gastone Manacorda, "Il primo ministero Giolitti," Pt. 1, *Studi Storici*, 2, no. 1 (January–March 1961): 88–103, and Pt. 2, *Studi Storici* 3, no. 1 (January–March 1963): 106–20.

Chapter 11: Social and Economic Dilemmas

The economic and social themes discussed in this chapter are fairly well covered in the literature. Gianni Toniolo's, *An Economic History of Liberal Italy 1850– 1918* (London and New York, 1990) is an excellent, clear, and brief treatment of the entire period covered by the author. On the agricultural crisis, see Emilio Sereni, *Il capitalismo nelle campagne, 1860–1900* (Turin, 1947), and P. D'Angiolini, "L'Italia al termine della crisi agraria della fine del secolo XIX," *Nuova Rivista Storica*, no. 3–4 (1969): 323–65. Shepard B. Clough's *The Economic History of Italy*, previously cited, provides a clear exposition of Italian economic development in its international context during this period. On public finance, see Isidore Sachs, *L'Italie, ses finances et son développement économique 1859– 1884* (Paris, 1885). Good general works covering the Italian economy of this period include Epicarmo Corbino, *Annali dell'economia italiana*, 5 vols. (Città di Castello, 1938), Gino Luzzatto, *L'economia italiana dal 1861 al 1914* (Milan, 1963), and, by the same author, "L'economia italiana nel primo decennio dell'unità," in *Rassegna storica del Risorgimento*, 1957. For local finances, see F. Volpi, *Le finanze dei comuni e delle province del Regno d'Italia, 1860–1890* (Turin, 1962); fiscal policy is examined in G. Parravini, *La politica fiscale e le entrate effettive del Regno d' Italia, 1860–1890* (Rome, 1958). The role of foreign investments is considered by Luigi De Rosa, *Iniziativa e capitale straniero nell'industria metalmeccanica del Mezzogiorno, 1840–1904* (Naples, 1968), and B. Gille, *Les investissments français en Italie (1815–1914)* (Turin, 1968).

On the question of economic growth and the tariff, see Alexander Gerschenkron, "Notes on the Rate of Industrial Growth in Italy, 1881–1913" *Journal of Economic History*, December 1955. Rosario Romeo provides a different version in *Breve storia della grande industria in Italia, 1861–1961* (Bologna, 1972). See also D. Morelli, *Il protezionismo industriale in Italia dall'unificazione del Regno* (Milan, 1920), and M. Calzavarini, "Il protezionismo industriale e la tariffa dognale del 1887," *Clio*, 1966. A good general idea of the issues involved in the economic question may be gained by reading Walt W. Rostow, *The Stages of Economic Growth* (Cambridge, 1960), and Alexander Gerschenkron, *Economic Backwardness in Historical Perspective* (Cambridge, 1962). A number of essays on the relevant questions are collected in A. Caracciolo, *La formazione dell'Italia industriale* (Bari, 1963). For an idea of the contribution by Marxist historians on the interpretation of the economics of this period, see *Problemi dell'Unità d'Italia. Atti del II convegno di studi gramsciani tenuto a Roma nei giorni 19–21 marzo 1960* (Rome, 1966). Luciano Cafagna's "L'industrializzazione italiana. La formazione di una 'base industriale' fra il 1896 e il 1914," *Studi Storici*, no. 3–4 (1961): 690–724, discusses the issue of retarded economic development. On the relationship between agricultural development and industry, see Renato Zangheri, "Agricoltura e sviluppo del capitalismo. Problemi storiografici," *Studi Storici*, no. 3–2 (1968): 531–63. Good studies on particular industries are too numerous to cite here, but a good review of the literature is G. Mori, "La storia dell'industria italiana contemporanea nei saggi, nelle ricerche e nelle pubblicazioni giubilari di questo dopoguerrra," *Annali dell'Istituto Giangiacomo Feltrinelli* II (1959): 264–366.

The literature on the North-South question is also abundant. See Shepard B. Clough and Carlo Livi, "Economic Growth in Italy: An Analysis of the Uneven Development of North and South," *Journal of Economic History* (September 1956): 334–49. Gustav Schachter, *The Italian South: Economic Development in Mediterranean Europe* (New York, 1965), gives an excellent perspective on the problem. Rosario Villari, *Il Sud nella storia d'Italia*, 2 vols. (Bari, 1966), has put together a very good anthology of writings on the subject. The demographic issues are discussed by Giuseppe Galasso in his essay "Lo sviluppo demografico del Mezzogiorno prima e dopo l'unità," in his *Mezzogiorno medievale e moderno* (Turin, 1965) and by M. Boldrini, "Un secolo di sviluppo della popolazione italiana," in *L'economia italiana dal 1861 al 1961* (Milan, 1961). In English, see Robert Dickinson, *The Population Problem of Southern Italy. An Essay in Social Geography* (Syracuse, 1955). Good statistics on emigration may be found in *Annuario statistico dell'emigrazione italiana dal 1876 al 1925, con notizie sull'emigrazione negli anni 1869–1875* (Rome, 1926). General statistics relating to the South are in Svimez, *Statistiche sul Mezzogiorno d'Italia 1861–1953*

(Rome, 1954), and Svimez, *Un secolo di statistiche italiane: Nord e Sud 1861–1961* (Rome, 1961). On southerners who returned and their impact, a theme emphasized by Gaetano Salvemini, see Dino Cinel, *The National Integration of Italian Return Migration, 1870–1929* (Cambridge, 1991).

Although the Mafia has attracted attention and there is a rich mine of memoirs and descriptions of social conditions, this important period is less well covered by scholars. See the relevant portions of Denis Mack Smith, *A History of Sicily. Modern Sicily after 1713* (London, 1968), Giuseppe Alongi, *La maffia* [sic] (Florence, 1886), and Raimondo Catanzaro, *Il delitto come impresa. Storia sociale della mafia* (Padua, 1988). Greater insight into the Mafia phenomenon may be gained through Eric Hobsbawm, *Primitive Rebels* (Manchester, 1959), and Anton Blok, *The Mafia of a Sicilian Village* (Prospect Heights, 1988). For a history of the Mafia, see Salvatore F. Romano, *Storia della mafia* (Milan, 1963). The Mafia's organization is described in Henner Hess, *Mafia and Mafiosi: The Structure of Power* (Lexington, MA, 1973). An excellent history of the island during this period is Francesco De Stefano and Francesco Luigi Oddo, *Storia della Sicilia dal 1860 al 1910* (Bari, 1963).

On the Catholic movement, see the classic work by Arturo Carlo Jemolo, *Chiesa e stato in Italia dalla unificazione a Giovanni XXIII* (Turin, 1965), Gabriele De Rosa, *L'Azione Cattolica. Storia politica dal 1874 al 1904* (Bari, 1953), and Fausto Fonzi, *I cattolici e la società italiana dopo l'unità* (Rome, 1953). Giorgio Candeloro's *Il movimento cattolico in Italia* (Rome, 1953) is an excellent work, while Giovanni Spadolini's *L'opposizione cattolica da Porta Pia al '98* (Florence, 1961) is the classic comprehensive history of the subject during the years under consideration. S. Secco Suardo concentrates on the intransigents in *I cattolici intransigenti* (Brescia, 1962), while Sándor Agócs examines the ideology and action of Catholic social activists in *The Troubled Origins of the Italian Catholic Labor Movement, 1878–1914* (Detroit, 1988). The school system is discussed by D. Bertoni Jovine, *La scuola italiana dal 1870 ai giorni nostri* (Rome, 1958).

The Anarchist movement has been examined with great acumen by Pier Carlo Masini in *Storia degli anarchici italiani. Da Bakunin a Malatesta* (Milan, 1969) and *Storia degli anarchici nell'epoca degli attentati* (Milan, 1981). The best general history of Italian anarchism during this period in English is Nunzio Pernicone's *Italian Anarchism, 1864–1892* (Princeton, 1993). There is also the ground-breaking older work by Richard Hostetter, *The Italian Socialist Movement. Vol I: Origins (1860–1882)* (New York, 1958). Bakunin's relationship with the Italians is the subject of a book by T. R. Ravindranathan, *Bakunin and the Italians* (Montreal, 1988). Aldo Romano's *Storia del movimento socialista italiano*, 3 vols. (Turin, 1954–56) exhibits a strong anti-Bakunin viewpoint. A general view of anarchism is Enzo Santarelli, *Il socialismo anarchico in Italia* (Milan, 1959). The early congresses of the fledgling Italian labor movement are the subject of Gastone Manacorda's *Il movimento operaio italiano attraverso i suoi congressi, 1853–1892* (Rome, 1953). Franco Della Peruta has examined the failure of Anarchist methods in "La banda del Matese e il fallimento della teoria anarchica della moderna 'jacquerie' in Italia," *Movimento Operaio*, no. 3, 1954. The Radicals have been examined by Giovanni Spadolini, *I radicali dell'Ottocento* (Florence, 1960), and by Stefano Merli, "La democrazia radicale in Italia (1866–1898)," *Movimento Operaio*, no.1, 1955. Important documentation on the movement has also been published: Liliana Delle Nogare and Stefano Merli, eds., *L'Italia Radicale. Carteggi di Felice Cavallotti, 1867–1898* (Milan, 1959); S. Ganci, ed., *Democrazia e socialismo in Italia. Carteggi di Napoleone Colajanni, 1878–1898* (Milan, 1959); and, especially, Pier Carlo Masini, ed., *La scapigliatura democratica. Carteggi di Arcangelo Ghisleri, 1875–1890* (Milan, 1960).

For the early Socialist movement, see Elio Conti, *Le origini del socialismo a Firenze (1860–1880)* (Rome, 1950), Felice Anzi, *Il movimento operaio socialista italiano (1882–1894)* (Rome, 1946), and, by the same author, *Origini e funzioni delle camere del lavoro* (Milan, n.d.). General considerations on Costa can be found in A. Berselli, ed., *Andrea Costa nella storia del socialismo italiano* (Bologna, 1982); the story of his party in the Romagna is told in Manuel Gonzales, *Andrea Costa and the Rise of Socialism in the Romagna* (Washington, D.C., 1980). Stefano Merli has published a collection of legal defenses by left-wing defendants, *Autodifese di militanti operai e democratici italiani davanti ai Tribunali* (Milan, 1958). Ernesto Ragionieri has studied the influence of German social democracy on Italian socialists in *Socialdemocrazia tedesca e socialisti italiani 1875–1895* (Milan, 1961). Luigi Cortesi's book, *La costituzione del partito socialista italiano* (Milan, 1962) tells the story of the PSI's foundation. Cortesi has also published a compendium of Turati's early works, *Turati giovane: scapigliatura, positivismo, marxismo* (Milan, 1962). The most monumental and detailed work on early socialism is the collected work edited by Giovanni Sabbatucci, *Storia del socialismo italiano. Volume primo: Dalle origini alla svolta di fine secolo* (Rome, 1981). The Sicilian *fasci* are examined in detail by Gastone Manacorda, et. al., *I fasci siciliani*, 2 vols. (Bari, 1975). For Anna Kuliscioff's early life as a Russian revolutionary, see Franco Venturi's excellent article, "Anna Kuliscioff e la sua attività rivoluzionaria in Russia," *Movimento Operaio*, 4 (March-April 1952): 277–86; see also the documents on Costa in the same issue. Kuliscioff's letters to Costa, with an excellent intoduction, have been published as *Lettere d'amore a Andrea Costa, 1880–1909* (Milan, 1976). On Antonio Labriola, the most important Marxist philosopher of this age, see Luigi

Dal Pane, *Antonio Labriola, la vita e il pensiero* (Rome, 1935). A contemporary work with living profiles of the Socialists of this period is Alfredo Angiolini, *Socialismo e socialisti in Italia* (Florence, 1900).

The following chapters in Edward R. Tannenbaum and Emiliana P. Noether, eds., *Modern Italy: A Topical History since 1861* (New York, 1974), offer good surveys on the issues considered in this chapter during and beyond the time span considered: Denis Mack Smith, "Regionalism," pp. 125–46; Jon S. Cohen, "Economic Growth," pp. 171–96; Nunzio Pernicone, "The Italian Labor Movement," pp. 197–230; Edward R. Tannenbaum, "Education," pp. 231–53; and Raymond Grew, "Catholicism in a Changing Italy," pp. 254–73.

Chapter 12: The Rise of Socialism and the Giolittian Era

The political, economic, and social questions of the years from 1900 to 1914 have given rise to a rich historical literature. The translation of Giolitti's memoirs has already been cited, but the original version, *Memorie della mia vita* (Milan, 1967), is far superior. In addition, Giolitti's parliamentary and extra-parliamentary speeches have been published, and most interesting is the archival collection of his correspondence with the prefects and crucial political leaders: Istituto Giangiacomo Feltrinelli, *Dalle carte di Giovanni Giolitti: Quarant'anni di politica italiana*, 3 vols. (Milan, 1962). Biographies of Giolitti are not plentiful in Italian and (so far) nonexistent in English. The most complete is the balanced Nino Valeri, *Giolitti* (Turin, 1972). Valeri, however, keeps in mind Giolitti's later role in the rise of fascism; a more recent attempt to look at Giolitti according to the statesman's own objectives is Sergio Romano, *Giolitti: lo stile del potere* (Milan, 1989).

The best biographies produced after Salomone's "rehabilitation" of Giolitti, overly influenced by this event but still essential for an understanding of the historiographical debate, are Giovanni Ansaldo, *Il ministro della buona vita* (Milan, 1949), and the work by Giolitti's friend Gaetano Natale, *Giolitti e gli italiani* (Milan, 1949). The pamphlet by Alfredo Frassati, *Giolitti* (Florence, 1959), gives a quick overview. On reevaluation of Giolitti and Italian politics during the period, the essential work is A. William Salomone, *Italy in the Giolittian Era: Italian Democracy in the Making 1900–1914*, 2d ed. (Philadelphia, 1960). This edition retains Salvemini's famous "Introductory Essay" and is enriched by a new section, "Giolittian Italy Revisited," bringing the discussion up to 1960. Salvemini's *Il ministro della mala vita* can be found along with his other writings on Giolittian Italy in Elio Apih, ed., *Gaetano Salvemini. Il ministro della mala vita e altri scritti sull'Italia giolittiana*, Opere IV, Vol. 1 (Milan, 1966). Salvemini's theses are at the origin of Antonio Gramsci's negative criticisms about an explicit northern "deal" between Giolitti and the Socialists to the South's detriment, a contention that can be found in Gramsci's *Il Risorgimento* (Turin, 1955). For the development of this thesis in Marxist hands, compare Palmiro Togliatti's scurrilous "Turatiana," in *Stato Operaio*, April 1932, and the same author's sophisms on the issue, after the publication of Salomone's book, in his *Discorso su Giolitti* (Rome, 1950). An author who believes that this conjunction between the reformists and Giolitti did not come about, at least not in the terms proposed by Communist historiography, is Brunello Vegezzi, *Giolitti e Turati: Un incontro mancato*, 2 vols. (Milan-Naples, 1976). Two useful collected works on Giolitti may round out various aspects of his tenure, *Istituzioni e metodi politici dell'età giolittiana* (Turin, 1979) and *L'Italia di Giolitti* (Milan, 1981).

The attempt to give a more articulated interpretation of the Giolittian period is achieved by Giampiero Carocci, *Giolitti e l'età giolittiana* (Turin, 1961), who argues that the Giolittian period arose from a need to liquidate the heavy-handed governmental methods of the nineteenth century. The most successful attempt to view the age in its own terms by examining in depth the details of governmental action and their relation to Italian life of the period has been made by Alberto Aquarone in *L'Italia giolittiana (1896–1915)* (Bologna, 1981) and in the posthumously published *Tre capitoli sull'Italia giolittiana* (Bologna, 1987). Aquarone also made an excellent exposition of his historical method in "A Closing Commentary: Problems of Democracy and the Quest for Identity," in the previously cited *Modern Italy: A Topical History since 1861*, pp. 355–76. An excellent and more popular treatment of the Giolittian "world" is given by Giovanni Spadolini, *Il mondo di Giolitti* (Florence, 1970). Ronald S. Cunsolo brings the historiographical issues up to date in "The Great Debate on Prime Minister Giovanni Giolitti and Giolittian Italy," *Canadian Review of Studies in Nationalism* 18, no. 1–2 (1991): 95–115. Denis Mack Smith discusses the kings of united Italy in *Italy and Its Monarchy* (New Haven, 1989).

On economic aspects of the Giolittian era, see Frank J. Coppa's positive treatment of Giolitti's policies in *Economics and Politics in the Giolittian Age* (Washington, D.C., 1971). For the effects of tariff policy, see the same author's "The Italian Tariff and the Conflict between Agriculture and Industry: The Commerical Policy of Liberal Italy, 1860–1922," *The Journal of Economic History*, no. 4 (1970). Coppa has also published an essay on Giolittian policies in the South in Frank Coppa, *Studies in Modern Italian History*, already cited, "Giolitti and the *Mezzogiorno*," pp. 59–78. A more strictly economic history is the excellent work by Valerio Castronovo treating the entire period after unity but particularly good on the early twentieth century, "La storia economica," in the Einaudi *Storia d'Italia. Dall'Unità a oggi*, Vol. 4 (Turin, 1975). Luciano

Cafagna discusses the formation of a modern industry during the period in "La formazione di una 'base industriale' fra il 1896 e il 1914," *Studi Storici,* no. 3–4 (July-December 1961): 690–724, already cited. General histories include the older but still useful Epicarmo Corbino, *Annali della economia italiana (1861–1915)* (Città di Castello, 1931–38), previously cited, Alberto Caracciolo, ed., *La formazione dell'Italia industriale,* 3d ed. (Bari, 1972), Rodolfo Morandi, *Storia della grande industria in Italia* (Turin, 1966), and Rosario Romeo, *Breve storia della grande industria in Italia* (Bologna, 1972). For economics and the changing nature of Italian imperialism, see Richard A. Webster, *Industrial Imperialism in Italy, 1908–1915* (Berkeley and Los Angeles, 1975; consult also the more extensive Italian edition). On industrial workers, Duccio Bigazzi's *Il portello: Operai, tecnici e imprenditori all'Alfa Romeo 1906–1926* is especially good on the workforce of one of Italy's most famous automobile firms.

For the effect of the Libyan War on the Giolittian system's breakdown, see Ronald Cunsolo, "Libya, Italian Nationalism, and the Revolt against Giolitti," *Journal of Modern History,* June 1965, and, by the same author, "Libya and the Undoing of the Giolittian System," in Frank Coppa, ed., *Studies in Modern Italian History,* previously cited, pp. 79–102. Maurizio Degl'Innocenti has linked the Libyan War, Socialist policies, and the collapse of the Giolittian system in *Il socialismo italiano e la guerra di Libia* (Rome, 1976). For the changes in Mussolini and Italian socialism as a result of Red Week, see Spencer Di Scala, " 'Red Week' 1914: Prelude to War and Revolution," in the cited *Studies in Modern Italian History,* pp. 123–33. Connections between the prewar revolutionary syndicalist movement and Fascist personalities may be found in David D. Roberts, *The Syndicalist Tradition and Italian Fascism* (Chapel Hill, 1979), and Renzo De Felice's first volume of Mussolini's life, *Mussolini il rivoluzionario* (Turin, 1965).

On socialism in general, Gaetano Arfé has written a good history up to 1926, *Storia del socialismo italiano (1892–1926)* (Turin, 1965), while Antonio Landolfi's work, *Storia del Psi* (Milan, 1990), comes up to the present and integrates the latest research. The most detailed work is Giovanni Sabbatucci, ed., *Storia del socialismo italiano. Volume Secondo: L'Età Giolittiana (1900–1914)* (Palermo, 1981). Z. Ciffoletti, M. Degl'Innocenti, and G. Sabbatucci's, *Storia del PSI. 1. Le origini e l'età giolittiana* (Bari, 1992) attempts to tell the history of the PSI from an integrated political and social viewpoint utilizing the latest scholarship. Other older, general histories include Giacomo Perticone, *Linee di storia del socialismo,* 2d ed. (Milan, 1944), Leo Valiani, *Questioni di storia del socialismo* (Turin, 1958), and the insightful essay by the same author, "Il partito socialista italiano dal 1900 al 1918," *Rivista Storica Italiana,* no. 75 (1963). Maurizio Degl'Innocenti's study of early Socialist structures, *Geografia e istituzioni del socialismo italiano* (Naples, 1983), is a valuable contribution to the field. The correspondence of Engels with Turati and Kulscioff, along with other writings, may be found in Gianni Bosio, ed., *Karl Marx-Friedrich Engles: Scritti italiani* (Milan-Rome, 1955).

The historiographical "rehabilitation" of Turati and a discussion of the movement's policies and problems may be found in Spencer Di Scala, *Dilemmas of Italian Socialism: The Politics of Filippo Turati* (Amherst, 1980). James Edward Miller discusses the nature of the prewar PSI and Mussolini's "innovations" in *From Elite to Mass Politics: Italian Socialism in the Giolittian Era, 1900–1914* (Kent, Ohio, 1990). The correspondence between Turati and Kulscioff, indispensable for an understanding of this and the period up to Mussolini's takeover, has been published, *Carteggio*, 7 vols. (Turin, 1949–78). Other correspondence may be found in Alessandro Schiavi, ed., *Filippo Turati attraverso le lettere di corrispondenti (1880–1925)* (Bari, 1947), and *Esilio e morte di Filippo Turati* (Rome, 1956); collections of Turati speeches at party congresses and some interesting writings are in *Le vie maestre del socialismo*, 2d. ed. (Naples, 1966). Schiavi has also written a short biography of Turati, *Filippo Turati* (Rome, 1955), and of his companion, *Anna Kulscioff* (Rome, 1955). Marina Addis Saba's *Anna Kulscioff. Vita privata e passione politica* (Milan, 1993) is a rare biography of the feminist and Socialist leader. Franco Catalano's *Filippo Turati* (Milan, 1957) is basically an overview. Two more recent long biographies of Turati may be useful for information but are biased and not very satisfactory: Renato Monteleone, *Turati* (Turin, 1987), and Franco Livorsi, *Turati* (Milan, 1984). On Kulscioff, see also the collection edited by Turati on the occasion of her death, *Anna Kulscioff, in memoria: A Lei, agli intimi, a me* (Milan, 1926). The essays in *Anna Kulscioff e l'età del riformismo* (Rome, 1978) provide an excellent idea of her influence on Italian socialism. Claire La Vigna's essay, "Anna Kulscioff in Italy," *Italian Quarterly* 20, nos. 77–78 (Summer-Fall 1976): 65–85 is a synthetic summary of her action in Italy. A sense of Turati's local political action and its relationship to national questions may be achieved by consulting Spencer Di Scala, "Filippo Turati, the Milanese Schism, and the Reconquest of the Italian Socialist Party, 1901–1909," *Il Politico* (March 1979): 153–63. Giuseppe Mammarella takes up the specific action of reformists and revolutionaries in *Riformisti e rivoluzionari nel partito socialista italiano, 1900–1912* (Padua, 1968), a question also examined by Brunello Vigezzi in *Il PSI, le riforme e la rivoluzione (1898–1915)* (Florence, 1981).

Less controversial than Turati, Bissolati has been treated better by historians, for example, Ugoberto Alfassio Grimaldi and Gherardo Bozzetti, *Bissolati* (Milan, 1983), and Raffaele Colapietra, *Leonida Bissolati* (Milan, 1958). See also the book by Bissolati's collaborator Ivanoe Bonomi, *Leonida Bissolati e il mov-*

imento socialista in Italia (Milan, 1929). Bonomi's own role has been examined by Luigi Cortesi, *Ivanoe Bonomi e la socialdemocrazia italiana. Profilo biografico* (Salerno, 1971). An examination of Arturo Labriola's revolutionary syndicalism is Dora Marucco's *Arturo Labriola e il sindacalismo rivoluzionario* (Turin, 1970). Gaetano Salvemini's influence on the Socialist movement may be measured by his collected writings on the South during this period collected by Gaetano Arfé, *Gaetano Salvemini. Movimento socialista e questione meridionale* Opere IV, Vol. 2 (Milan, 1963), and Massimo Salvadori, *Gaetano Salvemini* (Turin, 1963). Essential for an understanding of Salvemini's thinking are the most complete editions of his correspondence and an anthology of his writings of this period, edited by Enzo Tagliacozzo and Sergio Bucchi, *Carteggio 1894–1902* (Bari, 1988) and *Carteggio 1912–1914* (Bari,1984), and *Gaetano Salvemini. Socialismo riformismo democrazia* (Bari, 1990).

On the Socialist congresses, a compendium has been published by Franco Pedone, *Il partito socialista italiano nei suoi congressi*, 4 vols. (Milan, 1963). Gaetano Arfé has published an informative history of the Socialist party daily up to 1940, *Storia dell'Avanti!*, 2 vols. (Milan, 1956–58).

The Italian labor movement has received attention from two American scholars, Daniel Horowitz, *The Italian Labor Movement* (Cambridge, 1963), and Maurice Neufield, *Italy: School for Awakening Countries* (Ithaca, 1961). Carlo Cartiglia's view of the period's pioneer labor leader, *Rinaldo Rigola e il sindacalismo riformista in Italia* (Milan, 1976), is overly colored by Rigola's naive actions during the Fascist period. The documents of the Socialist labor union have been conveniently collected by Luciana Marchetti, *La Confederazione Generale del Lavoro negli atti, nei documenti, nei congressi 1906–1926* (Milan, 1962). Adolfo Pepe has written a history of the CGL up to the Libyan War, *Storia della Confederazione generale del lavoro dalla fondazione alla guerra di Libia, 1905–1911* (Bari, 1972). Elda Gentili Zappi's *If Eight Hours Seem Too Few: Mobilization of Women Workers in the Italian Rice Fields* (Albany, 1991) examines the attempts of Socialist leagues to find support among female workers. An exhaustive description of peasant conditions is provided by Giuliano Procacci, "Geografia e struttura del movimento contadino della valle padana nel suo periodo formativo (1901–1906)," *Studi Storici* 5, no. 1 (January–March 1964).

The 1898 crisis is analyzed by Umberto Levra, *Il colpo di stato della borghesia: La crisi politica di fine secolo in Italia, 1896–1898* (Milan, 1975). The social and political changes in Italy's most advanced industrial city during the same period are examined by Louise Tilly, *Politics and Class in Milan* (New York, 1992), and Volker Hunecke, "Comune e classe operaia a Milano (1858–1898)," *Studi Storici* 18, no. 3 (July-September 1983). Luigi Pelloux's memoirs, *Quelques sou-*

venirs de ma vie (Rome, 1967), are a fundamental and underutilized source. For insights on the operations of Parliament, see Salvatore Saladino's essay in the cited *Modern Italy: A Topical History*, "Parliamentary Politics in the Liberal Era," pp. 27–51, and the general history by the same author, *Italy from Unification to 1919* (New York, 1970).

On the Catholic movement, besides the works already cited, see Giovanni Spadolini's very informative *Giolitti e i cattolici 1901–1914* (Florence, 1960) and Gabriele De Rosa's biography of a major leader of the period, *Filippo Meda e l'età liberale* (Florence, 1959). For an overview of the relationship between Socialists, Catholics, and Giolitti, there is Spencer Di Scala, "Socialists and Catholics in the Giolittian Era," *La Parola del Popolo* 28, no. 69 (March-April 1977): 54–56. See also Frank J. Coppa, "Giolitti and the Gentiloni Pact between Myth and Reality," *The Catholic Historical Review* 53, no. 2 (July 1967): 217–28, which argues that the "pact" has been misinterpreted.

Chapter 13: The Culture of the New Italy

Material on private lives during this period must be culled from a variety of sources, especially correspondence, periodicals, and novels. In English, the short piece by R.J.B. Bosworth, "The Opening of the Victor Emmanuel Monument," *Italian Quarterly* 18, no. 71 (Winter 1975): 78–87, gives a taste of life in 1911. A good overview of the demographic growth and the changes taking place in the cities is provided by Luigi De Rosa, "Urbanization and Industrialization in Italy (1861–1921)," *The Journal of European Economic History* 17, no. 3 (Winter 1988): 467–90. Aldo Alessandro Mola's *1882–1912: Fare gli italiani. Una società nuova in uno Stato vecchio* (Turin, 1975) combines social analysis with documents and statistics. The multivolume Einaudi history of Italy includes two large volumes of relevance to this and other sections regarding social history and the development of science and technology. They are Franco Della Peruta, ed., *Storia d'Italia. Annali 7. Malattia e medicina* (Turin, 1984), and Gianni Micheli, ed., *Storia d'Italia. Annali 3. Scienza e tecnica nella cultura e nella società dal Rinascimento a oggi* (Turin, 1980). Mary Gibson discusses prostitution during this period in *Prostitution and the State in Italy, 1860–1915* (New Brunswick, 1986). The book edited by Edward Muir and Guido Ruggiero, *Sex and Gender in Historical Perspective* (Baltimore and London, 1990), includes one essay on the social relationships and the role of women during the time period discussed in this chapter.

A number of general works examine the literature of this period. The best include the collection of Benedetto Croce's essays, *La letteratura della nuova Italia*, 6 vols. (Bari, 1967); Gaetano Mariani and Mario Petrucciani, eds. *Letter-*

atura contemporanea italiana (Rome, 1979), vols. 1 and 2, which also include a discussion of dialectical literature; and the massive Gianni Grana, ed. *Novecento*, 10 vols. (Milan, 1980), which provides the economic and social context of the literature examined. Emilio Cecchi's *Letteratura italiana del Novecento* (Milan, 1972) is a high-level work, while Alfredo Galletti's *Il Novecento*, 4th ed. (Milan, 1967) in the *Storia letteraria d'Italia* multivolume set gives a particularly detailed view of this period. Piero Bigongiari, *Poesia italiana del Novecento* (Milan, 1978), provides an introduction to poetry. Brief histories such as J. H. Whitfield, *A Short History of Italian Literature* (Westport, CT, 1960), are less satisfactory but may serve as an introduction.

Works on the music of this period and biographies of the musicians cited are readily available, but an unusually good chapter on Verdi's politics may be found in Paul Robinson, *Opera and Ideas* (New York, 1985). An attempt to give a complete portrait of the great composer, faults and all, is Mary Jane Philips Matz, *Verdi. A Biography* (New York, 1994).

Specialized works on Italian painting of the age may be consulted. Albert Boime, *The Art of the Macchia and the Risorgimento: Representing Culture and Nationalism in Nineteenth-Century Italy* (Chicago, 1993), attempts a reevaluation of the international reputation of the Macchiaioli. In English also, Lionello Venturi's critical study, *Italian Painting* (New York, 1952), has a section on this period, while James Thrall Soby and Alfred H. Barr, *Twentieth Century Italian Art*, 2 vols. (New York, 1949), is more complete. Good general works include Emily Braun, ed., *Italian Art in the 20th Century* (Munich and London, 1989), Corrado Maltese, *Storia dell'arte in Italia, 1785–1943* (Turin, 1960), and Pontus Hulten and Germano Celant, eds., *Arte Italiana: Presenze 1900–1945* (Milan, 1989). See also Dario Cecchi's full-scale biography of painter *Giovanni Boldini* (Turin, 1962).

On futurism, consult Giusi Baldissoni, *Filippo Tommaso Marinetti* (Milan, 1986), which combines biography and criticism. Isabella Gherarducci, *Il futurismo* (Rome, 1984), gives good criticisms and readings, while Anna Elena Giammarco's, *Le forme poetiche nei futuristi* (Rome, 1977) is a short analytical work on the poetry. See as well Ester Coen, *Umberto Boccioni* (New York, 1988), Claudia Salaris, *Storia del futurismo* (Rome, 1985), and Pontus Hulten, ed., *Futurismo e futurismi* (Milan, 1986).

On architecture, see Richard A. Etlin, *Modernism in Italian Architecture, 1890–1940* (Cambridge, Ma, 1991).

Catalogs of exhibitions can sometimes be a good introduction to art; some that might be profitably consulted are: Maria Cristina Gozzoli and Fernando Mazzocca, *Hayez* (Milan, n.d.); *Arte moderna in Italia, 1915–1935* (Florence, 1967); Commisariato Generale d'Italia per l'Expo '86, *Futur-Balla* (Milan, 1986);

Maurizio Calvesi, *Boccioni prefuturista* (Milan, 1983); and Maurizio Fagiolo dell'Arco, *Severini prima e dopo l'opera* (Florence, 1983).

An idea of the Italian cinema within the general cinematic context may be gleaned in Gianni Rondolino, *Storia del cinema* , Vol. 1 (Turin, 1977). General histories that consider this period, among others, include Pierre Leprophon, *The Italian Cinema* (London, 1972), and Carlo Lizzani, *Il cinema italiano, 1895–1979*, Vol. 1 (Rome, 1979). Useful specific works on the early days of Italian filmmaking are: Aldo Bernardini, *Cinema muto italiano: industria e organizzazione dello spettacolo, 1905–1909* (Rome, 1981), *Cinema muto italiano: arte, divismo e mercato, 1910–1914* (Rome, 1982), and *Cinema muto italiano: ambiente, spettacoli e spettatori, 1896–1904* (Bari, 1980); Roberto Paolella, *Storia del cinema muto* (Naples, 1956); Mario Verdone, *Cinema e letteratura del futurismo* (Rome, 1968); and Riccardo Redi, *Ti parlerò d'amore. Cinema italiano fra muto e sonoro* (Turin, 1986). The film journal *Bianco e Nero* published a thorough review of Italian films of the 1920s in its issues of 1980 and 1981.

Emiliana P. Noether contributed an essay on "Italian Intellectuals" in the previously cited volume, *Modern Italy: A Topical History*, edited by Tannenbaum and Noether, which may serve as a general introduction to the period. Leone Bortone's chapter, "La cultura politica," in Nino Valeri, *Storia d'Italia*, Vol. 4 (Turin, 1965), is an incisive and exhaustive summary. Catholic modernism, with rich chapters on Italy and an analysis of Fogazzaro's important novel *Il Santo*, is considered by Michele Ranchetti, *The Catholic Modernists. A Study of the Religious Reform Movement* (London, 1969). Richard Drake, *Byzantium for Rome. The Politics of Nostalgia in Umbertian Italy, 1878–1900* (Chapel Hill, 1980), is best at tracing the development of intellectual resentment during this period and pointing out its link with the rest of Europe. In his long chapter on Italy in *The Generation of 1914* (Cambridge, 1979), Robert Wohl makes the link more apparent and establishes a connection with fascism. Walter L. Adamson examines the relationship of "modernist" culture in Florence—as expressed in journals such as *La Voce*—and Facist ideology and rhetoric in *Avant-Garde Florence: From Modernism to Fascism* (Cambridge, 1993).

Works providing an intimate view of the Nationalists are Enrico Corradini, *Discorsi politici, 1902–1923* (Florence, 1923), *Il nazionalismo italiano* (Milan, 1914), *L'ora di Tripoli* (Milan, 1911), and Pier Ludovico Occhini, *Enrico Corradini e la nuova coscienza nazionale* (Florence, 1925). An explanation of Nationalist desires is in Alfredo Rocco, *Che cosa è e che cosa vogliono i nazionalisti* (Padua, 1914). Giovanni Papini and Giuseppe Prezzolini explain their later nationalism in *Vecchio e nuovo nazionalismo* (Milan, 1914). Papini's autobiography, *Un uomo finito* (Florence, 1974), gives a precious insight into the workings of the mind of a rightist intellectual of this period. For an example of Nationalist views on Libya, look at P. Vinassa de Regny, *Libya Italica* (Milan, 1913), and Giuseppe Piazza, *La nostra terra promessa* (Rome, 1911); for an excellent contemporary analysis of the Nationalist role during this period, consult Gaetano Salvemini, *Come siamo andati in Libia* (Florence, 1914). Ronald S. Cunsolo combines interpretation and readings in *Italian Nationalism from Its Origins to World War II* (Malabar, Florida, 1990). The best work on the Nationalist Association is Alexander De Grand, *The Italian Nationalist Association and the Rise of Fascism in Italy* (Lincoln, NE, 1978), while the best essay in English on the rise of a "new" right in Italy is Salvatore Saladino's essay in Hans Rogger and Eugen Weber, *The European Right: A Historical Profile* (Berkeley and Los Angeles, 1966).

On D'Annunzio, see the biographies by Philippe Jullian, *d'Annunzio* (London, 1972), and the older but still useful Tom Antongini, *D'Annunzio* (New York, 1971 reprint). For a short critical introduction and guide to D'Annunzio's work, consult Anco Marzio Mutterle, *Gabriele D'Annunzio* (Florence, 1980).

Many good studies exist in English on Mosca and Pareto, and their works have also been translated. An excellent short introduction to Gaetano Mosca is Ettore A. Albertoni, *Mosca and the Theory of Elitism* (Oxford, 1985), and to Pareto, Joseph Lopreato, *Vilfredo Pareto* (New York, 1965). There is a good introduction by S. E. Finer in his edition of *Vilfredo Pareto: Sociological Writings* (New York, 1966). The essays in James H. Meisel, ed., *Pareto and Mosca* (Englewood Cliffs, NJ, 1965), are excellent and highly recommended. Richard Bellamy takes the long view in *Modern Italian Social Theory: Ideology and Politics from Pareto to the Present* (Cambridge, 1987). On Robert Michels's work and his connection with Italy, see the chapter putting that writer in Italian and German context, in Arthur Mitzman, *Sociology and Estrangement* (New York, 1973). Armand Patrucco has produced an excellent study on the effects of Mosca and Pareto's thought within the general context of the criticism of the parliamentary system, *The Critics of the Italian Parliamentary System, 1860–1915* (New York and London, 1992). On Croce's importance for Western thought, see H. Stuart Hughes, *Consciousness and Society* (New York, 1961); for a recent assessment of the philospher, there is David D. Roberts, *Benedetto Croce and the Uses of Historicism* (Berkeley, 1987).

Chapter 14: World War I and the Red Biennium

Students wishing to understand the general diplomatic situation before and during World War I would do well to consult the previously cited classic by A.J.P. Taylor, *The Struggle for Mastery in Europe, 1848–1918* (Oxford, 1965). The best book on the diplomatic issues leading up to and during the Libyan War is still William C. Askew, *Europe and Italy's Acquisition of Libya, 1911–1912* (Durham, NC, 1942). In addition to general European diplomacy and the war's outbreak, Italy's position is exceptionally well analyzed by Luigi Albertini, editor of the country's major newspaper who knew many of the Italian protagonists personally. His magisterial work has been translated as *The Origins of the War of 1914*, 3 vols. (Oxford, 1965). Albertini was an important figure in Italy and his memoirs, *Venti anni di vita politica*, 2 vols. (Bologna, 1969), may be consulted with profit on all issues of the day. The military aspects of Italy's connection with the Triple Alliance are treated in Fortunato Minniti, *Esercito e politica da Porta Pia alla Triplice alleanza* (Rome, 1984). Rino Longhitano, *Antonino di San Giuliano* (Milan, 1954), is a rare work on the Italian foreign minister. R.J.B. Bosworth's *Italy, the Least of the Great Powers: Italian Foreign Policy before the First World War* (London, 1979) is marred by the author's attempt to establish too close a "continuity" between the foreign policy of Liberal and of Fascist Italy, but it is nevertheless an interesting and informative book. Bosworth's collaborative effort with Sergio Romano examining Italian foreign policy from 1860 to 1985, *La politica estera italiana 1860–1985* (Bologna, 1991), includes some excellent essays and others that are less useful. Bosworth has also published a short work on *Italy and the Approach of the First World War* (London, 1983), but see also Roy Price, "Italy and the Outbreak of the First World War," *The Cambridge Historical Journal* 11, no. 2 (1954): 219–27. Also in English there is a W. A. Renzi's account of the neutrality period, *In the Shadow of the Sword: Italy's Neutrality and Entrance into the Great War, 1914–1915* (New York, 1987). Balanced views on Italian foreign policy by a protagonist are in Leonida Bissolati, *La politica estera dell'Italia dal 1897 al 1920* (Milan, 1923). Gaetano Salvemini's *La politica estera dell'Italia* (Florence, 1944) is a good work by one of Italy's leading historians. William C. Askew's "The Austro-Italian Antagonism, 1896–1914," in Lillian Parker Wallace, ed., *Power, Public Opinion, and Diplomacy* (New York, 1968), is an outstanding overview of the Austro-Italian relationship and the issues dividing the two "allies." Askew has also published "Foreign Policy and Diplomacy after Unification," in the previously cited Tannenbaum and Noether, *Modern Italy*. On Albania, Renzo Falaschi combines interpretation with an interesting set of Italian documents (translated also into English) up to 1921 in *Ismail Kemal Bey Vlora. Il pensiero e l'opera attraverso i documenti italiani* (Rome, 1985). James Burgwyn has published two valuable articles on Italian diplomatic activity in the Balkans on the eve of war and during the conflict, "Sonnino e la diplomazia italiana del tempo di guerra nei Balcani nel 1915," *Storia Contemporanea* 16, no. 1 (February 1985): 113–37, and "Italy's Balkan Policy 1915–1917. Albania, Greece and the Epirus Question," *Storia delle relazioni internazionali* 2, no. 1 (1986): 3–61.

The excellent book by John Thayer, *Italy and the Great War* (Madison and Milwaukee, 1964), provides a probing analysis of the Italian cultural milieu during the interventionist debate and in the period before the war.

The best work examining Italy's neutrality from all aspects is Brunello Vigezzi's massive *L'Italia di fronte alla prima guerra mondiale, vol 1. L'Italia neutrale* (Milan-Naples, 1966), while Isacco Artom's, *Iniziative neutralistiche della diplomazia italiana nel 1870 e nel 1915* (Turin, 1954) is useful for the diplomacy of the neutrality period. Relations with Germany during neutrality are expertly examined in Alberto Monticone, *La Germania e la neutralità italiana 1914–1915* (Bologna, 1971). Leo Valiani's, *Il partito socialista italiano nel periodo della neutralità 1914–1915* (Milan, 1963) is a classic work on the Socialist party during months of neutrality. For the impact of the interventionist crisis on the parliamentary system, see Spencer Di Scala, "Parliamentary Socialists, the *Statuto* and the Giolittian System," *Australian Journal of Politics and History* 25, no. 2 (August 1979): 157–68. A prominent diplomatic historian examines the negotiations and the Pact of London, Mario Toscano, *Il patto di Londra* (Bologna, 1934). H. James Burgwyn revises earlier notions of Italy's foreign policy under Sonnino in *The Legend of the Mutilated Victory: Italy, the Great War, and the Paris Peace Conference, 1915–1919* (Westport, CT, 1993). Of the writings left by the protagonists, consult Sidney Sonnino, *Diario 1914–1916* (Bari, 1972); Antonio Salandra, *La neutralità italiana. Ricordi e pensieri* (Milan, 1928), *L'intervento 1915* (Milan, 1930), and G. B. Gifuni, ed., *Il diario di Salandra* (Milan, 1969); Ferdinando Martini, *Diario 1914–1918* (Milan, 1966), and Giolitti's memoirs, previously cited. See also Brunello Vigezzi, *I problemi della neutralità e della guerra nel carteggio Salandra-Sonnino* (Milan, 1962). Documents relevant to Giolitti are in *Dalle carte di Giovanni Giolitti: Quarant'anni di politica italiana*, Vol. III (Milan, 1962), previously cited. The official documents relating to intervention have been published by Augusto Torre, ed., *I documenti diplomatici italiani*, Series IV, Vol. 12, and Series V, Vol. 1 (Rome, 1954).

The best military history of the war on the Italian side is Piero Pieri, *L'Italia nella prima guerra mondiale 1915–1918* (Turin, 1965); see also Emilio Faldella, *La grande guerra* (Milan, 1965), and the official history, Ufficio storico dello Stato maggiore dell'Esercito, *L'esercito italiano nella grande guerra 1915–1918* (Rome, 1927–1967). Piero Melograni has written the best political history of the country during World War I, *Storia politica della grande guerra* (Bari, 1969). An excellent work that captures the essence of the war effort and the country during the conflict is Mario Silvestri, *Isonzo 1917* (Turin, 1965). Rino Alessi, *Dall'Isonzo al Piave. Lettere clandestine di un corrispondente di guerra* (Milan, 1966), gives a picture of the climate after Caporetto.

On the Italian participation at Versailles, the best work in English is still René Albrecht-Carrié, *Italy at the Paris Peace Conference* (New York, 1938). A good source on the economic aftermath of the war, with a host of relevant statistics is the previously cited Shepard B. Clough, *The Economic History of Italy*. The work by Douglas Forsyth, *Monetary and Financial Policy and the Crisis of Liberal Italy* (New York, 1993), gives a good overview of the problems and their effects. On the relationship between economic and social issues during the period, see Luigi Einaudi, *La condotta economica e gli effetti sociali della guerra italiana* (Bari, 1933). Electoral statistics for the period are in Istituto Centrale Statistica e Ministero per la Costituente, *Compendio delle statistiche elettorale italiane dal 1848 al 1934*, 2 vols. (Rome, 1947), while economic statistics may be found in Ministero dell'economia nazionale, *Annuario statistico italiano, Seconda serie, vol. VIII, 1919–1921* (Rome, 1925). On the Socialist party during the red biennium, consult Gaetano Arfé, *Storia del socialismo italiano 1892–1926* (Turin, 1966). A Socialist protagonist, Pietro Nenni, wrote the excellent *Storia di quattro anni 1919–1922* (Milan, 1927). Debates in the Socialist congresses can be followed in Luigi Cortesi, *Il socialismo italiano tra riforme e rivoluzione* (Bari, 1969). A contemporary, Francesco Magri, followed the factory councils in *La crisi industriale e il controllo operaio* (Milan, 1922). Giovanni Pesce, *Da Lenin a Mussolini*, describes the impact of the Russian Revolution. On the workers, see G. Maione, *Il biennio rosso* (Bologna, 1975), and on the stiffening attitude of the employers to the disorders, M. Abrate, *La lotta sindacale nella industrializzione in Italia 1906–1926* (Turin, 1968).

Chapter 15: The Rise of Fascism

The interpretations of fascism's rise to power and its development have attracted enormous interest and have given rise to heated polemics. Important questions include whether the liberal state had reached the end of its rope and whether fascism was inherent in Italian society or came about as a result of the war and its aftermath. Before coming to conclusions on such issues, it behooves the reader to become throughly versed in the complex developments of the period.

Economic affairs may be studied in Clough's *The Economic History of Italy* and Forsyth's *Monetary and Financial Policy*, both previously cited, while the section on this period of Valerio Castronovo's "La storia economica," in *Storia d'Italia, Volume quarto: Dall'unita a oggi, I* (Turin, 1975), is particularly useful.

Roberto Vivarelli's *Dopoguerra in Italia e l'avvento del fascismo (1918–1922). I: Dalla fine della guerra all'impresa di Fiume* (Naples, 1967) is a very impressive and complete work that links events in Italy to the democratic interventionism of the United States and to the Communist Revolution. On the Fiume affair and its link to fascism, see Michael Ledeen, *The First Duce: D' Annunzio at Fiume* (Baltimore, 1977). Federico Chabod, *L'Italia contemporanea* (Turin, 1961), argues that fascism was a completely new movement holding none of the principles that had previously determined the political struggle. Chabod and Vivarelli believe that in the period under discussion are to be found the origins of contemporary Italy and emphasize the country's disillusion with the war despite its victory. This is a theme developed by Gaetano Salvemini in his Harvard lectures, published as *The Origins of Fascism in Italy* (New York, 1973), and in the earlier *The Fascist Dictatorship in Italy* (London, 1928). Ironically G. A. Borgese, Salvemini's fellow exile and professor at the University of Chicago, sought the roots of fascism in the remote Italian past in his *Goliath. The March of Fascism* (New York, 1937). Though not going back quite so far, Vivarelli also found it necessary to go further into the past in pursuing the reasons for the collapse of liberal institutions in his *Il fallimento del liberalismo* (Bologna, 1981). For more information on this point, Nino Valeri reviews the literature relating to the relationship between liberalism and fascism in his *Tradizione liberale e fascismo* (Florence, 1972).

For other views of fascism's rise to power, see the classic and extraordinarily clear Angelo Tasca, *Nascita e avvento del fascismo*, 2 vols. (Bari, 1965). This period is also covered by the controversial but convincing and informative Renzo De Felice, *Mussolini il fascista. I. La conquista del potere 1921–1925* (Turin, 1966).

Many protagonists of these years have left important works. An analysis by a leftist opponent is Pietro Nenni, *La lotta di classe in Italia* (Milan, 1987). Luigi Sturzo published *Italy and Fascism* (New York, 1967). The Anarchist leader Armando Borghi has left his memoirs, *Mezzo secolo di anarchia* (Naples, 1954). The former revolutionary syndicalist who served in Giolitti's cabinet, Arturo Labriola, published *Le due politiche, fascismo e riformismo* (Naples, 1924). Giolitti's memoirs have already been cited, but see also the letters on fascism published by Gabriele De Rosa in *Venti anni di politica nelle carte di Camillo Corradini* (Rome, 1957). Ivanoe Bonomi's recollection of this period is *From Socialism to Fascism* (London, 1924); see also Roberto Vivarelli, "Bonomi e il fascismo in alcuni documenti inediti," *Rivista Storica Italiana*, March 1960. On the Bonomi government's economic policy, see the work of the minister for industry, Bortolo Belotti, *La politica economica del ministero Bonomi* (Milan, 1923). On the Banca di Sconto affair, consult the musings of its head, Cesare Rossi, *L'assalto alla Banca di Sconto. Colloqui con Angelo Pogliani* (Milan,1950). An important memoir that presents important documents relating to the March on Rome is Effrem Ferraris, *La marcia su Roma veduta dal Viminale* (Rome, 1946). For the Fascists, see Benito Mussolini, *Tempi della rivoluzione fascista*

(Milan, 1930), and, for a flavor of the squads, the diaries of Italo Balbo, *Diario 1922* (Milan, 1932), and of Umberto Banchelli, *Le memorie di un fascista* (Florence, 1922). For the origins of the Fascist party, see Direzione del Partito Nazionale Fascista, *Le origini e lo sviluppo del fascismo* (Rome, 1928).

On leftist party activities, in addition to general histories, see the relevant sections of Alexander De Grand's parallel history of the Socialist and Communist parties, *The Italian Left in the Twentieth Century* (Bloomington and Indianapolis, 1989). See also De Grand's study of Angelo Tasca, *In Stalin's Shadow* (DeKalb, 1986). Serrati's politics are examined by Tommaso Detti, *Serrati e la formazione del Partito comunista d'Italia* (Rome, 1972). On Turati, see *Le vie maestre del socialismo* (Naples, 1966) and *Turati-Kuliscioff, Carteggio*, Vol. 5 (Turin, 1953), both previously cited. The Socialist congresses of this period are summarized by Franco Pedone, *Il Partito socialista italiano nei suoi congressi*, Vol. 3 (Milan, 1963), but see especially Direzione del Partito Socialista Italiano, *Resoconto stenografico del XVII Congresso Nazionale. Livorno 1921* (Milan, 1963). The birth and early life of the Communist party is chronicled by Paolo Spriano, *Storia del Partito comunista italiano. Vol I. Da Bordiga a Gramsci* (Turin, 1967); on the formation of the Communist party, an essential work is Palmiro Togliatti, *La formazione del gruppo dirigente del Partito comunista italiano nel 1923–1924* (Rome, 1971). On Gramsci, see John Cammett's fine work, *Antonio Gramsci and the Origins of Italian Communism* (Stanford, 1967), and Martin Clark, *Antonio Gramsci and the Revolution That Failed* (New Haven, 1977). Richard Bellamy and Darrow Schecter have published a short work on *Gramsci and the Italian State* (Manchester, 1993), which seeks to place the Communist leader within his Italian context. Dante Germino, *Antonio Gramsci: Architect of a New Politics* (Baton Rouge, 1990), argues that Gramsci owes his importance to his vision of a "new politics of the excluded." An interesting attempt to link the values and ideas of Gramsci and Turati has been made by Lelio Lagorio and Giancarlo Lehner, *Turati e Gramsci per il socialismo* (Milan, 1987).

Several good local studies exist on agrarian fascism. For an overview of local fascism and bolshevism, see Alexander De Grand's essay "Bolshevik and Fascist Attacks on the Liberal State, 1919–1922," in Frank Coppa, ed., *Studies in Modern Italian History* (New York, 1986). Paul Corner's *Fascism in Ferrara 1915–1925* (London, 1975) is a fine study. Frank M. Snowden connects the class struggle in Apulia at the beginning of the century up to 1922 in *Violence and Great Estates in the South of Italy* (Cambridge, 1986). Two studies of fascism in Brescia are Paolo Corsini's massive *Il feudo di Augusto Turati* (Milan, 1988) and Alice Kelikian's brief *Town and Country under Fascism. The Transformation of Brescia 1915–1926* (Oxford, 1986). Frank Demers has produced a good study on *Le origini del fascismo a Cremona* (Bari, 1979). N. Onofri's *La strage di Palazzo d'Accursio: origine e nascita del fascismo bolognese* (Milan, 1980) examines the origins of fascism in Bologna while Anthony Cardoza, *Agrarian Elites and Italian Fascism* (Princeton, 1982), links agrarian fascism in Bologna to a new group of commercial farmers who became more important after 1900. Other good studies of local Fascist movements include Raffaele Colapietra, *Napoli tra dopoguerra e fascismo* (Milan, 1962); R. Bernabei, *Fascismo e nazionalismo in Campania* (Rome, 1975); M. Francini, *Primo dopoguerra e origini del fascismo a Pistoia* (Milan, 1976); R. Cantagalli, *Storia del fascismo fiorentino 1919–1925* (Florence, 1972); M. Vaini, *Le origini del fascismo a Mantova* (Rome, 1961); and S. Colarizi, *Dopoguerra e fascismo in Puglia 1919–1926* (Bari, 1971).

On all of the events considered in this section, see the relevant parts in Paolo Calzini et al., eds., *Fascismo e antifascismo (1918–1936). Lezioni e testimonianze* (Milan, 1963). Guido Neppi Modona's work on the Italian magistracy also considers its role in the rise of fascism, *Sciopero, potere politico e magistratura 1870–1922* (Bari, 1969). The Fascist labor movement is examined in Ferdinando Cordova, *Le origini dei sindacati fascisti 1918–1926* (Bari, 1974). On the crises leading up to the March on Rome, and the march itself, consult Danilo Venerusso, *La vigilia del fascismo. Il primo ministero Facta e la crisi dello Stato liberale in Italia* (Bologna, 1968); Marcello Soleri, *Memorie* (Turin, 1949); Cesare Maria De Vecchi, "Mussolini vero. Memorie," in the weekly *Tempo*, November-December 1959; Cesare Rossi, *Trentatre vicende mussoliniane* (Milan, 1958); and Antonino Repaci, *La marcia su Roma* (Milan, 1972).

Chapter 16: Mussolini's Italy

Whoever treads into the field of Italian Fascist history will find a bewildering array of literature on practically every aspect of the *ventennio*, most of it emotionally charged and viewed from different angles that generally depend on the political viewpoints of the authors.

Books written on fascism during Mussolini's regime in Italy or outside must generally be approached with caution, since many of them were justifications of the regime. The best of them, however, are still useful and also give an idea of how fascism justified itself. For example, the book of a reputable historian, Giaocchino Volpe, *L'Italia in cammino* (Milan, 1927), argues that important developments of Giolittian Italy had a positive outcome in fascism. Anti-Mussolini literature must also be used with caution because it gives an opposite viewpoint, although here as well the best can be used profitably to understand the views of Mussolini's enemies. An example is Gaudens Megaro's critical biography, *Mussolini in the Making* (Boston, 1938), which sought to rebut Mussolini's apologists. A notable exception to the more polemical literature, despite his opposition to Mussolini and his feisty style, are the books of Gaetano Salvemini, now collected in his general works that have been previously cited. His best works in English are *The Fascist Dictatorship in Italy* (New York, 1967) and *Under the Axe of Fascism* (New York, 1936). Other early treatments of the Fascist phenomenon that still have value include Herbert W. Schneider, *Making the Fascist State* (New York, 1968); Herman Finer, *Mussolini's Italy* (New York, 1965); Carl T. Schmidt, *Italy under Fascism* (New York, 1939) and *The Plough and the Sword* (New York, 1938); William G. Welk, *Fascist Economic Policy* (Cambridge, 1938); and Frances Keene, ed., *Neither Liberty Nor Bread* (Port Washington, 1940).

Bibliographical articles include Emiliana Noether, "Italy Reviews Its Fascist Past," *The American Historical Review* 51 (July 1956): 877–99; Charles Delzell, "Italian Historical Scholarship: A Decade of Recovery and Development," *Journal of Modern History* 28 (December 1956), 374–88; "Benito Mussolini: A Guide to the Bibliographical Literature," *Journal of Modern History* 35 (December 1963); and "Mussolini's Italy Twenty Years After" *Journal of Modern History* 38 (March 1966): 53–58. Marxist interpretations of fascism may be found in John Cammett, "Communist Theories of Fascism, 1920–1935," *Science and Society* 31 (Spring 1967): 149–63. Charles S. Maier's "Some Recent Studies of Fascism," in the *Journal of Modern History* 48 (September 1976): 506–21, examines a number of historians writing about Italian and German fascism.

To get an idea of the specific events of this period, consulting a general history is recommended. These range from multivolume works to short books. The best in each of these categories are Luigi Salvatorelli and Giovanni Mira, *Storia d'Italia nel periodo fascista* (Turin, 1964), an unusually complete and balanced treatment; Danilo Veneruso, *L'Italia fascista (1922–1945)* (Bologna, 1981), Vol. 5 in the author's history of Italy from unity to the Republic, is less detailed but still very useful. In the short category, there are Alexander De Grand, *Italian Fascism* (Lincoln and London, 1989), noted for its clarity of organization and its theory of "hyphenated fascisms"; Alan Cassels, *Fascist Italy* (Arlington Heights, IL, 1985); Elizabeth Wiskemann, *Fascism in Italy: Its Development and Influence* (New York, 1969); and S. William Halperin, *Mussolini and Italian Fascism* (New York, 1964). To keep all the characters straight, it might be handy to have a copy of Philip V. Cannistraro, ed., *Historical Dictionary of Fascist Italy* (Westport, CT, 1982), mentioned at the beginning of this essay. *The Dictionary of Modern Italian History* (Westport, 1985), edited by Frank J. Coppa, picks up some people not mentioned in the previous reference work and is useful for important actors of the entire period covered in this book.

Documentary collections include the fundamental collection of Mussolini's speeches and writings, edited by Edoardo and Duilio Susmel, *Opera omnia di Benito Mussolini* (Florence, 1961), 36 vols. In English, an idea of the Fascist "mystique" may be gleaned from Adrian Lyttelton, ed., *Italian Fascisms from Pareto to Gentile* (New York, 1973), with a good introduction by the editor. Important documents are published in Benito Mussolini, *Fascism: Doctrine and Institutions* (New York, 1968). Interviews that had a major impact during the Fascist period are collected in Emil Ludwig, *Talks with Mussolini* (Boston, 1933). Charles F. Delzell has edited *Mediterranean Fascism, 1919–1945* (New York, 1970), which has many difficult-to-find documents on Italy. A good collection of translated articles reflecting some of the best Italian scholarship on fascism is Roland Sarti, ed., *The Ax Within: Italian Fascism in Action* (New York, 1974), while A. William Salomone's *Italy from the Risorgimento to Fascism* (New York, 1970) tackles the question of origins. Domenico Settembrini has authored an excellent book that deserves greater notice, which argues for the kinship between fascism and communism: *Fascismo controrivoluzione imperfetta* (Florence, 1978).

Biographies are a fundamental part of modern scholarship on fascism, especially those of Mussolini. The most important work here is Renzo De Felice's massive, multivolume *Mussolini* (Turin, 1966–93). De Felice considers Mussolini in the context of his times, trying to give him a fair hearing and going into minute detail to explain his actions. Not suprisingly this method has raised controversial issues and numerous debates. De Felice argues, for example, that fascism was forward looking while Nazism was quite different and backward looking. De Felice also distinguishes between the positive effects of fascism as a movement and the negative ones as a regime and maintains that Mussolini's policies had achieved "consensus" in the Italy of the 1930s. Some scholars, particularly of the left, have accused De Felice of whitewashing the Duce, but De Felice has held his own and, despite the contoversies he has generated, seems to be succeeding in depoliticizing postwar interpretations of fascism. The debate's parameters may be found in the Italian press, but De Felice puts them into sharp relief in his *Intervista sul fascismo* (Bari, 1975), edited by Michael A. Ledeen (published in an English translation in 1976 in New Brunswick, NJ). Ledeen has also written an article on De Felice's views, "Renzo De Felice and the Controversy over Italian Fascism," *Journal of Contemporary History* 11 (October 1976): 269–82. Other assessments in English of De Felice's work are Borden W. Painter, Jr., "Renzo De Felice and the Historiography of Italian Fascism," *The American Historical Review* 95, no. 2 (April 1990): 391–405, and a sympathetic study of his influence by Emilio Gentile, "Fascism in Italian Historiography: In Search of an Individual Historical Identity," *Journal of Contemporary History* 21 (1986): 179–208.

For a more neutral, although not sympathetic, view of Mussolini, see Gaspare Giudice's *Benito Mussolini* (Turin, 1971). A sympathetic biography instead is Giorgio Pini and Duilio Susmel, *Mussolini, l'uomo e l'opera*, 4 vols. (Florence, 1963). In English, Denis Mack Smith's *Mussolini* (New York, 1982) adopts a very negative and critical attitude, making him De Felice's counterpoint. Ivone Kirkpatrick's *Mussolini: A Study in Power* (New York, 1964) still stands out as a notable work. Paolo Monelli, *Mussolini. The Intimate Life of a Demagogue* (New York, 1954), is well worth reading for its insights into Mussolini's personality. Mussolini's widow has provided interesting glimpses of family life in Rachele Mussolini, *Mussolini. An Intimate Biography* (New York, 1977). Laura Fermi's *Mussolini* (Chicago, 1961) is readable but of little scholarly value. Other biographies that might be consulted are Christopher Hibbert, *Il Duce* (Boston, 1962), Richard Collier, *Duce!* (London, 1971), and Richard Lyttle, *Il Duce* (New York, 1987).

In addition to Mussolini, see biographies of the hierarchs, especially Claudio Segrè, *Italo Balbo, A Fascist Life* (Berkeley, 1987). Paolo Nello's two-volume biography, *Dino Grandi. La formazione di un leader fascista* (Bologna, 1987) and *Un fedele disubbidiente: Dino Grandi da Palazzo Chigi al 25 luglio* (Bologna, 1993), discusses the career of one of the most important Fascist leaders and his impact on Italy's foreign policy. Philip V. Cannistraro and Brian Sullivan's *Il Duce's Other Woman* (New York, 1993) is a work on Margherita Sarfatti that also provides an excellent view of the milieu in which Mussolini was formed. Sarfatti authored a hagiographic biography of Mussolini, *The Life of Benito Mussolini* (New York, 1925). On Bottai, see the interesting review of his ideas by Alexander De Grand, *Bottai e la cultura fascista* (Bari, 1978). Another author, Giordano Bruno Guerri, *Giuseppe Bottai un fascista critico* (Milan, 1976), argues that Bottai was the only Fascist who had an organic view of the hypothetical state that fascism wished to construct. See also Bottai's own *Venti anni e un giorno* (Milan, 1949) and *Diario* (Milan, 1988). For another hierarch, see Harry Fornari, *Mussolini's Gadfly: Roberto Farinacci* (Nashville, 1971).

On the consolidation of the regime, the most noted work in English is Adrian Lyttleton, *The Seizure of Power* (New York, 1973). In Italian, Giuseppe Rossini, *Il delitto Matteotti tra il Viminale e l'Aventino* (Bologna, 1966), and Ariane Landyt, *Le sinistre e l'Aventino* (Milan, 1973), confront the same theme. Doug Thompson, *State Control in Fascist Italy: Culture and Conformity, 1925–1943* (Manchester, 1991), discusses the transition from violent coercion during the early phase of fascism to nonviolent control of the country through legislation, mass organizations, and propaganda. On the organization of the Fascist state, the best work is Alberto Aquarone, *L'organizzazione dello stato totalitario*, 2 vols. (Turin, 1965). On the papacy and the Catholics during this period, see Francesco Margiotta Broglio, *Italia e Santa Sede dalla grande guerra alla con-*

ciliazione (Bari, 1966), and, most important, Gabriele De Rosa, *Storia del movimento cattolico in Italia, Vol 2: Il partito popolare italiano* (Bari, 1966). In English, there are P. Kent, *The Pope and the Duce: The International Impact of the Lateran Agreements* (London, 1981), and J. F. Pollard, *The Vatican and Italian Fascism, 1929–1932,* (Cambridge, 1985). Richard Webster's *The Cross and the Fasces* (Stanford, 1960) discusses Christian democracy's relations with fascism. The regime's suppression of the Catholic missionary organization Opera Bonomelli is discussed in Philip V. Cannistraro and Gianfausto Rosoli, *Emigrazione, chiesa e fascismo: Lo scioglimento dell'Opera Bonomelli, (1922–1928)* (Rome, 1979). The reaction of big business to fascism is discussed in some of the general works cited in this essay for the previous period. More specific works include Piero Melograni, *Gli industriali e Mussolini* (Milan, 1972), Roland Sarti, *Fascism and the Industrial Leadership in Italy, 1919–1940* (Berkeley, 1971), and Ernesto Rossi, *Padroni del vapore e fascismo* (Bari, 1966). On the army's attitude, see Giorgio Rochat, *L'esercito italiano da Vittorio Veneto a Mussolini 1919–1925* (Bari, 1967).

In addition to De Grand's general treatment, previously cited, the leftist parties during this period are covered in detail by Ariane Landuyt, *Le sinistre e l'Aventino* (Milan, 1973); Giovanni Sabbatucci, *I socialisti nella crisi dello Stato liberale (1918–1926),* Vol. 3 of the general history of Italian socialism already mentioned; Paolo Spriano, *Storia del partito comunista,* Vol. 1, already cited; Vittorio Vidotto, *Il Partito comunista italiano dalle origini al 1946* (Bologna, 1975), who publishes important documents relating to the PCI; Palmiro Togliatti, *La formazione del gruppo dirigente del partito comunista italiano* (Rome, 1962); and Giorgio Amendola, *Storia del partito comunista italiano, 1921–1943* (Rome, 1978). Alexander De Grand has also published a book on Angelo Tasca, *In Stalin's Shadow,* already cited. See Giuseppe Fiori's biography of PCI founder, *Antonio Gramsci: Life of a Revolutionary* (New York, 1971). Simona Colarizi has examined the more moderate democrats in *I democratici all'opposizione. Giovanni Amendola e l'unione nazionale, 1922–1926* (Bologna, 1973).

On Fascist economic policies and their results, see Giuseppe Toniolo, ed., *Lo sviluppo economico italiano 1861–1940* (Bari, 1973), Giorgio Mori, *Il capitalismo industriale in Italia* (Rome, 1977), and Ernesto Cianci, *Nascita dello Stato imprenditoriale in Italia* (Milan, 1977). Marco Maraffi, *Politica ed economia in Italia. La vicenda dell'impresa pubblica dagli anni trenta agli anni cinquanta* (Bologna, 1990), takes the story of Italy's public firms from the 1930s to the 1950s. Giampiero Carocci's short *Italian Fascism* (Harmondsworth, 1974) is at its most interesting on economic affairs. On the Corporate State, see the articles collected by Luigi Lojacono, *Le corporazioni fasciste* (Milan, 1935), and the works of Alfredo Rocco, *Scritti e discorsi politici*, 3 vols. (Milan, 1938). A good examination of Rocco is Paolo Ungari, *Alfredo Rocco e l'ideologia giuridica del fascismo* (Brescia, 1963). On Fascist attempts to mobilize the masses, see the fundamental work by Philip V. Cannistraro, *La fabbrica del consenso. Fascismo e mass media* (Bari, 1975), and Victoria De Grazia, *The Culture of Consent* (New York, 1981). A discussion of how the youth was mobilized is in Tracy Koon, *Believe, Obey, Fight: Political Socialization of Youth in Fascist Italy, 1922–1943* (Chapel Hill, 1985). Philip V. Cannistraro, "The Radio in Fascist Italy," *Journal of European Studies* II, 2 (June 1972): 127–54, and "Mussolini's Cultural Revolution," *Journal of Contemporary History* VII, 3–4 (July–October 1972): 115–39, analyze the themes and goals of Fascist cultural policy. The book by Edward Tannenbaum, *The Fascist Experience* (New York, 1972), delves deeply into popular culture. On a related theme, see Luisa Passerini, *Fascism in Popular Memory: The Cultural Experience of the Turin Working Class* (Cambridge, 1987). Ruggero Zangrandi, *Il lungo viaggio attraverso il fascismo* (Milan, 1972), gives a good idea of what it was like to live under fascism. Mussolini's attempt to eradicate the Mafia is studied by Christopher Duggan, *Fascism and the Mafia* (New Haven, 1989). Fascism's appeal to youth is discussed in Michael Ledeen, *Universal Fascism* (New York, 1972). Renzo De Felice, *Intelletuali di fronte al fascismo* (Rome, 1985), details how some prominent intellectuals reacted to fascism. Alexander De Grand has written on "Women under Italian Fascism," *The Historical Journal* 19 (1976): 647–88, while Victoria De Grazia has published a more ample treatment, *How Fascism Ruled Women* (Berkeley, 1992). Perry R. Willson, *The Clockwork Factory: Women and Work in Fascist Italy* (New York, 1994) traces women's work experience in a specific setting. Edward Tannenbaum's article on education in the cited Tannenbaum and Noether, eds., *Modern Italy*, pp. 231–253, treats education in general but gives a good synopsis of the Fascist period.

On aspects of popular culture, Mino Argentieri has written on the newsreels, *L'occhio del regime* (Florence, 1979), and Alberto Monticone has studied the radio during the period, *Il fascismo al microfono* (Rome, 1978). Giannni Isola, *Abbassa la tua radio. Storia dell'ascolto radiofonico nell'Italia fascista* (Florence, 1990), examines the impact of radio on the Italians during the Fascist era. On film during this period, consult Gian Piero Brunetti, *Cinema italiano tra le due guerre: fascismo e politica cinematografica* (Milan, 1975), and, in English, Marcia Landy argues that the postwar cinema had its origins in the Fascist era in her *Fascism on Film* (Princeton, 1986). James Hay, *Popular Film Culture in Fascist Italy* (Bloomington, 1987), also sees a "verist" culture in the filmmaking of the 1930s. On the PNF, the only full-length study in English, Dante Germino's *The Italian Fascist Party in Power* (Minneapolis, 1959), emphasizes the "social" aspect of the party but is outdated; Emilio Gentile has published the first volume of what will become the classic work on the subject, *Storia del partito fascista 1919–1922* (Rome-Bari, 1989). How the party was organized and how it functioned in practice is the subject of Ricciotti Lazzero's *Il Partito Nazionale Fascista* (Milan, 1985).

Fascism's appeal in other countries may be seen in John Diggins, *Mussolini and Fascism: The View from America* (Princeton, 1972), and Alastair Hamilton, *The Appeal of Fascism* (London, 1971). Relations between the United States and Italy up to the Ethiopian War are examined by Claudia Damiani, *Mussolini e gli Stati Uniti 1922–1935* (Bologna, 1980).

As might be expected, the interpretation of fascism has generated considerable heat. A general introduction to this subject is provided by Renzo De Felice, *Interpretations of Fascism* (Cambridge, 1977); see also his *Il fascismo. Le interpretazioni dei contemporanei e degli storici* (Bari, 1970). Federico Chabod, one of Italy's major historians, emphasized the conditions and the state of mind that produced the Fascist victory in the previously-cited *L'Italia contemporanea* (Turin, 1961). The idea of "modernization" has also been discussed as a contributor to fascism. See Roland Sarti, "Fascist Modernization in Italy: Traditional or Revolutionary?" *The American Historical Review* 75 (April 1970): 1029–45. Emilio Gentile, *Le origini dell'ideologia fascista* (Rome-Bari, 1975), has argued for a coherent ideological content to fascism, while Zeev Sternhell with Mario Sznajder and Maia Asheri, *The Birth of Fascist Ideology: From Cultural Rebellion to Political Revolution* (Princeton, 1994), contend that fascism was grounded in European civilization and was a coherent ideological opponent of both Marxism and liberalism.

A controversial view on the subject of ideology that has generally not been well received but deserves consideration is developed by A. James Gregor, *The Ideology of Fascism* (New York, 1969) and *Italian Fascism and Developmental Dictatorship* (Princeton, 1979). A good book to become acquainted with the Marxist viewpoint is Palmiro Togliatti's *Lectures on Fascism* (New York, 1976). Marxist views have been challenged by Rosario Romeo, *Italia moderna fra storia e storiografia* (Bari, 1977) and *L'Italia unita e la prima guerra mondiale* (Bari, 1978). Gino Germani, *Authoritarianism, Fascism, and National Populism* (New Brunswick, 1975), views fascism as a form of modern authoritarianism, while Charles Maier, *Recasting Bourgeois Europe* (Princeton, 1975), sees similar patterns of interest group representation in several European countries. A balanced view of Fascist ideology is given by Pier Giorgio Zunino, *L'ideologia del fascismo* (Bologna, 1985). A good article on the historiography of fascism (along with interesting documents) may be found in *Mussolini and Italian Fascism*, a special issue of the *Cesare Barbieri Courier* (Hartford, CT, 1980).

On the Jews during the Fascist period, the major work is Renzo De Felice, *Storia degli ebrei italiani sotto il fascismo*, 4th ed., (Turin, 1988). Meir Michaelis, *Mussolini and the Jews: German-Italian Relations and the Jewish Question in Italy* (Oxford, 1978), takes a harsher stand on Mussolini and the regime. A comparative view of Italian reaction to Nazi racial policies is offered in Ivo Herzer, ed., *The Italian Refuge* (Washington, D.C., 1989). Susan Zuccotti's *The Italians and the Holocaust* (New York, 1987) makes use of many interviews and concludes that the record was mixed. Alexander Stille, *Benevolence and Betrayal: Five Italian Jewish Families Under Fascism* (New York, 1991), successfully strives to provide a view of ordinary Jews during the Fascist period, including an examination of Jews who were an intimate part of the fascist movement from the beginning. Covering a longer period is H. Stuart Hughes, *Prisoners of Hope: The Silver Age of the Italian Jews, 1924–1974* (Cambridge, 1983). On the question of racism in the colonies, the most interesting work is Luigi Preti, *I miti dell'impero e della razza nell'Italia degli anni '30* (Rome, 1965). The conjunction between the two is discussed in Gene Bernardini, "Origins and Development of Racial Antisemitism in Fascist Italy," *Journal of Modern History* 49 (September 1977): 431–53.

A sampling of the views and actions of the Fascist opposition may be gleaned from the following: Istituto Socialista di studi storici, *L'emigrazione socialista nella lotta contro il fascismo (1926–1939)* (Florence, 1982); Gaetano Arfé, *Storia dell'Avanti! 1926–1940* (Milan, 1968); Stefano Merli, ed., "La ricostruzione del movimento socialista in Italia e la lotta contro il fascismo dal 1934 alla seconda guerra mondiale," *Annali Feltrinelli* 5 (1962); Giuseppe Tamburrano, *Pietro Nenni* (Bari, 1986); Aldo Garosci, *La vita di Carlo Rosselli* (Florence, 1977); Lelio Basso, ed., *Le riviste di Piero Gobetti* (Milan, 1961); Giovanni Spadolini, *Gobetti. Un'idea dell'Italia* (Milan, 1993)—a collection of Spadolini's writings on this anti-Fascist martyr; Paolo Spriano, *Gli anni della clandestinità*, (Turin, 1969), which is Vol. 2 of his general history of the PCI; Pietro Secchia, "L'azione svolta dal partito comunista in Italia durante il fascismo, 1926–1932," *Annali Feltrinelli* 11 (1969); Aldo Garosci, *Storia dei fuorusciti* (Bari, 1958); Frank Rosengarten, *The Italian Antifascist Press* (Cleveland, 1968); Santi Fedele, *Storia della concentrazione antifascista 1927–1934* (Milan, 1976); and Pier Giorgio Zunino, *La questione cattolica nella sinistra italiana (1919–1945)*, 2 vols. (Bologna, 1975–77).

Chapter 17: World War II and the Resistance

The fundamental documents on foreign policy on this and earlier years, *I documenti diplomatici italiani*, have been published by the Ministry of Foreign

Affairs (Rome, 1952–53 and 1954–1965). Another essential source for this period are the diaries of Galeazzo Ciano, *Ciano's Diary, 1939–1943* (London, 1947), and *Ciano's Hidden Diaries, 1937–1938* (London, 1952).

Alan Cassels has written the best account in English on *Mussolini's Early Diplomacy* (Princeton, 1970) and has also edited *Italian Foreign Policy, 1918–1945. A Guide to Research and Research Materials* (Wilmington, 1991). Works in Italian that cover a similar period are Giorgio Rumi, *Alle origini della politica estera fascista 1918–1923* (Bari, 1968), Ennio Di Nolfo, *Mussolini e la politica estera italiana 1919–1933* (Padua, 1960), and Giampiero Carocci, *La politica estera dell'Italia fascista* (Bari, 1969). Several older accounts of Fascist foreign policy are still solid and very important: Gaetano Salvemini, *Prelude to World War II* (New York, 1954), Elizabeth Wiskemann, *The Rome-Berlin Axis* (London, 1969), Mario Toscano, *The Origins of the Pact of Steel* (Baltimore, 1967), and Maxwell H. H. Macartney and Paul Cremona, *Italy's Foreign and Colonial Policy, 1914–1937* (London, 1938). Denis Mack Smith's *Mussolini's Roman Empire* (New York, 1976) labels Mussolini's foreign policy as senseless. There are two good essays on this period in Gordon Craig and Felix Gilbert, eds., *The Diplomats* (Princeton, 1953). A comprehensive and balanced work on the subject is Rosaria Quartararo's *Roma tra Londra e Berlino: politica estera fascista dal 1930 al 1940* (Rome, 1980).

On more specialized topics, there is an interesting book on Mussolini's attempt to bring Germany back into a "normal" relationship with the other powers, Konrad Jarausch, *The Four Power Pact* (Madison, 1965). William I. Shorrock's *From Ally to Enemy. The Enigma of Fascist Italy in French Diplomacy* (Kent, Ohio, 1988), while good on France, is less satisfactory on Italy. Angelo Del Boca, *Gli italiani in Africa orientale* (Bari, 1979), provides a comprehensive discussion of the Italians in East Africa. Claudio Segrè discusses Libya during this period in *Fourth Shore: The Italian Colonization of Libya* (Chicago, 1975). Robert L. Hess discusses *Italian Colonialism in Somalia* (Chicago, 1966). Many works have been written on the Ethiopian venture, but readers must remain aware of pro- or anti-Mussolini bias, especially in older books. The best book in English is George Baer, *The Coming of the Italian-Ethiopian War* (Cambridge, 1967); another account is Frank Hardie, *The Abyssinian Crisis* (London, 1974); see also the older work by Geoffrey Garratt, *Mussolini's Roman Empire* (New York, 1938). Franklin D. Laurens discusses the French position in *France and the Italo-Ethiopian Crisis, 1935–1936* (The Hague, 1968). On Italian colonial policies in Ethiopia, consult Haile M. Larebo, *Italian Land Policy in Ethiopia, 1935–1941* (New York, 1994) and Alberto Sbacchi, *Ethiopia Under Mussolini: Fascism and the Colonial Experience* (London, 1989). On the military and political preparations for the campaign, the most useful works are Giorgio Rochat, *Militari e politici nella preparazione della campagna d'Etiopia* (Milan, 1961), and A. J. Barker, *The Civilizing Mission* (London, 1968). For contemporary first-person accounts of the war, there are Emilio De Bono, *La conquista dell'impero* (Rome, 1937); Pietro Badoglio, *La guerra d'Etiopia* (Milan, 1936); Rodolfo Graziani, *Il fronte sud* (Milan, 1938); and Quirino Armellini, *Con Badoglio in Etiopia* (Milan, 1937). Some wider implications of the Ethiopian War are discussed by George Baer, *Test Case: Italy, Ethiopia, and the League of Nations* (Stanford, 1976), and Esmonde Robertson, *Mussolini as Empire-Builder* (London, 1977), discusses the European situation.

On Italian intervention in the Spanish Civil War, there is a good account in English that tends to debunk some of the myths in American academic circles about the supposed ineffectiveness of the effort: John Coverdale, *Italian Intervention in the Spanish Civil War* (Princeton, 1975). A good Italian work on the same theme is G. Ranzato, *Rivoluzione e guerra civile in Spagna 1931–1939* (Turin, 1975).

For the best discussion of the state of the Italian armed forces on the eve of Italy's entrance into World War II, see Lucio Ceva, "Le forze armate," in *Storia della società italiana dall'unità a oggi* (Turin, 1981). The army's historical office has also published an "official" history, Ufficio storico dello stato maggiore dell'esercito, *La politica militare italiana tra la 1a e la 2a guerra mondiale* (Rome, 1954); see also Emilio Canevari, *La guerra italiana. Retroscena della disfatta*, 2 vols. (Rome, 1948), and L. Mazzetti, *La politica militare italiana tra le due guerre mondiali* (Salerno, 1974). On the navy, see Ufficio storico della marina, *La marina italiana nella seconda guerra mondiale* (Rome, 1972); on the Air Force, consult G. Santoro, *L'aeronautica nella seconda guerra mondiale*, 2 vols. (Rome, 1957). For an understanding of the role that industrial production had in losing the war, there is Carlo Favagrossa, *Perchè perdemmo la guerra. Mussolini e la produzione bellica* (Milan, 1946).

On the war operations themselves, there exists a host of memoirs written by the main characters on particular episodes or areas; except for Pietro Badoglio, whose views are, for good or ill, fundamental, *Italy in the Second World War* (London, 1948), the accounts are too numerous to mention here. Good scholarly accounts of the general war effort are given by Giogio Bocca, *Storia d'Italia nella guerra fascista 1940–43* (Bari, 1969), Emilio Faldella, *L'Italia nella seconda guerra mondiale. Revisioni di giudizi* (Bologna, 1959), and Lucio Ceva, *La condotta italiana della guerra* (Milan, 1975). In English, the detailed book by MacGregor Knox, *Mussolini Unleashed, 1939–1941* (Cambridge, 1980), argues that Mussolini was set on war. Alberto Aquarone has written an article demonstrating how unpopular Italian intervention in the war was in the country, "Lo spirito pubblico in Italia alla vigilia della seconda guerra mondiale," *Nord e Sud* 11 (January 1964): 117–25.

The last phases of the Fascist regime, the March 1943 strikes, have been examined by Roberto Finzi, *L'unità operaia contro il fascismo. Gli scioperi del marzo '43* (Bologna, 1974). Gianfranco Bianchi's *Perchè e come cadde il fascismo* (Milan, 1982) is a detailed account of the preparations for Mussolini's overthrow on July 25, 1943. There are firsthand accounts of the Duce's fall, including Mussolini's *The Fall of Mussolini* (Westport, CT, 1975), and Dino Grandi, *25 luglio. Quarant'anni dopo* (Bologna, 1983). In 1994 debate raged on documents purporting to be Mussolini's secret diaries, but the jury is still out on their authenticity. Fundamental for an understanding of the relationship between Mussolini and Hitler and of the Salò Republic during this period is F. W. Deakin, *The Brutal Friendship: Mussolini, Hitler and the Fall of Italian Fascism* (London, 1962), and Dino Alfieri, *Dictators Face to Face* (New York, 1955), while Giorgio Bocca's *La repubblica di Mussolini* (Bari, 1977) is also an excellent account. On the breakup of the Axis, see Friedrich-Karl von Plehwe, *The End of an Alliance: Rome's Defection from the Axis in 1943* (London-New York, 1971). G. Mayda discusses the persecution of Jews under Salò in *Ebrei sotto Salò* (Milan, 1978). On the period between fascism's fall and the armistice, good accounts include Melton Davis, *Who Defends Rome?* (New York, 1972), Ruggero Zangrandi, *1943: 25 luglio-8 settembre* (Milan, 1964), Mario Toscano, *Dal 25 luglio all'8 settembre* (Florence, 1966), and Peter Tomkins, *Italy Betrayed* (New York, 1966). Silvio Bertoldi's *La guerra parallela. 8 settembre 1943–25 aprile 1945. Le voci delle due Italie a confronto* (Milan, 1966) is an illuminating collection of testimony by Resistance and RSI officials. D. Ellwood's *Italy, 1943–1945* (Leicester, 1985) is a good secondary source on the same period. On the debate over the armistice and its results, see Carlo Pinzani, "L'8 settembre: elementi di ipotesi per un giudizio storico," *Studi Storici* 13, no. 2 (April–June 1972): 289–337. An excellent account of Mussolini's end is given by two protagonists, Pier Luigi delle Stelle (Pedro) and Urbano Lazzaro (Bill), *Dongo: La fine di Mussolini* (Milan, 1962).

The best book in English on the Resistance remains Charles Delzell's *Mussolini's Enemies* (New York, 1974), a complete work that also covers the early opposition. Besides the works mentioned in Chapter 16, which carry over into the time period discussed in this chapter, see Frank Rosengarten, *Silvio Trentin dall'interventismo alla Resistenza* (Milan, 1980). Accounts of the Resistance abound, but the classic account of the movement in all its aspects is Roberto Battaglia's *Storia della Resistenza italiana, 8 settembre 1943–25 aprile 1945* (Turin, 1964). Claudio Pavone's *Una guerra civile* (Milan, 1992) is a breakthrough work on the Resistance because it introduces the concept of the Resistance as a civil war, in addition to its character as a war of liberation and a class conflict. Giorgio Bocca's *Storia dell'Italia partigiana* (Bari, 1977) is also excellent, while a good brief overview in English may be attained in Quido Quazza, "The Politics of the Italian Resistance," in Stuart J. Woolf, *The Rebirth of Italy, 1943–1950* (London, 1972). The passion of the Resistance comes out in full force in Piero Malvezzi and Giovanni Pirelli, eds., *Lettere di condannati a morte della Resistenza italiana* (Turin, 1965). Luigi Longo, head of the Communist forces, has published *Un popolo alla macchia* (Rome, 1974). On the northern Resistance movement and its aims, see Franco Catalano, *Storia del CLNAI* (Bari, 1956). For political developments during the waning days of the war, see Palmiro Togliatti, *La politica di Salerno* (Rome, 1969), Aurelio Lepre, *Storia della svolta di Salerno* (Rome, 1966), and Giulio Andreotti, *Concerto a sei voci* (Rome, 1945). Interesting also is the treatment of Italian-USSR relations at the end of the war up to the Popular Front elections by Roberto Marozzo, *La politica estera italiana e l'Unione Sovietica, 1944–1948* (Rome, 1985). Relations with the Allies during this period are cogently examined by Norman Kogan, *Italy and the Allies* (Cambridge, 1956), while the relationship between foreign and domestic affairs are analyzed by Elena Aga Rossi, *L'Italia nella sconfitta: politica interna e situazione internazionale durante la seconda guerra mondiale* (Naples, 1985). Finally Roy Palmer Domenico explains what happened to Italian Fascist leaders after World War II in *Italian Fascists on Trial* (Chapel Hill, 1991).

Chapter 18: The Structure of Postwar Italy

Some of the issues discussed in this chapter are well treated in Stuart Woolf, ed, *The Rebirth of Italy* (London, 1972), previously cited. General economic developments are examined by Shepard B. Clough, *The Economic History of Modern Italy*, Valerio Castronovo, *Dall'Unità a oggi*, Vol. 4, in *Storia d'Italia* (Turin, 1975), and in Michele Salvati's lucid *Economia e politica in Italia dal dopoguerra a oggi* (Milan, 1984). Important essays are also to be found in Frank J. Coppa and Margherita Repetto-Alaia, *The Formation of the Italian Republic. Proceedings of the International Symposium on Postwar Italy* (New York, 1993). Important party documents are readily available in Gabriele De Rosa, *I partiti politici in Italia* (Bergamo, 1981). Peter Lange has edited a useful bibliography, *Studies on Italy 1943–1975. Select Bibliography of American and British Materials in Political Science, Economics, Sociology and Anthropology* (Turin, 1977). Another bibliography for postwar Italy is Roland Sarti, ed. *A Select Bibliography of English-Language Books on Modern Italian History* (Amherst, 1989).

Elisa Carillo has published a good biography of Alcide De Gasperi, *De Gasperi: The Long Apprenticeship* (Notre Dame, 1965). An important testimony on De Gasperi's 1947 trip to the United States is Alberto Tarchiani, *America-Italia: Le dieci giornate di De Gasperi negli Stati Uniti* (Milan, 1947). Pietro Nenni's diaries for this period are a precious resource: Pietro Nenni, *Tempo di guerra fredda. Diari 1943–1956* (Milan, 1981). On the Socialist party, see Giovanni Sabbatucci, ed., *Storia del socialismo italiano*, vol. 5 (Rome, 1981), and, in English, the relevant chapters in Spencer M. Di Scala, *Renewing Italian Socialism. Nenni to Craxi* (New York, 1988).

For the Communists, in addition to the works that will be cited next, see Gianmaria Bottino and Aldo Brandirali, *La linea politica dei comunisti nella Resistenza e nel dopoguera, 1943–1953* (Milan, 1974), Livio Maitan, *Teoria e politica comunista nel dopoguerra* (Milan, 1959), Marcello Flores, *Fronte poplare e democrazia progressiva* (Rome, 1973), and Giuseppe Mammarella, *Il partito comunista italiano, 1945–1975* (Florence, 1976). Simon Serfaty and Lawrence Gray's *The Italian Communist Party. Yesterday, Today, and Tomorrow* (Westport, 1980) includes a good section on the early postwar period. Italo De Feo, *Diario politico, 1943–1948* (Milan, 1973), contains interesting interpretations of PCI policies during these years. Nello Ajello discusses the attraction that the PCI had for non-Communist intellectuals in *Intelletuali e PCI 1944–1958* (Rome-Bari, 1979). A trenchant examination of the PCI's "double track" politics by a number of prominent critics is in Mario Baccianini, ed., *Le ceneri di Togliatti* (Rome, 1991). The debate on whether Togliatti or Stalin first believed that revolution was impossible in Italy, thus imposing the "new party" policy, is referred to in an interesting review of Di Scala, *Renewing Italian Socialism*, by Sergio Bertelli, "Quando Togliatti a Mosca sognava l'abbraccio mortale," *Messaggero veneto*, June 25, 1991. On the general influence of Stalinism on the Italian left, see *Lo stalinismo nella sinistra italiana. Atti del convegno organizato da Mondoperaio. Roma 16–17 marzo 1988* (Rome, 1988), and the debate to which it gave rise in the Italian press of the period. David Kerzer, *Comrades and Christians* (Cambridge, 1980), discusses relationships between the two groups.

On Christian democracy, see Silvio Lanaro and Mario Isneghi, eds., *La Democrazia Cristiana dal fascismo al 18 aprile* (Venice, 1978); see also the older but still useful Mario Einaudi and François Gaguel, *Christian Democracy in Italy and France* (Notre Dame, 1952); Richard Webster, *Christian Democracy in Italy, 1860–1960* (London, 1961); and the chapters on this period in the more complete Giorgio Galli, *Storia della D.C.* (Bari, 1978). Santi Fedele, *Fronte popolare. La sinistra e le elezioni del 18 aprile 1948* (Milan, 1978), analyzes the left during the 1948 elections. The best work on the Uomo Qualunque movement that rapidly appeared and disappeared during the immediate postwar years is Sandro Setta, *L'uomo qualunque 1944–1948* (Rome-Bari, 1975).

The best books on U.S. policy toward Italy in the immediate postwar are James Edward Miller, *The United States and Italy 1940–1950* (Chapel Hill, 1986), and John Lamberton Harper, *America and the Reconstruction of Italy* (Cambridge, 1986). H. Stuart Hughes's *The United States and Italy* (Cambridge, 1979) is an older work that is still useful. Important documents for this period may be found in U.S. Department of State, *Foreign Relations of the United States, 1948, Vol. 3: Western Europe* (Washington, DC, 1974), and later volumes. On CIA involvement in Italian affairs, see Trevor Barnes, "The Secret Cold War: The CIA and American Foreign Policy in Europe, 1946–1956" *Historical Journal* 24, no. 2 (June 1981), and William Colby, *Honorable Men* (New York, 1978).

The documentary history of the Constituent Assembly is *La Costituzione della Repubblica nei lavori preparatori dell'Assemblea Costitutente*, 8 vols. (Rome, 1976). Pietro Scoppola puts the constitution in context in a short but trenchant volume, *Gli anni della Costituente fra politica e storia* (Bologna, 1980). Two books in English give an excellent idea of the structure and working of Italy's government and administration. John Clarke Adams and Paolo Barile's *The Government of Republican Italy* (Boston, 1966) is the more detailed, while Dante Germino and Stefano Passigli's *The Government and Politics of Contemporary Italy* (New York, 1968) is the more readable. David Hine's *Governing Italy: The Politics of Governed Pluralism* (Oxford, 1993) is a welcome addition to the literature and brings the story beyond the two earlier works. See also Norman Kogan, *The Government of Italy* (New York, 1962). Antonio Lombardo's work, *La grande riforma. Governo, istituzioni, partiti* (Milan, 1984), gives a good synopsis of the government, parties, and the chief areas for reform. Robert C. Fried has described the bureaucracy and the prefects in *The Italian Prefects: A Study in Administrative Politics* (New Haven, 1963). Two other important institutions in Italian society are examined in R. Canosa and P. Federico, *La magistratura in Italia dal 1945 a oggi* (Bologna, 1974), and R. Canosa, *La polizia in Italia dal 1945 a oggi* (Bologna, 1976).

Chapter 19: Postwar Politics: "Imperfect Bipolarism"

A number of general histories concentrating on Italy's postwar political history exist in English. Norman Kogan, *A Political History of Italy: The Postwar Years* (New York, 1983), excels for its tone and coverage. The general treatment by Frederic Spotts and Theodor Wieser, *Italy, A Difficult Democracy: A Survey of Italian Politics* (Cambridge, 1986), is also a very good treatment in a book of manageable length. John Earle's *Italy in the 1970s* (London, 1975) provides an overview of this period. A book that takes a partisan viewpoint but that can be used profitably for its emphasis on Italian society is Paul Ginsborg's *A History of Contemporary Italy. Society and Politics, 1943–1988* (London, 1990). Much information can also be gleaned from Donald Sassoon, *Contemporary Italy. Politics, Economy and Society since 1945* (London and New York, 1986), but is less satisfactory. Coppa and Repetto-Alaia's previously cited edited work, *The Formation of the Italian Republic*, includes several incisive essays on the questions this chapter deals with.

In Italian, general works include Antonio Gambino, *Storia del dopoguerra dalla liberazione al potere DC* (Bari, 1975). On De Gasperi during this period, see his daughter's biography, *De Gasperi uomo solo* (Milan, 1964) by Maria Romana Catti De Gasperi, who has also published a documentary collection, *De Gasperi scrive* (Brescia, 1974). Leo Valiani's *L'avvento di De Gasperi* (Turin, 1949) is an early view by an influential thinker. Books describing De Gasperi's policies include Pietro Scoppola, *La proposta politica di De Gasperi* (Bologna, 1978), and Giulio Andreotti, *De Gasperi e il suo tempo* (Milan, 1969). For the "early" DC and the issues with which it was concerned, see Gianni Baget Bozzo, *Il partito cristiano al potere. La DC di De Gasperi e di Dossetti, 1945–1954* (Florence, 1974). The excellent general history of the DC by Giorgio Galli, already cited, is fundamental for this and later periods: *Storia della democrazia cristiana* (Bari, 1983). For political relationships among all major parties during these years, and their policies, the first volume of Pietro Nenni's diaries is a fundamental source, *Tempo di guerra fredda. Diari, 1943–1956* (Milan, 1981).

As mentioned in the text, Giorgio Galli has interpreted the politics of this period as one of "imperfect bipolarism." See his *Il bipartismo imperfetto. Comunisti e democristiani in Italia* (Bologna, 1967) and *Dal bipartismo imperfetto alla possibile alternativa* (Bologna, 1975). Domenico Settembrini has focused on an interesting theme running through Italian history that should be taken into consideration when analyzing postwar Italian politics, *Storia dell'idea antiborghese in Italia, 1860–1989* (Rome-Bari, 1991). Joseph La Palombara's *Democracy Italian Style* (New Haven, 1987) views Italian politics as spectacle but seems unconvincing.

Several interesting books in English by political scientists exist on the postwar Communists. They include Donald Blackmer, *Unity in Diversity: Italian Communism and the Communist World* (Cambridge, 1968); Sidney Tarrow, *Peasant Communism in Southern Italy* (New Haven, 1967); Donald Blackmer and Sidney Tarrow, *Communism in Italy and France* (Princeton, 1975); and Donald Blackmer and Annie Kriegel, *The International Role of the Communist Parties of Italy and France* (Cambridge, 1975). Most of the essays in the previously cited Serfaty and Gray, *The Italian Communist Party*, deal with the the period covered in this chapter. The "different" nature of the PCI can also be understood in a long interview format, Giorgio Napoliano and Eric Hobsbawm, *The Italian Road to Socialism* (Westport, CT, 1977). Stephen Hellman discusses the historic compromise in *Italian Communism in Transition: The Rise and Fall of the Historic Compromise in Turin, 1975–1980* (New York, 1988). Relations between the Americans and the Italian Communists are treated by Mario Margiocco, *Stati Uniti e PCI 1943–1980* (Rome, 1981).

A detailed analysis in English of Socialist policy of the postwar period and on the American view during the Kennedy period, including important interviews, is Spencer M. Di Scala, *Renewing Italian Socialism* (New York, 1988). In Italian, see volumes 5 and 6 of Giovanni Sabbatucci, ed., *Storia del socialismo italiano* (Rome, 1981). A short but excellent history is Giorgio Galli, *Storia del socialismo italiano* (Bari, 1983). Antonio Landolfi has published both an excellent analysis of the sociological base of Italian socialism, *Il socialismo italiano: Strutture comportamenti valori* (Cosenza, 1977), and a general history of the party, *Storia del PSI* (Milan, 1990), cited previously. Nenni's diaries are, again, a fundamental source, *Gli anni del centro-sinistra. Diari 1957–1966* (Milan, 1982) and *I conti con la storia. Diari 1967–1971* (Milan, 1983). Interpretations of Nenni's work, including a contribution by Arthur M. Schlesinger, are in Fondazione Pietro Nenni, *Nenni dieci anni dopo* (Rome, 1990). See also the papers delivered to the International Symposium "One Hundred Years of Italian Democratic Socialism, 1892–1992," videotapes at the John F. Kennedy Library, the University of Massachusetts-Boston Library, and the Italian Consulate-General in Boston. Excellent insights on the relationship between the United States and Italy during the Center-Left in particular, but on the entire postwar period, are provided by a collaborator of Schlesinger who interviewed most of the important personages involved, Leo J. Wollemborg, *Stelle, strisce e tricolore: trent'anni di vicende politiche fra Roma e Washington* (Milan, 1983). The best analysis of the Center-Left period has been written by Giuseppe Tamburrano, *Storia e cronaca del centro-sinistra* (Milan, 1990).

Insights on the role of economic planning can be obtained from Joseph La Palombara, *Italy: The Politics of Planning* (Syracuse, 1966), and Valdo Spini, *I socialisti e la politica di piano (1945–1964)* (Florence, 1982). The Social Democrats are discussed in Giuseppe Averardi, *I socialisti democratici da Palazzo Barberini alla scissione del 4 luglio 1969* (Milan, 1977).

Italian labor is treated by Maurice Neufeld, *Italy: School for Awakening Countries* (Ithaca, 1961), Daniel L. Horowitz, *The Italian Labor Movement* (Cambridge, 1963), Joseph La Palombara, *The Italian Labor Movement* (Ithaca, 1957), and Joan Barkan, *Visions of Emancipation: The Italian Workers' Move-*

ment since 1945 (New York, 1984). Union stragegy is examined by Peter Lange, George Ross, and Maurizio Vannicelli, *Unions, Change and Crisis: French and Italian Union Strategy and the Political Economy, 1945–1980* (London, 1982). Electoral and political analysis is found in Howard R. Penniman, ed., *Italy at the Polls: The Parliamentary Elections of 1976* (Washington, DC, 1977), and later books in the same series, and Robert Leonardi and Raffaella Y. Nanetti, *Italian Politics: A Review, Volume I* (London, 1986), which is also an ongoing series. Giorgio Galli and Alfonso Prandi analyze *Patterns of Political Participation in Italy* (New Haven, 1970). Several books by political scientists examining political attitudes, party operations, techniques, and representation have been published; they include Robert Putnam, *Beliefs of Politicians: Conflict and Democracy in Britain and Italy* (New Haven, 1973); Sidney Tarrow, *Between Center and Periphery: Grassroots Politicians in Italy and France* (New Haven, 1977); Giuseppe Di Palma, *Surviving Without Governing: The Italian Parties in Parliament* (Berkeley, 1977); and Samuel H. Barnes, *Representation in Italy: Institutionalized Tradition and Electoral Choice* (Chicago, 1977).

Sidney Tarrow, in *Democracy and Disorder: Protest and Politcs in Italy 1965–1975* (New York, 1989), ties unrest in Italy to similar agitation in Europe and believes it strengthened Italian democracy. Luciano Pellicani has written an excellent book on the terrorist mentality in general, *I rivoluzionari di professione* (Florence, 1975). Richard Drake links modern terrorism to intellectual tradition in *The Revolutionary Mystique and Terrorism in Contemporary Italy* (Bloomington, 1989). Robert C. Meade, Jr., *Red Brigades: the Story of Italian Terrorism* (New York, 1990), deals primarily with the Moro case; he is adequate on the facts but weak on interpretation. Carla Mosca and Rossana Rossanda's *Mario Moretti Brigate Rosse Una storia italiana* (Milan, 1994) is a book-length interview of one of the most notorious Red Brigades leaders and kidnapper of Aldo Moro. A graphic description of one of the many kidnappings that afflicted Italian life during this period is Curtis Bill Pepper, *Kidnapped! 17 Days of Terror* (New York, 1978). The best works in Italian on terrorism are Giorgio Bocca, *Il terrorismo italiano, 1970–1978* (Milan, 1979), and Giorgio Galli, *Storia del partito armato, 1968–1982* (Milan, 1986). Two autobiographical works by leftists convey very well the climate of the time: Oreste Scalzone, *Biennio Rosso '68–'69. Figure e passaggi di una stagione rivoluzionaria* (Milan, 1988), and Mario Capanna, *Formidabili quegli anni* (Milan, 1988). Bocca has written a book on the Moro case, *Moro: Una tragedia italiana* (Milan, 1978), while Galli has taken up the question of possible involvement of the right wing in the Italian political crisis, *La crisi Italiana e la destra internazionale* (Milan, 1974). On the theme of possible American intervention in Italian affairs, the books by Roberto Faenza, *Il malaffare* (Milan, 1978), and by Roberto Faenza and Marco Fini, *Gli americani in Italia* (Milan, 1978), are interesting but contain a goodly dose of imagination.

For the 1980s, one must still rely on the press, journals, and documents, but secondary works are appearing. The papers in Giuseppe De Palma and Philip Siegelman, *Italy in the 1980s: Paradoxes of a Dual Society* (San Francisco, 1983), analyzed the country's contradictions at the beginning of the decade. For analysis of the relationship between Communists and Socialists just before that decade, see Giuliano Amato and Luciano Cafagna, *Duello a sinistra: Socialisti e comunisti nei lunghi anni '70* (Bologna, 1982). The Socialist attack on the undemocratic nature of Antonio Gramsci's ideology and of Italian Communist roots is contained in *Egemonia e democrazia: Gramsci e la questione comunista nel dibattito di Mondoperaio* (Rome, 1977) and in Craxi's famous article on the same theme, "Il vangelo socialista," *L'Espresso*, August 27, 1978. Good works on Craxi, his policies, and the nature of his influence include Guido Gerosa, *Craxi: il potere e la stampa* (Milan, 1984), and Antonio Ghirelli, *L'effetto Craxi* (Milan, 1982). The "rise" of Craxi can be followed in Eugenio Scalfari, *L'anno di Craxi (o di Berlinguer)* (Milan, 1984), while newspaper articles on him have been collected by Ugo Intini in *Tutti gli angoli di Craxi* (Milan, 1984). The Craxi government's program and goals have been published by the Presidenza del Consiglio dei Ministri, *Il governo Craxi* (Rome, 1983). Press reaction has been collected in *Craxi in prima pagina* (n.p., 1984).

On foreign policy issues, see the views of two protagonists, Alberto Tarchiani, *Dieci anni tra Roma e Washington* (Milan, 1955), and Carlo Sforza, *Cinque anni a Palazzo Chigi. La politica estera italiana dal 1947 al 1951* (Rome, 1952). Giovanni Di Capua presents a clear exposition of political attitudes surrounding Italy's entrance into NATO: *Come l'Italia aderì al Patto Atlantico* (Rome, 1971). On the issue of South Tyrol, see Mario Toscano's *Alto Adige, South Tyrol: Italy's Frontier with the German World* (Baltimore, 1975). There is a stimulating essay on the republic's foreign policy by Christopher Seton-Watson in Richard J. B. Bosworth and Sergio Romano, *La politica estera italiana 1860–1985* (Bologna, 1991). An ample section is devoted to foreign policy during the Craxi period in A. Benzoni, R. Gritti, and A. Landolfi, *La dimensione internazionale del socialismo italiano. 100 anni di politica estera del PSI* (Rome, 1993).

Chapter 20: The Economic Miracle and Its Effects

Besides Clough and Castronuovo, already cited, two older works on postwar Italian economic development may be mentioned as retaining their usefulness. These are Muriel Grindrod, *The Rebuilding of Italy: Politics and Economics*

(London, 1955), and Vera Lutz, *Italy: A Study in Economic Development* (London, 1962). Chairella Esposito, *America's Feeble Weapon: Funding the Marshall Plan in France and Italy, 1948–1950* (Westport, CT, 1994), is a recent study of the economic aid so essential to Italy's postwar recovery. Pasquale Saraceno, one of the country's major economists, has spoken out on the Reconstruction: *Intervista sulla Ricostruzione 1943–1953* (Rome-Bari, 1977). F. Roy Willis, *Italy Chooses Europe* (New York, 1971), discusses the issues with regard to Italian membership in multilateral trade organizations. Robert M. Stern, *Foreign Trade and Economic Growth in Italy* (New York, 1967), focuses on the role of exports in Italian economic growth. General economic developments for the period may be followed in Salvati, *Economia e politica in Italia*, previously cited, in Giuliano Amato, *Economia, politica e istituzioni in Italia* (Bologna, 1976), Napoleone Colajanni, *Riconversione grande impresa partecipazioni statali* (Milan, 1976), and Augusto Graziani, ed., *L'economia Italiana 1945–1970* (Bologna, 1972). A good short essay is Luigi De Rosa's "Italy's Second Industrial Revolution," in Coppa, ed., *Studies in Modern Italian History*, previously cited. For Communist economic views, see Eugenio Peggio, *La crisi economica italiana* (Milan, 1976), and Sergio Garavini, *Crisi economica e ristruturazzione industriale* (Rome, 1974). Raffaella Y. Nanetti argues that Italy's success in responding to the economic crisis of the 1970s was the result of a "unique response" to that crisis which involved institutional decentralization: *Growth and Territorial Policies: The Italian Model of Social Capitalism* (London and New York, 1988). Edith Kurzweil, *Italian Entrepreneurs: Rearguard of Progress* (New York, 1983), looks on the Italian entrepreneurs of the 1970s acting as innovators and adapting to new social and economic conditions.

Good treatments of economic and societal issues are also in the general works by Paul Ginsborg and Donald Sassoon, cited in Chapter 19. Works in Italian encompassing all aspects of the Italian Republic, including treatment of economic, social, and cultural issues, are Silvio Lanaro, *Storia dell'Italia repubblicana dalla fine della guerra agli anni novanta* (Venice, 1992), and the more concrete Aurelio Lepre, *Storia della prima repubblica. L'Italia dal 1942 al 1992* (Bologna, 1993). Excellent detailed essays on different aspects of Italian society, including women, youth, custom, culture, and ideology, may be found in *Dal '68 a oggi. Come siamo e come eravamo* (Rome-Bari, 1979). General living conditions are discussed in two older books, now surpassed but useful as a picture of their times—news correspondent Irving R. Levine's *Main Street, Italy* (New York, 1963) and Andrew Bryant's *The Italians, How They Live and Work* (New York, 1971). A recent examination of cultural stereotypes and economic realities may be found in the essays collected in Carlo Chiarenza and William L. Vance, eds., *Immaginari a confronto* (Venice, 1992).

Women's issues are treated in Maria Michetti, Margherita Repetto, and Luciana Viviani, *Udi laboratorio e politica delle donne* (Rome, 1984), and in Franca Pieroni Bortolotti, *Sul movimento politico delle donne* (Rome, 1987). See also the paper and response between Paola Gaiotti de Biase and Margherita Repetto Alaia, "The Impact of Women's Political and Social Activity in Postwar Italy," in Coppa and Repetto-Alaia's previously cited *The Formation of the Italian Republic*, and Repetto-Alaia's paper delivered to the International Symposium "One Hundred Years of Italian Democratic Socialism," cited in Chapter 19. For the 1970s, see *La donna e le scelte della società italiana per gli anni '70* (Rome, 1971); R. Spagnoletti, ed., *I movimenti femministi in Italia* (Rome, 1971); and B. Frabotta, *Femminismo e lotta di classe in Italia (1970–1973)* (Rome, 1973). Rosa Rossi has written an interesting essay on language as it relates to women, *Le parole delle donne* (Rome, 1978). Judith Adler Hellman has examined Italian feminism in *Journeys among Women: Feminism in Five Italian Cities* (New York, 1988). Other aspects of women's issues and roles in postwar Italy are examined in the books of Ann Cornelisen, most especially *Women of the Shadows* (Boston, 1976). On feminism and the women's movement, in English, see Lucia Chiavola Birnbaum, *Liberazione della donna. Feminism in Italy* (Middletown, CT, 1986). On women in various aspects of contemporary Italian culture, see Maria Cicioni and Nicolle Prunster, *Visions and Revisions: Women and Italian Culture* (Providence and Oxford, 1993), and Giuliana Bruno and Maria Nadotti, eds., *Off Screen. Women and Film in Italy* (London and New York, 1988), primarily concerned with the post-World War II era but with flashbacks to earlier periods.

The South is amply considered in the works cited earlier on the topic of economics; on the region's particular problems, see in addition, Paquale Saraceno, "La politica di sviluppo di un'area sottosviluppato nell'esperienza italiana," in Augusto Graziani, ed., *L'economia italiana 1945–1970* (Bologna, 1972); Judith Chubb, *Patronage, Power and Poverty in Southern Italy* (Cambridge, 1982); and Raimondo Catanzaro, "Mafia, economia e sistema politico," in U. Ascoli and R. Catanzaro, eds., *La società italana degli anni Ottanta* (Bari, 1987). A classic work on the Mafia and its roots is Michele Pantaleone's *Mafia e politica 1943–1962* (Turin, 1962). On Mafia structure and organization, refer also to the works cited in Chapter 11. The best treatment of the current structure of the Sicilian Mafia is Pino Arlacchi, *Men of Dishonor. Inside the Sicilian Mafia* (New York, 1993). Important works by the protagonists of the fight against the Mafia include Giuseppe Ayla, *La guerra dei giusti. I giudici, la mafia, la politica* (Milan, 1993), and Giovanni Falcone, *Cose di cosa nostra* (Milan, 1993).

Books on Italian film are plentiful in both Italian and English, although the English-language works tend toward more specialized topics. Packed with information, Peter Bondanella's book, *Italian Cinema from Neorealism to the Present* (New York, 1990), is the best general history in English and includes a valuable bibliography and rental information for videocassettes. Millicent Marcus examines *Italian Film in the Light of Neorealism* (Princeton, 1986) and the links with literary theory. An author who believes that neorealism had a fundamental influence on Italian cinema is John J. Michalczyk in his examination of *The Italian Political Filmmakers* (London and Toronto, 1986). Angela Dalle Vacche, *The Body in the Mirror: Shapes of History in Italian Cinema* (Princeton, 1992), explores how the uniqueness of Italian culture emerged onto the screen.

In Italian, Gian Piero Brunetta's massive *Storia del cinema italiano 1945–1982* (Rome, 1982) examines the topic from every conceivable angle and completes the job with a vast bibliography and excellent photographs. Briefer treatments include director Carlo Lizzani's *Il cinema italiano, 1895–1979* (Rome, 1979) and Bruno Torri's *Cinema italiano dalla realtà alle metafore* (Palermo, 1973). Franca Faldini and Goffredo Fofi have collected the comments of directors and actors in *L'avventurosa storia del cinema italiano raccontata dai suoi protagonisti 1935–1959* (Milan, 1979); Massimo Mida and Lorenzo Quaglietti focus on the transition from Fascist filmmaking to neorealism, reproducing essential documents, in *Dai telefoni bianchi al neorealismo* (Rome-Bari, 1980). Political and economic aspects are emphasized in Lorenzo Quaglietti's *Storia economico-politica del cinema italiano 1945–1980* (Rome, 1980).

A mine of information on modern Italian cinema, art, literature, and culture in general, including the themes discussed in this chapter, may be found in English in the pages of the *Italian Quarterly* for which a convenient index for articles up to 1971 has been published separately.

Good introductions to the lives and works of the three poets mentioned in this chapter are Frederic J. Jones, *Giuseppe Ungaretti: Poet and Critic* (Edinburgh, 1977), and Leone Piccioni, *Vita di Ungaretti* (Milan, 1979); Rebecca J. West, *Eugenio Montale: Poet on the Edge* (Cambridge, 1981), and G. Singh, *Eugenio Montale: A Critical Study of His Poetry, Prose and Criticism* (New Haven, 1973); and Michele Tondo, *Salvatore Quasimodo* (Milan, 1971).

General histories of Italian literature usually include a discussion of the period examined in this chapter. The best treatment of the postwar era is Gaetano Mariani and Mario Petrucciani's *Letteratura Italiana Contemporanea*, Vol. 3 (Rome, 1982). *Letteratura italiana. Storia e geografia. Volume Terzo. L'età contemporanea* (Turin, 1989), edited by Alberto Asor Rosa, is a detailed treatment that is heavy on social considerations, organized by region and literary category. Other good works include Romano Luperini, *Il Novecento. Apparati ideologici ceto intelletuale sistemi formali nella letteratura italiana contemporanea* (Turin, 1985). On women writers, see the collected work edited by Santo L. Aricò, *Contemporary Women Writers in Italy: A Modern Renaissance* (Amherst, 1990).

Short sections on Italian design may be found in English in Stephen Bayley, Philippe Garver, and Deyan Sudjic, *Style and Design* (New York, 1986). The scope and influence of Italian industrial design can be gleaned from the following catalogs with both English and Italian texts: Piero Sartozo, *Italian Revolution. Design in Italian Society in the Eighties* (Milan, 1982), *Compasso d'oro* (Milan, 1985), *Dal cucchaio alla città—From the Spoon to the City* (Milan, 1983), and *Design Process. Olivetti 1908–1978* (Milan, 1979). For an indication of the role of Italian fashion, see *Moda Italia. Creativity and Technology in the Italian Fashion System* (Milan, 1988), catalog of an exhibition held in New York City under the auspices of the Italian Institute for Foreign Trade (I.C.E.).

Works on science in the republic are scarce and the topic must be researched from many sources. The same is also true for more prominent scientists such as Enrico Fermi, who is due for a good, full-scale biography. Fermi's wife has written a book telling of their life together, *Atoms in the Family. My Life with Enrico Fermi* (Chicago, 1954), while his collaborator Emilio Segrè has attempted to put Fermi's life work into focus in *Enrico Fermi: Physicist* (Chicago, 1970).

Chapter 21: Conclusions: Where Is Italy Headed?

The discussion in this chapter is based on the press and on talks with Italian scholars and politicians. Since they are so close to the present, the events in this chapter are best followed in the Italian press, to be used with caution in anticipation of thoughtful scholarly works that will analyze the rapid-fire events of the "bloodless revolution." For different reasons, the English-language press has also been quite poor on the issues, but *The New York Times* and *The New Yorker* have carried articles. Two serious articles are Angelo Codevilla," A Second Italian Republic?" *Foreign Affairs*, Summer 1992, and John W. Holmes, "Can Italy Change Yet Remain Stable?" *Mediterranean Quarterly*, Spring 1993. Michael Ledeen's "Italy's Great Purge," *The American Spectator*, October 1993, gives a good account of the Italian situation up to that date but is overly preoccupied with American politics. The British publication, *The Financial Times*, has been much better than the American press. The following articles by Spencer Di Scala, in *The Christian Science Monitor*, may prove helpful for an analysis up to the dates when they were published: "Italy's Embattled Left," February 13, 1990; "Italy's Political Upheaval," April 15, 1992, and "Italian Political Reform Needs More Than 'Clean Hands'," April 15, 1993. In October 1992, despite the cool reaction of Bettino Craxi, a conference on the scandals and their significance was held at the initiative of the group responsible for publishing the party's ideological review, *Mondoperaio*. Their reports are published in the November 1992 issue of the journal.

A number of works examining the causes and results of the bloodless revolution have already appeared. Sergio Romano, *L'Italia scappata di mano* (Milan, 1993), gives some interesting ideas on its origins and developments. Giorgio Bocca, *Metropolis. Milano nella tempesta* (Milan, 1993), gives what purports to be the history of the real "Tangentopoli" ("Kickback city"). Gianpaolo Pansa's *L'anno dei barbari. Diario cattivo di come la crisi dei partiti ci ha regalato l'incognita leghista* (Milan, 1993) is the warning of a well-known journalist not to go from the frying pan into the fire. Luciano Cafagna also points forcefully to the potential dangers resulting from the reaction to "Tangentopoli" in *La grande slavina. L'Italia verso la crisi della democrazia* (Venice, 1993).

Books examining current developments in Italian politics include Stephen Hellman and Gianfranco Pasquino, eds., *Italian Politics: A Review* (Kent, Worcester, 1992); Robert D. Putnam, *Making Democracy Work: Civic Traditions in Modern Italy* (Princeton, 1993); Mauro Calise, ed., *Come cambiano i partiti* (Bologna, 1992); Gianfranco Pasquino and Patrick McCarthy, eds., *The End of Post-War Politics in Italy: The Landmark 1992 Elections* (Boulder, 1993); Carol Mershon and Gianfranco Pasquino, eds., *Italian Politics: Ending the First Republic* (Boulder, 1994); and Mark Gilbert, *The Italian Revolution: The Ignominious End of Politics, Italian Style* (Boulder, 1994). Works with an "institutional" focus include Sebestiano Messina, *La grande riforma* (Rome-Bari, n.d.). Anna Chimenti has written a work on the role of the referendum in contemporary politics, *Storia dei referendum* (Rome-Bari, 1993), while Primo di Nicola has published a work on the most influential current promoter of referendums, *Mario Segni* (Milan, 1992). The role of the referendum is also examined in Marcello Fedele's *Democrazia referendaria. L'Italia dal primato dei partiti al trionfo dell'opinione pubblica* (Rome, 1994). Alan Friedman's *Spider's Web* (New York, 1993) discusses the role of the Banca Nazionale del Lavoro in arming Iraq and gives a good idea of the links between Italian domestic politics, corruption, and foreign affairs. An excellent work on Craxi's political "demise" and the reasons for it is Antonio Padellaro and Giuseppe Tamburrano, *Processo a Craxi. Ascesa e declino di un leader* (Milan, 1993). Tamburrano, one of Craxi's earliest and harshest critics, is notable for his balanced tone in this book. Achille Occhetto, the person who led the Italian Communists into the postcommunist era, has published his reflections and judgments as *Il sentimento e la ragione* (Milan, 1994).

Ilvo Diamante has published a solid work on the Lombard League and the sources of its power, *La Lega. Geografia, storia e sociologia di un nuovo soggetto politico* (Rome, 1993). This book also has a bibliography valuable for the study of this new phenomenon. Other books on the League include Umberto Bossi and Daniele Vimercati's *La Rivoluzione* (Milan, 1993), a clear exposition of the

League's ideology and history; Luigi De Marchi's *Perchè la Lega* (Milan, 1993), an attempt to put the League and its ideas into world context; and Giulio Savelli's *Che cosa vuole la Lega* (Milan, 1992), which seeks to explain the reasons for the League's rise. For the League's "ideology," see the various works and interviews of Gianfranco Miglio, erstwhile official League "philosopher." His books include *Per un Italia "federale"* (Milan, 1990); *Una costituzione per i prossimi trent'anni* (Bari, 1991); *Come cambiare* (Milan, 1992); *Disobbedienza civile* (Milan, 1993); *Una repubblica migliore per gli italiani* (Milan, 1983); and *Così è andata a finire* (Milan, 1993).

On the South examined in light of the League's growing influence, see Isaia Sales, *Leghisti e sudisti* (Rome-Bari, 1993). Shorter treatments examining the issue of whether the League is a "federalist" phenomenon or not are James P. Cross's "The Lega Lombarda: A Spring Protest or the Seeds of Federalism?" *Italian Politics and Society*, no. 32 (Winter 1990–1991), and Micheal Thompson's "From Canoux to Bossi: The Roots of Northern Regionalist Politics," *Italian Politics and Society*, no. 39 (Spring 1993).

Since scholars have concentrated on the left, there is a paucity of good works on the recent development of the MSI, whose debates, however, can be followed in the Italian press. Some indication of MSI activities may be found in Norman Kogan's *A Political History of Italy* (New York, 1983), previously cited. There have been a number of books by rightist protagonists reflecting their own movement, usually printed by small publishers. Some interesting ones include Nino Tripodi's *Fascismo così. Problemi di un tempo ritrovato* (Rome, 1984), which seeks to reinterpret fascism in light of contemporary problems, and Adalberto Baldoni's *Noi rivoluzionari. La Destra e il "caso italiano" Appunti per una storia 1960–1986* (Rome, 1986), which argues against the political isolation of the right. Giano Accame maintains that it is possible to heal the divisions of Italian society by rediscovering fascism's "red" roots in his work with an apparently paradoxical title, *Il fascismo immenso e rosso* (Rome, 1990); this is the continuation of a theme found in the same author's *Socialismo tricolore* (Novara, 1983). There are also two books jointly written by rightists and leftists that seek to open a dialogue. They are E. Landolfi and F.M. D'Asaro, *Socialismo e nazione* (Rome, 1985), and Adalberto Badaloni and Sandro Provvisionato, *La notte più lunga della repubblica. Sinistra e destra ideologie, estremismi, lotta armata (1968–1989)* (Rome, 1989).

Berlusconi's rise is too recent to judge, but works have appeared. Pino Corrias, Massimo Gramellini, and Curzio Malatesta's *1994 Colpo Grosso* (Milan, 1994) is the story of Berlusconi's amazing climb to power and victory in the 1994 elections. Giovanni Ruggeri and Mario Guarino's *Berlusconi. Inchiesta sul Signor TV* (Milan, 1994) is an unfriendly journalistic "investigation" of Berlusconi's political and financial connections and a good example of the passion that the new leader engendered. The international press devoted a fair amount of attention, not all of it balanced, to Italian affairs following the first elections after the new reforms. For a good idea of the fiscal problems facing the new government, see "Berlusconi Confronts a Critical Challenge over Fiscal Reform," *The Wall Street Journal*, August 25, 1994. Finally, the political "geography" of the "Second Republic" is examined by Paolo De Lalla Millul, *Topografia politica della Seconda Repubblica. 1. La Destra* (Naples, 1994).

Candeloro's summary quoted in the text is in a long and interesting section of considerations on the development of modern Italy in the eleventh and last volume of his previously cited *Storia dell'Italia moderna*.

About the Book and Author

PRESENTING THE HISTORY of modern Italy from the 18th century to the present, this book begins with a brief introduction to the legacy of the Renaissance and the 17th century. Di Scala fills a serious gap in the field, synthesizing modern Italian history, placing it in a fully European context. He also critically re-examines certain traditional historical interpretations and assumptions. The "European context" ranges from the Enlightenment to unity, to liberalism, to the South, to Fascism, and to the Republic.

The book gives prominence to social, economic, and cultural developments while providing a picture of how ordinary Italians lived. Di Scala discusses the role of women and gives ample attention to the Italian South, not only in terms of the "problems" of that region, but also in terms of its active participation in the historical and cultural life of the nation.

Cast in a clear and lively style that will appeal to students, Di Scala's work makes a strong contribution to the field by providing different historical interpretations of events in Italian history by incorporating the most recent scholarly contributions in his analyses. The book includes a rich bibliographic essay designed to guide undergraduate and graduate students to further reading on the various topics under consideration.

Spencer M. Di Scala is professor of history at the University of Massachusetts—Boston. The author of numerous scholarly books and articles, he also writes frequently on Italian politics and culture for the *Christian Science Monitor*.

Index